# Spirit of Rebellion

# Spirit of Rebellion

## Labor and Religion in the New Cotton South

**JAROD ROLL**

<hr>

UNIVERSITY OF ILLINOIS PRESS

Urbana, Chicago, and Springfield

Library of Congress Cataloging-in-Publication Data
Roll, Jarod.
Spirit of rebellion : labor and religion in the new cotton South /
Jarod Roll.
p.   cm. — (The working class in American history)
Includes bibliographical references and index.
ISBN 978-0-252-03519-7 (cloth : alk. paper)
ISBN 978-0-252-07703-6 (pbk. : alk. paper)
1. Tenant farmers—Missouri—History. 2. African American
farmers—Missouri—History. 3. Labor movement—Missouri—
History. 4. Working class—Religious life—Missouri—History.
I. Title.
HD1511.U6M876     2010
305.9'6309778909041—dc22     2010005641

For T. L. B., in memory,
and
M. S. R., with hope

# Contents

# Illustrations

## Maps

## Figures

# Acknowledgments

Many helped me write this book, but a few deserve special mention. First and foremost, I thank Nancy MacLean, who lifted this project at a particularly rough time. Her tough reading, superb advice, and always-open door made this book much better than it would have been otherwise. I also appreciate the invaluable guidance and suggestions provided by Josef Barton, Steven Hahn, Dylan Penningroth, and Mike Sherry—all of whom shaped this book in different ways. Erik Gellman, Justin Behrend, Aaron Astor, Owen Stanwood, Kathryn Burns-Howard, Debs Cane, Carole Emberton, and Tobin Miller Shearer offered good questions, unfailing comradeship, and quite a lot of gallows humor. Bruce Moses, from the University of Texas at San Antonio, made the excellent maps. Michael Honey, James Barrett, Ken Fones-Wolf, Wayne Flint, Richard Follett, and Clive Webb all read the entire manuscript at a late date and contributed excellent ideas for improving it.

Nothing gets done without money, and I offer my gratitude to all those who funded this book at various stages: the Graduate School and the Weinberg College of Arts and Sciences at Northwestern University for a Graduate Research Grant, a Janet Mead and Thomas Unterman Dissertation Fellowship, and a Dissertation Year Fellowship; the State Historical Society of Missouri for a Richard S. Brownlee Grant; the Franklin and Eleanor Roosevelt Institute for a Beeke-Levy Research Grant; Phi Alpha Theta for a Doctoral Scholarship; the American Historical Association for an Albert J. Beveridge Research Grant; *Labor History* for the Best Dissertation in Labor and Working-Class History Award; and the Labor and Working Class History Association for the Herbert G. Gutman Prize for Outstanding Dissertation in United States

Labor and Working Class History. I would like to give special thanks to Stephen Burman, Clive Webb, and Richard Follett at the University of Sussex, who funded research trips and a term of leave that helped me complete the book. They are also superb colleagues.

At the University of Illinois Press, I am grateful to Laurie Matheson for her excitement and dedication to the project, Jennifer Reichlin for graceful assistance during the production process, and Kate Babbitt, a superb copyeditor who made me say things clearer and better and saved me from some dumb errors. Any that remain are mine alone.

But book writing is easy compared to the hard physical work that my parents, D. R. and C. R., have performed in their lives. While it may be true, as they often say, that it is better to turn pages than a wrench, their work ethic and defiant pride have taught me more about life and vocation than any book could. I salute them.

And lastly I thank R. S. and M. S. R., the brightest of lights.

# Abbreviations

| | |
|---|---|
| AAA | Agricultural Adjustment Act |
| AME | African Methodist Episcopal Church |
| CIO | Congress of Industrial Organizations |
| CME | Colored Methodist Episcopal Church |
| CRS | Committee for the Rehabilitation of the Sharecroppers |
| DHC | Delmo Housing Corporation |
| FBI | Federal Bureau of Investigation |
| FSA | Farm Security Administration |
| MAWC | Missouri Agricultural Workers' Council |
| MES | Missouri Employment Service |
| NAACP | National Association for the Advancement of Colored People |
| NFCF | National Federation of Colored Farmers |
| NLRB | National Labor Relations Board |
| OIBAPMW | Original Independent Benevolent Afro-Pacific Movement of the World |
| PMEW | Pacific Movement of the Eastern World |
| STFU | Southern Tenant Farmers' Union |
| UCAPAWA | United Cannery, Agricultural, Packing and Allied Workers of America |
| UNIA | Universal Negro Improvement Association |

# Spirit of Rebellion

# Introduction

In the cold of a January morning in 1939, more than one thousand men, women, and children piled their meager belongings in protest along the highway roadsides in the lowlands of southeast Missouri. Over the preceding decade, their lives as farmers had been decimated by environmental disaster, falling crop prices, worsening poverty and disease, national agricultural policies that favored wealthy landowners, and the mechanization of cotton production. They hoped that by dramatically displaying their plight they could compel the federal government to change its policies so they could earn their livelihoods by working the land. Most joined the protest through their involvement with the Southern Tenant Farmers' Union or the National Association for the Advancement of Colored People, though others came out of desperation or to support family and friends. They were there to resist the destruction of an agrarian way of life in a fight that many feared was the last stand in a long struggle that stretched back into the late nineteenth century. The men were fighting, union leader Owen Whitfield said, to "free themselves and their wives and children from wage slavery and get some of the things that God prepared for us from the foundation of the world, and that is Land for the Landless, Food for the Hungry, Freedom for the Wage Slave."[1]

The Tripp and Daniels families were among those seeking freedom and security. Both families were young: Mose Daniels was 28 and his wife Myrle was 23; Ike Tripp was 30, his wife probably younger. Both couples had three children, aged between 15 months and 7 years old. Neither family had any cash and together they possessed only enough food—a little flour, some lard, and a few pieces of salted meat—to last about a week. They came from farming families with deep ties to southeast Missouri and eastern Arkansas. Tripp had followed his father Henry into Missouri from Lee County, Arkansas, in the 1920s looking for available land. Tripp's landlord had recently forced him to leave the farm he had rented since 1936 because he wanted to work it with wage hands, people like the Danielses. They had worked for wages on farms ever since they had moved to Missouri from Arkansas in 1935, but they could no longer afford to rent a house. Desperate, both families clung to the social worlds that gave their lives meaning. They huddled on the roadside with friends, neighbors, and kin that included Ike Tripp's parents and Mose Daniels's father. Even in such dire circumstances, both men voiced a desire to keep farming. Tripp said he would accept "any kind of farm job where I can make an honest support for my family." Daniels wanted "to continue farming," and it made "no difference what section of country." He just wanted "to make a living and have a place to live."[2]

Comparing their common backgrounds, current crises, and visions for the future, one could not guess that the Tripps were black or that the Daniels family was white. In all, over 200 white farmers protested alongside their black counterparts that winter. Collectively the protestors demanded that the promised "New Deal" provide them access to food, shelter, work, and ultimately farmland. "We feel that we are entitled to this," they argued, "since we want to work and since we are Americans and since we helped to make America what it is today."[3]

A generation earlier, farming families like these had believed that southeast Missouri would be their promised land. More than 125,000 white and black farmers—small landowners and tenants alike—moved to the state's Bootheel lowlands between 1890 and 1925. They came for the opportunities offered by the reclamation project that transformed dense forests and fetid swamps into rich farmland. Life in the regions they came from—the Ozarks of Arkansas and Missouri, the hills of southern Illinois and Indiana, the Cumberland Plateau of western Kentucky and Tennessee, and the lowlands of Arkansas and Mississippi—had been upended by the intrusion of cash economies and the power of corporate agriculture. Those who worked the land sought a place to secure their autonomy and freedom from rising tenancy and expensive credit. They wanted to settle new Bootheel land, make it productive, buy it, and establish small family farms. African American migrants also sought escape from racial oppression and were eager to enjoy full citizenship in Missouri, where there were no disenfranchising Jim Crow laws. Although the two groups had divergent backgrounds and dreams—black farmers seeking justice after the failures of Reconstruction, whites hoping to regain autonomy lost in commercial markets—they both came to the Bootheel in pursuit of an agrarian future.[4] Informed by both rational and romantic notions, their agrarianism arose from the way that "living on the land . . . shaped a core of common values of hard work, self-sufficiency, and mutual aid," as one scholar put it.[5] This worldview, with its counterpoints of familial independence and community cooperation, endowed farmers, black and white, with "a sense of identity, a sense of historical and religious tradition."[6]

Yet the investors who financed the development of these alluvial lands envisioned vast and profitable plantations of cash crops, not small homesteads. Enticed by state and local governments, these railroad promoters, land speculators, and resource-hungry industrialists had first come to the Bootheel to cut the dense stands of old-growth forest that covered the land. Capitalist investors then financed the nation's most extensive system of drainage canals to eradicate the swamps and use the fecund soil thus exposed for large-scale commodity production. Theirs was a vision of rapid development that relied upon government favor, capital investment, and the mechanization of the countryside. Like the dreams of farming people, their plan, too, had elements of idealism, albeit of a different kind. Local boosters likened the Bootheel to the land of Canaan, a "modern promised land" wrought by the genius of American capitalism. As self-styled prophets of progress, local leaders touted the clear-cut swaths, the canals, and the ripe fields as the realization of providential design through human effort.[7]

They were not alone. The Bootheel was at the leading edge of a modernizing process in cotton agriculture that transformed the region's western frontier, including the lowlands of eastern Arkansas, the delta of northwestern Mississippi, and the bayous of northern Louisiana. In 1940, one government official looked back on recent history and summarized developments in the Bootheel this way: "The evolution of agriculture in Southeast Missouri recapitulates in a small area in a very short span of time the history of the development of commercialized farming in general."[8] The site of the emergence of a new rural economic and social order—a new cotton South—this modern frontier served as a battleground between visionary capitalists and tens of thousands of small or landless farmers hoping to secure agrarian livelihoods. In time, the conflict would spread to further frontiers: the coastal plain of Texas, the valleys of southern Arizona, and the irrigated fields of California. The story of this struggle in southeast Missouri marks one telling phase of the wider history of that new cotton South.[9]

Twenty years before the roadside demonstration, African American and white small farmers had clashed as they staked rival claims to freshly opened

Bootheel land. Whites from the hill country deeply resented the system of tenancy that accompanied cotton agriculture, but black farmers seized on it as an opportunity to rent good land, climb toward landownership, and live with dignity in a state where they could vote freely. Not content to be throttled again by the designs of more powerful men, landless whites, led by socialist and Pentecostal insurgents, contested their new dependence by organizing violent assaults against both their black counterparts and the white elite that hired them in the 1910s. African American farming communities, in response, closed ranks behind Marcus Garvey's black nationalism in order to defend their livelihoods and dignity. Very quickly, both groups retreated into social and political worlds defined by race. Just a generation later, however, black and white farming families joined in common cause to demand collective social and economic rights from the New Deal state. How do we make sense of this remarkable change?

This is the story of how two generations of farmers created grassroots rebellions against the rise of capital-intensive commodity agriculture and its political proponents in the first half of the twentieth century. It is the history of how ordinary rural people—small landowners, cash renters, sharecroppers, and casual wage workers—fought to carve out and protect agrarian livelihoods in the midst of wrenching changes using the resources, beliefs, and hopes that gave meaning to their labors on the land. From their decision to migrate to their efforts to build communities, the settlers created political movements that rejected the rising tenancy, expensive credit, and political dispossession that dogged rural southerners following the collapse of Populism in the late 1890s. Increasingly voiceless in mainstream electoral politics, some invested their hopes in civic groups like the National Association for the Advancement of Colored People (NAACP), others joined the Socialist Party or the Universal Negro Improvement Association (UNIA), and still others embraced vigilantism as a way to preserve their way of life. The ravages of tenancy, falling cotton prices, and displacement bankrupted these strategies in the 1920s and informed a new generation of rebels. Through groups like the Southern Tenant Farmers' Union (STFU), a renewed NAACP, and the Congress of Industrial Organizations (CIO), farm activists forged a new understanding of poverty and politics from which they developed a more expansive idea of democratic citizenship and the rights of working people.

Cooperation among landless farmers was rooted in a common ideological soil. Farming families made their rebellions out of shared faith in an agrarian cosmology that held sacred the right of small producers—"soil toilers," as they called themselves—to independent livelihoods on the land they worked.

They found support for this right in both American democratic ideals and the moral teachings of the Bible. One dimension of their belief system was an attachment to what historians have called "producerism," a moral logic whereby "free men rightfully received the 'fruits of their labor' and, conversely, that those who did not make a contribution to tangible production had no legitimate claims on its results."[10] By the 1890s, according to one historian, producerism "combined a 'labor theory of value' of mongrel republican origins with commitments to independence and the responsibilities of citizenship."[11] Rural people who sought to make good on the opportunities that appeared in Missouri's Bootheel drew upon the producerist ideas of the southern reform movements of the late nineteenth century—the People's Party, the Farmers' Alliance, the Knights of Labor, and the Agricultural Wheel.[12] Drawing on this shared democratic lexicon, white and black farmers alike spoke of their cause in terms of "equality of opportunity," "natural right," "just conditions," "security," and "freedom."

To their minds, citizenship required personal independence: the freest citizens were those who owned the land they worked. This foundational conviction underpinned rural notions of manhood and womanhood, parental authority, and family security, a complex relationship captured succinctly by Ike Tripp's desire "to make an honest support for my family." Male dominance was central to this formulation, since it structured the family economies of southern farms. For small landowners and sharecroppers alike, economic survival often required heads of households—almost always men—to serve up the productive labor of their wives and children. Many southern men believed that a man's inability to exert control over the labor of household members, whether due to landlessness or another reason, undermined his autonomy and foretold spiritual and physical calamity. Farmers like Tripp likened such a condition of dependence to slavery, the worst degradation imaginable.[13] To them, this "wage slavery" was "a condition against the spirit of our institutions and dangerous to popular government."[14]

The authority of this agrarian cosmology stemmed from a set of religious convictions and practices at the heart of evangelical Protestantism. By 1900 most southern believers, both African American and white, belonged to one of three evangelical traditions: Baptist, Methodist, or Presbyterian. Although serious theological and ecclesiastical differences separated the traditions, all shared a belief that the Bible was literal truth, that an individual's relationship with God was deeply personal, and that divine power was present in everyday life. Well versed in the New Testament admonition that it was "by works a man is justified, and not by faith only" (James 2:24), rural evangelicals commingled ideas of "agrarian purity and self-reliance."[15] Farmers experienced tilling the soil, cultivating it, and making it productive as a powerful spiritual duty. This theology of work also justified the punishment of sin. Farmers were just as familiar with the Apostle Paul's admonition "that if any would not work, neither should he eat" (2 Thess. 3:10). These religious views also carried political weight as central tenets of both the People's Party and the Knights of Labor; the People's Party 1892 Omaha Platform quoted Paul's command to support a plank declaring that "wealth belongs to him who creates it."[16]

Religious communion provided the moral thread that united rural people's ideas of work, kinship, community, and citizenship. An individual's commitment to personal righteousness and strenuous labor was in part a contribution to the fellowship of the church body, a group that included family members and neighbors. Duty linked believers well beyond formal church gatherings. Just as the business of a farm required the labor of an entire family, so some agricultural seasons—such as the times for chopping or picking cotton—encouraged cooperation between families. Individual morality thus became a communal matter, a social resource that ensured neighbors who likely attended the same churches that an individual was reliable. Religious fellowship enabled migrant settler families in the Bootheel to form new communities and organize politically. Churches, which often were the only meeting places available to rural people, became important civic spaces where a shared moral system that ordered ideas about families, labor, leadership, and belonging could be enunciated and enforced.

Yet the primacy of kinship in church groups also deepened racial division. The new friendships and neighborly obligations that men and women forged before and after sermons, in prayer meetings, and at baptisms were all formed along racial lines. Race was more than simply skin color; it was a means to knit varied family and kin groups into communities because it reinforced kinship structures, household economies, loyalties among trusted neighbors, boundaries of commitment, and the strength of tradition. Farming families in the Bootheel framed their agrarian ambitions within hierarchies that worked as they had for decades, through land tenure, gender, and age, with surprising similarities between the races. In both racial groups, older, more prosperous men controlled familial, financial, and social resources.[17]

In the 1890s, events threatened to cut the sacred ties that linked productive work, morality, and freedom. As the extension of capital-intensive agriculture accelerated, the failure of Populism seemed not only to defeat the farmer-labor alliance but also to decouple producerist politics from what historian

Michael Kazin called its "moral revivalism." That "parting of ways," as he described it, facilitated both the triumph of corporate influence in government and the centralization of religious authority in the main Protestant denominations.[18] According to historian Joe Creech, a southern evangelical culture "teeming with options for engaging society prior to 1900 was replaced by one that buttressed social, cultural, and political norms."[19]

Yet in the first decade of the century, a small group of southern Protestants set out to restore the connection between individual believers and "the power of the Holy Spirit" through Pentecostal-Holiness revivals.[20] "Spirit-filled" rebellion spread rapidly among rural blacks and whites hungry to resist denominational efforts to regulate worship, discipline members, and legitimate some preachers while debarring others.[21] Pentecostal-Holiness believers, driven to the margins of society and the edge of survival, sought in their revivals a radical spiritual transformation. Their vision of the future was shaped by Christian ideas of the millennium—Christ's 1,000-year reign of peace and justice on earth. Pentecostal-Holiness believers drew strength from a premillennialist version of this eschatology, whereby only divine intervention in human affairs could free the world from Satan's grip and so pave the way for Jesus to return. In most cases, premillennialism encouraged spiritual withdrawal, an introspective focus on personal purity while awaiting signs of the End Times.[22] In collective worship and personal witness, however, the faithful sought the daily blessings of the Holy Spirit as manifested in the power to heal, speak in unknown tongues, and prophesy about the fate of the world. Inspired by the Acts of the Apostles in the New Testament, evangelists preached that the intervention of such spirit-filled believers would hasten Christ's return.[23]

This kind of empowerment, given the circumstances, was pregnant with possibility. Rural activists trying to defend their agrarian way of life drew upon the popular awakening of Pentecostal-Holiness revivals for moral clarity and spiritual power. This righteous uprising was part of a larger tradition of American "religious populism." In the heat of rebellious fellowship, according to Nathan Hatch, poor people could create new "moral communities" to defend "those most vulnerable in a rapidly industrializing society."[24] Whether agrarian rebels pursued the socialist cooperative commonwealth, a black nation, or New Deal policies that would assure "the things that God prepared for us from the foundation of the world," they did so inspired at least in part by a prophetic religion that was democratic, oppositional, and explosive.[25] In their effort to protect their agrarian cosmology, they stood as prophetic witnesses against a world where the relationship between human effort and basic fairness had come unhinged. Unlike other movements centered on an individual prophet, spirit-filled revivals gave ordinary people access to "supernatural forces by means of dreams, visions, and special revelations" that they believed capable of working miracles.[26] They encouraged people, even if many church officials did not, to prophesy, to "stand apart" and "try to force an unwilling world to abandon sin," to seek the "restoration and reformulation of customary ideas and institutions."[27]

In the trials of the Great Depression, a social movement of landless farmers turned this prophetic critique into demands for a New Deal for the rural poor. Although recent scholarship demonstrates how urban industrial workers created a working-class movement that forced concessions from the federal government in the 1930s, few historians have explored similar attempts in the rural South.[28] This book shows how a generation of local leaders and activists, most of them religious rebels, turned the sense of righteous empowerment into an organized effort to realign the balance between their spiritual ethos and worldly institutions. Through groups like the NAACP and the STFU, rural working-class leaders fashioned a newly expansive democratic ideal based on the rights of all producers as citizens. Some began to build bridges, haltingly but surely, to their counterparts across the racial divide with the help of new political allies, particularly those in the CIO. Their rebellion, although often complicated by lingering attachments to past ideas of manhood and racial division, created common ground for a protest movement that sought to force federal agencies to recognize and act on the rights of producers to economic security, decent housing, and basic health. Culminating in the roadside protest of 1939, the Bootheel movement won unprecedented federal measures that established some justice in the cotton country.

This story reveals a forgotten lineage of agrarian rebellion that linked Populism to the rise of civil rights unionism in the 1940s. Scholars have mistakenly eulogized this tradition as ending with the People's Party. Nancy Cohen concluded that "by 1900 the producers' movements that had been so characteristic of nineteenth-century America had gone down to defeat."[29] Populism, Matthew Hild argued, "marked the valiant but failed last stand" of producerism, which, he claimed, "lost meaning and resonance" in the years after.[30] Yet, as the Bootheel experience shows, rural people in the South held on to producerist ideals in both secular and sacred contexts well into the twentieth century. They continued, moreover, to apply those ideals to political questions.[31] We have been blind to the strength of agrarian rebellion in part because of the decline of the People's Party after the 1890s but also because of the intense cultural trauma of the Depression. The "discovery" of southern poverty by journalists, sociologists, politicians, and artists in the 1930s, immortalized by Dorothea Lange and James Agee, has fixed a seemingly timeless portrait of the misery and powerlessness rural southerners experienced in those years. That portrait obliterated the memory of all that came before.[32]

Imagining communities of landless farmers as culturally and politically barren places, scholars have concluded that the rebellion of agricultural workers in the 1930s must have arisen from outside sources. Patricia Sullivan thus argued that "New Deal programs and legislation stirred the stagnant economic and political relationships that had persisted in the South, unchanged and largely unchallenged, since the dawn of the century."[33] For others, communism, socialism, or Garveyism was the animating force.[34] Harvard Sitkoff, in another view, concluded that African American farmers were immobilized by centuries of oppression and remained in the 1930s "enslaved by disease and disfranchisement, by dearth of opportunity for employment and education, by social disorganization and dormancy, by isolation and intimidation." Their "fear, weakness, and resignation," he continued, "bred a crippling paralysis of will to struggle."[35] This story shows quite the contrary: two generations of rural people with the resilience and "will to struggle" that helped them, if only for a time, preserve an ordering of the world that gave them meaning and hope.[36]

The story told here would not be possible without the groundbreaking work of scholars who have shed light on rural protest in this period. Their research hoed many rows but tended to focus on either African Americans or whites, rarely both together, and to interpret their uprisings using frames designed for other movements in other times. For James Green, the STFU was "a kind of Indian summer" of earlier radicalism. Nan Woodruff, Robin Kelley, Mary Rolinson, and Glenda Gilmore depicted the rural activism of the 1920s and 1930s as opening skirmishes in the long civil rights movement.[37] Although these scholars paid attention to the role of religion, they often rendered it simply as a social instrument that facilitated the transmission of ideas from elsewhere.

In moving beyond such a depiction, this book builds on the important work of historians who took seriously the potential of religious revival to generate social and political change. While Charles Payne and David Chappell have used this insight to interpret the modern civil rights movement, most studies remained focused on the late nineteenth century.[38] Where scholars of religion and those of the rural working class in the early twentieth century have met in dialogue, their exchanges have focused almost solely on the white evangelical liberals-turned-radical who trained in the social gospel at Vanderbilt University and Union Theological Seminary.[39] Similarly, historians of the African American working-class experience have shown the power of religious revival to ignite activism in an urban context, but they have located the roots of this radicalism in the process of migration to cities, not in the resources of rural life.[40] Yet as this story shows, the first half of the twentieth century was a time of religious upheaval in the rural South, an awakening. "Awakenings begin in periods of cultural distortion and grave personal stress, when we lose faith in the legitimacy of our norms, the viability of our institutions, and the authority of our leaders in church and state," contended religious historian William McLoughlin in his classic study *Revivals, Awakenings, and Reform*. This process, he concluded, leads to "a profound reorientation in beliefs and values" as people turn away from old leaders and standards to prophesy new directions.[41] More specifically, the prophetic revivals of the early twentieth century empowered believers to fashion a new "moral community." It enabled the children of white supremacists and black nationalists to come together on the roadsides in 1939 and make demands on the New Deal state. To interpret rural political rebellion as prophetic revival is to thus uncover dynamic social and cultural history where historians have previously seen only stasis and simplicity.[42]

While this book is the story of a long-obscured tradition, it is also the story of its demise. The mechanization of cotton production in the New South in the 1940s transformed agriculture and the lives of landless farmers. Hundreds of thousands of people who were forced off the land migrated to cities or more distant fields. Nothing about this outcome was foreordained. Rather, it emerged from struggle between rebellious small farmers and their liberal allies and an alliance of large landowners and conservative southern congressmen who initiated their own rebellion in the 1940s against the New Deal programs that landless farmers had secured. Ultimately the conservatives won, but not without a fierce fight. And despite their defeat, those who fled the fields took their religious and political traditions with them to places such as Memphis, Winston-Salem, and Chicago. For many former sharecroppers who became factory hands, the urban labor and civil rights battles of the 1940s and beyond extended and adapted the rural rebellions they had waged for years.[43] We cannot understand these central dramas of American history until we first reckon with how rural people fought against this new world even as it dawned.

# 1

# A Modern Promised Land

"On ground so flat and low and marshy," the English novelist Charles Dickens observed of the lowlands surrounding Cairo, Illinois, in 1842, "lies a breeding-place of fever, ague, and death." Looking toward Bird's Point, Missouri, opposite Cairo, he saw nothing but "a dismal swamp . . . teeming . . . with rank unwholesome vegetation." The trees "had grown so thick and close that they shouldered one another out of their places." This was a "jungle deep and dark, with neither earth nor water at its roots, but putrid matter, formed of the pulpy offal of the two, and of their corruption." This pageant of rot took place, Dickens noted, with "the hateful Mississippi circling and eddying before it." This "slimy monster hideous to behold" lorded over a land "uncheered by any gleam of promise," Dickens concluded.[1]

By 1910 these swamps and forests had become a promised land for industrialists, speculators, and tens of thousands of hill farmers. From his vantage point at Cairo, Dickens looked into the tangled wetlands of the southeast Missouri Bootheel, the northernmost point of the vast lowland frontier of the Mississippi River Valley. Long despised and avoided, this massive swamp extended south through eastern Arkansas, the Yazoo delta of Mississippi, and the Ouachita-Tensas delta of northeastern Louisiana. Between 1890 and 1910, intense capital investment and backbreaking manual labor—to expand railroad lines, extract timber, build levees, construct drainage systems, and clear land—transformed these lowlands into a new cotton South of rich, fertile soil. Backed by federal, state, and county governments, investors imagined this agricultural kingdom, like the industrial New South, as an engine of wealth. The members of the elite group that quickly gained control of this lowland frontier styled themselves as prophets of progress whose endeavors carried almost holy meaning. Their creation of fecund fields from the wilderness became for them the human fulfillment of a providential design for the perfection of American civilization, their accumulation of wealth a sign of God's favor. Yet they were not alone in seeing the new lands as a blessing. The availability of work and the emergence of new sweeping fields stirred the imaginations of struggling farmers in the surrounding hill country. They came in search of wages, land, and, ultimately, their independence from the powerful interests that increasingly dominated their lives. As the twentieth century dawned, the lowlands, especially the Bootheel, became a battleground between an industrial and land-owning oligarchy, independent local farmers, and thousands of poor people hoping to salvage something of the aspirations they brought with them from the hills.

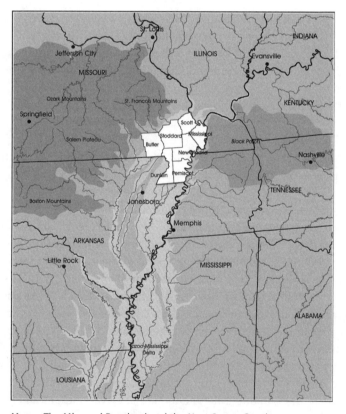

Map 1. The Missouri Bootheel and the New Cotton South.

*   *   *

The lowlands of southeast Missouri resembled Dickens's description well into the 1890s. The swamped forests of the state's seven Bootheel counties—Butler, Dunklin, Mississippi, New Madrid, Pemiscot, Scott, and Stoddard—offered a wild buffer between the Ozark hills to the west, the Black Patch of western Kentucky and Tennessee to the east, and the midwestern Grain Belt to the north. Prone to floods from the Mississippi and backwater from the meandering rivers coming from the Ozarks, the Bootheel of the last decade of the nineteenth century remained covered by standing water and impenetrable old-growth forests of cypress, oak, gum, and hickory. The Little River Swamp in the region's center was the largest and wildest of these ecosystems. This thick tangle of cypress and willow fed on labyrinthine roots that arched across stagnant lagoons teeming with malarial mosquitoes, poisonous water snakes, bears, wild turkey, deer, raccoons, and solitary panthers. Centuries-old trees, some thirty feet in diameter, rose 80 to 100 feet above this undergrowth. The Little River Swamp, the St. Francis River basin, St. John's Bayou, and other, smaller Bootheel wetlands characterized a vast lowland frontier of 15.5 million acres in the lower Mississippi River Valley.[2]

Prior to 1900, most of the farming in the lowlands of Missouri took place on ridges. Crowley's Ridge and the low sandy Kennett Ridge on the western side of the Little River extended south from Bloomfield in Stoddard County to Kennett and Cardwell in Dunklin County. To the east, Sikeston Ridge stretched south from Commerce in the Scott County hills to the town of New Madrid. The smaller Charleston Ridge ran down the middle of Mississippi County. Kennett Ridge divided the stagnant waters of the St. Francis and Little rivers, while Sikeston and Charleston ridges shielded the central swamp from the sloughs and bayous along the Mississippi River.[3]

Life was good on the ridges. Although half of ridge farmers rented land in the 1890s, they were relatively prosperous. Farmers on Sikeston Ridge cultivated more than 100 acres on average in that decade. They raised corn, wheat, and melons, which they sold in regional markets, as well as forage or subsistence crops. Regular church attendance and fellowship anchored their communities; one in three residents belonged to a church, the highest percentage of any county in the region. Roman Catholics, Southern Baptists, and Southern Methodists each made up about a third of churchgoers.[4]

Looking into the vast lowland forests from atop one of these ridges, northern investor Louis Houck saw untapped wealth where Dickens had seen only sickness and waste. Standing on a hillside near Dexter, Houck was "greatly impressed" by the "vast forest of timber on all sides" and began to "dream a dream."[5] His plan was to see that it was cut down. Houck was part of a cohort of capitalists that turned its attention to the immense untapped natural resources of the southern lowlands in the late nineteenth century. They sought to exploit the ancient virgin forests and ultimately open the land beneath them to the plow. Governments at all levels handed out vast grants of land and timber rights to railroad promoters and owners of lumber companies, who promised development and prosperity. States and counties sold hundreds of thousands of acres of swamped and overflowed lands for as little as $1.25 an acre, thus transferring a rich and vast public domain to the hands of a few men and large corporations. The new owners proceeded to construct a transportation network so they could ship resources to markets outside the region.[6] Houck later declared that "public opinion . . . and my own inclinations . . . compelled me to take hold of that enterprise in order to secure . . . as well as develop the material resources of" the Bootheel, including the thick timber stands he had so admired.[7]

Houck invested in railroad construction as the best means to make forested but swampy public land profitable. Railroad builders gained extensive rights of way through the swamps by assuring county governments that their roads would contribute in some way toward land reclamation. In 1895, Houck completed a railway line from Kennett to Caruthersville across the southern section of the Little River Swamp that would eventually extend south and west into Arkansas. He received 40,000 acres for completing this task. Similar transactions across the lowland frontier placed the land in private ownership and established connections to markets as far flung as St. Louis and Texas.[8]

Yet these investors faced constant threats to their interests so long as the floodwaters of Dickens's "hateful Mississippi" remained unchecked. Major floods swept through the lower Mississippi valley in 1890, 1893, and 1897, washing away railroad tracks and replenishing already impenetrable swamps and bayous. In order to protect against future floods and improve navigation in the valley, the federal government created the Mississippi River Commission to help local levee districts—controlled by landowners—build a more robust levee system along the river south of Cape Girardeau. In addition to receiving federal money, these districts also had the power to issue bonds and raise taxes for flood defenses. By 1897 levees of varying quality protected most of the lowlands from Missouri to Louisiana.[9]

After the railroads opened the swamps, the timber industry transformed them; Houck's dream was rapidly coming true. In the 1890s axes and mill

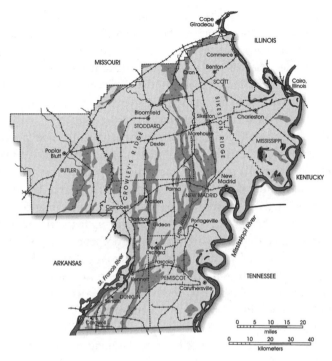

Map 2. The Bootheel, 1910: Land of Canaan.

blades followed the rails throughout the alluvial valley. Commercial logging companies looked to the southern forests for new sources of timber once they had denuded stocks in the woods of Wisconsin and Minnesota.[10] Again they found governments eager to sell public land, and they often bought timber tracts, land and all, for as little as $1.25 an acre. Would-be timber magnates and those who had invested in land and railroads shared mutual interests. In 1895, the heirs of Charles Luce, another railroad developer in the Bootheel, combined their 200,000 timbered acres with the Himmelberger-Harrison Lumber Company, a small stave and spoke mill in Stoddard County. Four years later, the new Himmelberger-Luce Land and Lumber Company bought an additional 150,000 acres in northern New Madrid County to become the area's largest lumber producer. That same year, William Deering, of Chicago-based International Harvester, acquired 60,000 acres of Pemiscot County timberland through his subsidiary Wisconsin Lumber Company to provide commercial lumber for tractor spokes. Similarly, the Gideon-Anderson Lumber Company acquired 15,000 acres in western New Madrid and northern Dunklin counties. In order to get to the tracts, timber companies needed railroads; likewise, timber became the main business of the railroads. Houck, who already owned one east-west line, constructed a line north and south through the Little River Swamp to connect the mills at Deering to the Himmelberger-Luce mills near Morehouse. He later joined this line to the Clarkton Branch of the Kennett Railroad, which provided a route to the Gideon-Anderson mills. Those rail lines were busy at the turn of the century.[11]

Before the mills could run, however, lumber companies had to reduce the swamp water that made much of the timber unreachable. Between 1895 and 1905, local governments created drainage districts on land owned by timber companies and land speculators. Often these districts extended to adjacent land. The unelected supervisors that operated the districts financed, through their power to tax, the construction of interlocking networks of canals and ditches that drained the brackish water into the deepened channels of existing streams, which eventually emptied into the Mississippi and Arkansas rivers. To accomplish this mammoth task, district supervisors invested heavily in new steam-powered dredge boats. These powerful boats allowed small crews of ten to twenty workmen to dig hundreds of miles of ditches in a short amount of time. However, the work progressed so rapidly that coordination of the massive projects could not keep up. Drainage networks often overlapped or emptied into one another, while competing districts sometimes taxed the same landowners.[12]

The corporations in control of the lowlands made windfall profits from industrial lumber production as their drainage schemes opened more tracts. Rates of timber and lumber cutting soared. In 1896, before the drainage districts were formed, Bootheel sawmills cut 80 million board feet of lumber. In 1899, after the first drainage districts were formed, the roaring mills cut 174 million board feet, 25 million more than the regional mills at Memphis handled in a year. As drainage progressed over the next six years, the Bootheel timber industry produced an average of 163 million board feet per year. The same pattern reshaped the lowlands of Arkansas, Mississippi, and Louisiana. Railroads opened the swamps to the timber industry, which then initiated drainage programs. As reclamation progressed, these companies cut down the old-growth forests with a fervor seldom seen. A federal forestry expert would later call the timber offensive in the South "the most rapid and reckless destruction of forests known to history."[13]

By the first decade of the twentieth century, then, a few large industrialists had acquired much of the lowlands in a process of government-backed resource accumulation that mirrored the national trend toward capital consolidation. Through friendly deals from county officials, corporations such as Himmelberger-Luce, Gideon-Anderson, and International Harvester had gained control of the Bootheel's natural wealth and transportation corridors. They controlled local governments through levee and drainage districts that had the powers of taxation and eminent domain. The result, the St. Louis Mirror charged, was the most "abominably rapacious monopoly in the State."[14] Their increasing power was merely a sign of the times. The nation's largest corporations gained unprecedented power and influence in these years, often with the help of the federal government. By 1904, as few as 300 trusts controlled as much as $7 billion in capital.[15] The reach of these corporations was staggering. International Harvester, for example, owned tens of thousands of acres of timberland throughout the lowlands. That timber was cut locally to make spokes for tractors, which were assembled in factories in Illinois and Iowa and sold to farmers across the country. James B. Duke's American Tobacco Company had even greater power. In 1900 Duke controlled 80 percent of the tobacco market as well as a large segment of the southern textile industry.[16] The cash economies these corporations created left an indelible mark on the lives of people in previously semi-autonomous rural communities.

By 1905 tobacco farmers in the Black Patch of Kentucky and Tennessee had become increasingly entangled in a web of debts, tax arrears, and defaulted mortgages. Traditionally, farmers in the region had grown enough of the cash crop to supplement their subsistence production. The coming of railroads after the Civil War, however, increasingly attached them to the price fluctuations and pressures of national commodity markets. American Tobacco took advantage of the agricultural crisis of the 1890s to entangle tobacco farmers further and take control of production in the Black Patch. Under monopoly conditions, prices soon fell below the cost of production. Initially, Black Patch growers grew more tobacco to compensate, which only glutted the market further and sapped the land. At the same time, the region's rural population was growing faster than this pitiful economic arrangement could support. Farmers had few economic or political alternatives. The pro-business, anti-union consensus of Kentucky Republicans and "New Departure" Democrats offered little room for an electoral challenge.[17] And so some farmers took up arms against Duke's agents and their supporters. According to historian Karin Shapiro, angry farmers in the Black Patch "emphasized the central importance of small-scale producers in American society" and believed that corporate monopolies "corrupted America's democratic institutions." Many left the Black Patch in the midst of the struggle to seek these ideals elsewhere.[18]

In less acute ways, farming families in the Ozarks and the hill country of southern Illinois and Indiana also experienced pressure from the cash demands of industrial capitalism. Since the 1880s, railroads had increasingly linked isolated Ozark communities to regional and national trade networks, which brought the power of distant markets to bear on established production, pricing, and trade systems. Turning away from subsistence practices, farmers by 1900 sold more of their produce for cash than they used for household consumption. In the eastern Ozarks, hill families experimented with cotton in order to generate cash, but the staple quickly exhausted the rocky weak soil and undermined the sustainability of already overpopulated communities. Similarly, farmers in the southern counties of Illinois and Indiana struggled to produce enough from the substandard hill-country soils to survive in an increasingly commercialized environment. Limited productivity, overpopulation, and rising demands for cash hit aspiring young men who were looking to establish their own farms especially hard.[19]

As one of the best and last sources of high rural wages and fresh farmland in the nation's midsection, the Bootheel attracted rural people from across the Ozark Plateau and the lower Ohio River Valley. Thousands of white migrants flooded into southeast Missouri seeking work in the booming mills; in stave, box, and spoke factories; on the cutting gangs in the forests; or on the railroads. Over 30,000 white people moved to the seven counties between 1900 and 1910.[20] "Workers flocked in from the hills," landowner Thad Snow would later recall, "some from the Ozarks but most from western Kentucky and Tennessee. Nobody advertised for them; the word got around and they came because they wanted to come." By 1910, nearly half of the Bootheel's residents had been born in another state; one in five came from Kentucky or Tennessee and one in six came from Illinois or Indiana. Two in seven of those born in Missouri came from the Ozarks. "They were poor people," Snow recalled, "and they came from poor hill country where the going was hard, and they showed it."[21] Ironically, the same process of corporate consolidation and monopoly power that had wrecked the lives of these migrants in the hills now offered the promise of better days in the Bootheel.

Only a small number of these migrants ever worked inside a sawmill; Bootheel timber companies employed relatively few mill workers. Only 125 workers ran the main Wisconsin Lumber mill at Deering in 1910, the period of its peak production. A similar number worked in the mills at Gideon, Pascola, and Morehouse. As in timbering operations elsewhere in the South, African Americans made up a large portion of the mill work force. Nearly 40 percent of those at Deering were blacks from Tennessee and Mississippi.

Wherever their origin, migrants soon found that the timber companies controlled nearly every aspect of life in the mill towns. At Deering, the location of Wisconsin Lumber, a series of whistle blasts roused everyone from bed at 4 A.M. and got them to work by 6 A.M. Wolves in the surrounding wilderness often howled back at the whistles. Workers shopped at company stores, got their hair cut by company barbers, and relaxed at the company amusement hall. African Americans lived in a special "Colored Town" on the outskirts of Deering where they had their own recreation facility, but there was no rigid segregation. Whites and blacks shopped at the same store and by all accounts received the same wages, which averaged a rather robust $334 per year in 1900.[22]

The vast majority of timber laborers lived and worked in logging camps near the cutting sites deep in the forests. The average camp consisted of five workers who cut and transported the timber. The camps were laid out in cut-over areas along the tram railroads and drainage canals that led to the mills and the timber face. Loggers, like those in the camp in northwestern Pemiscot County in Figure 1, lived in tents that could be moved two or three times a season as the cutting progressed. Choppers and sawyers worked in gangs. In most cases only the gang leader had any logging skill. Choppers who worked on undrained land had to wield their axes while standing in boats. Another team of workers would then transport cut logs back to the mills using tramcars, drainage canals, or draft animals. Loggers often lived with their families in the camps. Of the eight men who worked in the camp pictured in Figure 1, three were there with their wives and children. With the exception of the occasional odd job, members of a logger's family rarely worked for the timber company and paid rent to stay in the camps, where women cared for children and cooked for the other workers. Bootheel timber workers fed mills that produced an average of 228 million board feet per year between 1906 and 1912. Snow reckoned that they earned about 40 cents a day, less than half of the average wage of mill workers.[23]

The labor of this migrant workforce generated wild hopes in men such as land speculator Otto Kochtitzky, who believed that future riches lay beneath the cut-over swamps. "We [are] now at the beginning of a land trading era," Kochtitzky exulted, "inspired by the prospect of enhancing values resulting from reclamation of a large area of very fertile land situated at the center of the country . . . with the markets ready for its present forest wealth and its later assured agricultural products."[24] Despite the problems with the drainage districts, Kochtitzky and dozens like him sparked furious trading based on the prospect that farms would emerge from the muck. Values skyrocketed.

Figure 1. Logging Camp, Pemiscot County, ca. 1910. Source: Himmelberger-Harrison Lumber Company Papers, Special Collections and Archives, Kent Library, Southeast Missouri State University.

In one deal, Kochtitzky bought 400 acres of swampy forest in New Madrid County for $500. After it was included in a drainage district he resold it for $4,000. "The wet lands of Missouri are soon to become the most valuable of this State," promoter John Nolen boomed, "because their extreme fertility after having been reclaimed is sure to attract the attention of progressive people."[25] "My land is in a drainage district," Mercer Wilson informed potential buyers, "and the work is being rapidly pushed, and will be ready for cultivation before the land is cleared of timber." His land was a "great bargain" at $13–$18 an acre, he said, because similar land that had been in drainage for five years was worth more than $125 per acre.[26] Not every purchase was successful. Many small landowners could not pay the district taxes, which ranged from $1 to $5 per acre, and had to sell to avoid jail. These lands were soon picked up again in the investment cycle, usually by larger landowners or timber companies.[27] By 1905, timber companies controlled hundreds of thousands of stump-covered acres that were worth as much as ten times what they had initially paid.

As corporate interests consolidated their ownership of the land, they used their power in local government to expand reclamation plans. In 1907 the major landowners in the Bootheel created the Little River Drainage District, which would ultimately drain over 488,000 acres of the massive swamp that covered parts of every Bootheel county except Mississippi. The value of this land, most of which had sold for $1.25 an acre, grew to as much as $100 an acre almost overnight. District land that had also been cleared of stumps was worth as much as $225 an acre.[28] With large holdings in the Little River Drainage District, most timber companies established real estate divisions to improve and sell this land at a premium.

Creating wealth with seeming ease, industrial and land-owning elites interpreted their success as the fulfillment of God's plan. Bootheel investors expressed certainty that the richness and rapid profitability of the region's natural resources, from the timber to the alluvial soils, signaled divine blessing. They echoed a long line of postmillennial visions whereby "the climax and goal of human progress" is the triumph of Christ, "with human effort contributing to the realization of God's providential design."[29] "The Creator seems to have intended these alluvial deposits as a sort of endowment fund," Nolen told the Missouri General Assembly, and it was the destiny—even the duty—of those involved to unlock it. "It is almost impossible to comprehend the wealth-producing capacity of that area of land," International Harvester representative A. E. Chamberlain exclaimed to a congressional committee considering levee improvement. "It is the Nile of America . . . the best soil in America," he said. Chamberlain considered the Bootheel "a kingdom in itself" because of its "inexhaustible" wealth.[30] Even at an early stage, the agricultural production of the reclaimed land was already exceeding that of older lands. At the World's Fair in St. Louis in 1904, cotton from Dunklin County won first prize for quality and yield.

But before the new agricultural sovereign could rule, the remains of the old had to be removed. Lumber companies contracted families to clear whatever stumps, substandard timber, and waste remained on company land and prepare that land for cultivation. A single family group would agree to clear a plot of land for a piece rate per acre, usually between $6 and $12. These families lived in rough shacks or tents on the land they were clearing in conditions that were far below the standards of facilities in the logging camps. Their work—detailed land clearance by hand—was simple yet onerous. Working in family groups, husbands, wives, and children felled standing trees with cross-cut saws and piled and burned brush. Stump removal consumed most of their efforts. First, land clearers weakened stumps and root systems with dynamite, arsenic, or fire, after which they ripped the "stumpies" from the mud with mules or their bare hands. This work was easier in swampy areas where trees had shallower roots and stumps decomposed faster.[31] In this way, family groups transformed over a million acres of cut-over land into farms throughout the new cotton region of the South.

Once the land was clear of stumps, many of the families traded their saws and chains for hoes and cotton sacks. Timber companies, which were increasingly dealing in land, wanted to sell developed farmland in large tracts, not newly cleared plots, which were known to produce weak first and second crops. As part of land clearance contracts, large landowners such as Himmelberger-Luce gave families who cleared ten acres or more in a single year the option to farm the land for up to three more years rent-free. To families who came from the hills looking for a way to reclaim livelihoods working the land with some semblance of autonomy, this situation seemed promising. Thousands took advantage of it and planted their own corn and cotton crops, which they then sold for cash. After this contract expired, tenants could either move to another plot or stay on the land they had been cultivating and pay rent, usually between $4 and $20 per acre, depending on its fertility and how well it was drained. Meanwhile, real estate companies sought wealthy buyers for the land even as these families farmed it.[32]

This method of land clearance pulled tens of thousands of timber workers into agricultural labor—not as landowners but as tenant farmers who invariably grew cotton. By 1910, more than three of four farmers in Dunklin, New Madrid, and Pemiscot counties worked someone else's land, a rate that was much higher on newly reclaimed lands. Whether tenants needed cash to pay rent, to buy goods, or to save toward a land purchase, cotton offered an excellent means to earn it. Commodity prices boomed in the early years of the twentieth century. The price of cotton reached 14 cents per lint pound in 1910, a fifty-year high. Tenants took advantage of the high prices by doubling cotton acreages in Dunklin County, tripling acreages in New Madrid County, and nearly quadrupling acreages in Pemiscot County between 1900 and 1910. In that year, farmers in these counties raised over 75,000 acres of the staple and produced 0.60 bales per acre, a respectable yield given the newness of the land.[33]

Tenants did well enough on the back of high prices to maintain hope of securing their own land. Consider the best possible scenario for a tenant family in 1910 planting only cotton on a 45-acre farm, the average size. On the strongest land, they would have produced about 27 bales, worth approximately $1,890 if it was of highest quality. They would have paid $20 per acre ($900 for the year) to rent such land. They would have had $900 left—a lot of money for tenants at the time—to clear any debts accrued before the harvest as well as to buy clothes, tools, seed, and food for the next year and maybe even to make a bank deposit. In 1911, however, when prices fell to 9.7 cents per pound, they would have cleared only $400 and been dangerously close to relying on credit.[34]

The Bootheel's frontier workforce—timber cutters, ditch diggers, and tenant families—had few established social resources to rely on if hard times struck. Most had been in the area less than ten years and almost all moved from one place to another and from one job to another on an annual basis. Their lives and their labors were rude and rough, whether they ran a mill saw, chopped trees, prepared ground for a first crop, or cared for a family in a malarial swamp. Moreover, those making the transition from timber work to tenancy lived in relative isolation at the frontier's edge. Churches, the most common source of rural social fellowship, were rare in the lowlands. Less than 25 percent of people in the Bootheel belonged to a church in 1916, well below the state average of 41 percent. Since this figure included towns as well as ridge settlements, the rate of church membership in the lowlands was no doubt much lower still.[35] As a result, the migrants who remade the Bootheel had very little in common other than their experience as farmers who had left homes and kin to look for a new start in southeast Missouri.

Consider the paths of those living in Noah Pierce's boarding house in western New Madrid County in 1910. Brothers Alvah and William Gander were timber cutters, probably for the Himmelberger-Luce Land and Lumber Company. Both born in the 1860s, they had grown up on their parents' farm in Warrick County in southern Indiana. Neither, however, had been able to secure farms when they came of age. Sometime after 1900, the Gander brothers left Warrick County, where they had been working for local landowners as hired hands, or "servants," in the ungenerous estimation of the census official, to take their chances in the Bootheel. Otis Miller and Oliver Proffer were log loaders. Miller, who was born in 1886, had left his parents' rented farm in Williamson County in southern Illinois to pursue wage work in the Bootheel. Proffer, born in 1891, probably sent some of his earnings back to his widowed mother in the hills of Cape Girardeau County. Twenty-four-year-old Tully Raburn was from a tobacco-farming tenant family in Carlisle County in the Kentucky Black Patch. He now worked on the railroad. No doubt the rest of Pierce's boarders—as well as those in countless other boarding houses and makeshift shacks—came from similar circumstances and took similar risks by leaving their family homes.[36]

Entertaining more grandiose ambitions, local oligarchs were certain that their revolution would culminate in the perfection of American democracy after decades of sectional conflict and economic turmoil. Mercer Wilson believed that the Bootheel would play a key role in national reconciliation since it was "where North and South meet and greet with their excellency," not simply as a sectional border but also as a place where northern capital and southern resources created a potent new economic model. To Wilson's mind, the Bootheel was emblematic of the contemporary process of national healing through a renewed faith in white supremacy, economic prosperity, and America's divine mission to the world.[37] Kochtitzky agreed. He wanted future generations to know that the "effort and struggle" of men like himself were "the foundation of the rich reward to be had now from these alluvial lands." Like other wealthy industrialists and speculators of his generation, he believed that the "exemplary . . . standard and vision of these men" had set the region and the country on the course of progress.[38] When John Nolen looked to that future, he saw a robust republic. He envisioned the Bootheel as an American utopia full of "wells of pure water, domestic animals, churches, schools, fields of waving grain, orchards, cities and modern dwellings occupied by industrious, frugal, intelligent, contented, happy people."[39] It was a "modern promised land," according to C. F. Bruton, a Sikeston land agent. Like "the land of Canaan," the Bootheel's fecund fields were home to a new "children of Israel" who through their labor earned the bounty of God's favor. "If a man is blessed who makes two blades of grass grow where only one grew before," Bruton asked, "how much more blessed is the man who makes the swamp bloom and bring forth fruit as this land does, where, before they wrought and labored, only the frog and fish could live?"[40] Such imagery no doubt also filled the imaginations of those living at Pierce's boarding house.

Others were less optimistic. While small landowners and established tenants generally approved of land reclamation and improvement, they feared the implications of elite control. George Crumb, a ridge farmer near Bloomfield, shared his neighbors' reservations about the proposed Little River Drainage District, which he feared would extend the power of the few into the lives of nearly every Bootheel farmer. "We are all anxious to have drainage and at the earliest moment," he explained, "the only difference being in the method of organizing the work." Crumb was afraid that to have such a large district controlled by so few would shackle independent farmers "with liens which will ultimately drive hundreds of the pioneers from the homes which they have toiled amid many hardships and privations to build up." The oligarchs controlling the drainage district would have nearly absolute power to "convert the best parts of our counties into large 'Feudal' tenures tilled by a generation of tenantry." Such developments, Crumb argued, would be "against the spirit of our institutions and dangerous to popular government."[41] This is precisely what migrants to the Bootheel sought to escape.

Wedged between sites of timber extraction and land reclamation, ridge farmers in Scott County also felt these threats. The superheated transformation of the lowlands generated new demand for their land and raised their taxes to levels that favored only the wealthy. Tenancy rates crept upward, from 55 percent in 1900 to 60 percent in 1910. Meanwhile, the number of landowners declined slightly even though there were 8,000 more people in the county. Most of these migrants flocked to booming sawmill towns such as Morley, Oran, and Chaffee in the Scott County hills or to Sikeston, a growing trade and milling hub. At the same time, large landowners were in the process of planting cotton and thousands of tenants in the new lands of the nearby Little River Valley.[42]

Farmers on the ridge found few political alternatives to the power of the local oligarchs, who controlled both the Republican and Democratic parties. The influence of men such as Kochtitzky, Houck, and Wilson in regional affairs mirrored the pro-business designs of Republicans in the federal government between 1896 and 1912. Populist-minded Democrats such as Phil Hafner, a newspaper publisher and editor in Scott County, were lost in a political wilderness during these years. Raised in nearby Cairo, Hafner had prided himself on being the voice of the small corn and wheat farmers on Sikeston Ridge. Although he never affiliated with the People's Party, Hafner's Democratic newspaper remained a strong advocate of agrarian values throughout the 1890s. Yet the sweeping economic and social changes transforming the surrounding lowlands alarmed him like nothing before. Hafner and his neighbors feared the power that elites were massing through inequitable taxing structures, government favors for investors, and increasing corporate ownership of the land.[43]

Wary of the same "feudal tenures" that Crumb described, independent farmers sought a means to preserve and even enhance their livelihoods in the "modern promised land." Hafner gave voice to their powerful sense of unease in 1902 when he sold his Democratic paper and started an independent publication, the *Scott County Kicker*. From the start, the *Kicker* aimed to revive the "spirit" of popular government that farmers such as Crumb believed was threatened by monopolies. None of the popular reform movements of the late nineteenth century had established much footing in the Bootheel owing to its undeveloped isolation, yet the rapid transformation of the region after 1900 summoned inherited, if unarticulated, ideas about the proper relationship between work, independent manhood, and citizenship.

"The Scott County Kicker is the People's Paper," declared the masthead, and "it is not Muzzled!" Only by exercising their democratic voice could ridge farmers avoid being sucked into the whirlwind of wage labor and tenancy currently remaking the lowlands. Hafner challenged all independent farmers to read the *Kicker* and "wear no Man's Collar."[44]

Hafner and his readers were eager to perform their duty as free citizens to arrest these dangerous developments. Although repelled by the two main parties, they had faith in the electoral process and increasingly looked to the fledgling Socialist Party as an alternative. Led by Eugene V. Debs, himself from southern Indiana, socialists called for the great wealth of corporations, such as International Harvester, to be redistributed to the producers, the workers and farmers who had generated the wealth. Socialists also demanded that the government take ownership of the railroads and all public utilities.[45] "I am tired of choosing between the lesser of two evils," Hafner declared prior to the 1906 election. Instead, he pledged to "vote the ticket that comes nearest representing my ideas of government" and encouraged readers to join him in a "bold stand against the organized corruption of both old parties."[46]

Hafner, Crumb, and *Kicker* readers sought their own more equitable version of progress, not a return to some simpler past. Just as they held sacred the producerist ideas of work, citizenship, and freedom, Bootheel farmers were also "progressive people" who embraced modern development. The rural folk who turned to the Socialist Party were, one historian observed, "hopeful about the possibility of creating a new society in their own lifetimes."[47] Hafner and his readers had faith that their ballots could harness the power of progress to the will of the people, a faith that bore its own postmillennialist glint. "Change is sure to come," he declared, and "there is no heading it off." People could make a more perfect world, Hafner assured his readers, as soon as they "are convinced that the present system is ruinous and vote for a change."[48]

# 2

## Jerusalem

"I am carefully studying and watching and the Socialists are the only ones who have any sane plan of operations," Phil Hafner told *Kicker* readers in early 1907.[1] The national banking panic that year offered convincing new evidence that corporate tycoons could not manage their enormous power. "Fortunes that had been admired as evidence of the glorious opportunities in our happy land turned into exceedingly shaky exploits in thimble-rigging" once the bubble burst, journalist Charles Edward Russell wrote.[2] Yet elite industrialists and landowners in the Bootheel continued to drive forward their marriage of economic clout and political influence. In the midst of the panic, large landowners finalized plans for the ambitious Little River Drainage District, which would include parts of nearly every Bootheel county in the largest drainage scheme in the nation. Giving more authority to the rich in a time of poverty seemed like madness to Hafner, who feared that the captains of the drainage district would use their ability to tax and appropriate land to create a shadow government accountable to no one.[3] Taking to the stump circuit, Hafner argued that the unchecked power of these men posed a mortal danger to the independence of small farmers and that the Socialist Party offered the only democratic alternative. Without socialism, he warned uneasy crowds, producers would be "doomed to wage slavery." If that happened, Hafner demanded, "what better chance have your children?"[4] Local farmer H. P. Proctor agreed. "For 29 years I have voted, as I thought, for better times—but times get worse and worse and worse. Henceforth I shall vote—not for party—but for home and family," he declared in early 1908.[5]

Farmers in Scott County embraced the Socialist Party as a potent means to defend an agrarian way of life—what Proctor termed "home and family"— that valorized productive labor. Their agrarian producerism rested upon a popular rendering of the labor theory of value wherein work created wealth and those who labored possessed a natural right to a share of the wealth they generated. For most urban workers, the rise of wage work in the nineteenth century had undermined producerist ideas; work became a means to buy rather than an end in itself. Farmers, whether they ate what they grew or sold it in the market, continued to live by the fruits of their labor, which was a collective endeavor by members of households typically organized by a male head. In their world view, the hard-earned, God-given rights of producers legitimized claims to manhood, independence, and citizenship.[6] Like their artisan forbears, twentieth-century agrarians "linked freedom and independence with control over productive resources and portrayed the state as defender of the public good, as protector of communities of petty producers."[7] "Socialists propose a complete overthrow of present conditions," Hafner declared, a final triumph of producer's democracy, the reign of the "class that is useful and does the work of the world."[8]

Meanwhile, the spread of rural wage labor and permanent tenancy denied farmers access to the products of their labor and reduced them to a condition of dependence. Fearful of creeping wage slavery, many independent farmers looked to socialism for a "sane plan" to create a safe future. Led by Hafner and the *Kicker*, Scott County socialists organized an electoral political movement rooted in generations-old social forms to pursue the cooperative commonwealth, a vision articulated best by moderate socialist Eugene Debs as the transfer of "power from the corporate elite to those who produced society's wealth."[9] Scott County residents were among tens of thousands of farmers, lumber workers, and miners across Arkansas, Louisiana, Oklahoma, and Texas who joined the Socialist Party between 1900 and 1915. Together, voters in these states gave Debs nearly 100,000 votes in the presidential election of 1912.[10]

The migrants remaking the lowlands, meanwhile, were living the agrarian nightmare. Although their goal was to attain landed autonomy through extractive wage work, they were quickly caught up in the tumult of the rapid expansion of cotton production. By the early 1910s, their labor of cutting trees, digging ditches, and pulling stumps had made possible the rise of commodity crop agriculture on the new lands of Dunklin, New Madrid, and Pemiscot counties, where the widespread use of share tenancy dimmed migrant workers' hopes of autonomy. Unlike the ridge farmers of Scott County, migrant families had few social resources to fall back on. Their lives in the Bootheel were frantic and desperate. They lacked extended local kin networks, established church homes, and time-tested friendships in a dizzying and dangerous world where cutting accidents, drunken disputes, and deadly diseases were real threats to life. Worse still, very few were able to move from tenancy to landownership as they had planned.

In an effort to salvage some hope, landless families sought communal and spiritual meaning in the new Pentecostal revivals sweeping the southern countryside. Rooted in the Holiness movement of the late nineteenth century, Pentecostalism matured in what began as a small revival in 1906 in a poor area of Los Angeles, where it drew the attention of spirit-hungry preachers across the country. It offered seekers access to a latter-day outpouring of the prophetic power of the Holy Spirit. Rejecting what they saw as the sterility and formalism of the established denominations, Pentecostals crafted a new fellowship of ordinary believers empowered with spiritual gifts such as the ability to speak in unknown tongues, interpret divine messages, and heal the sick. Pentecostals foretold Christ's return and spoke of the justice that would be meted during the millennium as an imminent event. Rural people flocked to this insurgent religious movement and in it found the basis for common purpose in a time of fear and confusion.[11]

In the reciprocal cross-currents of socialism and Pentecostalism, workers in the lowlands fashioned a militant new social movement to resist the hegemony of cotton tenancy and wage work. Spilling over from local groups in Scott County, socialism spread rapidly among land clearers, timber workers, and tenants. Lowland socialists mobilized around opposition to share tenancy and its debilitating effects on their power as citizens, their household economies, their ideas of proper gender roles—and their notions of white supremacy. While upland farmers decried the effects of wage slavery, frontier workers labored on the edge of dependent relationships they likened to actual slavery, and they faced increasing competition from newly arrived African American migrants for the jobs that thrust them into these new work conditions. These rebellious white workers met in socialist meetings and in brush-arbor religious services—beyond the gaze of party and denominational leaders alike—to share discontent with the way the world was and to empower themselves to change it. As conditions worsened they would seek to achieve retributive justice with violence.

The rise of a millenarian, racist, and violent movement among the Bootheel's white work force highlights the ways ordinary rural people expanded their field of political action in response to the limitations of progressivism. Following the people's revolts of the late nineteenth century, progressive reformers sought an "ideal of classless social harmony," as Shelton Stromquist and others have shown. In doing so, "the Progressives hoped to marginalize and disarm an alternative politics of class" by narrowing the "circle of citizenship" through various methods of disenfranchisement.[12] Southern politicians, both progressives and quasi-populists, succeeded in fashioning a demagogic electoral politics that used rhetoric of universal white supremacy to secure elite control and the docility of "low white men." The 1912 election of President Woodrow Wilson, a progressive southerner who resegregated federal employment, seemed to consummate this alliance.[13]

Many rural whites like those in the Bootheel, however, refused to acquiesce to this regime and sought alternatives in social movements that promised to answer the corruption of ruling elites with the dawn of a new age. In doing so, new agrarian rebels—from the Bootheel to the Black Patch to the cotton fields of Oklahoma and Texas—cast themselves as the saviors of independent white producers.[14]

\* \* \*

Scott County socialists championed small producers in a world they believed was beset by monopolists. At the heart of their appeal lay a reverence for the natural, even divine rights of laborers. "Labor is honorable, exalted," Hafner wrote in 1906; it is "healthful and necessary to happiness." Relying on a commonsense reading of the labor theory of value, Hafner argued that "capital is that which labor creates. If you raise a crop of corn with your labor, the result is your capital. It should all be yours—every ear of it." This was a right rooted in biblical command, not some fancy new theory. "Under just conditions no man should have any product (capital) unless he creates it," because "the Bible directs that you eat your bread in the sweat of your face," Hafner argued.[15] No amount of economic or political power could change this. The right of producers was a "natural right," the *Kicker* declared, that "cannot be forfeited, nor by special privileges justly acquired." In short, "no man can give another the right to rob him."[16] Yet there were those in the Bootheel who did not "a lick of productive work, yet [they have] corn to burn, while you who raise the corn will have to mortgage your growing crop next spring."[17] The political system that allowed these affairs was "despotism," said Hafner.[18]

The *Kicker* argued that progressive politics made this corruption possible. Hafner lambasted presidents Theodore Roosevelt and William H. Taft for policies that valorized centralized economic management by a government of unelected business-friendly experts alongside a "hierarchical and exclusionary" interpretation of citizenship.[19] The attitude of such politicians that it was the government's power to decide for people "what is 'for their benefit'" was a form of "dictatorship," Hafner argued. He cited U.S. land seizures in the Philippines following the Spanish-American War as a warning about their domestic policies. Roosevelt was "a very depraved, heartless, blustering, and brutal man," and the policies he pursued created greater systemic blight in that he allowed corporations such as Standard Oil unprecedented access to the presidency. If it was up to Roosevelt and Taft "to decide when the Filipinos are fit for self-government, then it takes no long step to reach the point where a handful of trust magnates will decide that American workingmen are not fit for self-government," Hafner argued. "This has always been the working theory of capitalism," Hafner explained. "The workers are supposed to have no voice in the benefits to be conferred upon them. They are to be governed 'for their benefit' by those who exploit them."[20]

But there was hope. Socialism offered a modern means to restore the natural rights of producers. "It is the rising Socialist movement that has the mission to restore democracy," Hafner argued, "to make the best part of the Declaration of Independence something more than clanging brass, and to insure that a government of the people, by the people and for the people shall not perish from off the earth."[21] To achieve this mission, however, good citizens would need to take back their government. "What we need in office is men of our own class," socialist organizer J. W. Adams claimed. "There are but two forces—one that produces and consumes, and another that consumes without producing," he continued. "It seems to me that it does not require much effort for the farmer to discover to what class he belongs."[22] Socialism offered a new way, a compelling vision of the future that was free from past political attachments.

To transform frustration into action, Hafner adroitly challenged male heads of farming families to live up to their duty and responsibility as citizens and men. It was up to hardworking people to stand up for themselves, he declared. "There are hundreds of tenant farmers and wage earners who refuse to join a Socialist local because they are afraid of the landlord or boss," Hafner wrote. He implored them to be true men and "come out in the open and defy your landlords and bosses."[23] After all, the *Kicker* masthead urged readers to "wear no Man's Collar."[24] Adams, a Socialist Party candidate in Scott County, wondered rhetorically whether ridge farmers were too complacent to take control of their destinies. "If you are," he said, "take you[r] medicine, look pleased and say it is good. But if not satisfied, hunt the remedy."[25] The solution was the political triumph of socialism. "We can do at the ballot box what was formerly accomplished with guns," Hafner declared.[26] Farmers needed to follow men like H. P. Proctor and vote for "home and family."

But farmers had to act soon. Already, Hafner pointed out, the Scott County Milling Company controlled the processing of their corn and wheat. This control would pale in comparison to the power of land speculators, timber companies, and large landowners. "Farmers open your eyes!" Hafner demanded. "The big interests have subdued all but you, and they are now after you."[27] The *Kicker* appealed powerfully to readers' notions of independence and manhood by forecasting a future dystopia of wage slavery if citizens did not act. "On the Fourth day of [July] the orators of capitalism told the workers how free they are," Hafner reminded readers. "But no man is free so long as another man owns the means by which he must earn a living." While fifty years ago the "chattel slave power used the lash to drive men to work, today the wage slave power has substituted hunger and want for the lash," Hafner proclaimed.[28]

Agrarians saw the spread of agricultural wage labor as the greatest threat to their independence. When Hafner evoked wage slavery, he tapped a widespread rural abhorrence, rooted in antebellum America, of the dependent relationships created when one relied on another for work. The use of hired hands in seasonal farm work was common in both the North and the South, but those involved were usually young single men looking to become independent farmers in their own right; their dependence as hired hands was temporary. To the agrarian mind, farm workers who labored for wages on a permanent basis became perpetual dependents—became like slaves—and thus relinquished their claims to manhood and even citizenship. Hafner and others feared that the process of development in the Bootheel would force farmers and their children into such a condition permanently.[29] "Under chattel slavery the black man got his keep. How much more does the wage-slave get?" Hafner asked. "Sometimes—not often, I am awake when the whistle of the Scott County Milling Co. at Oran, blows at 4:30 a.m., and I can almost hear it say: 'Get up, ye slaves, and go to work—or starve.'" He concluded, "The tenant farmer fares but little better, if any, than the wage slave."[30] The *Kicker* insisted that through the power of socialism, "wage slavery is as surely doomed as was chattel slavery."[31]

By highlighting the threats to agrarianism, Scott County socialists transformed a doctrine that many farmers might not be inclined to trust into the last hope of a noble American heritage. If anyone was to be distrusted, Hafner suggested, it was the speculators, land barons, and mainstream politicians who robbed producers of the wealth they created. Socialism could correct this state of affairs because it would "eliminate rent, interest and profit." If farmers voted for the Socialist Party, Hafner contended, "the landlord . . . who does no useful work, and who now sits in his comfortable home . . . and forces the producers to bring him 'all above a living,' might have to hunt up a pick and shovel and apply for a job."[32] Socialism became a means for farmers to exercise their manhood, independence, and citizenship by challenging the power of prevailing elites.

Scott County farmers increasingly embraced socialism as a viable alternative because it also reaffirmed their public voice as citizen-producers through mass meetings, social gatherings, and public displays of discontent. Socialist events included local party meetings, speeches, debates, and barbeques. These meetings offered a way to bring in new members and reinforced feelings of solidarity and strength. Pleasant Valley members held a party meeting in the local church and reported that the "house was filled to its full capacity, and a rousing meeting was held." In such meetings "all over the country," Hafner added, "the Socialists are active, and when the workers take the bits in their own mouths, as they are doing, there is no doubt of the result."[33] "It was a great time the people had at Blodgett last Saturday at the picnic given by the Socialists," the *Kicker* reported in 1909. "A tremendous crowd had gathered, variously estimated at from 1,500 to 2,000 people. And the barbequed meat was fine."[34] Such events enticed farmers to take time out of their workaday worlds, make a trip to town, chat and gossip with other farmers in the region, and enjoy music, carousing, and good food. This method of organizing worked. With activists such as Hafner and Adams leading the campaign, socialists garnered 629 votes in Scott County in the 1908 election, 16 percent of all votes cast. More important, activists had organized thirteen party locals that boasted a total of 394 dues-paying members. Most of this support was concentrated along the Sikeston Ridge.[35]

A mood of pride and defiance was central to these public displays. Forthright and courageous, socialists evoked a heritage of independence and autonomy. Party speakers quickly gained a reputation for their scathing attacks on economic conditions and the established parties. "The Socialist speakers are the only ones that can draw a crowd," one correspondent told the *Kicker*.[36] Another boasted that one speaker in particular, J. K. Manion, delivered "sledge hammer blows with such precission [sic] and force that they never fail of good results."[37] Evidently the two major parties had difficulties meeting the socialist attack. The Socialist Party was "making open challenges to both the older parties," the *Kicker* exulted. While the Democratic press routinely accused socialists of atheism, free love, and social leveling among different classes and races, Democratic Party candidates seldom accepted challenges from Socialist Party members to debate. The Democrats always "squawk about 'dividin up,' 'agin religion' 'want intermarriage between blacks and whites,' and so on," Hafner complained, "but they won't toe the mark."[38] In short, socialists were real men; their opponents were not. Socialist Party meetings displayed respect for the intellectual capabilities of area farmers as opposed to the often crude appeals of mainstream politicians. Activists also used these gatherings to distribute Socialist Party literature other than the *Kicker*—particularly the national weekly *Appeal to Reason*—to people who wanted to know more.[39] Socialists' willingness to communicate with and educate ordinary people demonstrated their radical belief that tenant farmers, wage laborers, and their families deserved to be taken seriously.

The strength of the socialist movement soon shifted to the reclaimed lands of the southern counties. Scott County socialists reached their peak of strength in 1910 by polling 939 votes, more than 24 percent of all votes cast in the county. Significantly, however, the movement was spreading. That same year rural workers near Hayti in Pemiscot County organized the first local outside Scott County. Their candidate for county office lost badly in 1910, but they hoped to organize a second local soon. Meanwhile, members started new locals in Mississippi County and at Lilbourn in New Madrid County. In Scott County, however, the party slumped to 649 votes in 1912, a year that roughly marked the peak of socialism nationally. It is unclear why, but improving economic conditions on Sikeston Ridge likely contributed. Corn and wheat prices reached near-record highs in 1911, and many renters seem to have profited enough to buy land.[40] The industrial transformation of Scott County's countryside seemed to have halted just short of Sikeston Ridge. In Dunklin, New Madrid, and Pemiscot counties, meanwhile, things got worse by the day.

\* \* \*

White migrant families had few resources to gird them against the tribulations of the ever-harsher cotton tenancy system. Few came to the Bootheel with friends or kin. Rootless and suffering, these rural working families opened seams of collective discontent against local authorities through organized violence, prophetic religious revival, and emergent socialist groups. Deemed unfit and backward by area elites, frontier families sought to defend the remnants of a producerist worldview that upheld the importance of work, independence, and white supremacy.

As the industrial transformation of the lowlands gathered pace, landless migrants resorted to traditions of violence to shore up their visions of autonomy. Violence was so common in the Bootheel, one editor observed, that "a man who takes a fellowman's life can more easily escape punishment than one who steals a cow or a hog."[41] He was not far off the mark. Tenant farmers, lumber workers, and day laborers "were a rough, hard-working, hard-drinking lot" that was prone to settle disputes with force.[42] "They would take just so much abuse," area landowner Thad Snow recalled, "then they would sass you back, and perhaps pull a knife or gun."[43] Crime was difficult to report, Hafner noted, because it "is so common that it ceases to be news." A cursory examination of Scott County circuit court proceedings reveals just how pervasive lawlessness was.[44] In a two-month period, the court dealt with two cases of manslaughter, six felonious assaults, two robberies, three charges of carrying pistols, and one each of malicious trespass, dynamiting, gambling, carrying concealed weapons, murder, and disturbing religious worship.[45] In 1911 in Pemiscot County there were "three murders in a ten-day period in January, two in two days in March, and two more within ten days in September, to say nothing of numerous assaults in which victims survived."[46] More often than not, drunkenness played a part in the murder cases. "The fair this week started off fine," one reporter remarked, "only one man killed so far. It is said that whiskey and women caused the trouble."[47] Buffeted by powerful employers, dangerous work conditions, and social dislocation, frontier workers fell back upon rituals of violence rooted in the social world of the southern backcountry of the early nineteenth century. In that period, as Elliott J. Gorn has shown, "the material base of backwoods life was ill suited to social transformation, and the cultural traditions of the past offered alternatives to rigid new ideals," such as working for wages. That hard-drinking and hard-fighting culture, even though it impeded the creation of stable new communities, still offered resistance to modern "society's demands for sober self-control."[48]

Frustrated by the attempts of poor whites to retain autonomy, large landowners recruited African American farmers, who they hoped would provide a more docile and cheaper workforce. Prior to 1910, there were only about 6,000 blacks in the Bootheel; most of these farmed along the Mississippi River, although a few hundred labored in lumber mills. The expansion of agricultural production, however, attracted large numbers of farmers in the 1910s, when the black population increased by as much as 30 percent.[49] Like many poor whites, they saw wage work as a route to land. H. R. Post hired black workers in late 1911 to clear "wild land" and pick crops on his 1,300-acre farm near Parma. He did so in order for "the crops to be harvested now and to clear land that it is impossible to get white laborers to do." He was not alone in his preference for black farm workers. Most employers claimed that whites would not work at all, no matter what the wage scale was.[50]

In response to the influx of African Americans on area farms, landless whites moved from casual violence into vigilantism. Although it was fixed on the past, the backwoods culture of violence gave people a language and means of racialized political rebellion. After a white mob assaulted a meeting of black Republicans in Marston in March 1911, a landowner remarked that a "spirit of bulldozing and intimidating the negro seems to be growing in New Madrid County."[51] That began a wave of attacks against newly arrived black farm workers. In September 1911, members of a white mob fired shots into the shacks of cotton pickers near Marston. They wounded four and prompted many more to leave. A week later, Richard King, a black cotton picker, stabbed two white tenants during an altercation on a farm north of Caruthersville in Pemiscot County. White workers quickly formed a mob, but King eluded them.[52] Unsatisfied, the frenzied mob seized two black farm workers, A. B. Richardson and "High Pockets" Ben Woods, from the Caruthersville city jail, where they sat after being arrested for petty crimes. Richardson's body was fished out of the Mississippi River the following day and Woods was never seen again.[53] Repeated attacks continued almost nightly during November.[54] For white workers seeking a return to landed autonomy, vigilantism became a means to resist wage slavery as well as to punish African American competitors who not only provided a reminder of chattel slavery but whose presence actively undermined white claims to independence. Eric Hobsbawm has argued about premodern vigilantes that "though their movements are thus in many respects blind and groping," they nonetheless developed "a specific language in which to express" rebellion against more powerful foes. Vigilantes such as these did not "grow with or into modern society," he concluded; rather, "they are broken into it, or more rarely . . . they break into it."[55]

This campaign of racial violence galvanized landless whites in rebellion against the large landowners. Local elites described Tobe Oller, the alleged leader of the Parma vigilantes, as a former mill worker, a gambler, and a drunk. He and his ilk, landowner Seth Barnes explained, represented "the irresponsible, hoodlum element, that will work no longer than they can get a sack of flour and a piece of meat, and then they spend their spare time loafing and raising 'Hell' in the country."[56] The scarcity of pliable white workers suggests that resistance was spreading. Up to that point land-hungry migrants had provided an almost limitless supply of labor. But their desire for independence revolved around their aim to work for themselves as autonomous producers.

Poor whites could usually squat on uncleared land and survive on wage work when necessary.[57] Their refusal to answer to the needs of speculators and investors, however, threatened the pace of Bootheel development and profitability. The decision of landowners and developers to employ African Americans to undercut such piecemeal resistance precipitated the violent action of poor whites. J. S. Gossom was sure that the vigilante mobs "are composed of tenants and laborers, who think if the Negroes were out of the country they could get better wages for picking cotton and get cheaper rent."[58] Very quickly elites came to despise poor whites. Landowners frequently referred to the members of the mobs using derogatory terms such as "hoodlum" and reserved the label of citizen for themselves and even black farm workers. Nevertheless, the vigilante campaign of late 1911 marked the emergence of a movement among landless white men to defend their dream of being independent producers.

* * *

Into this violent world of cotton, mud, and blood arrived a group of white Pentecostal evangelists offering people radical new spiritual blessings and a hand in the millennium. In late 1910, preachers who had been organizing new churches in the Ozarks followed the migrant path out of the hills and began holding tent revivals in Senath, Cardwell, and Kennett. There they prayed that ordinary believers would receive spiritual gifts, including the power to heal and pray in unknown tongues, that would hasten Christ's return, according to the eschatology they subscribed to. Pentecostal services included sermons that featured literal interpretations of the Bible, particularly the New Testament book Acts of the Apostles; testimonials by laypeople; an unrestrained worship style; and intense prayer ending in a climactic call for salvation. At the altar, new converts, surrounded by believers praying in tongues, asked for Christ's grace and to be filled with the power of the Holy Spirit. This process could go on for hours, even all night. "Never before had people witnessed a Holy Ghost service," one observer of Pentecostal revival in the Bootheel noted, and "imaginations ran wild."[59] Bootheel evangelist Walter Higgins remembered that the first reactions to this new religious fervor were not always positive: "The rumors and tales about the so-called 'holy-rollers' were absolutely amazing."[60] But when onlookers saw "others shouting, dancing in the Spirit, falling under the mighty power of God, and hearing strange tongues spoken in ecstatic praise to God," they "were amazed and many believed and received."[61]

Pentecostals sought to emulate the prophetic powers the early Christians had received that both defined the early church and would signal Christ's return. Decrying what they considered the materialism, stagnation, and worldly concerns of mainstream Protestant churches, Pentecostals sought the restoration of the true church, unblemished by the trappings of wealth or worldly influence.[62] Pentecostal belief focused on the writings of the Apostle Luke, particularly the book of Acts, which described the formation of the early church as, in the words of one theologian, a "Spirit-inspired community, the New Israel."[63] The working of the Holy Spirit was centrally important to Pentecostals, not just as a means for salvation and initiation but also as "prophetic inspiration" that "equips the disciple for service." It was "an experience empowering for mission."[64] In the last days, Jesus promised His followers, "ye shall receive power" (Acts 1:8). He told them, "I will pour out of my Spirit upon all flesh: and your sons and your daughters shall prophesy, and your young men shall see visions, and your old men shall dream dreams" (Acts 2:17). With these powers, Pentecostals, like the Apostles, set out to "restore again the kingdom to Israel" (Acts 1:6).[65] Evangelists preaching this message achieved sustained success in the Bootheel. "The revival fires are burning here," Joseph Snyder, a minister in the Assemblies of God, reported from Kennett. "We held a series of meetings and the Lord was with us in power. . . . Sinners are begging us to come back."[66]

The teaching spread fastest among poor people because it gave them the power, both individually and as a collective, to confront evil. Pentecostals converted thousands of followers in the Bootheel in the early 1910s, most of them from timber camps, gangs of land clearers, and tenant families. In Dunklin County, tents overflowed as large crowds packed in to hear the message.[67] By 1912, an evangelist reported that he had personally baptized over 200 people.[68] Why was Pentecostalism so popular? Historians tend to dismiss faith in prophetic gifts variously as a numbing distraction, a psychic disorder, or, at best, an unreal expression of some more real discontent. This "tendency to understand religious language as expressing some reality separate from it, not as constituting a real world," Karen Fields argued, imposes ahistorical judgments informed by contemporary secularism. Fields cautioned that historians must try to understand the world as the faithful understood it, a world where "God is present and manifests Himself concretely—in the miracles of healing and deliverance, in fulfilled prophesyings, in the solidarity of believers, in tongues, in all the wonders of existence as well as in all its commonplaces."[69] The goal of Pentecostalism was to endow believers with the powers of the Holy Spirit; the exercise of such gifts would then prepare the way for Christ's millennial reign.[70] This was not simply a "chiliasm of the defeated," as some scholars have argued.[71] To the people involved, the empowerment was real.

As a collective experience that was unrestrained, Pentecostalism's potential for critiquing worldly authorities was also very real.[72] Precisely because of this unruliness, historical studies of early Pentecostalism often miss its radical political implications.[73] Indeed, police records can provide a better view of the rebellious possibilities at the frayed edges of revival than most church records do. Sensing what most historians have not seen and later church leaders have erased, local elites responded to the disruptive potential of Pentecostals by repressing them. Higgins and others had their meetings dispersed by police, received numerous death threats, and were often literally chased out of town. Taken together, the quest for spiritual power and the official backlash generated tremendous excitement in the Bootheel. "The more they persecuted us, the more they oppressed us," Higgins recalled, "the more the people would come."[74] In short, the revivals gave poor people a new means of resistance.

\* \* \*

At the same time that Pentecostal evangelists moved in from the Ozarks, the Socialist Party emerged as a viable alternative political voice of white working people throughout the reclaimed lands of the Little River Valley, particularly in Dunklin County. Organizers from Scott County, such as W. W. McAlister, were the first to target this terrain as a place to rejuvenate their movement. The election of 1912 gave a hint of real promise. In Dunklin County, Eugene Debs received 1,001 votes in support of his bid for the presidency. Although Woodrow Wilson carried the county with over 2,700 votes, Debs outpolled both William Howard Taft and Theodore Roosevelt. This second-place showing was due more to Debs's national popularity than to local organization, but the result nevertheless gave Bootheel socialists a boost. John G. Scott, who had run for the state senate on the Socialist Party ticket, looked to build on this uprising by founding *Justice*, a weekly paper that opposed the Bootheel's large landowners, industrialists, and speculators.[75] The goal of Scott and others was to channel the discontent that was emerging among lowland workers into a political organization capable of unseating the dominant Democratic Party. To accomplish this, socialists needed to mobilize emerging rebellious groups, whether religious or vigilante, for an electoral challenge. *Justice* quickly attracted the interest of white workers; within weeks of the first edition the paper boasted over 1,100 subscribers, a large number considering how poor most readers were.[76]

Lowland socialists tailored the rhetoric of producerism to appeal to farmers who were either landless or were doing wage work—people much worse off than the farmers on Sikeston Ridge. *Justice* especially attacked rent and interest, the most glaring marks of dependence for tenants. "Now rent is the chief way the master class of Dunklin County have of robbing the laboring people," Scott wrote. He argued that "in order to secure justice for the working people rents must be lowered and finally be abolished forever."[77] Landlords— those who cast producers into conditions of dependency—were especially heinous. "It is a grand thing to be the owner of yourself," McAlister wrote, "but the man that owns the land, the tools, and your job owns YOU. The liberty of one citizen ceases where the licence of another citizen begins," he concluded, and under capitalism, the "landlords licence never ceases therefore the tenants liberty never begins."[78]

This denial of the natural rights of producers was against Christianity. "Socialism says that God Almighty and labor produces all the wealth of this world," Scott explained, "and labor is entitled to all it produces, since God does not ask rent, interest, or profit on what he furnishes us." Any institution, religious or secular, that condoned this state of affairs was also unjust and ungodly. "Landlordism is ungodly and opposed to true Christianity," he declared.[79] Like Pentecostals, socialists pointed out that an unholy cabal of landlords and industrialists controlled the mainline Baptist and Methodist churches as well as local government. "A Baptist preacher, a landowner, a Christian (?) landlord," Scott reported, "uses the courts here in Kennett to help him drive poor tenants off his land. . . . How can he throw his brother out of the shack called his home and make him a wanderer on the face of the earth?" Like Jesus himself, Scott said, quoting Luke 9:58, "many a 'son of man' in Dunklin County 'hath not where to lay his head,' or tend a crop to make a living for next year" because of greedy landlords. For socialists like Scott, a landlord could not be a Christian, "preacher or no preacher."[80] "Just touch their pocket book nerve and the morality and Christianity of these 'our most eminent citizens' drops off like the veneer on cheap furniture," he explained.[81] Tapping into the deep strain of agrarian producerism that Bootheel farmers subscribed to, he wrote, "God made the land for all not for the few to own."[82] As if to prove Scott's critique, church leaders in Malden who were less interested in the false Christianity of their wealthy congregants attended to the more important business of laying "the corner stone of the $16,000 Methodist church."[83] If any of these old-line preachers denounced socialism as atheistic, one *Justice* correspondent advised, ask them "to preach from the following texts: 'In the sweat of they face shalt thou eat bread till thou return unto the ground' (Gen. 3:19), 'For when we were with you we commanded that if any would not work neither should he eat' (2 Thess. 3:10). We Socialists agree fully with these texts."[84]

Socialist use of religious rhetoric was more than simple propaganda, as some have argued; rather, it reflected the discontent already rumbling among rural poor believers such as the Pentecostals. Indeed, Scott and other correspondents used the Gospel of Luke to illustrate the sins of Christian capitalists.[85] "Read Luke 6:27 to 49 and then re-read 46," instructed "Thunderhead" in the pages of *Justice*, "then go out and compel your brother to give you a mortgage on everything he has." After reading these passages, which stress the kindness and mercy at the heart of Christian life, people who were truly "God fearing" would not debase others for profit.[86] "And why call ye me, Lord, Lord," Jesus asked in verse 46, "and do not the things which I say?" Devotion and righteousness had to be expressed through works toward mankind in order to have meaning.[87] The Apostles had organized themselves for the Lord's work on the day of Pentecost, Scott argued, when they became "of one heart and of one soul" in the service of Christ; the New Testament itself proved the "Socialistic character of the collective society of Christ's followers."[88]

*Justice* also carried frequent reports on socialist preachers. Scott praised a sermon given by a Rev. Friend that "was revolutionary and dealt with our unnatural, abnormal and unchristian social conditions." Scott felt that "we need more sermons like this," and he urged "everyone who loves righteousness and social justice [to] attend and encourage the minister in his work."[89] When Scott heard a "workingman preacher" deliver a Sunday sermon in June 1914, he reported that it was "the best sermon on true Christianity he ever heard preached."[90] By establishing socialists as the exemplars of radical preachers, Scott not only nurtured mutual sympathies with evangelists and reached out to those cramming into revival tents but also refined the Socialist Party's moral critique of Bootheel capitalism. Like their counterparts in Texas and Oklahoma, organizers in the Bootheel often became religious dissenters in their own right, and the two worlds of socialism and Pentecostal revivalism sometimes merged in the pages of the socialist newspaper *Justice*. The paper reported on a socialist meeting in 1914 that featured talks on "Who Owns the Earth" and "Christ's Earthly Mission."[91] Readers used the pages of the newspaper to advertise upcoming revival meetings. "There will be preaching [in Plum Island] this Sunday by Comrade McAllister on the 'Life and Teachings of Jesus,'" one *Justice* correspondent reported.[92] Socialist arguments for the restoration of the natural rights of producers meshed well with revivalist (especially Pentecostal) calls for a return to the apostolic church.

Like the Pentecostals, socialists offered a potent and compelling vision of a future that promised to empower ordinary people to change the world. While

Pentecostals looked to do so through the gifts of Holy Ghost baptism, Debsian socialists pursued the destruction of evil in the world and the "perfection of humanity" through Christian and producerist principles.[93] Bootheel socialists asserted the Socialist Party platform that capitalism was corrupt "and the source of unspeakable misery and suffering to the whole working class." Because they believed that "the longer sufferance of these conditions is impossible," socialists sought to "end them all," to purify the world by "the realization of its ultimate aim, the co-operative commonwealth."[94] The result of the commonwealth in rural areas would be the restoration of producers to their rightful place. "Socialism alone will rid our country of the curse of landlordism," stated the Dunklin County Socialist Party platform.[95] Unlike prophetic millenarians, socialists believed that building the cooperative commonwealth would be a gradual process. Yet they shared a faith in ordinary people as vessels of change. "The world's uplift must come from the forces underneath," Scott explained. "Only the toilers can free the toilers."[96]

Despite differences, the two movements reinforced one another: Pentecostalism lent strength to socialist moral arguments, while socialism supplied a political venue for the rebelliousness of Pentecostalism. Socialist "revival" meetings mirrored Pentecostal ones and were often advertised as both socialist and religious events. "A big Socialist revival meeting is now in progress," Scott announced in early 1914.[97] Not all of these involved religious themes, to be sure. In January 1914, Kate Richards O'Hare, a prominent party activist and co-editor of the socialist journal *Rip-Saw,* spoke to three large gatherings, including an overflowing event at the Dunklin County Courthouse, where 400 people had to be turned away for lack of space.[98] Later that year, over 5,000 people heard Debs preach the "gospel of Socialism" in Kennett.[99] The political frame of Bootheel socialism linked these secular events with rebellious religious meetings. "Vote as you pray," one correspondent instructed.[100] *Justice* was alone among area papers in commenting favorably on Pentecostal meetings. "George Smitson, penecost [*sic*], preached for us," reported a correspondent from Hunter; another writer used "Pentecost" as a pen name.[101] "We paid a visit to the south part of [Kennett] the other night where the Pentecosts are holding a series of meetings," wrote another correspondent. "They sure do have fun as compared with their long, sad-faced brethren of the old orthodox churches who sit around like someone was dead. Wonder if God ever smiles?"[102] "Ready Red," a correspondent from Senath, attended a service by Rev. King "at the Pentecostal mission" that compared heathenism in India to sinfulness in Dunklin County. "If he could have been in Kennett . . . at the Socialist speaking and heard that howling mob of Democrats and

Republicans he would think he could find plenty of heathenism without going to India," the writer remarked.[103] Many socialists in Missouri, Texas, and Oklahoma were Pentecostal believers. Area elites certainly considered both groups to be of the same ilk. "A Kennett land owner says he asks prospective tenants their politics and religion," Scott reported. "If they are either Socialists or Holiness they have to move on."[104]

Yet the sins of the Bootheel elite were pushing the socialist cooperative commonwealth further from view. By 1914, progress on the construction of the Little River Drainage District had encouraged landowners to scrap cash-renting agreements in favor of share-renting contracts. Renting new land on a cash basis had made sense because landlords were assured that they would receive a certain level of income no matter how the crop turned out. Share-renters, on the other hand, paid a fixed percentage of the crop, usually one-third of corn and one-fourth of cotton, as rent. For tenants, this was still a step above sharecropping, where a landlord provided the teams and tools and claimed half of all crops, but like croppers, share-renters had to defer to landlords about which crops they planted. A better drainage system made this gamble on crop prices worthwhile for landowners, who made sure their tenants planted cotton. But the deal went bad for both parties in 1914, when the price of cotton collapsed by 41 percent to 7.3 cents a pound when war broke out in Europe.[105] With their earnings nearly halved and with little food of their own, tenants faced a hard winter.

For lowland socialists, the real immorality of tenancy was that it attacked the manhood of producers by making them dependent and unable to fulfill their duties as heads of households. Activists blamed President Wilson and his New Freedom policies that gave administrative power to unelected executive agencies, such as the Federal Trade Commission and the Federal Reserve. "This Wilson's Democracy brand of new freedom is sure hell down in these diggings," one correspondent explained.[106] Rather than bring the hope of a new day, socialists claimed, Wilsonian progressivism gave more power to landlords and capitalists who sought to subjugate free men to a new form of servitude. "For my part I'd rather live under a king and give him a tenth," Scott blared, "than to live in hell as we do and give a third to the landlord, half of what's left to the speculator, 60 cents on the dollar to the merchant and then try to feed a family on what's left. It simply can't be did, boys."[107] The integrity of agrarian producerism rested on a man's ability to have the final say regarding the affairs of his household, especially concerning the labor of his wife and dependents. Reliance on a landlord stripped men who share-rented of crucial authority in the home and in the fields in ways that cash renting had not. Where cash renters paid their rent and got on with the work, share-renters had to obey a landlord's demands that certain crops be grown and often had to send their wives and children into seasonal wage work on other men's farms to earn cash. "A woman in Campbell takes her 4-year old and 8 months old babies to the cotton fields with her every day. There she hoes and scrapes in the dust and heat to earn a scanty living for the sucking babe," a *Justice* correspondent gloomily reported. "But if you kick and protest against such outraged motherhood you're branded as a fool."[108]

The cooperative commonwealth promised to restore agrarian men and women to their rightful places. "If you working men want to be respected," Debs challenged his Kennett audience, "you have got to begin by respecting yourselves" by abandoning the capitalist parties. "All these affiliations are calculated to strip you of your manhood, to reduce you to a condition where you are ashamed of yourself," he explained.[109] "Organize boys," *Justice* explained, "it will keep our wives and babies out of the fields and in the homes and schools."[110] If you just "swap one Democrat for another," Scott asked voters, do you expect that "little orphan girls will no longer drag a pick sack down the cotton rows in December barefooted"?[111] As "Debs told us at Kennett," he continued, "people must do things for themselves."[112] Rather than submitting or watching "their babies starve," organizer J. W. Campbell argued, landless men "should . . . organize, demand, and if necessary take what was needed to sustain life."[113] While local women had few public roles in the movement, they did exhort men to live up to their ideals. "We women are tired of all this," wrote correspondent Comrade X, "and should . . . urge our husbands to work harder for Socialism and for freedom from rent and the profit system."[114]

Threats to the independence and gender ideals of the Bootheel's white tenants and wage workers were also threats to their beliefs about race. Socialists channeled and inflamed the fears of tenants that powerful elites were attacking their rights as white citizens. They argued that tenancy was destroying the ability of poor whites to maintain the integrity, dignity, and independence rightfully due them. These arguments were particularly effective at a time when white supremacy was on the rise across the nation. Like the message of socialists in Scott County, this message centered on the idea that landless whites were being turned into wage slaves who were worse off than chattel slaves. *Justice* routinely compared the plight of white tenant farmers and laborers to slavery, albeit a romanticized and unrealistic version of that status. "Several slaves [are] hunting masters around here," *Justice* continued, "but they are not so fortunate as the niggers were who always had a master and grub furnished them."[115] The coupling of economic dependence with racial degradation terrified landless whites threatened by competition from black workers. "It is reported that Massa Frank Shelton will put all Socialists off his 2700 acres of land in Arkansas," *Justice* lamented. But "where will Massa Frank put all of those white niggers?"[116] Scott even reprinted Senator James Hammond's 1858 "mudsill" speech that accused abolitionists of enslaving members "of your own race" through wage work.[117] Similarly, *Justice* lambasted the Gideon-Anderson Lumber Company for the "the rankest hellishness" of the conditions its employees labored under in the mill and at the timber face. "We say to hell with a system that turns out an Anderson and his white nigger slaves," Scott boomed.[118] These arguments appealed powerfully to men such as William Cunningham who, although he worked as a hired hand on a New Madrid County farm, was listed by a census officer as a "servant," a term synonymous with slave as late as the 1830s. It continued to connote permanent dependence in the 1910s.[119]

Unlike their counterparts elsewhere, lowland socialists organized a defense of white small producers against both elite oppression and the encroachment of blacks. While most socialists nationally believed in the social separation of the races, they also recognized the common rights of producers, both black and white.[120] Not so in the Bootheel, where socialist racism focused popular animosities stemming from the vigilante movement of the early 1910s through the dark lens of threatened producerist manhood. Scott attacked the manhood of elites who opposed female suffrage at a time when landlords were looking to hire blacks who could vote in Missouri. They didn't want white women to vote, he argued, because they "like niggers better than their wives and mothers."[121] Tenant women pushed the issue. "We women are tired of being put beneath the negro who can stagger up to the polls and vote," two female correspondents wrote, "while we have to go to the fields and drag a pick sack and use a cross-cut saw in the woods."[122] Here the image of black men with more political rights than white women evoked the complete debasement of landless white families. The great champion of these families, Kate Richards O'Hare, perhaps the most militant racist in the party, was a favorite in the Bootheel. "Where is the Jim Crow law for the factory, workshop, mines or cotton field?" she demanded. O'Hare wondered why no politicians worried about racial equality when blacks and "white Democrats" worked together in the same degrading jobs. The current system, she argued, crushed the economic, political, and sexual integrity of whites; for her, Jim Crow did not work. Echoing the Bootheel woman's lament above, she pointed out that "in the cotton fields the white daughters of white voters drag the cotton sacks down the cotton row next to 'nigger bucks.'"[123] Back in 1892, Texas Populist Cyclone Davis had also railed against "the sight of a sweet white girl hoeing cotton on one row and a big, burly negro in the next row."[124] The relationships between manhood and womanhood, independence, and white supremacy had deep roots in agrarian producerist thought, as suggested by the consistency of this particular image across time and space. Like Davis, lowland socialists sought to turn these ideas against ruling capitalists.

Although agrarian activists continued to advocate action at the polls, their explosive rhetoric suggested that extralegal measures might be necessary. *Justice* admitted that "fighting must be done" but still believed that "ballots were better than bullets."[125] "If they fire us off the land" for voting socialist, one correspondent argued, "why a little of Christ's example would be good for the fellows who do the firing." Instead of suggesting that dismissed workers turn the other cheek, however, the writer reminded readers how "the Carpenter walked into the temple in broad daylight and scourged out the money changers."[126] Facing threats to their independence, their gender roles, and their white supremacy and with a racist vigilante campaign in recent memory, landless whites were primed for violence. "If our lords of the land refuse to rent to Socialists then we should see to it that they rent to no others, and if they do we should whip Heck out of them," Scott declared. "This is the class war."[127]

For all their electoral goals, Bootheel socialists evinced little confidence in established structures of power. "We hear around town that some people are becoming desperate, men wanting work and their families hungry," yet everywhere there is plenty, *Justice* angrily reported. "How long do you who hold our lives in your hands expect us to stand by and see . . . the wealth created by our toil piled up on every side? Your high sheriff, your laws, your militia don't scare a hungry man much," Scott continued. "We will not starve in sight of filled stores in Kennett."[128] They did not want to fight, but they would if forced to do so. "Now we Socialists are peaceful people, trying to get our rights peacefully at the ballot box. But if we are persecuted . . . we will do exactly what every other downtrodden class has done—revolt and fight," *Justice* warned area elites. "If you purposefully bring on trouble then the blood be upon your own heads."[129]

Trouble was indeed coming, but socialists were not the instigators. In 1914, a mob attacked John Scott in Kennett in broad daylight. Religious insurgents faced similar abuse. "Pentecost" reported that local elites "had the preachers beat up on the streets of Kennett, just like they did the Socialists."[130] These assaults heightened tensions. "If economic conditions don't soon change,"

Scott warned, the people "will stampede the storage houses and take back part of the product of their toil, robbed from them by rich speculators." And "Jesus will not find fault with them," he added.[131] He advised "every laboring man in Dunklin county to lay by a part of his earnings and invest in a good repeating rifle to keep in his home. . . . You can't do this too soon."[132] Socialists pointed out that this was an abominable state of affairs, the fault of greedy landowners and industrialists. "One poor Dunklin slave says he just has $1.30 in cash, a wife, six children and a revolver," Scott reported. "He may have to use the revolver to feed the family."[133] Bootheel Socialists had fused turbulent popular ideas about wage slavery, racial degradation, emasculated men, retributive violence, and Christian mission into a rebellious movement that continued to emphasize electoral victories.

The election of 1914 undermined the hope of socialists in the power of democracy. Despite rallying 5,000 people to hear Debs speak in Kennett that October, the party's regional vote dropped by 36 percent from the 1912 total.[134] In Dunklin County, the stronghold of the movement, socialists increased their strength by only eighty-one votes. Lower voter turnout in this midterm election does not account for the loss; overall, only 13 percent fewer people in the region voted in 1914 than in 1912. Socialists accused Democrats of fraud and intimidation. As early as June, Scott suspected that "the Kennett ring must be fixing for the election . . . the way the negroes are coming to town."[135] In the wake of the election, reports circulated that Democrats had stuffed ballot boxes, intimidated voters, and thrown out socialist ballots. Socialist candidates claimed that they had been robbed of rightful victories, particularly in the vicinity of Malden in northern Dunklin County.[136] They were not alone; political enemies cheated and intimidated socialist voters in similar ways in Alabama, Oklahoma, and Texas.[137] In this case, however, the election disaster rocked the local Socialist Party organization, and *Justice* soon ceased publication for a lack of funds. Before going silent, *Justice* declared that people "must live, work or no work, cotton sold or no cotton sold, gun or no gun, ballot or no ballot. We will not lie down and starve peacefully and quietly like you want us to. Arouse, ye slaves!"[138] In the final issue, Scott composed an elegiac farewell to Bootheel elites, citing the Gospel of Matthew 23:37–38: "Christ said to the people of Jerusalem: 'Oh Jerusalem, Jerusalem how often would I have gathered thy children together as a hen gathers her brood under her wings, and ye would not.'" Now, Scott warned, "your houses are left unto you desolate."[139]

\* \* \*

In 1915, the lowlands erupted with violence as white tenants and wage workers attacked African Americans, landlords, and the centers of corporate power. In February, a group near New Madrid launched nighttime gunfire raids on settlements of black farm workers.[140] A month later, in the lowlands of Scott County, the police broke up a group that called itself the Possum Hunters and was threatening to harm local planters and burn area towns if they were not offered higher wages and lower rents. In March, a vigilante group near Hayti issued death threats to all black laborers in Pemiscot County.[141] In October, a large group launched a terrorist campaign in the cut-over lands along the Little River in Dunklin, New Madrid, and Pemiscot counties. It began when eighty masked men on horseback rode through Tallapoosa threatening on-lookers and shooting wildly. On the night of November 1, 1915, twenty-seven masked white men pulled M. R. Adkisson, a large landowner, from his home south of Gideon and led him into a nearby cotton field, where they beat him with clubs and chased him off with shotgun fire.[142] The group, soon known as the Night Riders, punctuated these outbursts with public demands that the Gideon-Anderson Lumber Company increase wages from $6 to $10 an acre for land clearance and decrease rents for families working newly cleared land. They further demanded that employers discharge black workers and employ only white men.[143] The Night Riders threatened to burn the towns of Gideon and Clarkton and execute all company officials if their demands were not met. In late November the vigilantes waged a pitched nighttime gun battle with private detectives landowners had hired to infiltrate their ranks. Unable to dislodge the besieged company men and with five of their own wounded, the Night Riders retreated into the surrounding woodlands. Using evidence from the scene of the fighting, the detectives and police tracked down thirty of the alleged vigilantes within days and arrested thirty-seven more men in the weeks that followed.[144]

Because of the audacity of the Night Riders, local elites went to great lengths to punish them. The trial of the sixty-seven men plainly demonstrated the division of power in the Bootheel. Financing the prosecution was the New Madrid Citizens' Committee, a group of landowners who collectively controlled more than $1,000,000 and 200,000 acres, on which 5,000 tenant families scratched out a tenuous living. The Citizens' Committee rented the best hotel in New Madrid during the trial, where its members entertained journalists, law enforcement officials, and prosecution witnesses.[145] The trial was held in New Madrid's new courthouse building, which had just entered service. Featuring neoclassical columns topped with cornices decorated with cotton bolls, the structure announced the power of cotton agriculture in Bootheel politics. As the St. Louis *Post-Dispatch* observed, the oligarchs were "making every living effort to send to the penitentiary all of the 67 defendants."[146] That effort left a fascinating record.

At the time of the November attacks, the Night Riders consisted of six loosely connected groups from the Little River Valley. All of the 300 men who reportedly belonged to these bands lived in transitory camps while cutting timber, clearing land, or raising cotton in the cut-over area between the towns of Malden, Tallapoosa, and Peach Orchard.[147] Most of the sixty-seven suspects lived on land owned by the Gideon-Anderson Company near the latest point of canal construction for the Little River Drainage District. The Night Riders seem to have had the full support of their neighbors and co-workers. One witness, when asked if the defendants were members of the Night Riders, remarked, "Lord kno[ws] nearly everybody around Gideon belonged to that band."[148] The personal and political connections of the group's members extended along the drainage canals and railroads that facilitated the Bootheel economy. Defendants John Elder and Dick Gamble, leaders of the Peach Orchard and Gideon bands, called a number of witnesses from these marginal places. Their supporters, they said, could be found at Peach Orchard "on or near the tram railroad."[149]

Although the historical trail is dimly lit, the trial of these men suggests that as organized socialism failed, agrarian activists like the Night Riders transformed an older tradition of vigilante violence using the politics of agrarian socialism. In every case, the violence took place in areas of socialist strength and organization, often among people with links to previous vigilante organizations. The brothers Riley and Tude Miskell, both leaders of a band at Gideon, had belonged to a Socialist Party local in Scott County prior to moving to the lowlands. They had a long history of resistance to rural capitalism. They had fled to Scott County from the Black Patch, where they had taken part in raids against agents of American Tobacco.[150] Their contemporary Bootheel vigilantes also shared links to that conflict; the Possum Hunters of Scott County took their name from an armed group in the Black Patch.[151] "If we could get enough votes we could . . . get control of the government . . . and even send a man to the Legislature," Night Rider William Cunningham recalled being told. However, he admitted, the Night Riders had become impatient with electoral methods and "decided on revolution."[152] "Most of the men were Socialists," he said, "and some of them handed around Socialist papers."[153] The press blamed local party activists. The leaders of the Night Riders, declared the Sikeston *Standard,* "were Scott County Socialists who were followers of the teachings" of Phil Hafner, who "should be indicted along with the balance of the band" for his "rabid preachings."[154] Others blamed John Scott and *Justice,* which some called "the greatest menace known."[155] "It was this man Scott," the editor of the *Citizen* argued, "who proposed, advised and insisted on the tenant farmers and farm laborers to organize so as to force exactly what the night riders are demanding."[156]

Other extraordinary glints in the story of the Night Rider uprising, however, suggest that the campaign was a popular rebellion empowered by prophetic Pentecostal revival. During the trial, the prosecution and members of the Democratic Party elite pounced on links between the Night Riders and the insurgent socialists and Pentecostals. Among those caught "in the roundup" of suspected militants, the Sikeston *Standard* reported, were known "Socialists and Holy Rollers," the derogatory term applied to Pentecostals.[157] Both John Elder and Dick Gamble admitted in their testimony that they were preachers in the Pentecostal-Holiness Church of God. They began preaching at revivals in the area in 1914, one report stated, when they began to "organize the dissatisfied farmers and laborers to better their condition."[158]

How did the two become one? Socialists such as Cunningham had lost faith in elections as a means to a perfected world. At the same time, many people like Cunningham, who believed that God's power was real and present around them, sought to access divine gifts through Holy Ghost baptism. Socialists had already lent political direction to the ideology of Pentecostalism in their interpretation of agrarian producerism as a God-given moral system corrupted by worldly power and their sympathetic coverage of religious rebels who battled that corruption. Reciprocal exposure between the two movements combusted as a result of the collapse of cotton prices in 1914, physical harassment, and electoral fraud to ignite rebellion with the aim of bringing about a producer's commonwealth. Notes from other contemporary violent socialist rebellions offer confirmation of this dynamic in the Bootheel. "May the great god of heaven help us to secure our liberty and freedom," prayed a socialist farmer in Texas in February 1915. "He has promised to help those who help themselves." "I have known night riders to pray before they saddled their horses and reached for their Winchesters," remarked an Oklahoma socialist in 1915.[159] A single word from Cunningham's testimony illustrates the point. The Night Riders identified one another and their mission with a simple password: "Jerusalem." Theirs was not just a struggle to gain better wages and rent; it was also a movement to "restore again the kingdom to Israel," as the scriptures predicted.[160]

The outcome of the trial was also instructive. All sixty-seven men were convicted. Only eighteen, however, were required to serve their sentences, which ranged from two to five years. The ringleaders, the socialists, and the Pentecostals—including Elder, Gamble, and the Miskell brothers—all received the harshest penalty, evidence of how nervous they made local elites.[161] The rest were immediately paroled on good behavior so they could return to work. Shortly after handing down the verdict, the presiding judge addressed the visibly relieved men. "You are free to go home and live the lives of good citizens, the slate is wiped clean," he declared. "Hereafter," the judge continued, "when you have a grievance against your employers, go to them and talk it over. Remember that the laws of this country are too great to be overthrown by any band of men. We have a law that is based on the laws of the Bible, and under our Constitution, any citizen, rich or poor, can come into court and get justice."[162] The paroled Night Riders returned to their wives, their children, and their tenant shanties.

With that abrupt conclusion came the momentary end of landless white resistance to capitalist development in the Bootheel. The Socialist Party dwindled in subsequent elections; its vote in 1916 dropped 44 percent from the disappointing 1914 level. American entry into World War I, the Sedition Act of 1917, and war preparedness campaigns further constrained whatever organization might have survived. By 1917 Scott was gone and Hafner was dead. In 1918 Socialists could muster only 64 votes in Dunklin County and 23 votes in Scott County.[163]

Yet despite myriad defeats in the mid-1910s, landless whites seemed to have gained something from their rebellion. The best efforts of the Citizens' Committee notwithstanding, dozens of men who had plotted and carried out open assaults on the lives and property of area elites had gotten off with little more than a warning. The judge's lenient and reconciling verdict at the close of the Night Rider trial reaffirmed the claims of poor whites to the rights and privileges of citizenship. In addition, many African American farmers abandoned the area following the wave of violence. This could not but have boosted white hopes that they might now enjoy some of the benefits of their labor. In contrast to demagogues such as Ben Tillman, Cole Blease, and Tom Watson, who used images of a white yeomanry to build their own power, Bootheel rebels used agrarian producerism to argue for and partially receive a Jim Crow system that would deliver on its promises to all white people.[164]

# 3

## Saviors of Agriculture

Marcus Garvey offered little hope for the future of African Americans in the Bootheel. In his weekly address to the race from Harlem's Liberty Hall in early 1923, Garvey told his audience that thousands of black cotton pickers had been forcibly driven from Pemiscot County by white vigilantes. "Nigger, get to hell out of here," a note left for a black farmer read, "this is a white man's country." The following night the same farmer received another note, this time weighted to his front porch by a cartridge casing. "Nigger, if you cannot read—run," it ordered, and "if you cannot run, you are as good as dead." On the front page of *The Negro World,* the national organ of the UNIA, Garvey warned his followers that such attacks would continue and intensify in Missouri and elsewhere until "the poor Negro . . . has created for himself some haven of refuge." He declared that African Americans would always be unwelcome in "a white man's country" and urged his readers to fight "for the restoration of Africa to the Negro people of the world" and "to look forward to the building up of a country of their own," where they could determine their own lives. The program of the UNIA, Garvey concluded, offered the only good "alternative for the Negro . . . that of founding a Nation; that of developing a country for our own on the continent of Africa."[1]

In contrast to Garvey's pessimism, Alex Cooper, a black share-renter from Arkansas, saw opportunity in the Bootheel. In the early 1920s, land reclamation continued to open tens of thousands of acres of fertile farmland that was free of the soil depletion and insect infestation of the Deep South. Cooper, his wife Mary, and their eight children moved to Pemiscot County in late 1922 to rent (and, they hoped, buy) some of this new land. Over the next three years, more than 15,000 other African Americans did the same.[2] While most of them were successful sharecroppers, many were small landowners and prosperous renters who owned teams, tools, and equipment. They came from the lowlands of Arkansas, Louisiana, Mississippi, and Tennessee, regions where the shrinking availability of land, the boll weevil, and increasing white racial violence since the 1890s had undermined their ability to attain economic or political autonomy. They moved in extended family groups whose members shared a belief in the importance of working the land and were willing to keep moving in order to attain it. Most of these families had moved to the lowlands from somewhere else a generation earlier. Before renting land in Arkansas, for example, Cooper had owned a farm in Winston County, Mississippi.[3]

African American settlers looked to extend and defend an agrarian tradition rooted in the last half of the nineteenth century. As agrarians, their lives and labors on the land provided the foundation for stable kinship networks, community cohesion and leadership, and autonomy and dignity in the face of white oppression. This way of life was held together by the producerist notion that work was the lodestone of one's duty to self, family, and God, a set of ideas closely related to those of Booker T. Washington. As any farmer— white or black—could attest, everything had to come from individual hard work. Yet for African Americans whose freedom was elusive, the meaning of the rights of producers carried a different pitch than it did for whites. The power to control the product of one's labor was a means to self-possession and independence that for blacks offered a crucial counterpoint to family histories of enslavement.[4] Alex Cooper made sure that his grandsons learned this lesson. "Own something," he told them, even "if it's just one board over your head. That shows some progress. If you let everybody dictate to you what you should do," Cooper declared, "then you're not you."[5]

For the most part, historians have either dismissed or ignored the ambitions of black farmers who sought rural livelihoods in the twentieth century. An intense scholarly focus on the movement of black people to southern and northern cities has aligned studies of African American life after 1900 along urban and industrial lines. This "exodus" narrative has portrayed northward or urban migrations as irresistible forces building since 1890 and often suggested that agricultural life was only bondage in another form. According to this view, rural black life was a "depressing story of degradation, poverty, and hopelessness for the men, women, and children who lived in desperation and without alternatives."[6] Although farmers such as Cooper were not rich, they were not poor, degraded, or hopeless either. Rather, their faith in productive work underpinned rural worlds rich with meaning.

Although they ignored Garvey's warning, black settlers adapted the nationalist ideology of his fraternal organization, the UNIA, to reinforce and give new urgency to their agrarian ambitions. African Americans in the Bootheel established fifteen divisions of the UNIA in the 1920s. Altogether, southern farmers formed 354 divisions, half of all the divisions in the United States and a third of all divisions worldwide.[7] While most of these divisions were small (they had anywhere from seven to fifty members each), those who joined them had immense influence in their families and communities. Agrarian Garveyites were mainly prosperous men (and a few women): they were small landowners, successful renters, teachers, and preachers usually over 35 years old who owned personal property. Whether they owned large or small plots or simply mules and tools, their property provided important protection from white interference, insulation from expensive credit and from crop liens, and a sense of family and community autonomy. Many UNIA members headed large households and kinship groups and often employed family members to work land under their stewardship.[8]

Founded in Jamaica in 1914, Garvey's UNIA attracted wide support after he arrived in Harlem in 1916. From there he transformed the UNIA into a worldwide movement to build "a strong and powerful Negro nation" led by powerful black men.[9] Garvey argued that economic strength and autonomy was the best way for black people to realize "a country of their own where they should be given the fullest opportunity to develop politically, socially and industrially." This message captured a sense of urgency among African Americans after World War I. "If at any time in the history of the Negro race men were needed for service, that time is 'Now.' . . . Whatsoever my future is to be is my own creation," Garvey concluded, and "as of the individual so of the race."[10]

To some, Garvey among them, southern farmers must have seemed odd candidates for advancing the program of the UNIA. Their rural lives afforded them little opportunity to accumulate the education, capital, or cosmopolitanism needed to fill the professional, business, and diplomatic roles that Garvey envisioned as the future of the race. Likewise, the everyday lives of farmers, marked, among other things, by outhouses, livestock, and the rhythms of the seasons, clashed with the concerns of national UNIA leaders over social hygiene, progress, and the wonders of Harlem in the 1920s. Whatever Garvey had in mind, the UNIA was too weak as an organization to ensure consistency. The only regular contact that local groups had to the parent body was through *The Negro World,* which carried news, testimonies from members, and, most important, Garvey's speeches. In the absence of

Map 3. The UNIA in the Bootheel, 1925.

more institutional support, local members interpreted Garveyism through their own lived experiences and preexisting ideas.[11] In their own minds, the black farmers, teachers, and preachers who made the UNIA in the Bootheel upheld Garvey's ideals of race leadership.

In the UNIA, agrarian Garveyites combined the social resources of fraternal benevolent associations with the expansive spiritual power of churches, two main institutions of rural black life that had been moving toward one another since the rise of Jim Crow in the 1890s. Garveyism fused the "financial, social, and psychological resources available to black men" in fraternal orders with the "diversity, flexibility, and subtlety of black spiritual life" in service to the movement to liberate and redeem the black race worldwide—the *Cause Afric*.[12] This goal became the "great sentiment" of the organization, the kind around which "every great movement always centers," *The Negro World* declared.[13] The *Cause Afric* carried intense power; an African homeland that had been redeemed from colonial powers by the most devoted and faithful members of the race would usher in a new age, an epochal moment that would finally bring earthly peace and prosperity—a black millennium.[14] As leaders in the UNIA, the farmers who sought family and community autonomy in the Bootheel saw themselves as key actors in a collective movement that sought the autonomy of all black people and worked toward "founding a Nation" in Africa.

\*     \*     \*

The Bootheel, a site of agricultural boom during the years of the Great War, collapsed into depression in 1920. By 1921, cotton and wheat crops were worth half and corn crops worth a third of their 1919 value. While cotton prices rebounded, corn and wheat farmers remained mired in the slump. Farmers working heavily taxed Bootheel land could no longer earn enough to meet their obligations, which continued to rise following new levee construction and the completion of the Little River Drainage District. Cotton offered a way out. The region's grain growers experimented in 1922 by planting 198,000 acres in cotton, 95,000 acres more than the previous year. Their trial paid off, as good weather boosted yields to an average of 0.74 bales of ginned cotton per acre, a record high that more than doubled the national average. More important, cotton sold for 22.8 cents per pound, 7 cents above the 1920 price, while corn and wheat prices continued to languish.[15]

Cotton fever swept the remaining wheat and corn areas after the success of the 1922 experiment. The promise of high prices and high yields convinced many to devote their entire acreages to it. Farmers planted 355,000 acres of cotton in 1923, nearly double the previous high.[16] "Plant cotton! Plant cotton! Plant cotton!" one booster cheered his Scott County neighbors.[17] "Wheat," a Mississippi County farmer admitted, had left them "all but bankrupt, and we are forced to change this . . . to a cotton growing proposition."[18] Lumber companies fueled the frenzy. As the Little River Drainage District neared completion, tens of thousands of acres of cut-over land became available. Eager to sell it, companies advertised their holdings of cheap available land in "the best cotton section of the United States," a land that by virtue of its northerly position was free from the boll weevil.[19] Existing landowners took the opportunity to expand their holdings and cotton planters from further south moved to the Bootheel. Having made such a massive investment in cotton production, most of these landlords looked to "import a large number of experienced cotton growers" rather than employ existing white laborers. White landowners expected that these migrants would be "mostly colored families."[20]

Between September 1922 and spring planting in 1923, over 9,000 African Americans moved to the Bootheel to take up this opportunity.[21] Most of these newcomers were expert cotton farmers, whether as tenants or as successful sharecroppers, in search of rich, available land that was free of the weevil.[22] "Well dressed and every one of them self-sustaining and with bank accounts," these farmers had pioneered agricultural production in the lowlands of Arkansas and Mississippi in the first years of the twentieth century.[23] George Washington, a 33-year-old tenant, moved to southern New Madrid County from Louisiana via Arkansas and rented a large plot of land.[24] "Reliable and experienced cotton growing people were good citizens in their communities," newspapers in the towns they were leaving reported. They "were thrifty and dependable" and would be "sadly missed by their former landlords."[25] While some came looking for a fresh start, others came because their landlords had bought land in the Bootheel; as trusted tenants, their job was to make the new acquisitions profitable. Alex Cooper came as an agent of his Arkansas landlord, who rented Cooper part of his Pemiscot County holdings so that he could oversee the taming of those lands.[26]

Those who came of their own volition did so as a result of weevil infestation and the commodity depression of 1920–1921, although the postwar increase in racial violence undoubtedly influenced their decisions.[27] One recently arrived tenant reported leaving the vicinity of the recent massacre in Elaine, Arkansas because "conditions were so he could not make a living there." There was more to farming, however, than profitable crops. This man was glad to be in the Bootheel, where he could prove "that he was a good farmer and a good citizen."[28] Farmers such as this one believed in agrarian producerism as a way to autonomy. Economic independence had been central to black claims to citizenship from Reconstruction through to the Colored Farmers' Alliance: landownership, self-reliance, hard work, and personal sacrifice were necessary preconditions to individual and collective autonomy.[29] Booker T. Washington had called it "a wholesome desire to do something to . . . demonstrate the right of the negro, not merely as an individual, but as a race, to have a worthy and permanent place in" America.[30] These ideas did not begin and end with Washington. As Edward Ayers has observed, "Blacks had adopted Washington's strategy before they ever heard of him" and no doubt held to it after his death in 1915.[31] Migrants to the Bootheel seemed strongly committed to this idea and lauded Washington as its latest proponent; like thousands of other proud parents, George Washington named his first son Booker T.[32]

Whatever brought them, migrants arrived in kinship and community groups. Alex Cooper moved with his wife and eight children. "The past few weeks has brought hundreds of these families into this section," one account reported in early 1923, "and we will state that they are big families."[33] A landowner near Lilbourn, in New Madrid County, "counted 52 wagons and three trucks all right close together" bringing migrants and reported that "every freight train has from one to three cars" full of people and their goods. In one day alone, he recalled, "62 persons, including children, moved to Lilbourn."[34] Similarly, observers near Parma and Sikeston reported the arrival of over 500 and 600 settlers in their respective vicinities in December 1922. One landowner rented 250 acres to three families from Mississippi. Even whole communities seemed to move.[35] In late 1922 the Charleston postmaster received an inquiry from Mississippi about the availability of cotton land for rent. The postmaster referred it to the county agent of the U.S. Department of Agriculture's Extension Service, who replied "that there was much land for rent and that it was ideal for cotton." In response, thirty-one black families from one county moved to Mississippi County and reported that more were on the way.[36]

Settlers found themselves farming large swaths of the newly reclaimed lowlands. In less than a year, three main areas were completely transformed by black settlement and cotton cultivation: 7,500 blacks established farms in the recently reclaimed areas of the Little River Valley, 1,000 people settled in the lands bordering the river in Mississippi County, and over 1,000 more began working the area's best cotton soil bordering the river in Pemiscot County. Here the migrants seemed to find what they wanted.[37]

Small numbers of black landowners anchored these nascent communities. Although black landownership was negligible in 1920, the rate had rocketed by 1925, especially in Mississippi and Pemiscot counties, where blacks constituted 11 and 21 percent of all landowners, respectively. However, these percentages are somewhat misleading. Except in Pemiscot, where there were ninety-one black landowning families, their numbers were small, from twelve to twenty-five families in each county. And the holdings of these landowners were not large—usually they consisted of ten to thirty acres of half-cleared land.[38] Small numbers and small properties notwithstanding, these landowners embodied the benefits of agrarian producerism because they possessed the relative wealth and prestige to provide stability for those who lived around them. "It is difficult to overemphasize the self-respect and psychological freedom that landownership gave to African Americans," concluded oral historian Kim Lacy Rogers. "The possession of land, and prudent and successful farming practices, commanded admiration from African Americans, and even grudging respect from whites."[39] A generation earlier, Booker T. Washington had said, "We ought never to forget that in the ownership and cultivation of the soil in a very large measure we must lay the foundation" for the success of the race.[40]

The vast majority of newcomers, however, became share-renters or share-croppers. By 1924, no less than 96 percent of the rural black population in any Bootheel county were tenant farmers. These figures included families farming on both share-renting and sharecropping arrangements. Such arrangements were made based on the financial prosperity of a family, where they settled, and the situation of their landlords. Share-renters were the more prosperous and propertied and thus the smaller of the two groups, perhaps 25 percent of all tenants. Renters used their own tools, equipment, and teams to raise their crop, a quarter of which they paid to the landowner in exchange for occupancy rights to a house and land. Although share-renters planted mostly what their landlords wanted, they enjoyed some legal safeguards, primarily ownership of their crop, which allowed them to gin it and sell it where they pleased. Even though this freedom was often more potential than real, share-renters could still raise some garden crops and keep livestock for food. Migrant families with their own farming equipment stood the best chance of negotiating share-rental arrangements, especially where experienced cotton growers were most in demand.[41] When he came to Missouri, for example, Cooper, a share-renter, "brought his mules and his equipment, and some of his relatives, to work the land."[42]

Most of the migrants, perhaps 75 percent, were sharecroppers. Young families with ample labor but no property of their own were most likely to become members of this group. Typically working 40-acre plots, sharecropping families received the proceeds of half of the cotton crop as payment for their labor in addition to a house to live in for the year. They had no control over the ginning and marketing of their crop. Moreover, croppers were seldom allowed to devote precious land to subsistence foodstuffs. As a result they had to rely on loans of cash for food, clothing, and medical expenses, always running the risk of mounting debt.[43] Whatever their tenure, Bootheel farmers could be optimistic in 1923, given the area's overall shortage of cotton farmers, its robust land, and its freedom from the weevil.

Usually older men who were renters and owners led their kin and social groups. Their relative autonomy lent stability to the difficult work of rebuilding social relations and community institutions in a new location. The basis of their leadership was their relationships with family members and sharecroppers. Black renters and owners usually hired younger kin or the children of neighbors to work their crops. Alex Cooper employed his six sons as wage hands until they were grown, then they sharecropped on land he rented. Gideon Coffee, a 59-year-old renter in New Madrid County, employed his nephew, Dave Coffee, and his son-in-law, Peter Wilderness, as sharecroppers.[44] "Black landlords," historian Valerie Grim has argued, "considered themselves the communities' parents." Bound by a sense of paternal obligation, these landlords were more likely to allow their croppers certain liberties, such as garden space and some livestock. They "understood the impact of fair treatment, honesty, and respect on productive farming."[45] In return, however, black agrarians commanded patriarchal authority in their families and in their communities. As landlords and even as heads of households, agrarians needed to control their laborers to maintain economic viability, whatever the terms; the labor of family members and croppers were crucial components of their prosperity and their manhood.[46] Cooper, after all, had migrated with "some of his relatives" (his labor force) along with his "mules and equipment."[47] "It is difficult to understand southern African American culture," argued one historian, "without grasping this concept of personhood [manliness] through" property ownership, whether it was land or animals. Into the 1920s, the model of rural black manliness remained Booker T. Washington, who called on white Victorian ideals to cement the role of black men as "patriarchs or heads of families, protectors, and providers for dependents."[48]

Paternalistic relationships likewise framed community institutions, the most important of which was religious fellowship. On their arrival, migrants established church groups in homes, in brush arbors, in open fields, and (by the summer of 1923) in their own church buildings. The familiar rituals, beliefs, and codes of conduct of shared faith eased the migrants' transition and went some distance toward establishing trust between new neighbors. The new churches were almost evenly split between African Methodist Episcopal (AME) and Baptist denominations. By 1926, there were 792 AME church members and 971 Baptist church members in the Bootheel. The relative strength of the AME among Bootheel migrants is striking, since in other southern states at this time Baptists outnumbered AME members by about eight to one.[49]

The prevalence of AME churches reflects the widespread belief in the prerogatives of patriarchy among the settlers. The denomination was organized by an ecclesiastical hierarchy firmly controlled by a general council of bishops that exercised power over everything from doctrine to the robes ministers could wear. Church leaders claimed responsibility for the uplift of their congregations and for the masses generally. AME ministers interpreted their denominational history as "a parable of black men rejecting dependence within the white church and embarking on a journey toward the joys and challenges of 'manly' independence." AME leaders took seriously their right "to establish and preside over their own religious households—a privilege they guarded jealously from black women, as well as white men."[50] This religious structure framed much of black agrarian manhood.

That authority was under threat from renewed white violence in the 1920s. White elites had never quite forgotten the trouble landless white Night Riders had given them the previous decade. As they turned completely toward cotton production in the early 1920s, white landowners were determined to get rid of white tenants. Predictably, poor whites responded with venom—toward black farmers. Alex Cooper, who is quite possibly the farmer Garvey mentioned in *The Negro World,* found a note attached to his front gate that read "move out before we kick you out, KKK."[51] It was presumably from the same group that had distributed a handbill decorated with skull and crossbones in the runup to the 1922 election that declared it open to "White Voters Only." The handbill added "Nigger—You are not Wanted" and was signed "KKK."[52] As the migration of blacks into the area accelerated in early 1923, white tenants stepped up their attacks. After warning newly arrived families to "get out, and let white people live," vigilantes wounded four blacks with gunfire, including a young girl whose arm was blown off.[53] Violent attacks continued throughout early 1923. Near Parma, vigilantes punctuated the terror campaign by killing black tenant Tom Keaton while he slept.[54]

More than random violence, these attacks were part of a renewed revolt of white workers against large-scale cotton agriculture and black farmers.[55] Many of the militants claimed the land was rightfully theirs as producers. "The effort to rid Pemiscot County of negro laborers . . . was not the work of irresponsible white persons," one vigilante explained, but rather "was made by the class of people" who "came to this country when it was nothing but a God-forsaken swamp and we helped develop it." Now landowners were denying white farmers their share of the benefits of their hard work by pursuing cheaper labor. "We are not land owners," the vigilante continued, but we "have made our living working for land owners, scores of whom would now deprive us of that right in order to get a little more out of their land by employing negroes." Should whites sit idly by until the new laborers drove them out of their "own country?" he asked. "No," he answered, "it is not the nature of white men."[56]

These tactics only hardened the resolve of black migrants and white landowners alike. While some African Americans fled the violence, new migrants came, a county official said, "as fast as other negroes are going out."[57] The emerging cotton elite were determined to protect black settlers, who they described as the "saviors of agriculture in this section."[58] Angered by poor whites' appropriation of Ku Klux Klan (KKK) symbols, members of the official KKK informed Governor Arthur Hyde that they had nothing to do with the vigilante attacks. Rather, they were trying to stop them.[59] "You are directly responsible for outrages against Negro laborers," the Klan informed the militants, adding that "Pemiscot needs negro labor. . . . It does not need men of your stamp." Stop the attacks or be stopped, the message concluded.[60] The Klan posted similar warnings in shop windows throughout New Madrid and Stoddard counties.[61] Perhaps more important, influential Klan leaders convinced Governor Hyde, a Republican, to mobilize the Missouri State Guard to protect black workers near Parma after Tom Keaton was murdered. Twenty-eight armed soldiers occupied five large cotton farms on the Stoddard–New Madrid line for several weeks in April of 1923. The violence stopped.[62]

Armed protection, available land, and word of a big cotton crop brought hundreds more black families in the fall of 1923. In two days in October, 500 migrants arrived in Sikeston. Having made $19.5 million on cotton in 1923, area landowners planned further crop increases.[63] By the end of 1924, over 15,000 African American farmers had moved into the Bootheel, drawn by the promise of a reclaimed land.

* * *

During the period 1923 to 1927, the UNIA was the center of the new communities of African American settlers in the Bootheel. In addition to forming new churches, one of the first things the new migrants did was to establish UNIA divisions. The settlers had certainly heard of Garvey before 1923; the UNIA had attracted a strong following in the rural South as early as 1921, particularly in the lowlands of Arkansas and Mississippi, where most of the Bootheel settlers came from. Three UNIA divisions existed in the Bootheel prior to the big migration of 1922–1923: Hermondale 614, New Madrid 685, and Wyatt 449. Within a year settlers formed twelve more: Bertrand 797, Charleston 718, Commerce 860, Dexter 772, Essex 825, Lilbourn 719, Parma 787, Point Pleasant, Poplar Bluff 746, Risco, Saymos 706, and Tyler 704. Although these divisions were identified by the nearest town, they encompassed large rural areas. New Madrid division, for example, included members from around Kewanee and Matthews, an area of more than thirty square miles. These divisions would become among the most active of all those in the rural South: New Madrid's fifty-one members in 1926 were the most reported by any rural division to the UNIA's central division between 1925 and 1927. Extant membership records also indicate that only twelve rural divisions had more than twenty-five members; five of those were in the Bootheel.[64]

In some ways Bootheel Garveyites represented a vanguard of black agrarianism. They remained influential even after they had left the towns they had come from in the deeper South. For example, S. E. James of Bolivar County, Mississippi—itself the site of nineteen UNIA divisions—became interested in *The Negro World* because "a friend put me wise to this paper out in Southeastern Missouri." This kind of interaction says a lot about the sense of mission that drove Bootheel Garveyism.[65]

Garvey's doctrines of self-determination, independence, and self-defense seemed neatly suited for successful African American farmers trying to achieve prosperity and rebuild community institutions in a new land. Prosperous settlers dominated UNIA divisions in the Bootheel. D. D. Daniels, the first president of New Madrid 685, was a share-renter. Daniels, who was born a slave in Mississippi in 1851, had become a self-supporting farmer with some cash to spare; he regularly donated to UNIA causes, usually $1 or more.[66] Stonewall Jackson, a 63-year-old renter born in Arkansas, was also a regular contributor to the cause.[67] Another renter, Will Jones, who was born in Mississippi in 1885, presided over Wyatt 449 in the late 1920s and early 1930s.[68] His colleagues, James Milton and S. H. Marris, who had both served as UNIA officers in Mississippi County, were also renters.[69] Preachers—the other leading lights of rural black life—were similarly overrepresented; at least four preachers belonged to each division at Charleston, Lilbourn, and Wyatt; many of these men were AME. Schoolteachers were also highly visible. Professors (a common title for teachers) Farmer, Harrison, and Hunter were active in Charleston 718. On the whole, UNIA members were an educated lot. D. D. Daniels, Will Jones, James Milton, S. H. Marris, and probably all of the preachers and teachers were literate. They read *The Negro World,* wrote letters to the editor in polished English, and were familiar enough with French (or Creole) to use the code-switched phrase "*Cause Afric.*"[70]

Above all else, successful agrarians used the UNIA to highlight their economic authority within their communities. No member of the UNIA considered it an organization of the downtrodden or "the lowest economic class," as some historians have claimed.[71] In order to join, members had to pay 35 cents a month in dues. Most black and white tenant farmers and certainly all rural wage workers—truly the lowest farming class—could not afford such high payments. Yet between 1925 and 1927, the Bootheel divisions claimed at least 250 regular dues-paying members.[72] In addition, the UNIA frequently asked its members for money to support various causes, particularly Garvey's legal defense fund, annual conventions, and work in Africa. These constant requests for money elevated fund-raising to the most important task the divisions could do. "Remember the raising of the Fund means your liberty," Garvey told readers, "and the liberty of all Negroes now and forever." *The Negro World* rewarded those who contributed by printing their names and usually the amount given to "be circulated all over the world for everybody of the race and succeeding generations to know of the loyal persons who subscribed for the Freedom of Africa and the emancipation of Negroes."[73] During the period 1923 to 1926 these lists were full of contributions from Bootheel members such as D. D. Daniels. In 1923 and 1924, at least sixty-one different members from New Madrid 685 and Lilbourn 719 contributed a total of $62.80 to the UNIA.[74] In the summer of 1923 alone, sixteen people from these divisions together donated $10 to Garvey's legal defense fund. This would have been a challenge for any farmer, much less cotton farmers during the period between peak cultivating and picking seasons.[75]

What this meant was that one had to have money to be a race leader. As champions of hard work, property ownership, and patriarchy, black agrarians were, in the words of *The Negro World*, "the leaders in the social, the civil and the business life of" their communities. "They have the light and they should have the leading of the race into higher and better conditions," wrote one contributor.[76] Although comparatively few in number, these black farmers had by dint of hard work and determination secured a livelihood in the midst of Jim Crow repression. While northern Garveyites were mostly working class, southern Garveyites, both urban and rural, "measured economic success in terms of one's ability to purchase a home, open up a business, or acquire a small amount of land," historian Claudrena Harold concluded. They were "striving blacks."[77] As Mary Rolinson has shown, Garveyites did not learn new things in the UNIA but were "reminded of things they already knew and believed."[78] Agrarians shared with other black leaders the preoccupations of racial uplift, a set of beliefs that Kevin Gaines has catalogued as "self-help, racial solidarity, temperance, thrift, chastity, social purity, patriarchal authority, and the accumulation of wealth."[79] Although only a minority of black farmers belonged to the UNIA, the organization's influence spread to the mass of men and women who were the children, spouses, employees, students, and congregants of Garveyite leaders. The patronage of these leaders was enhanced by UNIA regulations that allowed local divisions to keep two-thirds of all dues for expenses and community needs.[80] Eager to emulate the example of leadership UNIA members enjoyed, many young Bootheel farmers such as sharecropper Owen Whitfield attended meetings even if they did not join.[81]

Agrarians found in Garveyism a cause that valorized their producerist beliefs. UNIA leaders stressed the duty of individuals to work hard for their own independence. Rev. L. W. Johnson preached to members of Wyatt 449 "in strong terms" against "the Negro depending upon God to do for them that which they themselves can do." According to the meeting reporter, Johnson inspired the assembled Garveyites "to do greater work."[82] Such messages echoed agrarian beliefs in the centrality of productive labor to personal and collective advancement. Garvey routinely declared that Christ empowered people to seek their own salvation not through faith alone but also through works. "If you do not exercise your own will on your own behalf," he cautioned, "you will be lost."[83] This was especially pertinent for black farmers who had acquired whatever property they owned through sheer determination despite the best efforts of whites to take it away. "Many Negroes," E. W. Pinkard of Hermondale 614 said, "are unwilling to bestir themselves to do one thing to aid the progress which a comparatively few struggling members of the race are trying to make. . . . Most Negroes are like grasshoppers," he complained, "they make lots of noise and then do nothing."[84] Work was the key to prosperity and independence. "A man who thinks that he is fitted for something better and is willing to work and suffer to get it," Pinkard wrote, "will eventually reach a higher plane. . . . We are masters of our destinies, and if we fail, we can blame nobody but ourselves."[85] Garveyites evoked a version of agrarian producerism that was remarkably similar to the one white socialists had voiced a decade earlier. (Recall how Dunklin County socialists, inspired by Debs, had declared that "people must do things for themselves.")[86]

Male farmers used the UNIA to assert their prerogatives and duties as men. As Barbara Bair has shown, Garvey conceived of the UNIA as a "new manhood movement."[87] Garveyite men were to be protectors and providers for family groups, through armed self-defense if necessary. "If some unfriendly acquaintance of yours threatens to burn down your house," Garvey advised after the Pemiscot County attacks, the sensible man "will surround himself and his home with sufficient protection as to make it impossible." The rural Garveyite took the protection of "himself and his family" seriously.[88] While the migrants were certainly familiar with racial violence, the appeal of this rhetoric would have been sharpened after the lynching of Roosevelt Grigsby, a migrant worker, in Charleston in 1924.[89] In addition, while Garveyites, like other black men in the rural post-Reconstruction South, were keen to protect women from the sexual predations of white men, their emphasis on the responsibilities of manhood was about far more than that.[90] Indeed, by associating true manhood with public "constructions of independence, authority, and power," rural Garveyites reinforced a patriarchal gender code negotiated in the early years of Reconstruction that, according to historian Susan O'Donovan, gave male heads of households authority and control over the labor of family members, particularly women.[91] In this sense, rural Garveyism was an old manhood movement.

By contrast, women in the UNIA provided a moral voice that upheld an "ethic of social responsibility."[92] Unlike in urban divisions, in rural divisions very few women held leadership positions. Although the UNIA constitution required that each division elect a "Lady President," no Bootheel division seems to have had one. Laura Burnett and Ann Clark, reporter and secretary of Wyatt 449 and Dexter 722, respectively, were the only female officers ever mentioned.[93] The work of Garveyite women was to exhort. At a July 4 meeting in Charleston, for example, ten of the twenty-two speakers were women. Only one of them (the wife of Rev. Marris) was married, a distinction carefully noted by the male secretary. The unmarried speakers addressed a mostly male audience that included their fathers.[94] Women also made public contributions to charitable and group causes.[95] More than one-third of Bootheel contributors to UNIA appeals were women. Three-quarters of these were listed alongside their husbands or fathers, their ability to give a reflection of male prestige.[96] These donors contributed most to the *Cause Afric,* whether they were supporting the African Redemption Fund, which was created in 1924 to raise money for the UNIA's programs in Africa, or Garvey's Defense Fund.[97] The UNIA described the latter as the start of "the fight for Africa's liberty." "Every Negro of loyalty and manhood is asked to subscribe," the appeal read, even when a substantial portion of the contributors were women.[98]

As the language "fight for Africa's liberty" suggests, agrarians looked to the UNIA for a grand purpose. In some ways the UNIA was like any other fraternal order, such as the Masons or the Odd Fellows, all of which were popular in the lowlands during the period 1880 to 1915. They were all select groups that privileged the participation of men of good standing, required the payment of monthly dues, observed elaborate rituals, and encouraged members to take the lead in communal affairs. Since the 1870s, according to one historian, fraternal orders had provided "a valuable resource for black men seeking new pathways to financial stability, social authority, and racial pride."[99] But they had limitations. Formed as a response to the roaring violence and fraud of the Jim Crow era, fraternal orders retreated from partisan electoral politics and necessarily looked inward.[100] At the same time, fraternal orders met resistance from the other main outlet for community action in the years of Jim Crow—the AME and Baptist churches. Gripped by mutual suspicion, churches and fraternal associations usually worked against one another to their mutual detriment. "The struggles could become intense and divisive," historian Steven Hahn observed, "based as they often were not only in conflicting sensibilities but also in rival kinship groups and community institutions that set clan against clan and lodge against church." By the time *The Negro World* began circulating among rural African Americans, fraternal groups and churches, the main civic bodies that framed black life in the South, were fragmented and fractious.[101] The UNIA seemed to shore up both, especially for African Americans trying to order their lives in the Bootheel.

Preachers from all denominations rallied to the UNIA. When he was founding the organization, Garvey had deliberately adopted the symbolism, ritual, and language of the church in order to galvanize the idea of a black nation. Division meetings were usually held on Sundays, often in churches; each division had a chaplain; and Garveyites sang hymns, heard sermons, and said prayers. And just as Garvey draped the UNIA in the garb of religiosity, so rural church leaders used Garveyism to reinforce and strengthen their own core beliefs and goals.[102] The Garveyite emphasis on individual effort gave another layer of meaning to agrarian ideas about the righteousness of work. Like the UNIA, AME and Baptist preachers taught that the keys to progress were "morality, sobriety, industry, and uplift."[103] This compatibility of ideas created broad consensus across rural religious groups at a time when congregations were still forming and fragmented. Consider the 1926 meeting of Garveyites at the AME church in Charleston in Mississippi County. Following the morning's sermon, it began "in the usual manner with religious services conducted by Mr. A. Mallory." He was followed by division president Rev. S. H. Marris, who made some remarks, and then Rev. McAdory delivered another sermon. More presentations followed throughout the afternoon, including those by Revs. Halling, Harmon, and Willis. The church choir provided entertainment.[104] Members then prayed and recited the UNIA's aims and objectives. To conclude, they chanted the Garveyite motto, "One God! One Aim! One Destiny!"[105] Garveyism had to be powerful to get so many men who were unaccustomed to sharing their pulpits to cooperate with each other.

These leaders saw Garveyism as a means to achieve new spiritual power in challenging times. The UNIA's interpretation of the redemption of Africa provided the expansive political goal that black agrarians sought after years of disfranchisement, retrenchment, and disagreement. Garveyite efforts were all aimed at returning the African "motherland" to glory.[106] To a much greater extent than urban Garveyites, agrarians transformed the *Cause Afric* into a kind of religious revival, a means to imbue their own authority as spiritual and community leaders with new significance. At a UNIA meeting in the Wyatt AME church, Rev. L. W. Johnson delivered a sermon-like "soul-stirring lecture . . . that reacted on the conscience of every un-believer and stirred the soul and mind of believers to the extent that they were inspired to achieve greater victories" for the cause. "Our hearts really did burn within us," reporter Robert Greyer declared.[107] "Our cause is based on righteousness," Garvey confirmed, "because God Almighty is our leader and Jesus Christ is our standard bearer."[108] Wyatt Garveyites assured themselves of their role in the quest for redemption by continuing to sing "From Greenland's Icy Mountains," an old missionary hymn the UNIA used in ritual (even though most divisions opted for the UNIA's official "Universal Ethiopian Anthem").[109] The hymn reminded believers that God's work could not be done without their dutiful labor:

From Greenland's Icy Mountains
From India's coral strand
Where Afric's sunny fountains
Roll down their golden sand
From many an ancient river
From many a palmy plain
They call us to deliver
Their land from error's chain.[110]

This fixation on the process of redeeming Africa revived a tradition of thought among rural Southerners in which Africa was "both a real and imagined site of black liberty," the symbol of a haven for all black people.[111]

The spiritual power of this mission flowed from God through Garvey, who his followers regarded as a "Black Moses," a model of manly leadership.[112] Garveyites in Cape Girardeau, just north of Scott County, opened their meeting with a reading of the third chapter of Exodus, which tells of God sending Moses to rally the elders of Israel to pray for deliverance "up out of the affliction of Egypt" and "unto a land flowing with milk and honey" (Exod. 3:16–17).[113] The role of Garvey as Moses was clear; they imagined themselves as the elders. Garveyites in Hermondale, meanwhile, conceived of Garvey's teaching as a Mosaic dispensation. "The seed which he sowed here continues to grow and will continue to grow until Africa is redeemed," they reported.[114] This sense of calling also strengthened rural hierarchies by imbuing the familial, economic, and religious authority of rural leaders with epic significance. Just as Garvey followed God and race leaders followed Garvey, so dependents should follow race leaders. Fourteen-year-old Emmanuel Street of Charleston portrayed Garvey as the Messiah whose appearance Ezekiel had prophesied in the Old Testament. "Let him as a shepherd seek out his flock that is scattered," he wrote, quoting chapter 34 of the book of Ezekiel, "and deliver them out of all places where they have been scattered in the cloudy and dark days."[115] Garvey would "bring them out from the countries and will bring to their own land and feed them upon the mountains, by rivers, and in all the inhabited places of the country," Street concluded, suggesting that a redeemed Africa was their Israel.[116] This precocious teenager no doubt learned the power of this biblical interpretation from the church leaders who led the ecumenical UNIA meetings in Charleston. His and their faith in Garveyite authority could not but have added to the power of agrarian men working to secure autonomy in places like the Bootheel.

These agrarians considered their efforts to build independent worlds in the Bootheel to be a small but vital part of the Garveyite project. Speaking in Lilbourn in 1923, W. M. Davis, a UNIA leader from Cairo, Illinois, emphasized "the importance of the work in which we are engaged, the greatest work of the century, the greatest and noblest task that any race could undertake."[117] That task was, as D. D. Daniels said later, "the great work of Negro Uplift and African Redemption."[118] Davis lauded the formation of Lilbourn division as another link in "the evergrowing chain of the U.N.I.A. which is encircling the globe."[119] So convincing were such "testimonies" that the division "enrolled fourteen new members to the *Cause Afric*" and everyone declared "to go on with the fight until Africa is redeemed."[120] Farmers in the Bootheel never expressed a desire to migrate to Africa, nor did they ever talk about what a redeemed Africa might be like. While they seemed to follow Garvey's advice in "building up a country for themselves," they looked to do so in the new lands of the Little River Valley, not in Liberia. They believed that their hard work and accumulation of property would generate the power needed to redeem the race in the United States. Always more interested in themselves than in Africans, rural Garveyites used the *Cause Afric* to magnify their own prestige and authority. As the most dedicated agrarians, Bootheel Garveyites were among the most visible in the UNIA; they wrote letters, gave money, and filed meeting reports at a rate above and beyond that of most other rural UNIA groups. Addressing the UNIA's national convention in Harlem in 1924, J. L. Simmons, a Mississippi County farmer, boasted to the gathered delegates from around the world that his division "was getting along nicely and becoming a power in the community."[121] Earlier that year, Simmons's division announced its ambitions when it informed *The Negro World* that it was "desirous for the world at large to know that it is functioning and will continue to function until our program is put over the top."[122]

While devoted to the redemption of Africa, rural Garveyites seem to have eschewed other means of improving the standing of African Americans within the United States. According to available reports, meetings in the Bootheel were dominated by talk of the *Cause Afric,* which served as a kind of blank screen onto which they projected their own ambitions and concerns. Unlike other Garveyites, especially those in cities, Bootheel Garveyites never recorded their thoughts about partisan politics or voting in general, even though African Americans could and did vote freely in the region.[123] Moreover, their devotion to the UNIA cut off potential support for the NAACP, even though there had been a robust NAACP chapter in Caruthersville in 1920.[124] During the period 1923 to 1927, several NAACP organizers attempted to rouse the settlers as they streamed into the Bootheel, but to no avail.[125]

Indeed, some Garveyites were so intent on bolstering their standing and so convinced of their divine purpose that they looked to leading whites, not the NAACP, for support. In nearby Blytheville, Arkansas, in 1924, local UNIA members claimed the "sympathetic consideration of the town authorities." The mayor went so far as to recommend the UNIA and its program "as being very good for the race."[126] As late as 1936, Joseph Gray went before Charleston's all-white city council and "presented the program so intelligently that the Mayor and officials endorsed his work there with the UNIA."[127] One can imagine white elites agreeing with the Garveyite message of the duty of individual effort, the value of hard work, and the importance of uplifting Africans. Such relationships with white authorities seem to have worked. Areas that had been tormented with vigilante violence in 1922 and 1923 suddenly became peaceful.

It is possible and plausible that UNIA leaders in the Bootheel received sustained protection from local planters who were members of the KKK. While there is no record of any local member meeting with Klan leaders, the absence of violence against Garveyite communities is curious, given the history of violence in the region. This is not to say that the Klan controlled the UNIA or that the two were particularly friendly, but both had goals and assets that were mutually beneficial. Bootheel Klan members controlled large amounts of land and political power and possessed the means to repress poor whites, while the UNIA included members who were the most successful cotton farmers, the "saviors of agriculture in this section."[128] Garvey himself carried on an odd, semi-friendly relationship with the Klan, even publicly applauding the Klan's pursuit of racial separation.[129]

The only time rural Garveyites used their "power in the community" to challenge leading whites was in support of Garvey. Bootheel Garveyites spent immense energy on appeals for Garvey's freedom after his 1923 trial and 1925 imprisonment on charges of mail fraud.[130] As Garvey's final appeals wound down, the Mississippi County divisions organized a day of meetings devoted solely to discussing Garvey's situation. "Four thousand and five hundred Negroes of Southeast Missouri have met in meetings at various places and have become grieved," they informed President Calvin Coolidge, "and pray that you will consider the appeal of this race for the clemency for our leader Marcus Garvey."[131] Another round of Bootheel meetings attracted more than 3,000 Garveyites.[132] Although these attempts failed, Garvey's plight hovered over local meetings. In late 1925, New Madrid 685 expressed a collective "wish and desire that he continue to be our leader as he has been in the past, to carry on the great work of Negro Uplift and African Redemption."[133] Local members continued to appeal to the government through 1926.[134] These efforts, as with so much that rural Garveyites did, were meant to defend the powerful within their communities (or, in Garvey's case, the most powerful patriarch) as a way of bettering their communities more generally.

*   *   *

The Great Depression came early to southeast Missouri. In the early morning of April 16, 1927, the worst flood ever to strike the Mississippi Valley swept away with apocalyptic ferocity the fortunes and futures of landowners, renters, and sharecroppers alike. The swollen river tore a 1,500-foot hole in the Dorena levee and soon most of Mississippi County was blanketed with muddy water. The towns of Wyatt, Anniston, and East Prairie were all submerged. Within days the flood topped the levee guarding New Madrid and forced its residents to flee. Meanwhile, the St. Francis River, engorged with backwater from the Mississippi, broke its levees in several places and inundated most of Dunklin County. The converging floods swamped the canals and ditches of the Little River Drainage District and slowly drowned the lands along the length of this central valley. The destruction of land was epic: 193,000 acres in New Madrid, 125,000 in Mississippi, 100,000 in Dunklin, 58,000 in Pemiscot, 26,000 in Scott, and 25,000 in Stoddard were devastated.[135] Whatever well-being and economic success African American farmers had attained in the 1920s were washed away.

The flood took its heaviest toll on the tenants and croppers living in the bottomlands. The water displaced over 31,000 people in the six Bootheel counties, almost nine in ten of which were tenants. Almost half of all African Americans in Mississippi and New Madrid counties were displaced.[136] Most lost everything as water swept away houses, barns, tools, and equipment. In many areas only the land remained, covered in sand and silt. "To be sure, there are a number of farmers who have lost their all, which was not much, because they were the tenant farmers who owned no land," a Lilbourn correspondent observed in the aftermath. Yet it would hurt them "as much as it would hurt a man who owned $10,000 worth of property and lost that."[137] Another onlooker declared that "the privation and loss suffered by these people can never be counted."[138]

Although the Red Cross came to the aid of flood refugees throughout the Mississippi Valley, black farmers in the Bootheel looked to themselves for support. The areas surrounding the UNIA divisions at Charleston, Commerce, New Madrid, Saymos, and Wyatt suffered the worst flooding. Rather than go into the white-controlled Red Cross camps, however, most displaced blacks took refuge in neighboring communities. Only 38 percent of black refugees went to camps, about half as many as in Arkansas. Significantly, most out-of-camp refugees congregated in unaffected rural areas that were home to strong UNIA divisions, particularly Parma, Risco, Kewanee, and Charleston. As centers of community leadership, prosperity, and kinship ties, local UNIA groups responded to the crisis by sheltering their own. In doing so, they enabled refugees to accept Red Cross food, clothing, and medical attention without surrendering their freedom of movement or association and avoided the abuses of planters further south who used Red Cross relief as a means to extend control over their tenants.[139] In the midst of disaster these agrarians could still exercise some autonomy.

But this show of self-sufficiency was short lived. The flood had devastated the land, disrupted the agricultural season, and exhausted the people. To compound matters, as refugees were returning to their land in early June, high water spilled through the unrepaired Dorena levee and flooded large parts of Mississippi County once again. That year farmers in the six Bootheel counties planted only 291,000 acres of cotton, the lowest amount since 1923. The reduced acreage and swamped soil stunted the crop, which yielded the lowest number of bales in the county since 1921. The weather in the spring of 1928 offered no respite. Heavy rains throughout the planting season caused yet more flooding and Mississippi County farmers lost 75 percent of their crop. Farmers in the lowlands of New Madrid County lost all of their crops during a June flood, and the county as a whole reaped only half of the crops it planted. Over 15,000 people in these three counties relied on the Red Cross for emergency food supplies to survive until cotton-picking season. The crop that year was only marginally better than in 1927.[140]

Relentless disaster reshaped the agricultural economy to the detriment of owners and renters, the bedrock of black agrarianism. Debt delinquency rocketed after the 1927 flood, from 33 percent in 1927 to 53 percent in 1928 to 80 percent in 1929. Foreclosure rates rose as rapidly as land values fell. In New Madrid County, the price of land fell by $37.60 per acre during the period 1924 to 1929, a 45.8 percent drop that ate 8 million dollars' worth of land value. Similar collapses struck Dunklin (–36.8 percent), Mississippi (–24.4 percent), Scott (–41.6 percent) and Stoddard (–34.9 percent) counties. This had two consequences: as insurance companies and gin operators bought up the cheap land, they employed sharecroppers, the most dependent of all farmers, to raise cotton, and elsewhere, smaller landowners grew less cotton because they lacked capital and credit. From 1924 to 1929, cotton planting fell by an average of more than 50 percent. The increased competition for cotton land led to bad deals for tenants. Share-renters had two choices: become sharecroppers or leave the area. Even with some outmigration, in 1929 black families in Mississippi and New Madrid counties worked an average of 30 acres, which was barely sustainable, while Pemiscot families farmed a miserable 22.7 acres.[141] Depression and disaster were turning lands once full of promise into sweeping plantations of hunger and poverty.

These successive crises shattered the basis of Garveyism in the Bootheel. The flood and ensuing economic disaster undermined the ability of agrarians to maintain their farms and families, let alone maintain UNIA divisions. Only six of the fifteen divisions survived into 1928: Charleston, Commerce, New Madrid, Poplar Bluff, Risco, and Wyatt. Dexter, Essex, and Hermondale divisions—which had each boasted between twenty-five and thirty-six members as recently as 1926, placing them among the largest of all rural divisions at the time—were now gone. Surviving divisions were dangerously weak. Commerce, which had thirty-one members in early 1927, could claim only ten dues-payers in 1928.[142] These Garveyites focused now almost solely on Garvey's plight in federal prison both as a point of discussion and as a symbol of their struggle to maintain authority in the midst of calamity. With death creeping all around them in the wake of the flood, Wyatt division resolved in August 1927 "that if our chief dies in Atlanta the spirit of him shall go on until Africa is redeemed." Despite these hardships, Rev. Strong urged the division to "carry on and on and never give up the fight."[143] Three months later Garvey was finally freed, only to be deported within days. Yet a year later, Wyatt division members remained optimistic about the UNIA program, even though their leader had been taken away and they faced crop failures and economic turmoil. Emboldened by Garvey's successful trip to Europe in 1928 and excited about a rumor that he would soon return to the United States, members anticipated that "there will be work and more work, and we are preparing ourselves to do our bit."[144]

But the authority of local Garveyites was slipping. In 1928 a group of merchants, cooks, mill workers, day laborers, and farmers from Charleston organized a chapter of the NAACP.[145] None of the Garveyites in Mississippi County records were listed on the application charter. After five years of monopolizing community leadership, local Garveyites were weak enough to be challenged by an organization devoted to equal rights for African Americans in the United States, a set of ideals antithetical to those of the UNIA and publicly derided by Garvey himself. For the most part, those who started the Charleston chapter represented a new generation of leaders. People like Marshall Currin, a 33-year-old café owner, were younger and had interests in occupations outside of farming. But their time to lead had not yet come; by early 1929 the chapter had collapsed. A. J. Halloway cited apathy toward NAACP methods and financial problems as reasons for the demise. "They don't believe in it," he lamented of his neighbors.[146] While the creation of the chapter suggested a willingness to engage in protest politics, the NAACP's gradualist legalistic approach did not yet satisfy the needs of black farmers.

In the meantime, Garveyite concerns became more and more limited and focused inward. In August 1929, Garvey split from the New York–based leaders who had managed the UNIA during his imprisonment and created a rival group, the Universal Negro Improvement Association of the World, August 1929 headquartered in Kingston, Jamaica.[147] Garvey continued writing for *The Negro World,* and his "New Organization" retained the devotion of some of his rural American followers, especially those around New Madrid, Poplar Bluff, Risco, and Wyatt.[148] The meetings of these groups were sporadic, however, and were attended by fewer and fewer people. They remained obsessed with loyalty to Garvey, their discussions heavy with a sense of besiegement and a yearning for better days. "Let's put all selfishness and foolishness out of our mind," pleaded L. E. Ridgel of Poplar Bluff 746, "and all have one desire, and that's for Africa to be redeemed."[149] President Will Jones of Wyatt division "asked the members to be loyal to the U.N.I.A. and the Hon. Marcus Garvey" at a meeting "filled with Garveyism." Desperate to defend Garvey's authority (and perhaps some of their own), division leaders demanded that "members obey your superior officers."[150] But the Black Moses would never return; his work of redeeming Africa would remain unfinished. By late 1930, the organizational UNIA was largely dead in the Bootheel. Only Wyatt and Charleston Garveyites made any further reports of their activity.[151]

Although the UNIA faded, something of Garveyism remained, strengthened even amid the suffering of the early Depression. A new generation of farmers, people such as Owen and Zella Whitfield, Peter and Vera Wilderness, and others, was coming of age in the Bootheel. Their life and work would never be the same as those of their fathers, tenants such as D. D. Daniels, Alex Cooper, and Stonewall Jackson. This new generation faced the daunting challenge of maintaining their communities, their kinship networks, and their dreams of agrarian independence in a world of catastrophe and sorrow. The ideas that made Garveyism so powerful, so respected—the desire for economic autonomy, the importance of duty to kin and community, and the sense of spiritual empowerment in a great cause—continued to fuel their hopes for a better future. Those hopes offered the only light against the descending, deepening darkness.

# 4

# No More Mourning

On a warm summer evening sometime in the early 1930s, Owen Whitfield, a black Baptist preacher and sharecropper in Mississippi County, sat alone with his mules in the cotton patch after a long day's work. Suddenly, the twilight quiet was interrupted by the pitiful cry of his daughter, who told him that there was no food left in the house for supper. Like thousands of other rural families, the Whitfields were on the precipice of catastrophe as the Great Depression pulled them into conditions ever more hellish and degrading.[1] They toiled for crops that were next to worthless; they ate less or went hungry; they wore ragged clothes they could not afford to replace; they lived in rented, dilapidated shacks that no one would repair; they grew sick from preventable diseases; and they watched helplessly as death consumed friends and loved ones. A local journalist described the effects of the crisis on a Scott County family. This "share-cropper has the trachoma and his whole family has the malaria," the journalist informed readers, and "his children always have worms." The family was large; his wife had been just 14 when she began bearing children. "It could have been larger though," the journalist reported. "There is a row of little graves." The reporter asked, "Who will save him" and his family?[2]

Although the election of Franklin D. Roosevelt in 1932 raised hopes, the new administration did not immediately take action to help families like this one. Instead, the early New Deal legislation most relevant to cotton farmers, the Agricultural Adjustment Act of 1933 and Bankhead Cotton Control Act of 1934, financed the recovery of planters at the expense of the landless. These laws reduced the number of acres that tenants could farm and provided few guarantees that tenants would be fairly compensated for their loss. Rather than simply shore up the old agricultural model, these developments gave rise to a new system of cotton agriculture characterized by absentee corporate investors who expanded and consolidated their holdings, seasonal wage workers that replaced tenants, and tractors that replaced human labor. New Deal policies destroyed the ties of both black and white tenants to the soil, while big landowners—backed by the government—profited handsomely.[3]

Hungry and exhausted and desperate, Whitfield fell to his knees and prayed to God for an answer. "You said the righteous and them that preached the Gospel would never go hungry," he chided. "But I done worked, behaved my self, kept Your precepts—and those that haven't is getting along much better." At some point during his lamentation an answer came to Whitfield from within, "like a common-sense part of me," he later said. "But you ain't been preaching the Gospel—just makin' a noise," the voice said. "I bless you with enough to fill many barns. Somebody's gettin' it. If you ain't, that's your fault, not Mine."[4] Whitfield's argument with God symbolized a growing sense of alienation among rural believers. While the Depression plunged farming families deeper into poverty and dependence, it also opened a social and cultural divide in religious communities that mirrored a contemporaneous pattern in urban areas. In the midst of crisis, at a time when the faithful needed support most, the main denominations—the Southern Baptist Convention; the Methodist Episcopal Church, South; and the AME—pulled back from rural areas in order to focus on flagging congregations in larger towns. As these churches began to reflect the expectations and concerns of their largely middle-class members, rural believers increasingly felt shunned and unwelcome because of their worship style, their lack of good clothes, and their desire for close fellowship. In response, rural believers such as Whitfield used older evangelical traditions and beliefs to fashion religious communities that would better speak to their needs. They increasingly rejected the top-down workings of the major denominations, the Calvinistic traditions of those denominations that explained prosperity as God's favor, and the local hierarchies of property, age, gender, and decorum. Instead they sought a greater experience of God that directly challenged reigning conceptions of social and ideological authority.[5]

Across the Bootheel, this search for more responsive religious fellowship generated an expansive revival in Pentecostal, Holiness, and schismatic Baptist congregations that together produced a dramatic devolution of spiritual power. The proliferation of new churches, many led by lay preachers and unconnected to any denominational body, unleashed a dispensation of spiritual gifts to ordinary people—through visions, speaking in tongues, and the laying on of hands—that would heal sick bodies, mend broken spirits, and (adherents believed) hasten Christ's triumph over evil in this world. For many believers, especially whites in Pentecostal-Holiness churches, the theological doctrines of which were three decades old by the 1930s, this outpouring of divine gifts signaled the impending End Times and fed a view that encouraged withdrawal from all things related to this corrupt world, especially politics. For others, especially rural blacks such as Whitfield, the spread of revival enlisted ordinary believers as agents who could fulfill God's will.[6]

This reorientation of rural faith communities around a personal experience of God reaffirmed a black theological tradition that emphasized the human role in social change, a shift that had profound political implications.[7] Grassroots "spiritual empowerment" unlocked protest-minded democratic political activism among rural blacks in the Bootheel. Given the centrality of religion to rural black life and the relative paucity of rural churches, revivalists armed with renewed moral power made manifest in the gifts of the Holy Spirit were able to claim the mantle of leadership and refocus the strategies of existing leaders, whether they were denominational preachers or former Garveyites, around the needs of ordinary people. The result was the creation of parallel mobilizations within rural black communities, one led by existing leaders that tried to use groups such as the well-established NAACP and the National Federation of Colored Farmers, a newer group, to continue long-term efforts to improve the condition of black people and another created by the rural poor who sought an immediate end to their suffering through volatile new protest groups.[8] Traversing this spectrum, Whitfield, after his discussion with God, pledged to stop "whoopin' and hollerin'" and begin serving the Lord through action, a change that reflected revivalist calls for "action and behavior" over formal theology. A preacher who will "tell you about Heaven and can't tell you how to get a loaf of bread here" was now a "liar" to Whitfield. "A sermon," he decided, "sends you home happy. The Gospel sends you home mad."[9] The ultimate conviction honed in the rural black revivals of the early 1930s was simple: although God would provide the power, he asked the faithful to save themselves.

*　*　*

In the summer of 1930, as banks and markets crashed nationwide, the Bootheel's soil and crops dried up in a record-setting drought that enveloped all or parts of Arkansas, Kentucky, Louisiana, Mississippi, Missouri, Oklahoma, Tennessee, and Texas.[10] As fall approached, clear skies and scorching sunshine burned food crops in the ground and baked cotton while it was still in the boll. After successive waterlogged years in the late 1920s, the drought seemed a new cruelty. Farmers in the Bootheel and surrounding states lost between 50 and 85 percent of their corn crop, which caused a shortage of corn meal, the main staple in the diets of landless families. In addition, the drought withered forage and pasture crops needed to feed livestock.[11] As cows, pigs, and goats starved and died, tenants lost essential sources of meat and milk that they could not afford to replace. Hungry families could only wait for cotton-picking time when they might earn enough to buy the high-priced food that sat on store shelves.

Cotton-picking season provided no relief, however. The drought ravaged crops and lives in the dust-eaten hills of the Ozarks and Tennessee as badly as it had in the lowlands. During the period 1929 to 1934, more than 12,000 whites from these areas fled to the Bootheel in search of wage work, most during the drought of 1930–1931. With so many eager to work, area growers lowered wages to a starvation rate of 50 cents per hundred pounds picked.[12] "Plenty of people in the surrounding territory have been badly in need of employment," a Caruthersville newspaper pointed out, "hence they are willing to come here and work for whatever they might be able to get."[13] To make matters worse, the drought had produced a cotton crop that was "way below normal," wrote a Red Cross official, making it "difficult for a picker to make more than a dollar a day on average, and in some counties they are fortunate if they can make fifty cents a day."[14] For tenant families relying on picking work to earn extra cash, low wages and low prices promised a winter of unending hardship. That fall a bale of cotton was worth $45, down from $90 a year earlier. A tenant family would have been hard pressed to cover their basic provisions for winter with this income, especially considering the high prices of groceries.[15]

The deprivation was so severe that the Red Cross began relief operations in southeast Missouri in December. By the end of the month, 2,000 families had received basic food supplies in Dunklin County; 1,000 in New Madrid; and 2,500 in Pemiscot. More than 5,000 blacks in Mississippi County relied on relief.[16] The crisis worsened throughout January and February, as any remaining provisions and money that tenants had hoarded finally ran out. By the time of spring planting, more than 75 percent of all people in the lowland counties had received some sort of aid, mostly food. Unlike their self-sufficient stand during the 1927 flood, nearly all of the black residents in the Bootheel—more than 19,000 people—lived in the shadow of famine and were dependent on relief committees controlled by local planters.[17]

Many of those planters were themselves struggling to survive. Fearful that the drought would persist, growers planted fewer crops in 1931. "Land owners in this section [New Madrid] are not operating on as large a scale as in earlier years and consequently a large number of farm laborers have been unable to secure employment," the Red Cross reported.[18] The crash of cotton prices to a new low of 4.6 cents per lint pound in 1932 made the staple nearly worthless. At this price, a 500-pound bale of lint cotton earned less than $25, down from $45 in 1930 and $90 in 1929.[19] To cope with acreage reductions and the piti-ful price, planters lowered picking wages to 40 cents per hundred and below. Many could not afford to pay even this paltry sum. Caverno reported that "the people who expected to farm this land are living in the houses on it with no means of support except day labor." But their labor was not needed and no one had any cash to pay wages if it had been. Caverno, usually a success-ful grower, defaulted on his taxes and his mortgage for the first time in 1932. Many owners went bankrupt and lost their land to financiers who planned to let the fields lay fallow rather than plant worthless crops.[20]

The rising control of absentee owners—insurance, gin, and lumber com-panies—decimated the ability of local landlords and renters to help their sharecroppers. Corporate owners acquired many thousands of acres. Gen-eral American Insurance alone owned over 250,000 acres in a four-state area, much of it in the Bootheel, by 1934. Where these growers decided to plant crops rather than leave the land fallow, they demanded higher rents or larger crop shares from the cash and share tenants who subcontracted their land.[21] One of the preferred tactics these companies used to maximize profits was to employ casual wage workers instead of tenants. Unlike share-croppers, wage laborers did not receive homes, credit, or any share of the crop and could be paid at prevailing wage rates. Andrew Puckett, a tenant in Pemiscot County, and his eight sharecroppers were driven from their land in 1933 when it was purchased by a gin company using day laborers. "There is plenty in the same neighborhood that has had to leave the same way," Puckett reported.[22] To Caverno, the transformation of the Bootheel from swampland to cropland had failed. "Most of our farmers," he said, "have gone through tremendous hardships in the clearing, draining, and developing of this country [only] to find . . . an invisible system which re-duced them to hopelessness and starvation."[23]

Government flood-control policy only made conditions worse. After the 1927 flood, the U.S. Army Corps of Engineers planned to construct a series of spillways along the Mississippi River that could be flooded if high water threatened the levees. In 1932, the first of these was completed; the 160,000-acre Bird's Point–New Madrid Spillway covered eastern Mississippi and New Madrid counties and surrounded some of the richest land in the Bootheel with a 60-foot-high setback levee that forever threatened farms within it with a devastating flood. The government bought flowage rights over the land for $15 per acre, a miniscule price for the ability to destroy land worth on average $214 per acre. Most resident landowners moved out of the rich and dangerous spillway or sold their holdings to speculators. The tenants who had lived and worked there since the early 1920s, most of whom were black, remained. However, their landlords stopped building new tenant homes or improving old ones because they would only be washed away.[24] The spillway region, once a promised land, had become a ghetto.

At the same time, the poverty and looming famine of 1930–1932 condemned landless families to increasing levels of disease and death. Thad Snow recalled that tenants "went cold and hungry." "Their shoes and clothes wore out and they could not replace them," he said, and "they lost weight and they lost color."[25] Life in the Bootheel had never been particularly healthy, given the swamps and humidity, but the deterioration of living conditions and diets during the hard years of 1927 to 1932 meant that more people died from endemic diseases. Over this period, the death rate from malaria in New Madrid increased from 10 to 13 times the state rate; in Pemiscot, it increased from 12 to 15 times the state rate. Similarly, in the period 1930 to 1932, the death rate from typhoid in Snow's Mississippi County rose from 19 to 31 deaths per 100,000, six times the state rate. Starvation and poverty hit the young hardest. The number of children under two years of age who died from diarrhea and enteritis grew from 81 deaths per 100,000 in 1928 to 115 deaths per 100,000 in 1932. By comparison, the rate for all of Missouri in 1932 was only 14 deaths per 100,000 people. During this period, African American families endured an average of 190 infant deaths (deaths of children under one year) per 1,000 live births, including 220 deaths in Pemiscot. In New Madrid and Pemiscot counties, white families experienced similar rates: 159 and 153 deaths per 1,000 births, respectively, an appalling level of mortality.[26] One white sharecropping woman, all too aware of the rising prevalence of child illnesses, explained helplessly, "We can't change our food, can't afford it. . . . We would eat differently if we could get it."[27]

*　*　*

The depth of the crisis prompted some rural black community leaders to explore more active political strategies. Save for the failed effort to organize an NAACP chapter in Charleston in 1928, no formal political organization had emerged following the collapse of the UNIA. The crushing blows of economic crisis, ecological disaster, and social dislocation of the early Depression years no doubt privileged survival over politics. By the final year of the Hoover administration, however, activist sentiment had begun to stir. In early 1932, according to a report in the *Chicago Defender,* "150 Race farmers" around Parma in New Madrid County organized a local group of the National Federation of Colored Farmers (NFCF), an organization created in the early 1920s to advocate cooperative marketing and buying, diversified farming, and the value of landownership among African Americans.[28]

The NFCF was a selective organization of largely successful farmers. In large part, its members sought to resuscitate the agrarian ambitions that had defined rural Garveyism. The group's concerns about cooperatives, diversification, and land buying all reflected an uncommon degree of prosperity made more remarkable by the dire economic circumstances. Although the Depression had shackled leading black farmers in the Bootheel with debts, some believed they could still regain their autonomy. Rev. M. T. Ghess, a founder of the Parma unit, reported that black farmers in the Bootheel raised "excellent crops this season and predicts that they will be able to liquidate many old debts and in some instances have a surplus to begin the next season with." They hoped to supplement these efforts by creating "an agricultural credit organization that will enable them to finance themselves."[29] The emphasis on cooperation resembled Garveyite calls for racial solidarity and self-determination. An Alabama member reported how local whites "are being aroused by the organization of our farmers for their advancement and thrift," language that closely matched rural Garveyite, indeed Washingtonian, rhetoric.[30] While it is unclear whether or not Ghess had been a member of the UNIA, Parma had been home to a successful UNIA division in the 1920s. Nevertheless, community leaders such as Ghess and Jack Battle at Parma, both of whom were preachers, and L. B. Boler, an Agricultural Extension Service agent and agricultural teacher at Charleston's Lincoln High School who would soon join the NFCF, still believed that self-sufficient communities led by prominent men and supported by leading whites could weather the storm. Boler preached the benefits of home production and encouraged tenants to "courageously approach the land owner for the permission to raise" foodstuffs as well as cash crops. Only "sacrifice, work, and co-operation from both landowner and tenant" would see them through the crisis, Boler declared.[31]

In this new, harsher climate, however, NFCF leaders broke with UNIA strategy and belief by calling on national agencies to ensure that rural blacks received the same aid as white farmers. In a daring step that resembled the strategies of the NAACP, J. P. Davis, national NFCF president, encouraged farmers whose applications for Red Cross assistance had been rejected to complain to the national office, promising that "the persons in charge of that branch will be dismissed," or so he had been assured by Secretary of Agriculture Arthur Hyde.[32] Davis's reliance on personal assurances rather than rights suggests that although some rural blacks looked to the government for help, they did so in the faith that elected Republicans would reward their loyalty at the polls.

Democrat Franklin D. Roosevelt's victory in November 1932 rendered this faith obsolete. He tallied massive vote totals in every county in the Bootheel: 82 percent in Dunklin County, 75 percent in Scott County, and between 64 and 69 percent in the remaining counties. Black voters, however, did not share the excitement of their white neighbors about Roosevelt. Over 88 percent of voters in Charleston's mostly black third precinct supported Hoover, as did significant numbers of African Americans in New Madrid and Pemiscot counties.[33] Although they were beginning to push for greater federal involvement in the rural crisis, African Americans in the Bootheel continued to place their bet with Republicans. This no doubt reflected traditional loyalties (the Republican Party, after all, was still referred to as "the party of Lincoln") as well as local attachments to sympathetic figures such as Secretary of Agriculture Hyde, who as governor in 1923 had dispatched the state militia to protect black settlers near Parma.

Their candidate defeated, some black leaders explored more aggressive tactics in 1933. Four groups of activists in Scott and Pemiscot counties tried to organize chapters of the NAACP, the first such attempts since 1928.[34] "The people of this section are very anxious to have a branch office," Rev. D. McNewerell of Sikeston reported.[35] The timing of this sudden surge in interest during and immediately following FDR's first hundred days suggests that some grassroots leaders, certainly more than historians have claimed, were warming to the NAACP's campaign for racial equality. It is possible that the proliferation of New Deal initiatives aimed at combating the economic crisis led people to reevaluate the efficacy of the NAACP's strategy of lobbying the federal government for reform. In contrast to years of relative Republican inaction, the Democrats were doing things, which raised expectations that political engagement might now be worthwhile.[36] Whatever the reason, their efforts broke with the separatism of the UNIA. However, no new NAACP chapters were established in the Bootheel in 1933. No organizer could find fifty people, the number required to charter a chapter, with enough money to pay dues.[37]

Despite Roosevelt's popularity among white voters, the agricultural policies of the New Deal seemed to confirm the suspicions of African Americans. The most relevant legislative creation for tenants, the Agricultural Adjustment Act of 1933, was designed to raise the prices of commodities, including cotton, to 1914 "parity" levels by reducing the amounts produced and pay compensation to growers for the reduction. The new law came into force after cotton had already been planted in 1933 and called for farmers to voluntarily plow up part of their crop, for which they would receive a payment that would be divided among those with a stake in the crop in proportion to their share. Most sharecroppers should have received half of any federal payment, but many did not. The Bankhead Cotton Control Act of 1934 gave even more power to landowners and did not have proper mechanisms to safeguard the rights of tenants. Moreover, it made acreage reductions of 40 percent mandatory for all growers and restructured the balance of compensation for reducing production. Under the provisions of the Bankhead Cotton Control Act, landlords who had sharecroppers or share tenants who were not managers would receive 90 percent of the government payment for allowing land formerly used to grow cotton to lay fallow, while those working on shares would receive 10 percent. Meanwhile, cash tenants would receive 100 percent of the payment, and share tenants who were managers would receive 50 percent of that payment (landlords of the latter received the other 50 percent).[38] The determination of who would be considered a "managing share renter" was left to local AAA committees controlled by the biggest planters. They were free to demote managing share tenants to the nonmanaging type, and they now had financial incentive to do so. They could even go a step further to demote sharecroppers to wage laborers; the latter had no claim to any part of the payment.[39] Paragraph seven of the law, meant to prevent this kind of deceit, required landowners to "endeavor in good faith" to carry out the reductions with the least amount of social disruption, to maintain the same number of tenants, and to allow tenants continued use of housing, rent-free. This was binding unless the tenant became a "nuisance or a menace." With such equivocal language and biased committees, there was little real protection for tenants and sharecroppers.[40]

The cut in acreage, without adequate compensation, pushed tenants of all classes to the breaking point.[41] "A 40 percent cut in the cotton crop," Caverno warned, "will not leave a family living for these families."[42] Thad Snow reported that the Bankhead Cotton Control Act made his sharecroppers "deeply resentful." Outraged that the government seemed to so flagrantly attack their livelihoods, they "labor[ed] under a sense of injustice and betrayal."[43] Simply having land to work was now a luxury, however, as the use of wage laborers increased. Growers in Dunklin, New Madrid, and Pemiscot counties responded to the incentives of the Cotton Control Act by employing wage laborers to plant, cultivate, and pick their cotton, a trend reflected in larger average farm sizes despite an increase in the rural population in these counties.[44] More wage workers meant lower wages for sharecroppers who used peak labor seasons as a source of additional income. "There are too many pickers of a day to make any money," a white sharecropper who picked cotton for additional income in Dunklin complained. "They just fill up the field with them."[45]

Restructuring the cotton economy tore apart tenant communities. In order to find work, neighbors and kin had to move. Families who had become tenants since the onset of the Depression were the most mobile. In early 1935, for example, 42 percent of all tenants in the Bootheel had been on their farms less than a year, 15 percent for one year, and only 7 percent for three years. Some families, however, showed surprising resilience: 18 percent of tenants worked the same land as they had in 1928. While a minority remained rooted in place, the high rate of mobility for others strained kinship, work-sharing, religious, and other networks of social fellowship as families drifted from farm to farm.[46]

In addition, the health of tenants was deteriorating further. Housing conditions worsened markedly because landlords, especially absentee owners, considered improvements a waste of money. By the mid-1930s, two-thirds of black and half of white sharecroppers lived in strip houses, a type of shack made of vertical planks with paper or rubber strips over the cracks. Most tenants got their drinking water from surface sources that were easily contaminated since nearly all families used open or unscreened outdoor toilets. Moreover, about two-thirds of tenant houses had no screens to keep out the mosquitoes that transmitted malaria.[47] Inside these hovels, tenants ate meals of corn pone, salt pork, dried beans, molasses, and greens that were deficient in vitamins and protein. Few families had substantial gardens. As a result, 84 percent of African American families preserved fewer than the 80 quarts of food they typically needed to make it through winter. Almost half of white tenants canned too little.[48] This decline in the quality of rural lives and weakening of rural communities seemed to offer little hope for an agrarian future.

\* \* \*

The denominational church bodies that had long been the central institutions among African American and white farmers buckled under the strain. Many small rural congregations could not afford to sustain a preacher or a meeting place and simply folded. In response, most Southern Baptist Convention and Methodist-affiliated churches consolidated congregations in area towns to make them more financially viable.[49] As a result, rural people who had worshipped in unprepossessing country churches now faced the prospect of attending services in town among people who were more prosperous, who wore better clothes, and who expected their middle-class decorum to reign. Rural people often felt unwelcome. They could not afford to contribute to the offering, they sensed the opprobrium of the better-off for not "being dressed up," and they felt cold in more restrained and text-based services. All of this contributed to a growing sense of spiritual dissatisfaction, even alienation. "The 'old line churches' are evidently not meeting the needs of a certain class of people," sociologists working for the Resettlement Administration in the Bootheel noted in 1935.[50] Among African Americans, the more elite and hierarchical AME and Colored Methodist Episcopal (CME) churches suffered most. In 1926, the AME had been central to community life; the denomination had claimed 45 percent of all black churchgoers in the Bootheel. By 1936, the AME could claim only 13 percent and had almost 200 fewer total members than a decade earlier. Poverty-stricken landless farmers no longer felt connected to churches like the CME Beebe Chapel in New Madrid, where the minister in 1930 earned an annual salary of $800, almost three times the average yearly earnings of sharecroppers.[51] Rural whites in the Bootheel also grew apart from the old denominations in this period, and Southern Methodist and Southern Baptist churches lost members.[52]

Thousands of rural Baptists, white and black, established independent churches that placed a traditional (what some called "primitive") emphasis on absolute congregational autonomy. Traditional Baptists insisted on "the right to appoint their own preachers . . . set their own styles of worship and music; and recognize spiritual authority in a variety of ways, including supernatural communication."[53] In the years 1926 to 1936, Southern Baptist churches in the Bootheel lost over 2,000 members, while the ranks of unaffiliated white Baptist churches, both rural and town, increased by more than 5,000. Likewise, African American Baptist churches gained almost 3,000 new members over this period.[54] Most of these congregations identified themselves as Missionary Baptist, claiming a tradition that was fiercely insistent on local autonomy as well as an emotional, auditory, and physical Afro-Baptist liturgy as the basis for simple and direct communion with God.[55] Whitfield, who variously described himself as a Primitive Baptist or Missionary Baptist, took an active part in the revival of this tradition when he confronted God in the cotton field. Like those who left the AME, these believers rejected the pretensions of the leading black Baptist churches in area towns, such as those that hosted the Third District Baptist Association meeting in 1934 in Charleston. "The affair was one of the grandest ever witnessed in this city," read one newspaper report, noting the elaborately laid tables, fresh flower arrangements, and "menu which was very appetizing" at the meeting.[56] Displays such as this amid the worst suffering in living memory could only have hastened the efforts of independent Baptists to get closer to God.

Thousands of others sought new communion altogether in the Pentecostal-Holiness congregations that collectively sparked a revival that would go far beyond the one of the 1910s. The first wave of revival had left about ten stable congregations of white believers in Dunklin and New Madrid counties. These churchgoers were split between two denominations, the Assemblies of God and the Pentecostal Holiness Church. By 1930, these churches owned property, paid regular preachers, and participated in larger ecclesiastical bodies.[57] The revival of the early 1930s, however, was bigger, more widespread, and more diverse than the initial Pentecostal-Holiness revival of the 1900s and 1910s. In the period 1930 to 1936, Spirit-filled preaching extended the reach of these existing churches while giving rise to an array of other Pentecostal-Holiness groups. The new churches in Mississippi County included a Church of God, an Original Free Pentecost Church, two Churches of God in Christ, and an Assembly of God. In Pemiscot County, there was a new United Holiness Church, two Pilgrim Holiness Churches, a Church of God, a Church of the Living God, and other Assemblies of God and Pentecostal Holiness Churches. By 1936 in Dunklin County, meanwhile, there were fourteen Pentecostal congregations. Unlike in the 1910s, African Americans were at the heart of this movement. Black believers founded new congregations in the sanctified tradition, which included Pentecostal, Holiness movement, and Apostolic churches that despite doctrinal differences all emphasized the process of sanctification and the working power of the Holy Spirit. The most prominent of these churches in the Bootheel were the Church of the Living God, the first black Holiness group, and the Church of God in Christ, a Holiness church that would become the largest black Pentecostal denomination in the United States.[58] "New-sect" congregations in the Bootheel, whether white or black, were by 1935 "made up chiefly of share croppers, tenants, or farm laborers."[59]

Eschewing the formalism and perceived materialism of the older denominations, revivalist groups worshiped wherever they could find space, whether in storefronts, in cotton fields, in brush arbors, or in shacks.[60] The Kennett Victory Temple Church of God in Christ, founded in 1930, met in a house and then in a workshop.[61] When members were asked why they chose these services, they usually responded that they did not have to be dressed up and felt welcome.[62] Worship services were often led by untrained lay preachers—who were likely tenants themselves—who felt the call to preach and took no regular salary. "It was the general opinion among most of the orthodox church ministers," one sociologist recorded during her fieldwork in the Bootheel, "that these sporadic branches meet the religious needs of a people that [the mainline denominations] cannot or do not care to draw into their churches."[63] White evangelist John Huffman announced in 1930 that his Pentecostal Church of God in Sikeston would be a "church for farmers . . . a house of worship for working men and women and they can come in their common clothes."[64]

To an even greater degree than Missionary Baptists, black and white Pentecostal-Holiness believers reclaimed traditions of spirit possession, prophecy, and vocal worship. Although they worshiped under an array of denominational affiliations, they all placed a central emphasis on the inspiration of the book of Acts, particularly the ability to speak in tongues, to heal, and to interpret prayers, dreams, and visions.[65] These deep-rooted vernacular forms took on new meaning in the context of the early 1930s. In the first half of the twentieth century, Pentecostal-Holiness believers and many Baptists considered this outpouring of spiritual gifts to be a sign "of God's power and action in the church and the world," a "prophetic endowment," according to Pentecostal theologian R. P. Menzies, that would enable them to "participate effectively in the mission of God."[66] While that mission's main thrust was salvation, it also called believers into the fight against Satan and his minions, who remained in rural folk traditions very "real spiritual beings intent on destroying God's creation."[67] In the context of the Depression, beliefs in the supernatural, both for good and evil, not only explained sickness and starvation but also provided a remedy. Revivalists in the Bootheel, for example, increasingly relied on faith healing instead of professional medical help, which they struggled to afford.[68]

The dynamics of Spirit-filled revival, whether in Pentecostal-Holiness or independent Baptist churches, offered ordinary people a new source of power in their efforts to confront evil in the world. In many ways, the revival cast this struggle in spiritual terms. Pentecostal-Holiness faithful fervently believed that they were living in the last days and that Christ would soon return. The suffering, death, and dislocation they saw all around them was their chief evidence; this kind of social chaos, the Bible said, was a clear sign that the End Times had arrived. This belief that the millennium was about to begin was strongest in the older Pentecostal-Holiness churches, especially the Assemblies of God, where believers saw no use in political action, given the closeness of the millennium.[69]

The early 1930s manifestation of spiritual power, however, destabilized reigning ideas of authority in rural communities. Believers in revivalist churches had broken fellowship with their old church homes and claimed their own destinies in a process that had potential political consequences. "Being relatively less integrated into the larger community," Liston Pope observed of contemporary revivalist churches in Gastonia, North Carolina, "they are more easily enlisted for campaigns that challenge prevailing conditions." While most remained aloof from economic questions, he noted, "their indifference passes occasionally into sharp antagonism."[70] Spirit-filled believers "were empowered in the social context of the religious collective," theologian Peter Althouse wrote, "which allowed them to confront oppressive social conditions."[71] Their efforts to "to reproduce the Christ-like character" privileged the "pre-eminently moral power" of the individual and bound those individuals together in new groups directed by the Holy Spirit.[72] As a result, revival had the potential to subvert hierarchies of class, gender, and even race. The primary aesthetic appeal of these churches was the erasure of class-based codes of dress, behavior, and worship. Moreover, women found their voices in revivalist churches, "in the pulpit, in prophesying, and in church leadership."[73] Perhaps most subversive of all, as historian Paul Harvey noted, was the common participation of whites and blacks in the religious practices and rituals of Pentecostal-Holiness churches, even if they were segregated.[74]

In the midst of the suffering and economic inequalities of the early New Deal years, the moral power of the Bootheel revivals was beginning to produce what Liston Pope called "sharp antagonism" among landless farmers. Revivalist groups were beginning to "cause problems by playing up socioeconomic difference," said sociologists from the University of Missouri. "They appeal to prejudice and emotion and capitalize on unrest and all forms of inequality," particularly "in relation to such factors as education, health, and improved agricultural practices."[75] While the precise details that led to this appraisal were not recorded, it suggests that those who attended Pentecostal-Holiness churches were not as otherworldly and apolitical as some historians have insisted.[76] The politics of revival seem to have been most explosive in rural black communities that were still groping to find leadership and a collective voice after the collapse of the UNIA. The application of religious ideas to political problems, however, was combustible; it could lead to democratic protest, violent retribution, messianic nationalism, or all three at the same time. In the summer of 1934, the editor of the *Charleston Spokesman,* a middle-class black newspaper, got wind of "radical propaganda" circulating in some local churches. Cryptically, the editor warned readers that this preaching threatened to sow "seeds of discord" that would undermine "the good neighborly feeling, and the cordial relations existing between the races."[77]

\* \* \*

The summer of 1934 was likely the worst time most landless black families in the Bootheel had ever experienced. They were sick, tired, and increasingly angry. Some leaders were attempting to protest these conditions through fledgling NFCF and NAACP groups. Thousands of rural people were joining Pentecostal-Holiness and independent Baptist revivals. Potent ideas about the power of believers to hasten the end of suffering coursed through the countryside. Amid this tumult, a man called Ashima Takis appeared who used language that evoked Garveyite slogans, claimed he had the power to heal the sick, and offered, of all things, the power of imperial Japan as a liberating force. His popularity demonstrated the extent to which the Depression and revivals expanded popular ideas among rural blacks about the necessity for and possibility of radical social and political change.

In late March, C. D. Wilson, a worried white planter from Mississippi County, informed the Department of Justice that two men, one Japanese and the other "a Negro named White," had been organizing African American sharecroppers in the area into "a secret society called the Original Afro Pacific Organization." Although the two advocated the "advancement of the Negro," Wilson was suspicious because they also talked about "certain social and economic injustices" and repeated disturbing mottos, such as "Asia for the Asiatics, Africa for the Africans at home and abroad." He reported that "the Negroes are going for it nearly 100 percent" and suggested that a "little secret work among the Negroes might save a surprise later on."[78]

Ashima Takis caused a stir wherever he went. Since mid-1932 he had been telling poor black people across the country that Japan was the "champion of the colored races" and would crush white supremacy. To accomplish this, Japan needed American blacks to fight alongside it, one day against the United States.[79] "You are the most oppressed people on Earth," he informed a meeting of black communists in St. Louis in June 1933. But "if you will join the Japanese and other colored races, you will be in command of the whites."[80] Later that year, he proclaimed, "Within two years, the colored races must fight the white for self-determination, and American negroes should be ready to support Japan."[81] They could start by joining his organization, the

Pacific Movement of the Eastern World (PMEW). As a reward, Japan would provide its supporters with land in Japan, Brazil, and Liberia.[82] Sometime that winter, Takis relocated PMEW to St. Louis and quickly won the support of some former Garveyites, who told him about the once-strong UNIA divisions in the Bootheel. For reasons that are unclear, while in St. Louis Takis created another organization, the Original Independent Benevolent Afro-Pacific Movement of the World (OIBAPMW), as an offshoot of the PMEW.[83] Soon after that, he and colleague James Malachi White set out for the Bootheel.

Takis had immediate success. By July he had organized OIBAPMW lodges in Charleston, Crosno, Sikeston, Matthews, and Wardell. The lodges at Sikeston and Matthews claimed 105 and 149 members, respectively, while the Charleston lodge marshaled over 600 members.[84] In late August, OIBAPMW members rallied 2,500 people at a meeting in Mississippi County.[85] Takis's magnetism derived in part from his ability to evoke black nationalism with his discussions of solidarity among people of color, self-determination, and the liberation of colonized people in Africa and Asia. His speeches and organizational literature overflowed with Garveyesque shibboleths, such as the general goal of "inculcat[ing] into the mind of the peoples to love its race" and encouraging the downtrodden to "establish a government of their own in the land of their fathers."[86] Meetings even included the presentation of "Liberty," a weekly short essay modeled on Garvey's Liberty Hall speeches. One example paraphrased Psalm 68:31 to announce global ambitions ("Ethiopia would stretch forth her hand and rule the world").[87]

Despite his public claims that he was building a peace movement, Takis preached preparation for a coming race war. In the combustible climate created by reactions to the Cotton Control Act in the summer of 1934, Takis urged his listeners to challenge the "social, economic and interracial maladjustments" afflicting them.[88] Whitfield later recalled that "this jap specialized in pointing out to Negroes the unfairness and brutality heaped upon us by the American white man." People responded with "great bursts of applause," he said, when Takis "pointed out the great things that awaited us when Japan would come to America to free its black brother from modern slavery."[89] This was the "radical propaganda" that worried the editor of the *Spokesman*.

Takis combined this militant message with messages of empowerment similar to those people heard in revivals. He urged members to act "according to the will of God."[90] Takis often cast himself as a spiritual leader. He claimed he had the ability to cure the sick by laying his hands on them.[91] This was an attractive proposition to people who watched loved ones die from starvation and disease. In addition, Takis deployed a vision of the end of time that contrasted with the gradualist vision of the UNIA. His colleague White, for example, made much of his middle name Malachi, no doubt a reference to the book of Malachi in the Old Testament, which foretold the arrival of the prophet Elijah and deeply influenced apocalyptic black nationalists.[92] Takis promised blacks that they could hasten their own deliverance from oppression. Japan was poised to strike the United States soon, he said, but it needed the help of awakened followers to achieve final victory. This promise of mass empowerment placed pressure on existing leaders. Whitfield later admitted that his congregation "threatened to throw me out of my church at Charleston" unless he joined. He did.[93]

The OIBAPMW bridged religious revival and political protest. At a meeting in a rural church near Blytheville, Arkansas, for example, George Cruz, a Filipino cook and organizer, declared that the "world belongs to the colored races" and promised that if the audience would "join us . . . hell will soon pop around the corner for the white man."[94] By the end of the summer, Takis had established additional lodges in Caruthersville, Bragg City, Pascola, Portageville, and Hermondale.[95] These lodges had strong links to previous mobilizations. Marshall Currin, a Charleston café owner, played a leading role in the Charleston lodge. While he had never been a member of the UNIA, he had been part of the failed effort in 1928 to establish an NAACP branch and by 1934 was also the president of Charleston's NFCF unit.[96] His involvement with Takis suggests that the currents of revival in the Bootheel, the efforts on behalf of the NFCF and NAACP to engage with the federal government, and the remnants of Garveyite thought, particularly the *Cause Afric,* were beginning to meld in the context of the Depression. Some members were ready for more than mere talk. In early September, landlords near Wardell reported "outcroppings of unrest among negroes." Soon after, black cotton pickers launched wildcat strikes, refusing to pick for less than $1.25 per hundred pounds of cotton.[97]

During the strike, a preacher from Steele, ten miles north of Blytheville, told local police that if OIBAPMW organizers were allowed to continue, Pemiscot would soon see open revolt.[98] His complaint joined a chorus of white voices seeking the eradication of whatever element had inflamed black farmers. In response to the preacher's complaint, the Steele police arrested four African Americans who were in the area from St. Louis. They were carrying letters from black internationalists in Jamaica, Haiti, and Liberia; speeches calling for black revolt against servitude; lynching statistics; and newspaper clippings related to the case of the Scottsboro boys. The police charged them with "unlawfully organizing Negroes."[99]

In the ensuing trial, the prosecuting attorney raged against these "niggers" for "coming down to Steele in high powered Chryslers and trying to stir up the Negroes who were all right as long as they were in their places picking cotton."[100] The judge found the organizers guilty later that same day. With a surprising knowledge of Takis's ideas, the judge berated the defendants for issuing "a call to arms for all of the Negroes to unite with the race of the Far East to overthrow the present system of government and to make the white race subservient to the Negro race and to set up a government by the Negroes."[101] As a warning to others, he sentenced them each to one year in county jail and a $1,000 fine.[102] He then left the courtroom. In an instant, with the sheriff and constables looking on, the enraged white audience surged forward swinging blackjacks, fists, and pistols. The judge rushed back to find that "all the four defendants were lying stretched out on the floor." None of them was conscious, and everyone else had left the room.[103]

The OIBAPMW collapsed in the wake of the Steele debacle. Fearing conviction, Takis fled to New York, where he helped found the Ethiopian Peace Movement. White disappeared. The police, meanwhile, warned local lodges that any further meetings would be considered a public menace and that members would be arrested. Caruthersville lodge voluntarily disbanded and destroyed its literature and records.[104] Others did likewise. In Sikeston and Matthews, the police raided the homes of members and recovered correspondence and membership lists.[105] Whatever "cordial relations" had existed between blacks and whites seemed to evaporate in the backlash. Recriminations abounded. Some former members claimed that their neighbors had forced them to join. "It will be hell if you don't," they had been told. Others explained that they had been promised "transportation back to their ancestral land of Ethiopia."[106] As suddenly as it had roared to life, the OIBAPMW was dead.

Against this backdrop, the demands of leading black farmers for government assistance gained traction. In October 1934 the Charleston unit of the NFCF, which claimed over 200 members, "some of whom are progressive owners of good farms," hosted the organization's annual meeting.[107] More than a thousand delegates gathered at the city's all-black Lincoln High School to discuss the convention theme—whether the New Deal "has been a curse or a blessing to Race farmers."[108] This was not necessarily an idle exercise, since Henry A. Hunt, the assistant to the governor of the Farm

Credit Administration and a member of Roosevelt's "black cabinet," was in attendance.[109] Not yet ready to condemn the Roosevelt administration outright, the NFCF was nevertheless developing a stronger stance on racial equality in public policy to accompany its traditional advocacy of landownership and cooperatives. In the run-up to the 1934 meeting, NFCF secretary Leon Harris announced that "the organization fights debt-slavery, injustice, and persecution. It is the only national farm organization in which the Race farmer has a voice and a vote."[110]

The resolutions of the Charleston annual meeting, reprinted in the *Chicago Defender,* articulated black agrarian demands in a platform of constructive protest politics. Although they were still committed to the ideals of self-sufficiency, leading black farmers now sought cooperation with the federal government in their struggle to maintain rural livelihoods. The NFCF "urged support of the national government and its efforts to assist farmers." This support, however, would be conditional on the government helping farmers achieve landed independence. Delegates "condemned the sharecropping system" and "urged [NFCF] units to continue the practice of cooperative purchasing, production, and marketing." The convention called on the government to reinforce the goals of black agrarians by establishing "at least one model Race farm community in each southern and border state." While they praised the administration for appointing people such as Hunt, the delegates demanded wholesale change in the government's farm policy, beginning with the "repeal or important revision of the Bankhead Act." Delegates demanded that the government give black farmers, tenants and owners alike, direct representation on the "AAA county committees." Finally, and most succinctly, the NFCF "requested that every effort be made by the government to widen land ownership by Race farmers."[111] Although the NFCF was still fixed on landownership, its platform charted a middle way between the lobbying efforts of the NAACP and the separatism of the UNIA.

Charleston NFCF members pointed to themselves as models of the potential of this approach. The leaders of the Charleston unit, Currin and L. B. Boler, announced that since the beginning of 1934 thirty-seven members of their unit had purchased farms ranging "in size from forty to 120 acres," much of which was still not cleared of stumps and brush. The national organization had negotiated the terms of purchase, they reported, and "no help was requested from the Federal government except a few applications were made for small crop production loans." The farmers then "went to work like pioneers, clearing, grubbing and building cabins." They pooled their stock and tools as well as their labor and apparently had a successful year. But their plan had limited efficacy. Ever true to the producerist creed, they continued to rely heavily on individual and cooperative hard work as a route to independence and were obviously reluctant to claim much help from the government, even though the central problem remained that hard work alone was not sufficient to overcome the trials of the Depression.[112] It was becoming increasingly clear that the solution would have to encompass many, not a few; farmers needed help from Washington. The NFCF was on the right track with its 1934 resolutions, but its leaders in the Bootheel were not yet ready to go so far as asking for wholesale assistance from the federal government.

The balance sheet of 1934 confirmed the need for more robust federal help for the rural poor if any semblance of popular agrarianism was to survive. Landowners profited handsomely from the Bankhead Cotton Control Act. In Pemiscot, New Madrid, and Mississippi counties, farmers received $830,000, $547,000, and $274,000, respectively, in compensation for reductions. At the same time, limited production raised the price of cotton to 13 cents per lint pound.[113] For the first time in a long time, Snow recalled, landowners "made real money."[114] Many used their subsidies to expand. By the end of 1935, land-owners held over half of the 1,800,000 farm acres in the Bootheel in blocks of 200 acres or more and a fourth of this area in blocks of 1,000 acres or more.[115] Caverno believed that 1934 was "the most prosperous agricultural year that Southeast Missouri ever had," a time when landowners could "jingle money in their pockets." Everyone, he continued, was "beginning to think about their new mules, wagons, and farm machinery, and automobiles and warm clothes, and money in the pockets or the bank, or the old teapot."[116] Everyone, that is, except the tenant families who planted, cultivated, and picked the crops. Their income continued to plummet. In 1935, the mean yearly income for white cropping families was only $415, while white wage-working families earned an average of $264 that year. Black sharecropping and wage laboring families combined earned an average of $251.[117]

* * *

The political activism of the OIBAPMW and the policy proposals of the NFCF emboldened landless black farmers as they continued to look for ways to protest their plight, which grew worse by the year. They turned to the NAACP and the STFU, organizations that encouraged ordinary people to make direct demands on the federal government through collective action, whether that meant signing petitions, demanding food aid, or going on strike. For the first time in more than a decade, communities of black farmers formulated political strategies that reflected the needs and concerns of the majority and called on the Roosevelt administration to address those needs. This broadening of voices would not have been imaginable without the revivals of the early 1930s. The rejection of old ways, the creation of new churches, and the claiming of "spiritual empowerment" was a moral awakening, an opening of democratic possibilities.

The STFU aimed to give ordinary people the power to change the structure that controlled their lives by mobilizing against the injustices of the cotton system, decrying the complicity of the government in improving the lot of large landowners, and emphasizing the importance of popular protest. Founded in northeastern Arkansas in the summer of 1934, the union took its initial inspiration and leadership from white socialists (especially locals H. L. Mitchell and Clay East) and national Socialist Party of America leader Norman Thomas. But it gained traction from the courageous involvement of thousands of landless farmers, particularly African Americans.[118] The centrality of grassroots efforts stemmed in part from Mitchell's decision "to build and mobilize opinion through existing networks and beliefs."[119] Encouraged to shape the union struggle to meet their own concerns, members waged a successful cotton-picking strike in Arkansas in late 1935 that earned the STFU national renown and boosted STFU membership—in Arkansas, Mississippi, Oklahoma, Tennessee, and Texas—into the thousands.[120] Perhaps of equal importance, the union's sudden growth attracted the sympathies of many liberals in the Roosevelt administration. Tenants rallied to the union's short-term plans for alleviating the suffering of farmers and its long-term plan of reforming government agricultural policy, beginning with the cotton control laws.[121]

The STFU's first stirrings in the Bootheel bore the imprint of revivalism. John Handcox, a black Arkansan who had been dispatched to Mississippi County to organize it for the union, arrived in late May 1936 to find that sharecroppers had already began an informal union group near Charleston and wanted official membership in the STFU. To Handcox's surprise, most of these activists were women who had already sent "for a women charter."[122] Although it was initially dismissive about female involvement, the union followed a policy of local autonomy that allowed units to segregate by race or gender (or not) as they saw fit. Rural women were often at the forefront of these locals.[123] The women who made these bold claims for leadership in Charleston and elsewhere were responding to changes in their communities that were beyond the capacity of male union leaders to anticipate or understand, most especially the erosion of paternalistic hierarchies that had dominated the UNIA and churches like the AME. These women's sense of authority and empowerment was unprecedented except for in revivalist churches. For them to write to a white man to ask for union membership was unusually bold. Handcox left his initial meeting with these aspiring union members convinced "that we will have a good success up here."[124] Within a week he had organized a local on Thad Snow's farm. Savannah Warr, Elzora Bynum, and Daisy Himms were among its leaders.[125] Other people who had never led anything before were also asking to lead. Tom Carson, "that little man that made a talk in the meeting at Charleston," Handcox reported, wanted to be an organizer.[126] It soon became obvious why these tenants were so eager to join. "The planters up here wont allow the labor to have chicken cow hog or a row of corn," he reported. Having seen hard times aplenty in Arkansas, Handcox admitted that even he was "really supprise to see the condition like they is up here." Facing desperate times, rural people were increasingly willing to take stronger measures. By July, Handcox had organized six locals in Mississippi County.[127]

The campaign was awash with spiritual urgency. Although not a Christian himself, union co-founder H. L. Mitchell used a familiar religious structure for union activities. STFU members opened meetings with prayers, sang hymns, and read scripture.[128] Rather than simply tap into a timeless rural church as Mitchell expected, however, the STFU opened itself to the dynamic influence of revival. "When they first started taking about the union I thought it was a new church," a white sharecropper in Arkansas said.[129] In a way, Handcox was just another evangelist, seemingly called by the same Luke-Acts tradition that animated new-sect revivalism, particularly Pentecostal-Holiness revivals.[130] "I have raise my hand to God," Handcox said of his activist commitment, "and I will not turn back."[131] Admittedly not a good speaker, Handcox relied on his talents as a musician and poet to spread the union message. In church, Handcox later explained, hymns prepared people for the preaching to follow, so it made sense to use labor songs to prepare people for his message.[132] "We'd usually start with a song and then a prayer," he said. "Singing is inspirational, more inspirational than talk. . . . It arouses people more, makes them feel a part of things."[133] Many of his songs were adaptations of well-known hymns. In "No More Mourning," Handcox changed the second line of the chorus of the spiritual "O Freedom" so that the liberating freedom of Christianity was gained through the union struggle rather than through death and heavenly reward. Handcox changed the traditional chorus:

And before I'd be a slave
I'd be buried in my grave
And go home to my Lord and be free

to end with these more empowering lines:

I'll be buried in my grave
Take my place with those
Who've loved and fought before.[134]

These songs presented the union as the way to salvation and encouraged people to "convert," or join the STFU, to achieve their own redemption. The song "In My Heart" made this conflation explicit. Handcox transformed the lyric, "Lord, I want to be a Christian in my heart," into "Lord, I don't want to be like the planters in my heart."[135] In "Join the Union Tonight," Handcox evoked the tone and tenor of a revival meeting. This song catalogued the abuses (or sins) of the Agricultural Adjustment Administration with a rousing call for tenants to "join the union tonight":

In 1933 we plowed up our crops
Join the union tonight. . . .
Oh, get enrolled, stop toting such a load.
Join the union tonight.[136]

The song declared that if listeners wanted justice, it was their responsibility to seek it. Just as individuals at revival meetings had to accept Christ to achieve salvation, tenants had to choose to join the STFU to achieve their economic goals. Moreover, this decision was not something that could wait; it had to be taken "tonight," since tomorrow or next week might be too late. Handcox stressed that once people joined, union members would gain life-changing power. The song "Roll the Union On" announced that organized workers were an undeniable force, no matter how strong the opposition might be.[137] Religious-style enthusiasm alone, however, did not make a political movement.

Landless farmers found the STFU to be an appealing vehicle of protest because the union's structure and goals melded their sense of spiritual urgency with popular demands for justice based on the principles of agrarian producerism. At its second convention in January 1936, the union declared that "the land is the Common heritage of the people" and demanded that "all actual tillers of the soil be guaranteed the possession of the soil either as individual working farm-families or cooperative associations . . . so long as they may use and occupy the land."[138] Although Mitchell and other union leaders advocated large cooperative farms as opposed to small holdings as the future of southern agriculture, most members sought their own farms, either as owners or renters. While the STFU leadership interpreted the agricultural crisis as a class problem, the older language of producerism, especially the idiom of enslavement, continued to resonate with the rank and file. Handcox excoriated the landlords who oppressed farmers; he and his audience knew farmers were the real producers of wealth. In the song "The Sharecropper and the Planter," he evoked the core of producerism:

The planter says he inherits his wealth from birth
But it all comes from the poor man who tills the earth. . . .
No worse place to be do I crave
But I want to be something more than a planter's slave.[139]

Like "No More Mourning," this song used the rhetoric of slavery, both to condemn conditions and to challenge people to take action.

The STFU's notion of collective suffering provided the terms for a consensus within black communities about protest politics that traversed the kind of social divisions that had limited the reach of earlier groups. Poor sharecroppers, former Garveyites, and supporters of the NAACP and NFCF worked together to organize locals; the Depression made all equal. Will Jones, who had been president of the Wyatt UNIA division, became the first president of Snow's STFU local. The Depression had hit Jones hard. In 1936 he was given notice by his landlord to leave the land he had rented since 1923. In the STFU, Jones shared leadership with sharecropping women like Warr, Bynum, and Himms.[140] Similarly, Marshall Currin, a former member of the NAACP and the OIBAPMW and continuing member of the NFCF, opened his restaurant outside Charleston to union meetings.[141]

The unprecedented nature of the STFU's message also brought African Americans and whites into political cooperation (albeit limited) in the Bootheel for the first time. Handcox tried to defuse the racial tension of early meetings by reading aloud from Sharecropper's Voice, the STFU's newspaper, at union meetings. This source offered a neutral text (it was written for and by both blacks and whites) that explicitly argued against racial division. Religious commonalities also helped. Handcox prepared for these readings by singing and praying.[142] Despite the recent history of racial animosity and violence, Handcox made progress in organizing an interracial union. By the end of July, he had recruited a local white organizer, J. C. Kirkpatrick, who had previous union experience with the United Mine

Workers. At Deventer, not far from Crosno, once home to an OIBAPMW lodge, Handcox and Kirkpatrick organized a mixed-race local that conducted integrated meetings. They were also enthusiastic about a local at Pin Hook, a white area just south of East Prairie, that had "a fire that will burn for ever."[143] Even in the former Garveyite stronghold around Wyatt, J. W. Davis, the black president of Cooper Local, reported, "We have some white people to join with us," both men and women.[144] The spirit of racial cooperation was novel for both sides. Many whites were still hesitant about joining a mainly black group, though. "I think we need a white organizer up here," Handcox confessed.[145]

Mitchell sent Rev. Claude Williams, a radical white preacher from Tennessee, to address a mixed-race union picnic at the Charleston city park, a remarkably bold and subversive thing to do. "Everybody had a plenty to eat," Handcox reported, "and it were not serve as white and colored but as a big family dinner."[146] This peaceful public event was so striking that Handcox would still describe it as a big "family reunion" fifty years later.[147] Williams impressed the crowd with his talk about the righteousness of the STFU cause.[148] Commenting on Handcox's revision of traditional hymns, Williams preached that "these are new words for old songs—because we have to build to the Kingdom of God on earth. The Kingdom of God is not of this world, but it is in this world."[149] The STFU represented a "a new Pentecost," he said. Just like the Apostles, who, after "Jesus was lynched," "were told to go to Jerusalem and wait until they got the power. How did they get it?" They received the power of the Holy Spirit, he affirmed, "when they were organized" on the day of Pentecost. "Pentecost is unity," Williams preached, and unity was power.[150] Williams was so popular among Bootheel unionists that local organizers urged him to return for a series of follow-up meetings, which he held in November. One of these took place at Owen Whitfield's church near Deventer. Whitfield joined the union shortly thereafter.[151] By the end of the year, there were fourteen locals in Mississippi County. "Nearly every night," *Sharecropper's Voice* reported, "trucks loaded with Union members and organizers make some schoolhouse and set up a new local."[152]

The STFU, however, was not the only option. Some rural activists looked again to the NAACP as a means to achieve political goals. What had begun earlier in the year as two separate campaigns to organize chapters in Essex in Stoddard County and Marston and Portageville in New Madrid County had merged by December into a unified movement. While the group waited for its official charter, it began holding meetings in late 1936. With sixty-four members, all of them farmers, the chapter brought together people of all stations, much like the STFU. George Washington and Menard Washington, both successful renters near Portageville, joined; so did B. L. Randolph and Peter Wilderness, Menard Washington's sharecroppers in 1936. The NAACP chapter shared with STFU locals an overtly religious mission; local preachers D. C. Johnson, D. W. Wherry, A. M. Mitchell, and J. R. Bell were at the forefront of the effort. They called the group "Rising Sun," which evoked the hope of a new dawn as well as Psalm 113:3 ("From the rising of the sun unto the going down of the same the Lord's name is to be praised.") However, there were some significant differences between the new NAACP chapters and the STFU. Leading men, mainly mainstream preachers, retained control of the group's activities; only four women were listed on the initial application.[153] The ideas of the new NAACP chapters about tactics also differed from those of the STFU. One of their first actions was to draft an appeal to Missouri senator Harry Truman for his support of the anti-lynching legislation before the Congress.[154]

The STFU and the new NAACP groups were a clear departure from former agrarian movements in the Bootheel. Economic crisis, environmental catastrophe, and unfavorable legislation had badly damaged rural communities in the early 1930s. No institutions, whether political, social, or religious, escaped the impact of the Great Depression. As their old standards failed to meet the needs of the day, rural people reached out to new and unproven ideas and associations for help. A renewal of Pentecostal-Holiness revival informed this grassroots effort to make sense of the suffering and dislocation of these years. Particularly for African Americans, the wave of revival encouraged an expansive, and at times explosive, search for alternatives to the status quo. While more dangerous choices such as the OIBAPMW quickly faded, rural blacks emboldened by revival rejected the aging charters of groups such as the UNIA and the NFCF in favor of the more democratic dynamics of the STFU and the NAACP, both of which encouraged members to exercise their rights as citizens and producers. This "new Pentecost," as Williams called it, empowered ordinary people to combine political protest with religious conviction in order to confront unjust authorities and make this world more like the Kingdom of God. Driven by a resurgent religious zeal, that effort now included halting but earnest attempts to bring blacks and poor whites together in condemnation of the hellish conditions in which both groups now lived. This dramatic development left little space for groups such as the NFCF, which again held its annual convention in Charleston in 1936, less than a week after Williams made his second trip to Mississippi County. In stark contrast to the Spirit-inspired gatherings that Williams addressed, the NFCF convention took its most enthusiastic support from leading whites. E. E. Oliver, the mayor of Charleston, gave the welcoming address. Other speakers included official representatives from Governor Junius M. Futrell of Arkansas, Governor Eugene Talmadge of Georgia, and the Agricultural Adjustment Administration, including a message from Cully Cobb, who headed the Cotton Section. None of these officials were friendly toward landless farmers, to say the least.[155] Considering that STFU members had only the week before gathered to denounce the policies these people endorsed, it is not surprising that white elites looked to embrace the more cautious NFCF. Determined to serve the Lord through action, hundreds of African American and some white farmers were now ready to demand justice in important new ways.

# 5

## Bear Our Burdens Together

C. H. Williams, a sharecropper and local STFU leader, wrote a simple letter in early 1937 to Gardner Jackson, the union's representative in Washington, making an audacious request: government support for his ability to continue an agrarian way of life. The winter had been hard. Williams and his Mississippi County neighbors had cleared some money from their 1936 crop, but "not enough to carry them through." "We are in a suffering condition now," he informed Jackson. Williams believed in the power of the union to help and had scraped together enough money to attend the STFU's convention in Oklahoma that January. There he had learned about Jackson's efforts to secure federal relief for croppers like him. Williams urged Jackson to "get with our Misouri man that is up there in Washington and convert him in the care of we poor people at Charleston, Mo. and Mo. in general." He and the other families did not want charity, he explained, only the ability to fulfill their duties as producers. They needed "a helping hand in the way of work to make an honest living," something they were now unjustly prevented from doing. Williams himself wanted "some land to grow cotton—corn—and food stuff for my self and family and the publick."[1]

Four days later, emboldened by his massive electoral victory the previous November, President Roosevelt outlined an ambitious vision for his second term that promised to finally extend the New Deal to the nation's poorest people, sharecroppers like Williams. "I see one-third of a nation ill-housed, ill-clad, ill-nourished," Roosevelt said. Foremost among these, he said, were poor southerners locked in "an un-American style of tenant farming." It would be unwise, Roosevelt warned, for the nation to allow them "to go along as they do now, year after year, with neither future security as tenants nor hope of ownership of their homes nor expectation of bettering the lot of their children."[2] If Williams was listening, it must have seemed that the president was answering him personally.

The following day, January 21, the federal government announced it would intervene in Mississippi County, but not in the way Williams imagined. The Army Corps of Engineers would come to the county to relieve pressure on the levees guarding the city of Cairo, Illinois. Hours after the announcement of the army's impending action, the temperature plunged below freezing and sleet covered the ground in hard ice. That night the army began evacuating the residents—almost all of whom were tenants—of the eastern half of the county, the Bird's Point–New Madrid Spillway. Over the next three days several thousand tenants and sharecroppers struggled to secure hay in barn lofts and rescue household goods, tools, and livestock. Freezing temperatures and icy roads made this task nearly impossible. Most simply left with what they could carry. On January 25, the army dynamited a gaping hole in the riverfront levee, rattling windows in Charleston, twelve miles to the west and sending a cascade of muddy, icy floodwater across the best cotton land in the Bootheel.[3] Williams and his neighbors would have to wait for their New Deal.

The spillway flood embodied the injustices that poor rural southerners were raising their voices to condemn. To many despairing agrarians, the Roosevelt administration was now governed by an ungodly and immoral economic calculus that was destroying their way of life. In order to prevent a big flood and protect the powerful, the government flooded those who actually worked the land. In the same way, the AAA and Bankhead Cotton Control Act crippled landless cotton farmers in order to save those who owned land. Despite new legislation meant to ensure the economic security of working people such as the Wagner Act and the Social Security Act of 1935 and Roosevelt's gallant rhetoric, Williams and his neighbors knew little of the federal government other than the iniquities of the Cotton Control Act, the work programs that discriminated against them, and now total disaster through the army's flood. Rather than relieve the "suffering condition" that Williams had described to Jackson, the New Deal was making it worse.[4]

Their homes, belongings, and crops destroyed by a blast of federal dynamite, the spillway refugees demanded a New Deal for landless farmers. Gathered in relief camps, the refugees saw the scope of the result of federal policies as they encountered thousands who shared their misery. The view suggested not just collective tragedy but also common cause. When the Red Cross, the U.S. Public Health Service, and the Resettlement Administration rushed clothing, medical care, and food to the displaced, local STFU organizers John Handcox and Owen Whitfield argued that if the federal government could offer relief in response to a disaster it had created with dynamite, it should address the disaster caused by its legislation. They knew that the New Deal had been good to other workers. The Wagner Act gave industrial laborers the right to organize collectively and so provided factory men the chance to earn a "family wage." Agricultural workers did not get these rights under the act; all the New Deal had brought them was access to the socially stigmatized, need-based poor-relief provisions in the Social Security Act and programs like the Works Progress Administration, which was administered by racially discriminatory county committees.[5] Eager to exchange pity for entitlements, Handcox, Whitfield, and other local activists, including the leaders of the Rising Sun NAACP chapter, began organizing to force the federal government to recognize and protect the rural producer's equivalent of the family wage: the right to work the land on secure terms for a fair reward. They wanted decent housing, improved health, and the ability to raise subsistence foodstuffs.

These demands asserted that New Deal policymakers were partly to blame for the agricultural crisis in the Bootheel. In many ways the political extension of the religious revivals of the early 1930s, the STFU facilitated this challenge by encouraging ordinary people to confront unjust power. Its broadly inclusive racial and gender policies were matched by an inclusiveness in political strategies; the union adhered to a permissive structure that allowed (if it did not directly encourage) local activists to shape the content and direction of their protests.[6] Many members, a union leader admitted, "didn't even know the address of the [main] office in Memphis."[7] As a result, Bootheel activists in the STFU called for bold policies that far exceeded the goals of their national leaders.[8] When activists such as Williams and Whitfield sought an end to their "suffering condition," they envisioned a restored agrarian setting whereby rural producers could reap the benefits of their work and lead healthy lives. This formulation drew upon a host of past grassroots mobilizations, particularly Garveyism, the NFCF, and socialism. It was leavened by a rural black theological understanding that although "unmerited suffering is intrinsically evil" it "can have redemptive consequences." Redemption could only be achieved, however, when God and man were "coworkers in the struggle to remove moral evil."[9] In this view, although the government was a source of many wrongs, it could become the source of a greater good. The STFU supplied a new means of struggle and federal policy became the battleground.

Rural activists intensified their hopes when the STFU voted to affiliate with the United Cannery, Agricultural, Packing and Allied Workers of America (UCAPAWA), a new union of agricultural workers in the Congress of Industrial Organizations (CIO), in late 1937. In the minds of landless farmers, the CIO offered them the power of a national network of unionists whose collective clout had recently won stunning gains in the automobile and steel industries.[10] Championing the industrial and political influence of the CIO, Whitfield led an organizing drive that transformed the various STFU locals into a regional political movement under its banner. Once, before the flood crisis, local activists like Williams had pleaded for the federal government to remember them. Now they demanded a New Deal of their own.

*    *    *

The refugee crisis was worse than anyone had expected. Relief providers strained to cope with the emergency. By mid-February more than 12,000 displaced people crowded into the seventy-five Red Cross centers in the area. The size of the group in need belied the army's woefully inaccurate estimate that only 2,000 to 3,000 people would be affected. At East Prairie alone, 3,500 refugees, 1,100 of them black, crammed into all available buildings, including high schools, local churches, warehouses, and cotton gins. Ultimately, the Red Cross transferred all black refugees to tent camps in Charleston. Because of overcrowding, several thousand more refugees sought shelter in private homes.[11]

Nearly all of the refugees, over 7,000 whites and 5,000 blacks, had been either tenants or sharecroppers on cotton plantations operated by absentee owners. After the completion of the spillway, only the landless lived in the flood zone, including almost all of the county's black farm population.[12] Most left all of their belongings behind. The flood displaced nearly all of Missouri's STFU members, including the Whitfields. Thomas Carson, a local union leader, told union secretary H. L. Mitchell "of my bad flood struggle." He "had to come out of the water and leave every thing," including his clothes and bedding.[13] H. Laws, another local leader, reported that most of his "members was evicted from their homes by the flood waters" and "all are poorly and on the relief."[14] The flood dislocated nine locals with 250 paid members and their families—more than 1,250 people.[15]

Despite the disruption, activists quickly resumed union work. In late January, STFU leaders in Memphis instructed members to cooperate with relief agencies and help direct refugees to the camps and distribution centers. In addition, H. L. Mitchell instructed officers and organizers to watch for irregularities in the distribution of relief.[16] In response to Mitchell's "notice for looking after the flood of the Union," W. H. Nelson and Queen Esther Nelson, officers of Braxton Local 53, reported that most members were now located in Charleston and that they had established committees to maintain communication.[17]

Within weeks, the committees had reconstituted most of the locals, which began holding regular meetings in the camps. They agreed that conditions were unjust. Members of Mule Ridge Local 195 acknowledged "getting some kind of help but not [what] we should." People who were able to rent rooms in Charleston were faring much better than those in the camps, who, they said, were "no[t] doing so well."[18] Handcox agreed. He found that people living outside the camps received either $3.95 or $5.10 a week, depending on the size of their families. Those in the camps, however, were "a horriable sight."[19] Members of the Mule Ridge local reported that the food was poor and "very little," consisting of a few "slices litebread, and little krout" and some apples. Moreover, the tents themselves were inadequate. Refugees slept on straw ticks over rough lumber laid on the ice-covered ground. The cold wreaked more havoc, Mule Ridge reported, because "women and children stand out in zero weather for hours to get" their food. Contrary to Red Cross claims, Mule Ridge members complained that "the sick here is not getting the tretement."[20] Handcox warned that if conditions in the camps didn't change "we will have to have a hunger march or something."[21] All were confident in the STFU's power to help. The Mule Ridge local was sure that "things can be change if the STFU say so."[22]

Improvements in the quality of care after these rumblings convinced many of the STFU's power, even if it was not directly responsible for the changes. In fact, better relief resulted less from union protests than from Red Cross efforts to stabilize a chaotic situation. After centralizing the black refugees, the Red Cross embarked on an ambitious effort to provide shelter, food, emergency clinics, and clothing to those in its care. Federal agencies provided vital backup; the Red Cross used Resettlement Administration offices in Sikeston to house its staff. To supplement clinical care, the Red Cross and the U.S. Public Health Service offered an immunization and vaccination program to prevent disease in the camps. The program targeted diseases endemic to the area, such as smallpox, typhoid, and diphtheria. Nurses also offered classes in health, nutrition, sanitation, and home economics to those who were interested.[23] Refugees left the camps with the distinct idea that New Deal agencies were helping them.

Handcox and other STFU leaders in the camps parlayed the improved care into a massive effort to bring in new members. During the first week of February, Handcox met with a representative from the Resettlement Administration, who promised that union members would receive proper assistance after they left the camps. Handcox reported that as a result, "we taken in a number of members," even if many of them had no money. Now was the time to "put the program over," organizer Scottie Spears believed, because "we have the people gather[ed]" in the camps. He quickly enrolled thirty-two new members.[24] STFU president J. R. Butler authorized Handcox to admit new members without charge for one month if they had been washed out by the flood.[25]

Indeed, the combined Red Cross/Resettlement Administration response to the flood crisis, however imperfect, provided local leaders with a vision of what the federal government could do for poor farmers. They had seen firsthand the destructive potential of federal power in the Agricultural Adjustment Act and the Cotton Control Act and the army's decision to flood their homes. During the refugee crisis, however, they saw another side of government power in the tent camps, the vaccination programs, and courses offering practical knowledge. It seemed that federal agencies could be made to intervene again if they saw the crisis in the cotton fields. With this in mind, Handcox and Whitfield called together local STFU leaders in mid-February to discuss their position.[26]

At the meeting, the Official Council of the STFU Refugees, as they named themselves, constructed a list of demands to area landlords and the federal government that essentially was a declaration of principles for the budding working-class movement in southeast Missouri. Handcox, Whitfield, Carson, Spears, and Rev. J. Emmanuel, among others, attended the meeting; all were black and all were refugees. Their declaration began by resolutely blaming their current plight on the federal government, not just the army. "The U.S. Government," they said, "blast[ed] the levee releasing the Ohio flood water into the Spillway in which we lived [and] swept away the cabin[s] in which we lived taking our household good[s] with them." In "the most disastrous flood in the history of our country," the government's action had "taken from us almost every thing we possessed."[27] Those who had been displaced had lost all they had struggled to acquire as landless farmers—not only household goods but also poultry, livestock, farming implements, and seed.

Since the government had caused this grievous situation, the council declared that federal agencies were responsible for remedying it. "We the members of the STFU and refugees" vowed not to return to the spillway and raise a crop until certain conditions were met. They demanded full federal support for their agrarian aspirations. They wanted the right to raise corn on the same 50–50 shares as cotton rather than on the current 25–75 basis. They demanded to be allowed to own hogs, cows, and poultry for their own consumption and sale and the right to maintain enough land for gardens. They called for assurances of "sanitary houses an out houses with screen window and door to protect our health" and "adequate cash furnished [at] a legal rate of interest with the privilege of trading where we please." In addition, "we as farm labor[er]s and citizens" had the right to modern school buildings and the same equipment for their children that white students had. Finally, the council insisted that the Resettlement Administration issue cash loans and grants to small landowners and landless farmers affected by the flood. They held the federal government, particularly the Resettlement Administration, responsible for seeing that their demands were met.[28] Union members distributed the declaration throughout the camps and to federal relief officials in Charleston. *Sharecropper's Voice* featured it on the front page.[29]

The program of the refugee council marked a departure for the movement in Mississippi County. Although the STFU had long outlined some of these demands in its membership literature, the union by 1937 focused almost solely on strikes to secure better wage scales and legal efforts to end planter abuse of New Deal agricultural laws.[30] Now the council looked to give life to the dry bones of earlier union calls. It held the federal government responsible for creating a new life for its members based on fair tenure agreements that would allow tenant families to provide for themselves by raising subsistence foods and livestock. Council members also believed that their New Deal should include their physical health. They wanted screened windows and doors and sanitary latrines to protect them from the malaria and dysentery that engulfed their families, sapped their energy, and shortened their lives. Calling for health, housing, food, and land, the council tapped deep currents of agrarian ideology to articulate a new vision of what the future should be for faithful rural producers.

Tenant women actively participated in the STFU's efforts by providing evidence of their experiences to support the union's demands. After all, it was they who struggled to balance field work, maintain dilapidated housing, and feed their families on meager diets. More and more black women took up leadership roles in the wake of the refugee crisis. Queen Esther Nelson, Dorothy Enochs, Savannah Warr, Mary Pratt, Pauline Moore, Estella Walker, and Ruth Sharp, among others, emerged as leaders in their locals. By 1938, at least ten black women held union leadership positions in Missouri; altogether forty-one females were local leaders in the STFU.[31]

As the floodwaters receded, the government seemed to respond. Supplied with assurances from the Red Cross of shelter for as long as necessary and provisions for two weeks, the refugees went home for the spring planting. The Resettlement Administration announced it would extend loans to landowners so they could reconstruct farm buildings, including tenant houses, and issued monthly subsistence grants in cash for tenants and sharecroppers from the time they left Red Cross care until they secured "gainful employment." These ranged from $10 to $25 a month, depending on the size of the family.[32] The Red Cross distributed garden seed and provided, with army help, over 700 tents for families without houses. After the Red Cross hospitals closed on March 1, nurses and doctors joined a home visit and follow-up program started by the U.S. Public Health Service to finish inoculations, check on former patients, and report on the well-being of the refugees.[33]

These tangible results added momentum to the STFU's organizing efforts. "I think that we'll be able to enroll all of the colored refugee[s] at Charleston [the] next meeting or two," Handcox informed the national office.[34] Fish Lake Local 142, which organized the day after the initial meeting of the refugee council, elected C. H. Williams as its president and Dorothy Enochs as secretary. In just over a month, Williams had gone from pleading with Gardner Jackson for emergency handouts to helping to lead a movement whose goal was to force changes in federal policy.

Elsewhere in the Bootheel, the Rising Sun NAACP chapter made its first demands on the government in the days following the flood. Writing on behalf of "the For-gotten negro" and the "Soil Toilers," the chapter's leaders, Rev. D. C. Johnson, Rev. D. W. Wherry, and Dollie Wherry, called on Senator Harry S. Truman to denounce violence against African Americans by voting in favor of the anti-lynching bill and addressing rural poverty. They made clear their belief that they deserved his support. "As we remembered you in our many different Counties in the past election," the committee argued, "now, We are asking you to remember us in the many unfair conditions under which we are laboring." Theirs had been a long struggle and the time had come "to bring about justice to all man kind." "We want our affairs remembers from the year 1866," they concluded, "Which means thus 'Partially towards none, Justice to all man kind, For God is no respecter of persons.'"[35] These were mainstream preachers and church leaders who came from communities formerly devoted to Garveyism; in years past they had remained aloof from making such demands on politicians. The flood crisis gave them new direction. Rev. A. M. Mitchell, an organizer in New Madrid, took up his work with urgency in February.[36] Unable to continue NAACP meetings because "the water is got the peoples scared," he instead focused attention on the plight of flood sufferers, who were badly ignored as the Red Cross and federal agencies focused their attention on the spillway. "Even the flood sufferers cant get thing that they lost unless some white man vouch for them," he explained.[37] The quick response of local NAACP leaders—acting well ahead of the national organization— signaled the broadening of grassroots protest against poverty, displacement, and unfair government policies.[38]

In Mississippi County the STFU mobilization had incorporated local concerns and relationships so thoroughly that Owen Whitfield soon eclipsed John Handcox, who hailed from Arkansas, as the primary union leader in the area. Despite their brilliant collaboration during the crisis, the two possessed very different strengths. Handcox was an outsider in Missouri, a worker for the union who always aimed at union goals. Whitfield, a local sharecropper and preacher, was tied into local social and political networks that reached back to the first days of black farming in the Bootheel. He and his family had lived and farmed in Mississippi County since 1923. During that period he preached in five different rural churches, where he had experienced at first hand the suffering of his congregations, the jolt of revival, and the stirring of protest. He had also been close to UNIA and OIBAPMW groups. After joining the STFU in late 1936, Whitfield laced his preaching with the union's message. When the STFU had to revoke the commissions of its national organizers, including Handcox, for financial reasons in April 1937, the union appointed Whitfield as a part-time organizer in Missouri. Outraged, Handcox accused the union of abandoning him despite his tireless work and predicted dire consequences if Whitfield was left in control; he feared that Whitfield would not have time to organize because "he's farming and pastoring 3 or 4 churches."[39] It was precisely Whitfield's local responsibilities, however, that would allow him to reorient the Missouri locals around the demands laid down by the STFU's refugee council.

*   *   *

Although landless blacks were becoming more politically confrontational, the budding NAACP and STFU movements remained disconnected from one another and from landless whites. As families returned to their homes after the flood to begin spring planting, Whitfield found it difficult to balance the task of resettling his family and doing organizing work, especially without Handcox. He filed no reports until mid-June because he had "been so busy working in the fields all day and roming around at night trying to get these locals to functioning again."[40] Moreover, despite the STFU's apparent success in securing flood relief the union had not grown much beyond the spillway. Local NAACP leaders, meanwhile, stopped sending reports to the national office in June. With members struggling with the difficult work of rebuilding their lives, both groups lost organizing momentum that summer. Although a few individuals had joined both groups, Whitfield looked for ways to enliven and broaden the movement, especially to include white farmers.[41]

Events elsewhere offered the potential to do just that. In June, Whitfield received a notice from Gardner Jackson about a CIO convention to be held in July for the purpose of establishing an umbrella union of agricultural workers, the UCAPAWA. The new agricultural and food workers union, which also included the Alabama Sharecroppers' Union and the Louisiana Farmers' Union, both of which were communist-led, was created as part of the CIO's efforts in the years 1936 to 1938 to expand the organization into new fields throughout the country. Excited about the opportunity, Whitfield hoped "to be elected as a delegate from Mo," which he was.[42] At the convention, he immersed himself in the culture of the CIO, discussing the plight of rural workers with experienced organizers, including the union's highest leadership. The experience impressed upon Whitfield the potential organizing power of the CIO. The STFU delegation voted to join the UCAPAWA, and Whitfield left the convention confident that the strength of the CIO was now his strength. Renewed and empowered, he launched an intense organizing campaign once he returned to southeast Missouri.

In the meantime, local organizers continued to tout the STFU's work during the refugee crisis. Following its plan to issue grants to refugees, the Resettlement Administration announced in April 1937 that it would buy several tracts of land in Mississippi County for the purpose of relocating landless farmers in resettlement farming communities.[43] It seemed to landless farmers that the STFU's efforts were bearing fruit, as the Resettlement Administration appeared to be meeting the demands of the refugee council. Although the connection was more apparent than real, hopeful farmers besieged activists for more information about the Resettlement Administration's plan. Rev. W. M. Harvey reported that tenants were asking "every where what will be an out come of the land here that the Government expect to sell to tenant farmers" and what they should do to acquire a place on the land.[44] Riding the momentum created by the the Resettlement Administration's announcement, Harvey organized several new locals, including a white local near Deventer in the spillway.[45] In July, Congress passed the Bankhead-Jones Farm Tenant Act, authorizing the Department of Agriculture to recharter the Resettlement Administration as the Farm Security

Administration (FSA). The mandate of the new administration was to re-locate selected landless farmers on government-owned cooperative farms and issue loans so that others could purchase land.[46] Although government policymakers had been working on these plans for months, local tenants associated the announcement with union demands. Most important for the STFU, black union leaders now could boast to white farmers about their seeming ability to pressure the federal government and receive friendly policies in return. The announcement of federal programs that so closely matched the earlier demands of the refugee council provided convincing, independent verification of the claims that STFU organizers like Harvey and Whitfield were making about the union's power.

White tenants had shown little interest in the STFU prior to the Resettle-ment Administration's announcement. The lack of union strength among the white refugees confounded Handcox. While the "colored people seem to be pushing forward," Handcox reported, whites seemed to be going backward, despite his initial successes with them in late 1936. "The white members have lost all interest in the union," he said, and he could not get them to meet.[47] Black union members recognized that white workers would not join unless there were white organizers to convince them. "There are a lot of white people up here day laborers and sharecroppers," Braxton Taylor, a black member near Charleston reported, but "we need an organizer among the white people to show and tell them about the Union."[48] Handcox had tried unsuccessfully to groom local white organizers. With no tradition of interracial political cooperation in the Bootheel, white tenants could scarcely imagine joining black locals that were deeply intertwined with black community and social networks, let alone heeding black leaders who had been involved in separat-ist groups such as the UNIA, the OIBAPMW, and the NFCF. White refugees eventually warmed up to the STFU because of the Resettlement Administra-tion's promise to resettle landless farmers. This concrete promise appealed powerfully to the white refugees at Deventer. After organizing a local under Harvey, the Deventer whites asked him not to return, suggesting they were much less excited about a black leader than about the prospect of securing STFU membership.[49] Moreover, this was the first STFU local formed in the Bootheel without the direct influence of participants in new-sect revivalism. "The white people of this county is ready to join" activist preachers like Harvey, new member Lee Munday said, "but they want to be in local to their selves and let the negro be to their selves and all work for the same thing."[50]

Meanwhile, tenants in Pemiscot County organized their own union locals, which were racially integrated and independent of older mobilizing networks.

In early July, thirty-one white and three black tenants near Cottonwood Point, Pemiscot County, reported having "gotten our selves together without an organizer of the STFU" and requested that the union send someone to their next meeting.[51] Tenants formed interracial locals in Cooter and Caruthersville in the same manner.[52] White tenants seemed to have less trouble associating with blacks when they controlled the locals and when both groups were confronted with cheaper imported labor. T. H. McConnell, a white tenant, a WPA worker, and a leader of the Pemiscot locals, warned Mitchell that landlords in the county were offering a starvation wage and would not hire union men at all during the upcoming picking season. Their stated goal, he said, was to evict all union members from area farms and replace them with "foreign scab labor" from Arkansas, Mississippi, and Tennessee. This was not the familiar pattern of black pickers replacing whites. Pemiscot landlords had recruited hundreds of whites from Tennessee, Mexicans from Oklahoma, and blacks from Arkansas to replace both white and black tenants. Not sure whether to organize the incoming pickers or "run them out," McConnell set out to mobilize other communities in the county.[53]

McConnell established fast-growing locals in Holland and Hayti. The Holland local grew from an initial membership of sixteen whites and five blacks in July to forty-five whites and thirteen blacks by September.[54] Encouraged, McConnell expected to soon "have the thing solid west to the Dunklin Co. line."[55] To bring coherence to this mobilization, McConnell planned a mass meeting of area locals for mid-September. But his organizing success prompted stiff resistance from Pemiscot elites. Planters had no intention of allowing this show of solidarity to occur. Members of the Cooter local, who gathered five days before the planned assembly, were met by twenty vigilantes armed with pistols, shotguns, and clubs. The next day thugs beat McConnell in broad daylight in Caruthersville and threatened to kill him if he continued his union activities. The planters' offensive in the fall of 1937 nearly stopped STFU activity, and the union lost credibility because of its seeming inability to respond.[56] McConnell cancelled the mass meeting, and the locals at Cottonwood Point and Cooter "were torn up on account of inadequate defense. . . .We realize we need a Union," McConnell said, but we "need a substantial one."[57]

Whitfield returned from the founding convention of UCAPAWA in July aiming to build that "substantial" union. "Whitfield come here," Harvey reported, "and said in a speech to cooper local that his credentials come now from the C.I.O. or the agricultural cannery union which was united with the C.I.O." Shocked by Whitfield's new allegiance, Harvey wondered, "What has happen in the convention that Whitfield met in Colorado?" Before Denver,

Whitfield had relied on his role as a local religious leader. But he realized that the CIO could link community-based groups to a much broader network of several million working-class activists who were united in their collective search for justice. Moreover, the CIO offered an expansive idea of democratic empowerment that meshed well with the developing local struggle to secure rights from the federal government.

While Whitfield had great faith in the CIO, his colleagues, as Harvey's comments make clear, were less certain. It would not be easy to overcome the deep attachment that many activists now felt with the STFU, an attachment that bore some of the qualities of religious devotion. Harvey responded to Whitfield's call for local farmers to affiliate with the CIO by vowing to advise "members of the STFU to stick to the call of the STFU until she goes to heaven with Butler in the lead."[58] Others, however, were as enthusiastic as Whitfield about CIO affiliation.

Burning with his new message, Whitfield crisscrossed the Bootheel, testifying to the new power the STFU would have if it affiliated with the CIO. In one eleven-day period, he convinced—"lined out," in his words—the STFU spillway locals near Pin Hook, Anniston, Deventer, Mule Ridge, Wyatt, Bird's Mill, and Snow's farm of the benefits of CIO affiliation. He also held a mass meeting of all area locals at Texas Bend to attract new members. In Sikeston, he organized a local of eighty-two members, all black, who elected Rev. T. S. Washington as president. By the close of picking season, Whitfield had overseen the expansion or solidification of eighteen locals in Mississippi County and two in Scott County. By the fall of 1937, the STFU boasted twenty-seven locals in southeast Missouri, including six locals in Pemiscot County and one in New Madrid County. These locals contained a combined membership of up to 2,000 paid members.[59]

Keeping these locals running, however, proved difficult in the midst of an economic crisis made worse by the 1937 recession. By December half of them were dormant or had disbanded. The Pemiscot locals had folded after violent vigilante assaults.[60] Others collapsed because their members could no longer pay dues as household costs consumed their meager earnings.[61] After the close of picking season, tenants and wage workers had few means to earn cash, especially to pay union dues. Without dues, the locals could not pay for the handbills, gasoline, and food needed to hold meetings, which made it difficult to enroll new members.

To make matters worse, a new catastrophe stalked the cotton counties as 1938 approached. In December 1937, planters notified several hundred tenant families, black and white, throughout southeast Missouri that they would be evicted on the first of the year. That month, the Sikeston *Standard* reported that the Missouri Social Security Commission found that 18,700 agricultural workers and their families were "living in a condition of wretched destitution" in the Bootheel. The commission counted 11,587 people on direct federal relief in December, mostly sharecroppers and day laborers. It predicted that after January 1, 20,000 people would be on relief. By early January, the St. Louis *Post-Dispatch* reported that landlords had already served 800 eviction notices—affecting 5,600 people—and Whitfield feared that as many as 10,000 people would be displaced.[62]

Since 1933, the Agricultural Adjustment Administration had given planters incentive to replace tenants with wage laborers, but never on this scale. The escalation of displacement at the end of 1937 reflected the concern of planters about the new Agricultural Adjustment Act of 1938. Rewritten after the Supreme Court declared the first Agricultural Adjustment Act unconstitutional in 1936, the new law was still intended to raise commodity prices but unlike the earlier version gave tenants stronger legal claims to parity payments and slashed the allowed cotton acreage in the Bootheel by 30 percent.[63] To compound matters, the new law did not make allocations for land brought into production after 1933. Many planters were left with insufficient acreage allotments to sustain their tenants, some of whom farmed as few as five acres of cotton. For example, E. P. Coleman, a Sikeston-area planter, reported that a 164-acre farm he owned that was worked by five tenant families received a total allotment of forty-nine cotton acres and none of corn. Similarly, Xenophon Caverno was allotted only fifty-eight acres of cotton on his 1,286-acre Headlight Plantation.[64] Many planters responded to the decreased allotments by employing wage laborers who had no claim to any of the crop. Planters could then take the entire parity payment and use the money to invest in labor-saving machinery such as tractors or to purchase more land. In the period 1936 to 1939, the use of wage laborers on farms larger than 480 acres increased by 85 percent. On farms of less than 120 acres that were being consolidated, wage labor increased by 325 percent.[65] At the same time, the use of tractors on the largest farms soared, averaging almost two per farm in 1938; 83 percent of these were 1936 models or newer. Counter to the intent of the AAA of 1938, the result was an obvious trend toward larger mechanized farms worked by casual day laborers.[66] As this strategy accelerated in late 1937, planters urged relief officials to expand the rolls to prevent a "stormy hunger uprising" by those who had been evicted.[67]

Sharecropping families who were forced into waged labor on farms faced harsh conditions. Wage laborers earned less than tenants of all classes. After buying food and clothes and paying medical bills, a sharecropping family might clear $100 at the end of an average year, and they received rent-free housing as part of the deal. In contrast, the members of a family of regular wage laborers working year-round in the Bootheel in the late 1930s earned at best a combined income of $330 a year, out of which they had to pay for housing, transportation, food, clothing, and health care. Members of families of casual laborers, who found work only in peak chopping or picking seasons, brought an average of only $254 into their households. Eviction was particularly devastating. When large landholders switched to day labor, as many as 500 people could be ripped from their neighbors and their community institutions overnight. Those who took wage work would likely move to nearby towns, where they faced horrid living conditions bereft of informal support structures. In Charleston, for instance, a reporter found nine white families of day laborers living in a dilapidated ten-room house and six families of black wage workers living in a shed.[68]

In addition to physical misery, the demotion to wage work dealt a catastrophic blow to the ideological basis of agrarian producerism. Wage work undermined producerist conceptions of manhood by making it impossible for men to support their families and thus function as legitimate heads of households. The wife and children of a wage worker had to work outside the home and beyond the direction of the male head of the household, sometimes separated from one another on different farms.[69] No longer insulated within household economies, workers from these families faced all sorts of vulnerabilities, particularly physical ones ranging from beatings to sexual violence. For rural men, wage work—or wage slavery, according to the idiom—connoted dependence and impotence. As a result, much of what rural activists demanded from the New Deal was shaped by adherence to a household model that would allow tenant men to provide for their families. C. H. Williams, for example, had wanted a federal "helping hand" to provide food and shelter for his family.[70] Eviction also threatened the connections between production and citizenship in the agrarian cosmology. Thad Snow observed that the tenant "loves his crop deeply. He is not only bodily improved so he fills out his clothes better, but his self-regard is also improved by his having a crop. His proud half-ownership of a crop makes him a different man from a day hand, so that under an observant eye he may be seen to expand both bodily and spiritually."[71] A man who was unable to produce, therefore, was at risk of failure on multiple levels.

Rev. Whitfield went to Washington in December to demand that the federal government halt the impending evictions. Writing to the Charleston

*Enterprise-Courier* upon his return, he explained that he made the case against eviction to New Deal officials "personally" and had sought "adequate relief measures for this mass of people, white and black." Whitfield reported receiving sympathetic assurances that the government would offer help. The moment was critical, he continued, and sharecroppers could not keep silent any longer about their poverty. In years past, he explained, the rural poor had kept too quiet, so quiet "that many people at large who would help us know nothing of our plight." Although they were well meaning, allies like Gardner Jackson could never adequately comprehend their struggle. "No one knows our condition as we ourselves know it. We are compelled to cry out," he said. As a "gospel minister," he had for too long condoned silence and contented himself with "preaching peace on earth and good will to all mankind." His awakening in the revivals of the preceding years now made it impossible "to preach a gospel of peace and good will to people facing eviction, and facing winter without food!"[72] In fact, his congregations would no longer accept such nostrums after their experience of revival.

Unscrupulous landlords had brought on this unrest, Whitfield explained, by crushing tenants' ability to provide for their families. Big farmers who sought to replace their sharecroppers with wage laborers were especially callous. Their decision to displace thousands, Whitfield said, "is causing the farm worker to become more and more susceptible to radicalism, and communism and all the other 'isms.'" The flirtation with outright revolt in the OIBAPMW in 1934 weighed heavily on him now. Whitfield reassured readers that no one wanted extremism in the Bootheel less than him, but without a change in how landowners treated tenants he was not sure he could contain tenants' growing desperation. Cannily positioning himself as a moderate representative, Whitfield encouraged planters to meet his reasonable demands before the union rank and file made more radical ones. Planters could prevent such an uprising by giving "the farm worker a lease on life as we once had" by keeping tenants on the land and allowing them "to raise corn, pigs, chickens and molasses." Give us access to healthy, sustainable lives and "the right to till the soil that we fought and shed blood for," he demanded, "and thereby keep the spirit of Democracy foremost in the minds of the workers." This was the first time Whitfield linked the demands of the Official Council of the STFU Refugees to the threat of political action. If the basis for agrarian conceptions of citizenship was demolished, he was saying, the loyalty of poor farmers to the democratic principles of the United States might be eroded as well. This new approach shows how influential the two major events of 1937—the refugee crisis and the STFU's entry into the CIO—had been on rural activists. By framing his letter to the *Enterprise-Courier* within the context of the impending eviction crisis, his meetings with New Deal officials, and the moral imperative to "cry out," Whitfield announced to readers in Mississippi County and beyond that the movement he represented would confront the federal government with conviction of conscience. "Remember," he reminded readers, "you have God to answer to some day."[73]

Whitfield framed the producerist cause as a drive for a family wage for tenants. At the most basic level, Whitfield argued, male heads of tenant households wanted to "feed their families." If the planters could not "pay a wage that will give the workers a decent living for himself and family," he explained, then they should understand that "neither can the worker work for a wage that will starve himself and family."[74] Farmers had not just the right but the moral obligation to rebel if they were prevented from reaping the just rewards of their hard work. Although it was based on a deep-rooted agrarian ideal and was framed using the language of the New Deal and urban labor, this defense of producerist manhood and its family wage rhetoric smuggled a patriarchal idiom into a democratic movement for justice that was inspired and led to an unprecedented extent by women.[75] This rhetoric was useful, however, because it harnessed male fears about their eroding responsibilities as heads of households to women's interests in providing for the family; together these formed a coherent argument about the way landlords and federal cotton control laws denied tenant farmers the ability to fulfill what they saw as their agrarian duty to produce. Meanwhile, grassroots calls for government protection of family farms clashed with the STFU's aim of developing communal farms.[76] Although the STFU policy was more attuned to the realities of consolidation and mechanization in the cotton economy, it was in many ways too radical for farmers who held to the producerist dream of independent homesteads.

Despite efforts such as Whitfield's, area landlords evicted several thousand people in early January 1938. Although the total fell short of the number that Whitfield had feared, the results were devastating, especially among union members, whom planters seemed to target. Sid Mitchell, a former spillway refugee, said his "condition was awful narrow" and admitted that he was "naked and bare of all things a person need."[77] A preliminary survey conducted by the STFU confirmed that 258 people in fifty-one families had been evicted in Sikeston, Wyatt, and Bertrand alone.[78] Clifton Dickerson of Wyatt reported that union members "have been given [notice] to get out at once [and] they are unable to find a place."[79] STFU members who were targeted for their union activity wanted assistance. James Lomax informed

Mitchell that "we are all members of the STFU and we are having a tough time. . . . We works hard and then cannot make it, and the relief is very very poor here." We "want to see if something can be done," Lomax said.[80] The STFU's national office helped ease the situation; H. L. Mitchell informed Whitfield that he had "made it possible for your people in southeast Missouri to get relief through the WPA or Farm Security," although the help was temporary.[81] The number of people hoping to receive this relief was overwhelming. When the offices administering it opened, fifty-three former sharecroppers applied in one day alone at East Prairie and 475 applied in the first four days at Charleston.[82] This temporary fix could not meet the large need, leaving little cause for hope.

*　*　*

In the face of the eviction crisis, Whitfield launched a new organizing campaign. He later recalled that it was in the first few weeks of 1938 that he grasped how politics worked. In subsequent speeches he described a vision of working-class political mobilization that had come into focus, sharpened by the attacks of landlords on unionists. Whitfield told audiences that the rural poor had to "organize for power." That January he set about organizing sharecroppers and day laborers into a phalanx that would give them "the balance of power." He explained to potential members that they could not just join a "Santa Claus" union and then get "land, mules and hogs. We must organize for power before we can obtain these," he argued.[83] The STFU had not been strong enough to protect its members in 1937, and Whitfield was increasingly convinced that farmers' only hope lay with the CIO.

Whitfield began to see the CIO as a model for emulation as well as an ally. As Handcox and others revealed, one of the biggest obstacles to the growth of the STFU was mistrust between white and black farmers. After decades of conflict and involvement in separatist groups such as the UNIA, the KKK, the NFCF, and the Socialist Party, farmers were skeptical and even fearful of interracial cooperation. To varying degrees, the same was true of white and black workers nationwide. The STFU tried to avoid racial animosity by allowing segregated locals and by forbidding any talk of partisan politics. The CIO, by contrast, cultivated a "culture of unity" in order to mobilize a diverse working-class movement that could achieve political as well as economic goals. While white racism often complicated and corroded these larger aims, as Bruce Nelson and other historians have shown, the CIO still achieved unprecedented successes due in large part to organization across the color line. Although it was not a movement for racial integration, the

CIO promised white and black workers deployable power if they would view one another with solidarity when it came to common concerns.[84]

Whitfield urged area farmers to abandon racial traditions and "organize for power" in the CIO. Contrary to what some historians have claimed, African Americans were in many ways just as averse to such alliances as whites.[85] Whitfield called on area blacks during the eviction crisis to suspend support for the Republican Party and to pledge "ourselves to not be swayed politically by the ghosts and skeletons of men of bygone days. . . . We shall hold our votes in our vest pocket," he concluded, "and shall hand them to men that will hand us a square deal in return," a point he reiterated to 1,500 blacks gathered at Charleston's annual Lincoln Day celebration, normally a banner occasion for Republicans.[86] However, in his speeches to poor whites Whitfield combined such declarations of openness with assurances that working together in a union would not necessarily lead to racial mixing. What rural black men did not want, he informed white crowds, was "social equality"; political cooperation did not mean interracial sex or marriage. "No social mixture," Whitfield said, "we don't desire that." "You are satisfied, I am sure, with your white women," he told white male listeners, "and I am tickled to death with my tea kettle brown." Even though he wasn't interested in what he called "social mixing," he argued that "you and I must unite for a higher standard of living through collective efforts and we can better our condition."[87] To illustrate his point, Whitfield frequently carried a cartoon to union meetings with one frame showing two mules, one black and one white, pulling toward two piles of hay in different directions. The second frame showed the two mules hitched together pulling toward one pile, then the other.[88] Even though blacks and whites might have separate goals, neither group would reach their goals unless they worked with the other group.

Whitfield's argument seemed to work, as white tenants from New Madrid, Pemiscot, and Scott counties clamored to join the growing regional movement.[89] Energized by affiliation with the UCAPAWA, McConnell began reorganizing the Pemiscot locals that had been destroyed the previous fall. He reported to Mitchell that evictions there had left "at least 10,000 in Pemiscot Co. on starvation." Few had been able to get WPA work or relief during the fall because area planters had cleared the county relief rolls in order to ensure plenty of cheap picking labor. "Starving the labor into gathering the crop cheap has opened the laborer's eyes," McConnell said.[90] Many had growing confidence in the CIO's ability to defend them. "The C.I.O. is proclaimed by the laborer here as their only friend . . . and medium between them and starvation," he continued, a belief that was enhanced by the fact that the local elite "as a whole fear and dread the C.I.O."[91] Elsewhere, this new energy led E. L. Hughes, the black leader of the STFU local in Oran, to form a committee to agitate for the right of sharecroppers to raise subsistence foodstuffs, a key demand of the STFU's refugee council. The committee's "Let Scott County Feed Itself" campaign argued that politicians could ease the burden on relief agencies by making it possible for "tenants to have a cow, pigs, chickens and a few acres of truck gardens to tide them over the winter months."[92]

Despite the local momentum, however, the leaders of the STFU and the UCAPAWA were on the verge of open warfare. H. L. Mitchell and J. R. Butler, the socialist leaders of the STFU, had deep misgivings about affiliating with the UCAPAWA, which was led by Donald Henderson, a communist. The STFU leaders also resented the CIO's strict policy on dues payment and felt that the dues were too expensive for rural people. Furthermore, they feared that Henderson wanted to take control of the STFU, which had retained its autonomy in the alliance. Henderson, on the other hand, considered the STFU leaders to be politically naïve, parochial, and ineffective. This mutual mistrust was deep-seated. Throughout the spring of 1938, Henderson sought to impose CIO standards on the STFU and Mitchell and Butler threatened to secede. The issue split the Executive Council of the STFU between those who believed CIO affiliation was vital and those who feared communist domination.[93] Although the disagreement was confined to the upper echelons of leadership, it threatened to undo local organizing successes.

Whitfield sought desperately to reconcile the two camps by arguing that the STFU needed the UCAPAWA for access to the CIO. "It gives [the STFU] more power," he told the STFU annual convention in Little Rock, Arkansas, in February 1938, by giving "us recognition all over America." More important, "it gives us not 40,000 but 40,000,000 voting power." To illustrate his point and reiterate the religious roots of the movement, he gave the STFU convention a sermon. "Let me tell you the story of a ship in a storm," Whitfield preached. "The ship was wrecked and a man was swimming about tossed this way and that," grasping at bits of wood that sank until he "felt something solid and held onto it for it was a rock and he was saved. My brothers that story is just like our union," he concluded. "We have been tossed about by many storms and often our support has disappeared from us . . . but we reached out and found a rock to cling to and I say to you brothers . . . that rock is the CIO!"[94] Whitfield's parable referenced scripture that emphasized faith in the redeeming and saving power of God, particularly Psalm 62:2, "He only is my rock and salvation; he is my defence; I shall not be greatly moved."[95] This was a reference churchgoers would have been familiar with;

they would have understood the religious implications of the secular parable Whitfield told at the union meeting. Whitfield had a strong motive for working so hard to convince his fellow unionists to support affiliation with the CIO. "I'm done in Missouri if we are not connected with the C.I.O.," he admitted.[96] The STFU-UCAPAWA alliance survived.

While the movement grew at the grassroots level, Whitfield maintained his pressure on state and federal officials. Activists in southeast Missouri were attracting attention. After a meeting in Jefferson City with Governor Lloyd Stark, who offered to place him on a special committee for the welfare of blacks, Whitfield wrote directly to President Roosevelt to protest the Bootheel evictions and demand that the federal government prevent more from occurring.[97] By early spring, Whitfields' efforts had begun to produce results. In late March, FSA representatives called on Whitfield to get "the lowdown on the conditions of the homeless people in S. E. Mo." Virgil Bankson, a National Labor Relations Board investigator, also visited his home, "getting the fact[s] on the farm labor situation in regards to wages & hours, housing, food, clothes, etc."[98] Whitfield interpreted Bankson's visit as evidence of the movement's impact, although it could have been seen as an empty gesture since agricultural workers were not protected by the National Labor Relations Board. Shortly afterward, Whitfield again went to Washington to lobby the administration. In the meantime, the FSA unveiled a model solution to the problems of rural poverty in southeast Missouri: a cooperative farm in New Madrid County called La Forge Farms.

Opened in June 1938, La Forge housed 100 sharecropping families—over 500 people—with the purpose of lifting them out of poverty and setting them on the path to landownership.[99] Technically the project was open only to residents of New Madrid County. Hans Baasch, the project director, announced that the families chosen had been living on the land when the federal government had purchased it. The FSA wanted to "find out whether these run-of-the-mill share-croppers could make a decent, secure living if they had a chance under different conditions," he explained.[100] La Forge consisted of 6,700 acres of cotton land, split into plots averaging fifty-five acres with a four- or five-room house for each of its sixty white and forty black families. These scattered (rather than centrally grouped) homes each came with a barn for equipment and livestock, a newly drilled well, sanitary latrines, ample garden and pasture land, and electricity supplied by the Rural Electrification Administration. In addition, the FSA loaned each family $1,300 to purchase feed, seed, tools, and equipment and provided training in diversified farming and home economics. Although it was segregated, La Forge had a shared community center where clients formed a "cooperative association" for self-government, buying and selling goods, and overseeing the sale of the group's crops. Above all, La Forge provided secure land tenure for desperate, vulnerable landless farm families.[101]

The first year at La Forge was an overwhelming success. By reducing their cotton acreages by 50 percent, farmers on the project were able to plant a range of additional crops, including wheat, hay, legumes, and garden vegetables. The vegetables provided a daily reminder of the new freedom La Forge offered during the growing season and after; by December, women on the project had canned over 20,000 quarts of home-grown produce. In addition, each family bought mules for fieldwork, a milk cow, fifty chickens, and a sow and two shoats (young pigs) for future meat. By the end of the first year, after repaying the loan and paying rent and other costs, each family cleared an average of $350 with a large store of food for the winter. Amid these material improvements, residents supported two new schools, one for whites and one for blacks. Although no blacks held elected offices in the settlement's cooperative association, black residents organized a "Negro Planning Council" to represent them in the association. The council arranged night classes for adults, recreation, and clubs for men and women. It also oversaw the construction of the school, which also served as a church. The Negro Planning Council also organized a Good Citizens League, led by Rev. Whitfield, to keep black residents abreast of current political issues.[102]

While it is not clear how Whitfield secured a place at La Forge, he took full advantage of his time there. Baasch was well aware of Whitfield's career with the STFU and encouraged him to use La Forge as an organizing hub.[103] While preaching the gospel to his fellow residents, he urged groups such as the Good Citizens League to support union demands for political action, in particular demands for more FSA projects like La Forge. In many ways, La Forge offered a perfect solution for the long-term protection of the values of agrarian producerism, since it stabilized family labor systems and enabled tenant women to be housewives rather than field hands. Indeed, one report listed "women's activities" as "mother, nurse, religious teacher, club member, good neighbor, American voter, recreation advisor, landscape gardener, cook, canner, seamstress, truck gardener, farm hand (not encouraged), milk maid, poultry raiser, and interior decorator."[104] In other words, women who had formerly worked in the fields now had the ability to devote their labor to providing for their children's health and welfare. La Forge's protection of individual ownership within a cooperative structure with diversified farming techniques and its emphasis on health, subsistence, and independence offered a strategy to create lasting change for the rural poor while preserving familiar gender roles and social structures.[105] However, only 100 families benefited from this federal experiment.

The La Forge example magnified the potential impact of the CIO for organizers trying to recruit new members. "I am busy now reconstructing the old locals," Whitfield reported to Mitchell, to "begin functioning after the great exodus," referring to the recent evictions.[106] Even though the CIO requirement that members pay regular dues complicated Whitfield's organizing work, tenants flocked to meetings.[107] Whitfield and white organizer W. B. Moore spoke to packed churches near Wyatt and Sikeston and to an overflow gathering at Mt. Carmel Church near Charleston. The meetings were a great success, with many rushing forward after the speeches "to shake hand with the speakers" and declare "that they will carry the message to their communities in a effort to stir up the spirit of unionism."[108] They attracted "good crowds" around New Madrid, previously NAACP territory, and launched an interracial local at Dorena in the southern end of the spillway.[109] Most crucially, Whitfield reorganized the Rising Sun NAACP chapter as two new STFU locals in New Madrid and Stoddard counties.[110] NAACP activists such as Dollie Wherry and Peter Wilderness became officers in the new locals.[111] Thad Snow noticed the upswing in union activity when he returned from abroad in mid-1938. His sharecroppers informed him that "croppers from all over the Delta had been getting together in an organized way for the purpose of talking over their affairs and exchanging information" and "were having lots of meetings."[112] Finally it seemed that a generation of white and black rural working people was coming together.

As cotton-picking season neared in 1938, the union movement in the Bootheel consisted of well over thirty locals with more than 4,500 dues-paying members. Missouri now had the largest membership in the STFU, following those of Arkansas and Oklahoma. Cotton workers from all three tenure groups—share tenants, sharecroppers, and day laborers—had joined.[113] Among them were promising local organizers, including W. M. Fischer of Dorena, who joined the STFU's National Executive Council.[114] The largest growth was among farm wage workers after the 1938 evictions.[115] Incorporating this volatile group helped diffuse competition, reestablish social ties among displaced people, and enable damaged communities to accommodate migrants from other regions. Whitfield and Moore were able to organize new locals in previously weak or new areas, reenergize the Pemiscot locals, and bring NAACP groups into the movement.[116] But another crisis loomed.

Map 4. The STFU and NAACP in the Bootheel, 1938.

In July, reports emerged of a large round of evictions planned for the beginning of 1939. "I am writing you to let you no we are expected to be out of
doors the first of the year," one East Prairie sharecropper told Butler. "If you
have any influence with the President," he pleaded, "I wish you would please
get him to do something for us."[117] Despite Whitfield's organizing success,
planters were not slowing their switch to day labor; they again said evictions
were necessary because of the provisions of New Deal cotton control laws.[118]
To speed up the transition, area elites purged people from the WPA work
relief rolls before the 1938 picking season. All able-bodied men, white and
black, were warned by the county WPA committees that they had three days
to find cotton-picking work or they would be permanently discharged from
WPA work.[119] Thousands of unemployed men, many from area towns, glutted
the cotton fields. Growers were delighted and lowered wages for picking.

This was too much for many to take. Refusing to pick for starvation wages,
hundreds of STFU members in Mississippi County staged a strike in late September. When fliers announcing a cotton-picking strike meant for Arkansas

arrived in Missouri, local union leaders around Charleston and Matthews, the latter led by Rev. R. H. Bradford, eagerly joined the strike action. The strikers demanded picking wages of $1 per hundred pounds and called for all potential pickers, union members or not, to stay out of the fields until their demands were met. The strikers could not match the power of the planters, however, who brought in scab pickers from neighboring Cairo to crush the strike and (they hoped) the STFU. Many strikers, desperate for work, ultimately returned to the fields to pick at the planters' wage, 75 cents per hundred. Within a week the strike was over and planters were as resolute as ever in their decision to switch to day labor.[120] Most planters blamed Whitfield for the disturbance and many planters called for the dismantling of the STFU.[121]

Whitfield answered their threats in a public letter that disowned the strike yet defended the right of the rural working class to organize. "I had nothing to do with calling the strike," he assured readers; "personally I am against strikes." But Whitfield pointed out that there were good reasons behind it that the planters themselves had created when they forced more than 500 WPA workers from their jobs through their control of county WPA boards "without taking under consideration the fact that most of these men had large families, rent to pay, fuel to buy, and clothing to provide for half clothed children—and winter just around the corner." As a result, he said, the expelled WPA workers, many of whom were white, joined the union. "Don't you think it about time that we poor devils, both white and black, that are being evicted and thrown out on the mercies of the world more and more," he asked, "get together for protection of ourselves and our families?" Whitfield and his followers "wish to make it plain that we are not organizing to come in possession of the big man's wealth and land." He can keep his land "and as far as we are concerned he can work it." The union's goals, Whitfield concluded, were "land for the landless, clothes for the naked, food for the hungry, and freedom from the wage slavers."[122] Although the language of wage slavery had long connoted rural fears of dependence, unmanliness, and lost citizenship, Whitfield's use of it in the midst of demotion, eviction, and displacement moved the meaning of the words from rhetoric into an all-too-real context.

Desperate to prevent the planned evictions, Whitfield decided that large-scale federal intervention would have to be forced by a dramatic display. "The union must fight through the government," he argued.[123] Using La Forge as a model solution, he began a "speaking and organizing campaign getting the people in readiness for a drive on the federal government" in July. His goal was to force the "FSA to continue its homesteading projects such as we have in New Madrid County." In August, after a conference with Baasch, Whitfield contacted John Clark, head of the St. Louis Urban League, for help. His reasons were simple. He wanted to see that the thousands of people being evicted got "back to the soil where they belong and they so desire to be." Since so many of the displaced were moving to southern and northern cities, he thought it imperative to "carry the fight into St. Louis and other northern cities" with a "speaking tour and put the plight of these homeless people before the nation." Whitfield reassured Clark that he had "no desire to go out as an official or organizer of any labor" union; he only wanted to give witness "as the voice of a people that is homeless and is drifting from place to place," a "people who wants to work and earn their living as they always has in the past."[124]

Throughout the fall, activists cast about for a plan. In October, Whitfield held a series of meetings with union members to discuss possible strategies and decided that a speaking tour by him alone would not be powerful enough to carry the plight of Missouri farm workers to the nation.[125] The rural poor themselves had to give their collective testimony to make the public take notice. At one of these meetings, a sharecropper facing eviction joked that after the New Year his family would have to camp out on the side of the road for lack of a place to go.[126] Whitfield latched onto the idea; the landless could use their greatest trouble—eviction—as a weapon. A roadside protest in the dead of winter of homeless, destitute families, he reasoned, would publicize their plight and issue a moral call for action. A display of human suffering on the order of the suffering after the spillway crisis would ignite public passions, attract media attention, and force the federal government to intervene.[127] By November, local unionists were busy making preparations.

Whitfield worked hard to win outside support for the demonstration. In late November, he, Fischer, and Johnnie Moore, a black leader of Matthews Local 384, spoke before the St. Louis Urban League and a number of other religious and civic organizations "in an effort to obtain moral support." On December 1, Whitfield told Mitchell that they were busy "trying to prepare ourselves for what will happen on the first of January" when "about 900 union familys will be evicted." "They are planning to pile their household goods on sides of the highway and see what happens," he said.[128] In mid-December, Whitfield told the St. Louis CIO Industrial Union Council that he was planning a "mass meeting."[129] Shortly afterward, he attended the annual UCAPAWA convention in San Francisco, where he told Henderson and other national CIO leaders about the demonstration. They were enthusiastic about the plan and pledged full CIO support. At the meeting Whitfield was elected as a vice-president of the UCAPAWA.[130]

With CIO support assured, Whitfield returned to the Bootheel to join his colleagues in their preparations for the demonstration. He also took time to fulfill his duties as the director of La Forge's black choir, which was due to perform at the project's official dedication on December 20. At the dedication, P. G. Beck, the assistant regional director of the FSA, delivered the keynote address. La Forge, he said, offered "another chance to men and women whose courage and ability is worth the effort" to obtain "the security, the abused but cherished anchor we call 'Home.'" Following Beck's speech, the choir took the platform and faced an audience filled with family members, fellow sharecroppers, local politicians, and federal officials. The choir's choice of songs, "Reap What You Sow," "Don't Drive Me from Your Door," "God Don't Like It and I Don't Either," and the finale, "Swing Low, Sweet Chariot," must have seemed somber amid the celebrations of the day. If the local and federal officials in attendance could have known what was coming, they might have understood this choice of songs.[131]

While Whitfield was away, local union leaders had organized the groundwork for the demonstration. This group, which included Fischer, Moore, Hughes, Wilderness, Bradford, Willie Scott, and others, represented the wide array of community groups working together. A movement that had begun among black refugees in the spillway was now made up of activists—white and black, men and women—from throughout the Bootheel. Their plan for the demonstration reflected the grassroots foundations of their movement: in the early hours of January 10, the last day of grace for evicted families to vacate their homes, those participating would move their belongings to pre-arranged meeting places on the sides of U.S. Highways 60 and 61. The camps would be made by community groups near their former homes and would be led by respected local tenants such as Wilderness, Fischer, and Moore.[132] Built from the ground up, this protest was waged by friends, neighbors, and kin determined to lead healthy, happy, and secure lives on the land. They wanted what the refugee council had demanded almost two years before: garden patches, sanitary latrines, screen doors, and the right to keep chickens and pigs. In short, they sought a New Deal for the rural poor. Until 1937, the New Deal had only harmed landless farmers, a fact driven home by the spillway flood. That crisis, however, also pointed a way forward. The rush of Red Cross and federal aid to provide shelter, food, and public health safeguards had given the refugees new hope that the federal government might actually provide the help their condition demanded.

Plans for the protest complicated relations with the STFU's national leaders. Bradford and Moore, who were busy galvanizing support, advised fellow members and other local union leaders not to send delegates to the STFU's annual convention, which was to be held from December 29 to January 1.[133] Whitfield supported their decision and informed the union office, somewhat unconvincingly, that he could not attend because he was too busy trying to locate a team of mules that had gone astray. He added that he was for "the STFU 100%."[134] The sudden cooling of Missouri unionists toward the national STFU is curious. At the very least, these developments suggest that the Bootheel members were frustrated with the lack of progress or help from the STFU during the previous year's battles. It also hints that local members believed their planned demonstration carried more potential than the ideas national leaders had offered. Or, more seriously, this rejection of the STFU could have stemmed from Whitfield's trip to the UCAPAWA convention in San Francisco.[135] Did Henderson and others convince him to abandon the STFU? The record is unclear.

On January 1, as expected, planters evicted several thousand sharecroppers. To steel the resolve of the protestors, Whitfield drew upon the revivalist roots of the movement. He invited 350 core union activists to a special meeting at the Sikeston First Baptist Church on the night of January 7. He also invited Thad Snow and *Post-Dispatch* reporter Sam Armstrong.[136] With Armstrong in attendance, Whitfield knew he had one chance to reveal to the public the moral imperatives behind the protest before planters denounced it. He took the pulpit that night and spoke not just to the gathered crowd but also to the nation.

Between prayers and hymns, Whitfield used Luke's rendering of Christ's final journey to Jerusalem to frame the protest. Quoting Luke 9:58, he said: "The foxes have holes and the birds of heaven have nests; but the Son of Man hath not where to lay his head." Knowing execution and ascension to be imminent, Jesus said this, according to Luke, after his rejection by the Samaritans in order to warn his followers about the difficulties of discipleship.[137] "How many of you got a notice to move?" Whitfield asked. Hands shot up. "How many have got a place to go?" The room went silent. "That's why we're here," he thundered, to "bear our burdens together." All would depend upon that collective mission. Once a new departure had been made, Whitfield suggested, it could not be undone. Those in attendance would have understood the commitment they were making, just as they knew the verses of Luke's gospel that followed Whitfield's quotation: "No man, having put his hand to the plough, and looking back, is fit for the kingdom of God" (Luke 9:62).[138]

"Where we goin' to go?" he asked. Whitfield's audience, both black and white, shouted enthusiastically "Sixty-one highway!" They should not fear, Whitfield said. Just as the Lord had freed Moses and the Israelites from Egyptian tyranny, so they would find their freedom now. "We also must make an exodus," he exclaimed. "It's history repeatin' itself in 1939!" "You've got no place to go," he concluded, "and the only thing left for us is to move quietly like good citizens to the highway." It was time to testify, to make people "see what we're up against."[139]

# 6

# On Jordan's Stormy Banks

On the morning of January 10, just after midnight, Alonzo and Mary Julian, clutching their six children, a little food, and a pile of tattered clothing, climbed onto a neighbor's flatbed truck a few miles west of Marston and headed for Highway 61. Huddled with his family against the cold, Julian must have felt a powerful uncertainty as his eyes searched the pitch-black darkness of the cotton fields, dreading the trouble that would surely visit him and his fellow protestors. As he caught the outline of the tent his family had called home since their tenant house burned in July, he was surely lifted by the fact that they had little left to lose. His landlord, Walter Richardson, had not rebuilt the house because the day laborers he had decided to employ had no right to houses; he had given the Julians their eviction notice later that fall. They had not been alone when they were evicted, and the Julians knew they would not be alone on this night either. The truck carrying them made two more stops, gathering other sharecropping families evicted by Richardson. As they reached the end of the six-mile trip to Lilbourn, they began to make out the dim glow of campfires ahead.[1]

Upon reaching the camp near Lilbourn, the Julians entered a throng of demonstrators busily constructing their new residences on the highway shoulder. They draped blankets and sheets over stick frames to erect makeshift tents. They moved whatever clothing, food, and belongings they had brought into their new shelters, including, for the lucky ones, pots, pans, wood-fired cooking stoves, and even a few squawking chickens. From old automobiles and trucks they unloaded straw ticks and corn-shuck mattresses, parking the vehicles close to their camps to provide better shelter for children and the elderly. Before unloading, the Julians met first with the local STFU leaders in charge of the camp, Peter Wilderness and Willie Scott, president and secretary, respectively, of Good Hope Local 385.[2] Scott and Wilderness found the families a place to settle and then reminded them of the code of conduct Rev. Whitfield had put in place to govern the demonstration—be peaceful and polite, he had said, and "let our camps do the talking."[3] Once this was finished, all the Julians could do was sit, talk things over with their neighbors and fellow union members, and wait for the nation to wake up.

By noon over 1,000 demonstrators occupied U.S. Highways 60 and 61 in thirteen different ramshackle camps, ranging in size from three to sixty families each, across Mississippi, Scott, New Madrid, and Pemiscot counties. Union members from the spillway established four camps along Highway 60, near Wyatt, Charleston, and Bertrand in Mississippi County, and west to Sikeston in Scott County, where fifty landless families, including a group of whites from Dorena, staked a camp.[4] Two more camps were located on Highway 61, where another 120 people took up residence opposite Matthews.

Figure 2. Landless farming families gathered along the highway, January 1939. Source: Farm Security Administration—Office of War Information Photograph Collection, LC-USF33-002927-M1, Library of Congress. Photograph by Arthur Rothstein.

The second camp of 175 people on Highway 61 was the one at Lilbourn that the Julians joined. Scores of additional demonstrators swelled the camps later on the first day, more than 100 more people at the Lilbourn camp alone. Although the camp populations fluctuated daily, 400 families—more than 1,500 people in all, 200 of them white—took part in the demonstration from January 10 to January 15.[5]

The dramatic protest shocked the nation. Within hours of the first encampments, print and radio journalists; newsreel crews; local, state, and

Figure 3. More than 200 white farmers joined the protest in January 1939. Source: Farm Security Administration—Office of War Information Photograph Collection, LC-USF33-002929-M3, Library of Congress. Photograph by Arthur Rothstein.

Figure 4. The demonstrators demanded the opportunity to work. Source: Farm Security Administration—Office of War Information Photograph Collection, LC-USF33-002927-M5, Library of Congress. Photograph by Arthur Rothstein.

national government officials; representatives of religious organizations; and agents of the STFU and the CIO all rushed to the Bootheel. Investigators from all corners interviewed the demonstrators, talked with planters, and struggled to comprehend the wrenching poverty and the sustaining vision of dignity that the protest summoned. Arthur Rothstein, a photographer from the Farm Security Administration's Historical Section, took the most vivid and startling photographs. The Historical Section's main goal was to galvanize political and public support for the FSA through the "exposure of the ill fed, ill clothed, and ill housed in need of agency assistance."[6] Rothstein had been in the Bootheel to document the success of the nearby La Forge project in order to help justify its budgetary requests in Congress. His pictures over the next few days captured the bravery and desperation of the demonstrators and accompanied nearly every news report of the protest.[7] A battle was waged in these reports, as planters and local officials worked feverishly to discredit the stories of eviction, displacement, and broken dreams the tenants told.[8] The display of the roadside camps, carefully crafted by local activists for Rothstein and others to broadcast, caught the attention of the federal government. Eleanor Roosevelt wrote about the demonstrators' plight in her newspaper column in the weeks that followed.[9] Likewise, President Roosevelt urged Secretary of Agriculture Henry Wallace "to do everything within our power to assist the families of the sharecroppers, farm tenants and farm laborers in southern Missouri who 'went out on the road.'"[10]

Although the demonstrators had captured the sympathies of the Roosevelts, the rural New Deal that they hoped to achieve faced mounting challenges. Acceleration in the use of wage labor and machines in cotton agriculture made a federal program for small producers an increasingly impossible achievement. Despite Roosevelt's urging, Henry Wallace and others saw nothing special in the Bootheel situation. From California to Florida, Wallace said, the ditches and roads were lined with "sharecroppers or tenants who have been forced off the land by mechanization and other technological developments."[11] These unfortunate people were a surplus farming population, Wallace explained to Eleanor Roosevelt. She did not share his fatalistic appraisal. Rather than try to help, should we just "drown the surplus population?" she angrily asked in reply.[12] Will Alexander, director of the FSA, still believed a solution could be found to the crisis but was pessimistic about the politics of doing so. "As a satisfactory long-term solution," he believed that a massive expansion of resettlement programs like La Forge "would eliminate much of the suffering" and "stabilize the agricultural economy in this area."[13] But that was a tall order. The bloc of planter-backed southern Democrats in Congress presented the main obstacle to such an expansion. Conservative pressure meant that Alexander was already fully occupied with defending successful projects like La Forge and was not in a position to create new ones. The roadside demonstration had put the needs of displaced Bootheel farmers at the center of policy debates in headlines, editorials, and the White House, but a long road remained between the demonstrators and their promised land.

Having showed people "what we are up against," Bootheel activists were only halfway to their goal. At their most audacious, the demonstrators were also now at their most desperate. The resources that had guided rural mobilizing in the Bootheel thus far—a shared commitment to farming, an outpouring of righteous outrage, and witness to the corruption of wealthy planters and corporations—had shaped the vision that led them onto the road. But in order to secure large-scale federal intervention on behalf of rural producers, the protestors would require help. As activists came to rely more and more on the national leadership of the STFU and CIO for support, so the political goals and ideology of those allies took on increasing importance among the protestors. In the political infighting that ensued, the religious roots of the agrarian movement rapidly began to die.

*　*　*

Despite the rallying power of CIO affiliation during the grassroots organizing campaign of 1938, the roadside demonstration began primarily as a protest of local groups, of families, co-religionists, friends, and neighbors. Following Whitfield's speech at the January 7 meeting at the Sikeston First Baptist Church, local unionists took over the demonstration.[14] The leaders of the main camps, all union officers, represented the breadth of the movement. Will Jones and T. J. North came from black locals in the Mississippi County spillway; William Fischer led white unionists from Dorena, in the south of the spillway; E. L. Hughes brought demonstrators from Scott County; Johnnie Moore and Rev. R. H. Bradford directed the campers near Matthews; Will Travers camped alongside white union members in Pemiscot County; and Peter Wilderness and Willie Scott led the Lilbourn camp, which included unionists and former NAACP members from Portageville, Marston, Lilbourn, Catron, Parma, Kewanee, and New Madrid, an area of ninety square miles. They followed a simple set of organizing principles established at the Sikeston meeting: maintain order and peace, do not force anyone to demonstrate, and let the visual statement of the camps speak for itself. On January 8, Whitfield and these leaders rallied the demonstrators in a series of small local meetings throughout the area.[15] The next day Whitfield left for St. Louis to coordinate outside support. Before going, he notified the STFU office in Memphis that the demonstration was under way and urged the union to "keep out." He later explained that if the STFU got involved, it would be obliged to support the protest financially, something he knew it could not do.[16] The protest was now in local hands.

The experience of being evicted and thus demoted from tenant status to laborer status united the demonstrators. When journalists asked Will Jones, leader of the Sikeston camp, what the protest was about, he replied, "We have no place to go." Echoing Whitfield's line, Jones declared, "We don't know whether this will do us any good, but it will show the people what we are up against."[17] To federal investigators working undercover, the demonstrators explained themselves in full. Of the eighty-seven demonstrating families interviewed by officials from the National Youth Administration who rushed to the Bootheel as part of the government's response, over 63 percent reported they had recently been evicted. Many others had been evicted in January

1938. The vast majority of these eviction notices were oral or "virtual," an arrangement in which the planter allowed the workers to stay on the farm, either without work, which was unsatisfactory for both parties, or as casual wage laborers.[18]

When asked by federal agents what they wanted to achieve with the protest, the demonstrators were unequivocal: they wanted to continue working the land under secure tenure agreements. Ninety percent wanted to keep farming; most were eager to return to sharecropping or renting.[19] Melvin Smith and his wife wanted to rent or buy a farm so their family wouldn't "have to move all over the country." Peter Wilderness said he wanted "to stay on a farm in this vicinity." Walter Johnson, of Deventer, wanted to rent or buy a farm in Missouri because, he explained, "I'm really a farmer, a renter." Others wanted access to productive land, as tenants if need be, and the right to raise subsistence foodstuffs that would allow them to better provide for their families. Ike Tripp would move anywhere in the area where he could "make an honest support for my family and won't have to be moving so much." Daniel McClenton and his wife, who were protesting with their ten children, were content to sharecrop if they could raise their own corn and chickens. Alonzo Julian wanted to farm "any good place" with good land.[20]

To a person, the demonstrators believed the federal government, through the FSA, should help them find that "good place."[21] A Red Cross official informed Governor Lloyd Stark that the campers believed "they are entitled to some form of Federal agricultural relief assistance."[22] Dave Coffey wanted to live on "Government land."[23] "We want a project like the one at La Forge homes and land," Elijah Moore said.[24] Most shared this desire, which is not surprising given the role La Forge had played in the previous year's organizing effort. The FSA project was compelling because it preserved the social worlds of small farmers on independent homesteads. "We want to be homesteaded as they are on the La Forge Project," Alonzo Julian said, where his family would have access to good schools and churches and be able to "raise plenty food stuff." "We only want a chance to live for ourselves," he explained, echoing the desire for autonomy that had guided black settlers to the Bootheel in 1923 and informed their subsequent involvement in the UNIA and NFCF.[25] This desire for independence, which stemmed from an agrarian cosmology with deep roots in the nineteenth century, had merged with the realization that the federal government owed its citizens assistance during a crisis, when New Deal agencies helped farmers displaced by the army's flooding of the spillway in 1937. One state official recognized as much when he reported that many of the campers believed they should be "fed and sheltered similar to the way they were taken care of during the flood of 1937."[26]

But just as during the spillway crisis, the demonstrators of 1939 did not want charity. They only wanted the opportunity to earn the rewards of productive work. "Give me a hand," Elijah Moore requested, "and I will make my living like other men." They needed federal help, he explained, because they were "in need of every thing[:] house, more land, food, clothing, and other things."[27] Irene Nickerson concurred, saying that, "We don't want relief[;] we want to work and make our own living."[28] These demonstrators were struggling to hold together a whole way of life that defined their labor as well as their relationships with kin, neighbors, and friends. Over 40 percent of the demonstrators said they were "fed up" with the horrid conditions they and their neighbors lived in. For example, Dan Warren, a white day laborer, told investigators from the Federal Bureau of Investigation that he couldn't stand to live any longer in the squalor low wages had forced upon him and his family. His house had no sanitary facilities and had "cracks in the walls so large that a cat could be thrown through them."[29] Floyd Topps, a black wage worker, left the farm of P. M. Barton because he "could not make a living at $1.00 a day for the poor kids."[30] Similarly, Charlie Rogers, a 21-year-old wage worker, took to the roadsides with his wife and daughter because he could not earn enough. "I could have stayed there," he explained, "but I might as well be here or in the graveyard."[31] These men believed profoundly in their duty to provide for their households and agonized over their inability to do so. Another 15 percent of those interviewed explained that they were protesting out of solidarity with friends, kin, and neighbors who had been recently evicted.[32] At Lilbourn, thirty day-laboring families, including the Topps and Rogers families, were among the over 170 people who walked off P. M. Barton's sprawling cotton plantation near Catron.[33] Many of these decided to join the protest during the small meetings organizers had held throughout the region on January 8. Henry MacAdory, 74, joined his kin because he had little left to lose.[34] Over 100 people had attended the January 8 meeting in New Madrid, demonstrator Booker T. Clark later recalled, many of whom "weren't even members of the union." "When they saw others moving," he explained, "they moved too."[35]

The power of these social relationships derived, in part, from their roots in the long process of rural community formation in the Bootheel. Contrary to accusations by area planters that the demonstrators came from out of state, the vast majority of those interviewed by the NYA officials—over 78 percent— had lived in southeast Missouri since before 1934, many since the early 1920s. After migrating to the area in 1923, Peter Wilderness had sharecropped near Marston in close proximity to his parents, brothers, and sisters. His eviction in 1939 threatened to destroy this social world. In some camps, three generations of kin protested together. Fathers and sons such as Henry and Ike Tripp and John and Spencer Nesbitt and their wives joined one another on the roadsides. These social connections extended beyond family. The Tripps, who had farmed near Essex and Morehouse since the 1920s, joined many of their recent and past neighbors in the protest. For example, the Tripps and 23-year-old Tommie Clark had sharecropped together on a farm outside Essex in 1934–1935.[36] Likewise, 64-year-old B. L. Randolph and 30-year-old Wilderness had been neighbors near Marston since 1923; now, in 1939, they camped together at Lilbourn. The pull of past connections was strong. H. P. Miller and his wife elected to join their former neighbors from Essex and Morehouse at the Matthews camp instead of protesting at Lilbourn, which was much closer to the land they had farmed in Portageville in 1938.[37]

Prior shared activism reinforced these social relationships. Old ties ran though the camps, particularly at Lilbourn, which brought together former NAACP members from Portageville, Parma, and Marston. Wilderness, Richardson, and Clark had all belonged to the Rising Sun chapter that Randolph had helped found in 1936.[38] In the same way, the camps near Charleston and Sikeston brought together members from the spillway locals, many of whom

Figure 5. Many entire families joined the protest. Source: Farm Security Administration—Office of War Information Photograph Collection, LC-USF33-002924-M2, Library of Congress. Photograph by Arthur Rothstein.

shared several layers of past experience. Will Jones, leader of the Sikeston camp, had been a local officer in the UNIA division at Wyatt and the first president of the STFU local on Thad Snow's farm.

The demonstrators relied on the support of community members who were not on the roadsides. Tenants with trucks or other large vehicles moved the demonstrators to the roadsides that first morning swiftly and quietly. Once on the road, the campers kept in constant contact with their home communities, who sent firewood and food. Willie Scott, known among the Lilbourn protestors as the "writing woman," used her literacy to pass messages and keep campers abreast of news. Other union women, such as Queen Esther Nelson, coordinated information networks with people like Willie Scott in the camps. Many families, like Scott and her husband, sent their young children to stay with friends for the duration of the demonstration in order to ensure their safety and provide some peace of mind. The eighty-seven families who were interviewed by the NYA claimed 413 immediate family members, only 293 of whom were in the camps; the rest stayed with friends and kin elsewhere.[39] Tenants such as Julian who owned valuable tools and work animals also left them in the care of others.[40]

Certain of the righteousness of their cause, the protestors turned their roadside camps into makeshift revival meetings to both reinforce their moral critique and maintain morale. "Religious meetings were held about many campfires under the direction of preachers" or, in some cases, lay camp leaders, the *Post-Dispatch* reported. Whether led by an ordained or lay preacher, many whites "joined in the service and knelt with" African American activists. "The Lord will take care of you," Rev. S. J. Elliott, pastor of St. James AME church, told them. "He was able to deliver the children of Israel, to save Daniel in the lion's den and to rescue the three Hebrew boys from the fiery furnace. He will not forget you," he preached. After Elliott had finished, the demonstrators continued their worship, singing "On Jordan's Stormy Banks I Stand" and other hymns late into the night:

On Jordan's stormy banks I stand,
and cast a wishful eye
to Canaan's fair and happy land,
where my possessions lie.
I am bound for the promised land,
I am bound for the promised land.
Oh, who will come and go with me?
I am bound for the promised land.[41]

The multiracial and grassroots nature of this service recalled the Spirit-in-spired revivals of the early 1930s. The support of preachers from the AME church, long the bedrock of black communities, provided evidence of how the spiritual power of those revivals had reoriented leaders of long-standing and more mainstream institutions around the needs and demands of the rural poor. Those grassroots voices had become so loud by 1939 that many churches delivered aid to the camps in league, however uneasily, with local juke joints. Most of the provisions the protestors used had to be stolen from area landlords. To avoid police patrols, these supplies were delivered at night, a task organized by area "juke men," owners of black dancehalls and roadhouses; their employees undoubtedly expedited the theft of landlord property.[42] In addition, a juke joint near Charleston also provided shelter for young and elderly campers during the cold nights.[43]

From the morning of January 10 to the morning of January 14, the demonstrators controlled the roadsides. The support networks functioned perfectly. Women cooked food, preachers preached, and leaders maintained order within the camps. Away from the roadsides, community members cared for the demonstrators' children, nursed the sick, and collected needed supplies. Meanwhile, the protest attracted immediate federal attention and gained the sympathy of the Roosevelts. What is more, the demonstration caught local planters and state officials completely unaware. In St. Louis, Whitfield planned an ambitious nationwide speaking tour to raise money and support for the demonstrators. But local authorities did not take long to respond.

*   *   *

Local officials first tried to break the demonstration by cutting all outside aid to the camps. Planters insisted in public pronouncements that any relief, especially from the federal government, would only encourage the protestors and "result in having the Highways lined with people from Charleston to the Arkansas line."[44] In large part this pressure worked. The army refused to provide tents to the campers because the "CIO was involved."[45] In addition, General Means of the Missouri National Guard urged William Baxter of the Red Cross not to intervene. Baxter concurred; he knew that the protest was a "man-made disaster" that "hardly . . . fell within the scope of responsibility of the Red Cross."[46] The district officers of the Federal Surplus Commodities Corporation, a division of the Agricultural Adjustment Administration that distributed agricultural surplus to local relief agencies, refused to deliver supplies to the camps because the campers had not made personal applications at one of their offices.[47] Likewise, the Missouri State Welfare Organization refused to deliver aid directly to the camps.[48] To make matters worse, state and local police officials blockaded the camps. Believing the demonstration a product of outside agitators, the police detained STFU officials trying to reach the campers and escorted them back to Arkansas.[49] They slackened their cordon at night, however, perhaps to stoke fears of vigilante attack. Little did they realize that this tactic facilitated nightly deliveries from the juke men, which provided just enough food and fuel to sustain the protest.

That the blockades did little to break the demonstration prompted state officials to bring the machinery of state to bear on the tenacious campers. After touring the camps on January 13, Harry Parker, the state health commissioner, declared them a "menace to public health" because they lacked clean water and sanitary toilets. He instructed Colonel Casteel of the Highway Patrol to remove them at once before epidemic disease broke out in "a state-wide and national health menace." If Casteel could not find homes for the campers, he said, "the proper action would be" to place them "in concentration camps" where they could be immunized and vaccinated.[50] "I don't know where we would put them," Casteel told reporters, "but if they threaten public health they must be moved somewhere."[51]

Acting on Parker's orders, the state police arrived to dismantle the Lilbourn camp on the morning of January 14 using trucks donated by the Barton Gin Company.[52] Scott and Wilderness refused to leave. Unprepared for such obstinacy, the police left but warned that resistance would only invite a "massacre." Tired of hearing threats, demonstrator Henry MacAdory, a former military officer who had served during World War I, responded that the Lilbourn campers were "just like a tree planted by the water, and we will not be moved," quoting the traditional African-American spiritual that again showed the religious dimensions of the protest.[53] The police were not the only ones threatening the demonstrators; vigilante attacks were also a looming threat. Yet MacAdory was resolute. If the vigilantes decided to attack, he said, the camp would respond in kind. "There will be a few sharecroppers lying around here," MacAdory admitted, "but there will be some of the mob lying here too." That night he organized men armed with shotguns in a defensive perimeter around the camp and moved the women and children into nearby fields. No attack came and the camp held.[54] The Sikeston and Matthews camps also resisted dispersal. Altogether, more than 800 people defied Parker's order and remained on the roadsides that night. "They are stubborn and reluctant to make preparations to move," one highway patrolman remarked, "until we finally convince them there's no alternative."[55]

The next day the authorities deployed new methods of persuasion. When the Barton Gin Company trucks arrived at the Lilbourn camp the following morning, they were led by the New Madrid County sheriff, who was accompanied by twenty-five armed civilian "deputies," some of whom carried state-issued rifles fixed with bayonets. There were no state police present.[56] Claiming that the campers were armed, the sheriff forced the protestors across the road at gunpoint while his "deputies" destroyed their tents. Finding the campers' shotguns only enraged the "deputies," who turned their attention to body searches of the demonstrators. Demanding compliance, one of the sheriff's men clubbed a camper in the face with the butt of his pistol. The blow tore a deep gash down the man's face. The sheriff arrested another protestor. The presence of Herbert Little, an NYA representative, and two other unidentified federal investigators who were sympathetic to the demonstrators constrained the mob's rage somewhat. After forcing the campers into Barton's trucks, the sheriff announced that he was moving them to a tract of county land in the spillway. Barton and the other landlords, he said, had refused to take back such ungrateful workers. When Little asked if the county would provide for the campers at the new location, the sheriff replied that "no one would care for them."[57] The whole scene, Little said, was "a little bit like Harlan County," where the notorious violent conflict between Kentucky unionists and militias supported by mine owners had taken place.[58] Where the state had failed, local authorities and an armed mob had succeeded. The police demolished the remaining camps on January 15.[59] Demonstrators who left peacefully were distributed to area farms whose owners would take them, but without promising them work. These people were essentially back where they started before the demonstration began. The sheriff took demonstrators who refused to leave to new "concentration camps," as Parker called them, one at a black school near Charleston and the other in the spillway.[60]

The New Madrid spillway camp was the largest of the detention centers.[61] On the afternoon of January 15, the sheriff and his men unloaded the remaining residents of the Lilbourn, Sikeston, and Matthews camps, over 500 people, onto a swampy piece of county land that provided no better health safeguards than the roadsides did.[62] But it was out of view and under the sheriff's control. "They took us eighteen miles back in the woods on the New Madrid Spillway," Clark recalled, "and dumped us. We didn't have nothing."[63] To maintain control, the sheriff ordered local officers and "deputies" to guard the camp around the clock to keep visitors out and campers in. Despite the presence of white families among the group, the guards refused to allow the demonstrators to fetch drinking water from a nearby white school; he thus forced them to drink muddy water from drainage ditches.[64]

Figure 6. Demonstrators being removed from the Lilbourn camp, January 15, 1939. Source: Farm Security Administration—Office of War Information Collection, LC-USF33-002975-M2, Library of Congress. Photograph by Arthur Rothstein.

Renaming their new camp "Homeless Junction," the demonstrators rebuilt their battered shelters of blankets, quilts, and wood scraps.[65] They had enough food to last a few days, despite the obstruction of relief. Horrified by the removal, President Roosevelt ordered the local Federal Surplus Commodities Corporation depots to immediately make all food supplies available to the campers.[66] In addition, the FSA, at Roosevelt's urging, announced that it would deliver tents to the camp and begin issuing emergency cash grants to the demonstrators and processing them for relocation loans.[67] The weakened but unbeaten demonstrators seemed poised to fight on, aided by the president of the United States.

Local authorities, however, were not about to let the federal government sustain the demonstrators. On January 18, after learning of the FSA's plan to deliver tents and money, local police tore down the spillway camp.[68] This time they scattered the demonstrators on farms throughout four counties, sometimes many miles away from their home communities. Authorities sent some into the black districts of area towns and dumped others on back roads to fend for themselves. Local officials hoped to prevent the FSA or any aid agency from finding them again.[69] Dispersal broke apart the internal organization the demonstrators had built, separating them from one another and their leaders. Hidden from the federal government without food or fuel, with no central leadership and with publicity waning, their dogged stand neared collapse.

Yet hundreds of campers re-formed in small groups and established new camps on community spaces. The largest was at the Sweet Home Baptist Church, a black congregation located between Charleston and Wyatt. The state police had placed a group of recalcitrant Homeless Junction campers led by Walter Johnson and Will Jones there. Word of the refuge attracted others. By the end of January, thirty-three black families were living at Sweet Home, most of them from the spillway communities. Many knew one another well. One-third, including Johnson, had been evicted together from land owned by O. Reeves near Deventer. Others had been neighbors around Wyatt and Charleston.[70] Demonstrators also re-formed camps on the Mississippi River levee at Dorena, in Charleston at Bethlehem Church and at Baby Red's juke joint, in a large shack near Hayti, and at scattered farmhouses near New Madrid, Matthews, and Morley. After Sweet Home, the Bethlehem and Dorena camps were the largest, with sixty-one blacks and twenty-eight whites, respectively, while the others consisted of from three to five families.[71] Food and shelter at these places proved barely adequate, however. Campers at Baby Red's lived in stalls without windows or proper ventilation, and all of the camps lacked sufficient toilet facilities.[72] "Our people are suffering," Whitfield told NAACP lawyer Thurgood Marshall, "but they are determined to stand."[73]

Having reached the limit of community support, the demonstrators looked increasingly to the STFU and CIO for help. Local union leaders organized the remaining groups into "demonstration committees," not unlike during the spillway crisis, and through them tried to restore order to what was now a shattered protest. To begin, the committees issued public statements that reiterated their commitment to a future for agrarian producers. "We ain't goin back," Walter Johnson told a journalist, "not until we can make a real living, raise cows, hogs, and corn. Not until we can improve ourselves."[74] Some committees established direct communication with the STFU office. Willie Scott held a meeting in New Madrid with the unionists she could find and instructed them to wait for further word from the STFU in Memphis.[75]

What the committees wanted to hear from the union was how to get food, shelter, and medicine after two brutal weeks spent out of doors in January. The meetings the demonstrators held in small groups and in relative isolation, however, gave rise to unrealistic expectations about what the union should or could provide. Out of both desperation and hope, committees fostered beliefs that the STFU or CIO would provide food or even homes and land.

These beliefs were no doubt influenced by word that Whitfield was busy gathering support from people around the country. Recently mobilized union members around Lilbourn and Matthews were especially likely to express requests based on such beliefs. Daniel McClenton, a member of Scott's committee, reported that campers were asking him daily what they must to do secure the "food and cole" the STFU had gathered. They also asked "When will you have a place set up for us to move?" Their camp was growing daily, he reported, and "we need tents and something if its not possible the houses will not be ready for us to move in."[76] Alonzo Julian requested that the STFU help him meet his FSA loan payments, otherwise he feared losing the tools, livestock, and seed he had accumulated since 1936. He also wanted the union to find him forty acres of land to rent, preferably with a stand of corn.[77]

Others contended that the STFU and the CIO were obligated to help in return for their sacrifice on the roads. An unknown supplicant from Charleston who had "lost every thing . . . out on the highway" wanted the STFU to send food for his starving family.[78] Ike Tripp requested that the STFU "help us with some aid . . . till we can get holder to some thing that we can make a earness living for our family." Holed up near Matthews with his father, Tommie Clark, and five other families, Tripp spoke for the group when he said, "We aint trying to hurt no one we just want some thing for our work. . . . The law put us out here and we cant get no aid from no where." "We don't want no day work," he concluded, "we want some where to farm where we wont hafter move every year."[79] Still others simply wanted union reinforcements. R. A. McAdory of the STFU's local in Matthews demanded that the union send "tents, provision, and a camping place" because the planters were "planning to oppress my people."[80] Such high hopes undoubtedly helped the campers sustain morale and hold their small groups together. But such hopes also set them up for later disillusion.

Both the STFU and the CIO launched relief operations soon after the protest began, but state repression and logistical difficulties plagued those efforts. Initially, union leaders lobbied the federal government to provide tents and surplus commodities to the demonstrators. Although the FSA failed to supply tents, it did issue checks for emergency grants. In addition, both the STFU and the CIO's Industrial Union Council in St. Louis, with Whitfield's help, organized relief committees that attracted large donations of money, food, and clothing from sympathizers. The STFU originally planned to distribute its supplies from Sikeston, but because of police pressure it opened its relief operations in Blytheville, Arkansas, nearly ninety miles from the furthest demonstration site in Charleston, on January 20. Blockades hampered these deliveries. The STFU could distribute supplies only if the demonstrators themselves made trips to Blytheville. As a result, almost all of the material collected by the STFU, including all of the clothing, went to people in the southern counties, which were closer to Blytheville.[81] The distribution of CIO aid was similarly limited. Spearheaded by the Committee for the Rehabilitation of the Sharecroppers (CRS), a St. Louis–based relief group Whitfield, former Alabama communist Al Murphy, and author Fannie Cook had organized, the CIO relief operation reached only as far south as Sikeston and Charleston because of police obstruction.[82]

Local authorities wanted to stop all outside help. In early February, the Mississippi County Citizens' Committee lodged a formal complaint in the House of Representatives through a local congressman to challenge the amount of FSA aid being given to area tenants. They charged that 17,500 people out of 20,000 in the county received some sort of government money and that 2,000 sharecroppers received "outright gifts of money" from the FSA, a situation that Citizens' Committee members felt threatened to destroy the work ethic and cause a "first-class race riot."[83] Under heavy pressure from an increasingly hostile Congress in which conservative southern Democrats were stepping up their attacks on the perceived use of relief money for political purposes, the FSA stopped its grant payments in the Bootheel on February 8 pending an investigation to certify that all recipients "deserved" the money.[84] With its funds and mandate controlled by the planter-friendly U.S. Department of Agriculture, the FSA ceded this particular battle in order to protect the agency's larger goals.[85] To make matters worse, ten inches of snow fell in the Bootheel that day, the largest snowfall in twenty-two years.[86]

The Citizens' Committee's offensive had a direct and harmful effect on the protestors. Savannah Warr, a union veteran from the spillway, reported that "the landlords were working hard to get the grant checks stopped." She asked the STFU on behalf of her members to help preserve this vital source of income because "we are real in need for them."[87] Harlan McField begged the STFU to help the campers at Bethlehem Church by supplying tents. "We are suffer," he explained, "it is seven in my family and we just been able to get one little flour since we been out here."[88] They needed the union to do more than distribute aid from Blytheville. Charleston leader Houston Turner captured the growing frustration when he admitted that "the temporary relief in Blytheville is good," but "most of our members have no way to get to Blytheville."[89] Fischer reported to the CRS that the campers at Dorena faced "a crisis because of lack of food, most of the Government aid having ceased."[90] These conditions pushed the southern camps even closer to the wall. Peter

Wilderness admitted to STFU president J. R. Butler that his fellow campers near Marston "were having a hard time for something to eat they is stop the relief and our F.S.A. check and we can't get nothing to eat." He hoped the union could help because his people "want to no what we is goin to do for some to eat." Confident that the STFU "is one hundred per cent with us," however, he reported they were "still encourage to go to the end."[91]

At the depth of this crisis, Rev. Whitfield reappeared to reassure the demonstrators. In two letters to the Missouri locals written in early February, he praised "our people who stood up like men and women in the face of mean men." "You have fought the biggest fight you ever fought in your life," Whitfield exclaimed, "and you have won." He knew that the authorities had tried "to starve you to death" and to "make you lose faith in me and the union." He promised them that neither he nor the union would fail. Whitfield said that in his travels to St. Louis, Chicago, New York, Boston, and Washington, he had found people committed "to help the Southern Tenant Farmers' Union fight to get land and homes for all of the union people," and he advised them "to get busy and build our frontline trenches and continue our fight for freedom from wage slavery." He urged the protestors to press forward and demand that their local congressmen restart the FSA programs, assuring the campers that "we are going to win."[92]

Encouraged by Whitfield's promises, the demonstrators believed that the STFU was coming to their aid, though their desperation was outpacing their patience. In Dollie Wherry's efforts to secure supplies for her Essex members, she reassured the STFU that "we are going to stand by you" as long as you "stand by us."[93] However, the strain of hunger was undoing this loyalty. Exasperated, Wilderness asked "[Is there] nothing else can the union do for us?" His local had beseeched its congressmen to ask the FSA to resume its grants program without success. "We do believe that the union people is duing all they can for us," he said, but "the people here sure do need help here now."[94] A week later, the STFU declared that the crisis stage of the demonstration was over and closed its relief center in Blytheville, which by this point was receiving few donations. STFU leaders H. L. Mitchell and J. R. Butler wanted to put the protest behind them in order to focus on the upcoming National Sharecropper's Week, the union's main fund-raising event. This poorly timed move infuriated the demonstrators.[95]

At this critical hour, UCAPAWA leaders launched long-simmering plans to expel the STFU leadership while retaining its members. Tension that stemmed mainly from political differences had plagued the alliance since it was forged. Although it was largely unrelated to this ongoing dispute, the roadside demonstration had provided an excellent field for battle. In light of perceptions that the STFU had failed the demonstrating farmers, UCAPAWA head Donald Henderson accused Mitchell and Butler of malfeasance, incompetence, and deceit. He emphasized the inability of the Memphis office to get relief to the northern camps and accused the STFU of obstructing CIO efforts to provide relief supplies to demonstrators in the southern counties.[96] In the face of these charges, the STFU leaders did not acquit themselves well. In response to Houston Turner's complaints about the distance from Charleston to Blytheville, Mitchell angrily responded that "the Union has done and is doing all it can for you people in Missouri." If there was a problem with distribution, he added, it was due to local failures.[97] If all the STFU could manage was little more than nothing, Turner must have thought, what was the use? Henderson wasted no time exploiting this dissatisfaction. On February 23, he notified all of the Missouri locals that the UCAPAWA had decided to expel the STFU for violating the provisions concerning dues in the union constitution. Henderson instructed members that they would have to decide in an upcoming convention in St. Louis whether they would stay with the CIO or "stand alone with the STFU."[98]

\* \* \*

The decisions of local STFU members would not be so clear-cut. Some had joined the STFU in the pre-CIO days; others had joined because of the power of the CIO. Some of the demonstrators had received their aid from the STFU; others from the UCAPAWA. With the demonstration still ongoing, people starving, and planting season approaching, this fight must have been difficult for demonstrators to comprehend. Local activists did seem sure of one thing, however—that their allies had not done well. Rev. Whitfield, in particular, came in for heavy criticism. With his unfulfilled assurances that help would come from the STFU still fresh in their minds, many unionists told him "to go to hell."[99] Stunned, Whitfield fell in with the UCAPAWA assault. He assured the demonstrators that they had not received the aid "that I have worked and are still working so hard to get for you" because the STFU had botched the job. He now announced that he would leave the STFU and asked for their support at the upcoming referendum. Whitfield urged members to "go on with the great labor movement in America and continue to fight for the blessings of life and the higher standards of living." The CIO was the union for this fight, not the STFU. "Are you with me," he asked, "or are you against me?"[100] The spirit of righteous fellowship and witness that had reigned in the early days of the protest was now in little evidence, and the moral community that had inspired it was now facing dissolution.

The convention turned out to be a one-sided UCAPAWA affair. Twenty-one locals sent representatives and all voted to remain in the CIO alliance. At least five locals stayed with the STFU and did not bother to vote. Whitfield reorganized those that remained in the UCAPAWA into a subsidiary union, the Missouri Agricultural Workers' Council (MAWC). The new union elected William Fischer as president and Owen Whitfield as secretary.[101] The new union was diverse. In addition to the all-black spillway locals, Fischer's white colleagues from Dorena joined. T. J. North, from near Charleston, reported that "50% of the people in his district were affiliated with his Union" and "that no one any longer belonged in the STFU."[102] Much of this loyalty stemmed from the drawing power of the CIO. Johnnie Moore, who had been a part of the Rising Sun NAACP chapter, informed the STFU that his Matthews local would remain with the CIO because "all of our members wants to be thoroughly identified with the big democratic labor movement." "We found a welcome door open," he explained, "and we have entered in it."[103]

For some, the welcome was less certain; Good Hope Local 385 split in two. Willie Scott remained fiercely loyal to the STFU. Scott, who had been living in New Madrid since her days at Homeless Junction, reestablished contact with many members of her local. "My local are doing fine but they are scatter so bad," she reported. "I walk 7 miles" a day, she said, "trying to plead with the people to stick by the S.T.F.U." She distributed STFU food and clothing to those she found and assured STFU leaders that they could "bet on 35 in the state of mo being STFU" because "the STFU only one done any thing for us."[104]

Peter Wilderness, the other leader of Lilbourn camp and former president of Local 385, joined the MAWC. After his time at Homeless Junction, like Scott, he went back to his Marston community and tried to relocate union members in order to coordinate further action and secure relief. Wilderness and his homeless family found refuge with Dave Richards, an old friend from the NAACP. From Richards's home, Wilderness was able to locate other Marston demonstrators, including the Julians, his former neighbors. B. L. Randolph and James Monroe, both fellow NAACP friends and Lilbourn campers, helped him link up with other committed demonstrators in the various camps, including Minnie Washington in Portageville.[105] Their ties were both political and personal. As Johnnie Moore had suggested, the NAACP connection was crucial since the activists in the Rising Sun chapter had joined the STFU as a means to access the resources of the CIO. They were also friends, neighbors, and kin. When the STFU failed in the eyes of a few, as it had for Julian and Wilderness, it failed among them all.[106]

Widespread anger at the STFU galvanized support for the MAWC. Whitfield kept these wounds open. He blasted the STFU policy of making demonstrators "come way to Blytheville and pay our own gas and oil money to get a little relief." He accused the union of using its relief center to secure support for itself rather than "for relief of those that really needed it."[107] It was not hard to convince those at Sweet Home, Bethlehem, and Matthews of these failures. CRS member Fannie Cook wrote to Eleanor Roosevelt that the people in these camps "turned against the STFU because they felt the STFU did not stand by them with courage or loyalty during the January 1939 demonstration and because in general they had lost confidence in the STFU leadership."[108] Johnson, leader of the Sweet Home camp, "remembered bitterly his personal experiences in trying to get supplies all the way from Blytheville last winter."[109] Wilderness, the Julians, and Moore had all begged the union for food, money, and protection but had received very little from it. The image of weakness doomed the STFU.

The activists who joined the MAWC were eager to continue their protest. In late March, the new union organized a petition to state and federal officials reminding them that their demands were unsatisfied.[110] Without federal help, the MAWC warned, a humanitarian crisis loomed. Many of those forcibly scattered to area farms, they said, had been given death threats; others cramped in crowded tents and churches struggled to survive. They had all been left to "get out and scout for ourselves or starve to death."[111] Citing a preliminary FBI report that described the roadside demonstration as a locally planned response to what the Department of Justice called "economic slavery," the petitioners demanded that the government "do whatever is in your power to furnish some tents for us and enough land to form a camp of us so that we will be free from this brutality."[112] Although a number of women signed, the MAWC petition adhered to the rhetoric of agrarian manhood; it called for food relief or WPA work so that the protestors might "feed our wives and children until something can be worked out for us, the homeless people." Despite the chaos of the preceding months, their goals remained clear and coherent. They sought federal help to preserve the core elements of the agrarian producerist ideal that shaped their world: the ability of men to work hard for fair reward, care for their families, and function as full citizens. It was the duty of work at the heart of that cosmology, the petitioners argued, that made these legitimate rights, not privileges. "We feel that we are entitled to this," they explained, "since we want to work and since we are Americans and since we helped to make America what it is today."[113]

Although infighting had obscured the religious imperative guiding the movement, activists were looking for ways to refresh their moral critique. In a letter to the MAWC, Whitfield urged the protestors to remember that theirs was a "movement to free themselves and their wives and children from wage slavery and get some of the things that God prepared for us." It had been a trying year, he acknowledged, but said it was time to "be up and about our Father's business." By any account the STFU-UCAPAWA affair had not been godly. "Let's fight on," Whitfield concluded, so we will go "to the grave as men and women, mothers and fathers, husbands and wives, white and black—that have done their duty."[114] No longer content with a cessation of evictions and tenancy agreements that were more secure, Whitfield now called on his supporters to demand the outright "abolishment of sharecropping and tenancy" and government guarantees of the "INDIVIDUAL ownership of land" in cooperative frameworks like that at La Forge. This sharpened goal marked a full rejection of proposals by the STFU and communists such as Henderson for the collective ownership of land and equipment. Although it was in many ways an impossible aim, the MAWC's new demand retrenched the movement in the bedrock of agrarian ambition.[115]

*   *   *

The miserable condition of the remaining protestors belied Whitfield's optimism for making evicted tenants into landowners. After visiting the camps in April, Fannie Cook described it as "an experience that makes Dante's *Inferno* an understatement."[116] She found starving, sick people living in squalid conditions with no toilets, privacy, or clean water. As many as eight people lived in one room. Even in such conditions, the campers at Sweet Home had stood strong for three months behind the leadership of Walter Johnson. "We ain't goin to make a crop until this here is settled," they informed anyone who asked. Their defiance was rooted in the belief that the church was theirs. That confidence crumbled when area planter J. D. Byrne produced title to the building and surrounding land. He initiated eviction proceedings against the "squatters" in county court and sued them for back rent for good measure.[117]

Convinced by Cook that something had to be done, the CRS solicited donations for the purchase of land to resettle the remaining demonstrators. Two days after the Mississippi County Court delivered its verdict against the Sweet Home campers, Whitfield announced that they would move to a 90-

acre tract of land purchased with these funds. Located in the Ozark foothills of Butler County, the sixty-five wooded and twenty-five cleared acres "will be used as a temporary relief station for other homeless families" as well as the Sweet Home campers, Whitfield said.[118] He invited to the camp "all of those that are huddled in those dirty Camps such as Churches, old dance halls, or any place where you are not wanted and cant have peace" and those in "old waste houses where you were put against your will and are being mistreated."[119] Crucially, only the members of the MAWC received his notice; loyalty to the UCAPAWA now defined the protest. By the end of the summer, eighty black and fifteen white families had moved to the settlement, which they dubbed Cropperville. They elected Walter Johnson as the camp leader, although the white settlers still followed William Fischer, who had prestige as the MAWC president. To simplify matters, the white group established camp a little removed from their African American colleagues. Segregated living arrangements lessened friction within the camp and with the whites of Butler County; Johnson and Fischer could lead their followers without igniting racial anxieties.[120] Other union leaders, including Will Jones, Harlan McField, Dave Nixon, and Alfred Williams, some of whom were veterans of the spillway, were among the first settlers.[121]

Now with a measure of security, the Cropperville unionists issued new petitions that reiterated their demands for an agrarian New Deal. "We as American born citizen do hereby call upon this Great Government and its great people for help in such ways that we can secure shelter and food," they declared. "We also ask for some kind of W.P.A. work that may be established in this neighborhood so that we can secure the *things* which we desire," the petitioners continued.[122] They had not received a warm welcome from the small farmers nearby, and the local sheriff had expressed reluctance to defend them. They wanted protection. "We have been herded about like so many animals in the last 15 days," they said, but finally had land that was theirs. "It is the only spot of ground we have on God's earth, and here we have taken our last stand," the petitioners threatened, "and if we are not given some protection we will be forced to fight back for self preservation." In a last appeal to President Roosevelt, rooted firmly in the belief that hard work deserved justice, they reasoned that "surely this administration will help a people who are struggling to help themselves."[123]

This renewal of agrarian goals lent momentum to MAWC organizing efforts. By the summer the union claimed over 4,000 members in twenty-nine locals.[124] Most of the veteran activists lived at Cropperville, so these locals relied on four key leaders: Johnnie Moore in Hayti, E. L. Hughes in Morley, and Peter Wilderness and Booker Clark in Marston. "All of us want FSA Co-operative farms," Wilderness and Clark reported, "and as soon as we build our membership somewhat larger we are going to have FSA Cooperative farms here in South east Missouri," like the one at La Forge. Their members resolved "to make our own living for our families" and "we mean to fight for our rights until Hell freezes over."[125] Although pulled by sectarian union allegiances, activists continued to draw on the religious and civic ideals at the core of their agrarian cosmology; their intertwined notions of independence and righteousness remained strong. An enthusiastic recruit to Hayti Local 609 gushed, "Thanks be to God, the new day is dawning and the yoke of bondage has broken and the prisoners set free!"[126] Similarly, in a rhetorical flourish akin to powerful preaching, the Marston leaders declared in a letter to the *UCAPAWA News* that the "UCAPAWA has brought a new day for the Negro and poor white sharecropper in the cotton belt. . . . The sun has risen and the light is shimmering everywhere. Now we have waked up and we no longer sleep."[127] These ideas proved compelling beyond the confines of the Bootheel. Jesse Burton, secretary of UCAPAWA Local 285 in Alabama, echoed this sentiment almost word for word in his own contribution to the next issue, writing that "UCAPAWA has brought a new day for us. A new light is shining and we are all waking up and will sleep no more."[128]

Meanwhile, the STFU regained some strength in the southern Bootheel counties during the spring and summer. W. M. Buck, a new white organizer, raised fifteen new locals in Dunklin, New Madrid, and Pemiscot counties to go along with the five that remained after the split with the CIO.[129] Organizer J. F. Hynds reported that "all I hear around Wardell and community is the union."[130] The organizing base seemed solid. The locals at Portageville, Kennett, and Wardell had both black and white members. Former members Scottie Spears and Rev. R. H. Bradford, who had initially gone with the MAWC, rejoined; Bradford himself admitted that this "might come as a surprise."[131] Moreover, members were managing to pay their dues. In August, the Missouri locals raised more dues money than those in Oklahoma and Arkansas combined.[132]

Old problems died hard, however. That fall, STFU activists in the Bootheel pushed for a picking strike. The union's national leadership worried that fresh conflict after the year's upheavals might wreck their recovery and refused to sanction it. The decision to avoid trouble disappointed local activists and led some to abandon the STFU again.[133] Meanwhile, deteriorating living conditions at Cropperville hindered the work of the MAWC. Arriving late in the planting season, the settlers had not grown sufficient food on Cropperville's rocky, wooded hillsides. They had received surplus commodities from state relief officials and FSA grant checks, but these were running out.[134] In September, UCAPAWA representative John Day held an emergency meeting; "member after member took the floor and testified to their belief that the union was the one thing that could help them overcome their present slavery." "We are hungry," they said and "there ain't been one full meal at the camp since we have been out here." What they wanted to know, Day reported, was whether or not "there any way this union or the people outside who are friends can help us until we get . . . something to help ourselves."[135] Most troubling for all, however, was the news that planters had started issuing eviction notices for January 1940.[136] Early estimates predicted that 500 more tenant families people would be displaced. The demonstration had done little to alter the trend toward mechanization and if anything had only steeled the resolve of planters to forge ahead with plans to replace tenants with wage laborers.[137]

*  *  *

After months of pressure by the STFU and the UCAPAWA, the FSA announced in mid-December a new "five-point" plan to address the crisis of landless farmers in the Bootheel; it consisted mainly of programs to increase affordable loans and emergency grants. The FSA's most radical proposal was for two rehabilitation housing schemes. The first, a scattered home project, would build individual houses for rural wage workers on small tracts of land leased by the government from landlords, where families could raise gardens and livestock.[138] The second was modeled on a STFU plan in which the FSA would construct collective "labor camps" to house 200–300 wage workers near area farms.[139] The FSA plan offered nothing to prevent further evictions and it would not provide for individual farms. Governor Stark endorsed the FSA proposal in the hope of avoiding a repeat demonstration in response to the new eviction crisis.[140] In order to negotiate an orderly resolution, he convened a conference in St. Louis in early January with representatives from the FSA, the U.S. Department of Agriculture, and the Missouri Employment Service; two Bootheel planters; and Rev. Whitfield.[141]

On the morning of January 7, the second day of the conference, motorists driving along Highways 60 and 61 in the Bootheel encountered large, clearly worded signs where landless families had camped to protest their evictions a year earlier. "Lest You Forget," the signs read, "One Year Ago, sat on this roadside, 1,500 croppers shelterless for days in snow and freezing cold." Since then, the message continued, little had changed, except "the abuses remain and grow." Simultaneously, residents of towns and villages throughout the Bootheel awoke to find their main streets blanketed with handbills, all bearing the name of the MAWC. "Is it right to give double payment to the planter who kicks his croppers out? Is that the New Deal?" the pamphlets asked. "We croppers call it a Raw Deal and it makes us desperate." Unless the government took action, the MAWC warned, protest would erupt again.[142] The well-organized and costly display not only made clear the MAWC's dogged commitment to fight but also reflected the continuing financial support of the CIO.

The symbolic protest lent new urgency to the FSA's plans. The following day, Governor Stark, backed by all the delegates, called on landlords to postpone evictions until February 1 so that the Missouri Employment Service could establish a register of families that needed work and try to match them with planters who needed workers. In addition, the delegates requested that the FSA redraft plans for a more expansive program in the Bootheel. Whitfield reported that the MAWC would postpone further protests pending the implementation of the conference's recommendations. Members who attended this conference planned to meet again in a month's time to review the revised FSA scheme.[143] While attending the UCAPAWA convention in Washington later that month, Moore, Fischer, Hughes, and Whitfield delivered a petition to the White House signed by 20,000 CIO-affiliated workers that protested impending evictions across the South and demanded new federal programs to aid landless farmers. Eleanor Roosevelt met with the contingent and was sympathetic to the struggle of landless farmers, Whitfield told the press.[144]

In Jefferson City in early February, the FSA announced a new, more generous program. In addition to loans, grants, and the homes for laborers, the plan would finance small cooperative associations, provide new funds for rehabilitation loans to small landowners, and, most important, provide group homes that would be built in eight communities on government-owned land and leased to displaced farming families. In addition, Stark announced that landlords would again postpone planned evictions until March 1.[145] Implementation began immediately. The scale of the crisis had not been exaggerated. A Missouri Employment Service survey found 925 families with no tenure arrangements for 1940, all of which the FSA registered for relief. Soon after, the FSA chartered two associations for leasing and purchasing land: 2650-acre Portage Farms in Pemiscot County and 2055-acre Independence Farms in Dunklin County.[146] These associations enabled members to rent between forty and eighty acres on reasonable terms for a period of five years, during which time they could raise food and cash crops and participate in cooperative ventures. By early March, the FSA had dispersed an additional 568 labor rehabilitation grants and loans to displaced Bootheel farmers through its Scattered Workers' Homes Project, which also promoted subsistence food production.[147]

This influx of federal support culminated in June when the FSA unveiled plans for Delmo Security Homes. Initially, the plan called for the construction of 502 homes in eight settlements across the Bootheel for the neediest displaced families. Small plots of land accompanied each home and the settlements included community washing, toilet, and meeting facilities. "The Delmo Homes are located in the heart of the cotton area," the FSA explained, "where the residents can obtain cash income for cotton chopping and cotton picking, to supplement home products produced on their tracts" in exchange for a small monthly rent.[148] Construction began immediately. Although Delmo resembled La Forge, it did not provide clients with their own farms; it was to be a settlement for wage workers. Even though the FSA had abandoned plans to create family-owned farms, its programs marked a significant victory for activists in the Bootheel. However, the new programs also marked the fading of hopes of landless farmers that they could someday be landowners.

Bootheel unionism staggered through the end of 1940. The STFU reeled in Missouri after the FSA announced its new programs. By March only ten locals were paying dues, half as many as the previous fall.[149] But the MAWC was also struggling. Although Cropperville hosted an open-air meeting of 2,500 farmers in June, activists spoke more about the desperate need to find more dues-paying members than about recent successes.[150] When Rev. Whitfield left in August to organize for the UCAPAWA in Memphis, Cropperville fell apart. William Fischer, still president of the MAWC, tried to wrest control of the camp from Walter Johnson, whom he accused of favoring the original Sweet Home settlers. When Fischer failed, he tried to organize a second local at Cropperville. A few people joined and followed the Fischers, by now the only remaining white family, to a rival camp on a nearby hill. Distraught over the infighting, Johnson resigned as camp leader in November and left the settlement. The main group elected Will Jones, the ex-Garveyite from Wyatt, to replace him.[151] Johnnie Moore, E. L. Hughes, and Peter Wilderness continued to work through their locals, but they were uneasy. Wilderness urged workers to fight low picking wages that autumn and lamented "seeing the poor class people suffering so much"—to the point that he could not "rest in my bed at night." He exhorted his fellow unionists to pull together to "organize the unorganized." "Let us," he concluded, again "sing 'I shall not be moved,'" like they had in the roadside camp near Lilbourn.[152] Wilderness bemoaned the loss of solidarity as well as fellowship based on a righteous cause. Although Whitfield and others worked to maintain the spirit of rebellion, any sense of community based on shared moral principles was now hard to find.

* * *

Yet in early 1941 it seemed that the New Deal programs that Bootheel activists had won on the roadsides would become the keystone of a new federal program to reduce rural southern poverty. In January, the FSA finished building the Delmo Security Homes. Delmo, as it was soon known, provided 539 single-family homes for landless farmers in eight separate settlements, at least one in every Bootheel county. Initially the FSA allocated five communities solely for whites: fifty homes near Gray Ridge in Stoddard County, fifty near Kennett in Dunklin County, sixty near Morehouse and fifty south of Lilbourn in New Madrid County, and seventy near East Prairie in Mississippi County. The FSA also planned two black communities: eighty homes south of Wardell in Pemiscot County and sixty north of Lilbourn. The Delmo project at Wyatt was technically integrated, although a drainage ditch divided its eighty white and thirty-nine black families.[153] Because of the poverty and casual employment of its clients, the FSA charged each family a low monthly rent of $3. Clients of working age were also required to provide four hours of community labor on the project. In addition, the FSA had constructed an additional 337 houses through its Scattered Workers' Homes Project.[154] More than just the fate of these families rested on Delmo's gleaming white cottages. "If group labor projects in this district are successful," FSA regional director P. G. Beck observed, "the program will be extended throughout the South."[155]

With so many programs now running in the Bootheel, the FSA added an experimental program to provide comprehensive medical insurance for clients in the area. Unveiled in late 1941, the Southeast Missouri Health Service was open to all 4,418 FSA client families. Designed to provide people with affordable access to routine and emergency medical care, the service required each participating family to contribute 6 percent of its monthly earnings toward the program's general fund. Upon visiting any of the sixty physicians or nine hospitals that initially joined the service as professional partners, members would pay only a small portion of their medical bill while the service's general fund would cover the remainder, including prescription medication.[156] Although the plan was not designed to become fully operational until 1943, over 1,220 families signed up early.[157] The plans had potentially far-reaching implications. The FSA now considered the Bootheel a "laboratory for the Cotton South" where it could refine housing and health programs before expanding them over a much larger area.[158]

As a focal point for progressive policy, Delmo attracted powerful enemies, none more determined than Democratic congressman Orville Zimmerman, a Dunklin County native and the Bootheel planters' man in the House of Representatives. Zimmerman had been wound tight since the roadside demonstration, which he called "a diabolical effort of a certain group" from St. Louis and elsewhere to "create an embarrassing situation." This subversive "crusade," he claimed, had drawn "reporters in there from all over the United States," many of whom "wrote some of the darnedest stories that were ever printed." To him the demonstration was "a perversion of the real situation in southeast Missouri."[159] Delmo, the main achievement of the protest, threatened to stand as a lasting reminder of that embarrassment. In February, Zimmerman launched a campaign to have the Wardell Delmo Homes reallocated for white families. Armed with protest letters and petitions from his white constituents, Zimmerman argued that Wardell was a predominately white area with a large number of worthy poor white farming families, all of whom opposed the construction of homes for blacks. Summarizing Zimmerman's position, the postmaster at Wardell demanded this change because "this is a white man's country, settled years ago by white people, cleared and drained by white people." Echoing a refrain that dated back to the 1910s, these campaigners stated defiantly that the Wardell section "will remain a white man's country."[160]

Johnnie Moore and his MAWC local in Pemiscot County rallied to defend their New Deal from Zimmerman's attack. By early 1941, Hayti local consisted solely of black farmers, and Zimmerman's plan targeted them directly. Delmo's racial apportionment was already skewed against black families and if the Wardell project went to whites, African Americans would be left with fewer than 100 homes in Delmo. "We, the Colored sharecroppers, tenant-farmers and farm day laborers, are making a strong protest to our Seat of Government, at Washington, D.C.," the group declared. They reminded New Deal officials that Bootheel farm workers had agreed to call off another planned roadside demonstration in exchange for the expanded FSA program that produced Delmo; most of those who had threatened that protest were black. "We have waited patiently," the petition continued, for "the better day to come when the Government would give us a place to stay, so that we could begin life all over again as decent citizens." They had been hit hard by demotion; the number of African American tenants in the county had fallen by 62 percent between 1935 and 1940.[161] Because "we have suffered most" and "we have suffered longest," the petitioners demanded their rightful place at Delmo.[162] "If this petition is ignored, we . . . shall depart from this County in [a] body on March 20, 1941," they said. Such a boycott would have deprived landlords of day laborers in the middle of spring planting. Other MAWC members declared that potential African-American Delmo clients elsewhere would refuse their placements with the FSA as long as "their brothers in Pemiscot County are denied the homes due them."[163]

Threatened on both sides, the FSA struck a compromise. To keep the MAWC from making a fiasco of the opening of Delmo, the FSA maintained its original plan for a black settlement south of Wardell. In order to placate Zimmerman, a dangerous congressional enemy, the FSA expanded its plan to include a white project north of Wardell. Delmo would now house over 600 families in nine communities. On March 6, Robert and Edna Wicker, white former sharecroppers, moved into their new home at the Wyatt project.[164] Robert Wicker, who had written to the STFU in 1936 expressing solidarity with the "disinherited sharecroppers," had finally found refuge with his family.[165] There were still thousands who had not, however. Although the MAWC called off its boycott, local activists did not relax their organizing efforts. The MAWC viewed Delmo as a temporary solution that would do little more than "give 500 families a better roof over their heads than they now have." "You can's [sic] eat them houses," one woman remarked at Cropperville during a meeting to discuss the projects. "I want to know how we can keep our stomachs fed" without the land to make a farm, she said.[166]

Her question marked a growing recognition among landless farmers that the old agricultural system was gone forever. By 1941, wage workers had little prospect of becoming tenants or even year-long residents in the same county. Between 1935 and 1940, the tenancy rate in the Bootheel fell from 77 percent to 64 percent, the lowest level since 1920.[167] Over the same period, spending on wage labor increased 168 percent. The use of day labor increased twice as fast on large farms as on small ones.[168] "Today," the FSA concluded in December 1940, "farming in Southeast Missouri is rapidly being mechanized." Farms now "operate on a factory basis, employing only a few tractor drivers for most of the year, but depending on large numbers of day laborers for a few months in cotton-chopping and picking seasons," it reported.[169] Many of these new wage earners now worked in regional fruit, vegetable, and cotton harvests. For example, 60 percent of cherry pickers in Berrien County, Michigan, and the majority of the 2,900 migrant laborers surveyed in the Union County, Illinois, peach harvest that year had come from the Bootheel.

Most of these workers would return to their homes in Missouri in time for the cotton cultivating and picking seasons before leaving again to follow other harvest work.[170]

Delmo clients were well placed to exploit these harvest opportunities. In 1941, one family on the Kennett project left the Bootheel after the close of cotton-chopping season to pick strawberries in southern Illinois and Indiana before returning. Near the end of summer, they went back to Illinois to pick peaches with several other wage hands who had paid to ride along in their truck. They all returned to Dunklin County in time for cotton picking. Local FSA administrators considered them one of the most financially secure wage working families in southeast Missouri and perhaps anywhere in the South. "The head of the family," P. G. Beck reported, "stated that the fact that he lived in the Farm Security Administration group labor home community gave him a feeling of security and encouraged him to seek migratory farm work."[171] Although these farmers had fallen to the bottom of the agricultural hierarchy, their access to secure homes, subsistence plots, and freedom from tenancy agreements gave them the independence to prosper in the new agricultural economy.

*   *   *

Faced with the reality of a rural wage system, union activists gradually abandoned the hope of a landed future—long central to ideas of agrarian independence—in order to organize around the interests of wage workers. Noah Graham, a white STFU member in Pemiscot County, reported that everywhere he tried to organize, wage workers asked what the union was doing for them. He did not know what to say. Along with colleague B. S. Beck, Graham called a District Council meeting in early May 1941 of representatives from all active STFU locals in Missouri for the purpose of establishing a union wage scale for cotton chopping.[172] Twenty-three locals sent delegates to the meeting near Kennett. These activists claimed that of the more than 4,000 people in their communities, at least 3,400 worked exclusively for wages, while only seventy-three still sharecropped.[173] In support of Graham and Beck, the national office dispatched J. E. Clayton and F. R. Betton, black organizers from Texas and Arkansas, respectively, to the Bootheel to help J. F. Hynds, the national organizer already there.[174]

The District Council demanded that a cotton chopper's pay for a 10-hour day be raised from $1 to $1.75.[175] Chopping constituted around 20 percent of all labor needed to produce cotton, second only to picking. In late spring, workers with hoes were needed to cut away, or chop, smaller cotton plants and weeds to ensure that the largest plants grew to full size. Everyone, unionist and planter alike, knew the importance of good chopping work to a big crop. Wage workers still had clout if they could control the labor supply. "No strike of farm labor is contemplated in Southeast Missouri," an STFU press release announced, "but it is possible that members of the STFU may later be notified to stay out of the fields until the wage increase is granted." Although planters did not meet the full union demand, they raised the wage to $1.25.[176]

Although this was a small victory, the concession gave local activists new momentum. During June, Betton and Clayton held several mass meetings throughout Dunklin, New Madrid, and Pemiscot counties and reported good results among both blacks and whites. Buoyed by early success, they focused their main energies on organizing people in Delmo. Before visiting the clients there, Betton and Clayton first got the permission of the camp manager. This orderly plan worked, and by the end of the summer the STFU had locals in the white projects at Kennett and Wardell and there was growing interest among African Americans at the south Wardell project, the one the MAWC had worked to save. Although it was still very weak, the STFU now boasted 203 paid members in Missouri, the most since late 1939.[177]

Local MAWC organizers, following their defense of the black Wardell project, also aimed to rebuild around Delmo clients. On June 14, the MAWC hosted the annual meeting of the Southern States Cotton Council at Cropperville, which brought together UCAPAWA activists from throughout the South to discuss the progress of the CIO's southern unions. The MAWC invited clients of the different Delmo projects, white and black, to send delegates to the meeting to hear guest speakers representing the National Negro Congress, the NAACP, the FSA, the CIO, and the Social Security Board. Their speeches dealt with the implications of the European war, the UCAPAWA's efforts to increase FSA spending, and plans to find land for the landless. "You in these Group Homes have good houses and good conveniences," the MAWC pointed out, "but don't forget you cannot feed your families on good homes alone." "The battle" for economic security "has just begun."[178]

A battle had indeed begun, but perhaps not the one they imagined. In late June, Nazi forces invaded the Soviet Union. This stunning end to the Molotov-Ribbentrop Pact of 1939 shocked the communists in the UCAPAWA and other CIO unions. Labor activists who had opposed the Allied war effort for two years were now suddenly asked by the Communist Party to defend and support it. President Roosevelt also demanded that the CIO support the war effort once mobilization began that summer. By the fall, American communists had joined other CIO leaders in readying themselves to do whatever the government needed to defeat fascism.[179] All expected rural workers to follow their political lead.

Owen Whitfield, who had relocated to St. Louis, launched what he called a Four Point Working Program to prepare the MAWC for this environment. The plan's points emphasized the need to "teach people to use the ballot to their advantage and build solidarity for political campaigns" and "to teach economic co-operatives and self-sufficiency." The program would bring together activists from groups such as the MAWC, the CRS, "and all other such organizations whose purpose is to help the dispossessed farmers and agricultural workers," as well as the FSA. Each group would nominate a representative to take part in county committees that would oversee the formation of cooperative communities that met federal aid requirements "thereby enabling the GOVERNMENT to help us help ourselves."[180] Significantly, Whitfield intended the committees to include the STFU, with which he had agreed to a truce at an April meeting with organizers J. E. Clayton and F. R. Betton.[181]

Whitfield's plan recast rural wage workers as patriotic producers essential to national defense. In a gesture toward traditional aspirations of landownership, he said that the program was intended to alleviate the "the present condition of the soil tillers who have no soil to till" and whose only desire was to "get back to the soil where they rightfully belong, and earn a living by the sweat of their brow, as god said do." The main goal, however, was to prepare rural wage workers to qualify for and take advantage of FSA projects such as Delmo. If the plan worked, Whitfield explained, it would help "these people reestablish themselves in the good old American way of life, and become self-supporting and useful citizens." He was convinced that agricultural workers would have new political leverage in coming months. With that in mind, Whitfield hoped his program would "intrench these people (economically) so that they will be in a position to stand as good American citizens during the Great Crisis" that was sure to come.[182] Although Whitfield's thinking was attuned to the needs of wage workers, it was still based on the producerist assumption that productive labor legitimized citizenship rights.

For the first time in a long time, cotton farmers made money in late 1941. War in Europe again raised prices, which benefited sharecroppers. Meanwhile, regional harvests and booming war industries in Memphis, St. Louis, and Chicago pulled rural wage laborers away from the Bootheel. With cotton fetching 18 cents per lint pound in a shortened market, growers suddenly feared that there would not be enough pickers. The MAWC seized the opportunity to launch a strike for higher wages. With wide support from nonmembers, the strikers quickly won their demand for $1.50 per hundred pounds. Accustomed to lean times, they had underestimated the market. By the end of the season, the MAWC had secured $1.75 and even $2 on some farms. The crop was the largest since 1935, and high prices and high wages meant a windfall for tenants and wage hands. Eager to spend this hard-earned cash, they bought cars, radios, and new clothes. Charles Colman and his family, black sharecroppers near Charleston, earned enough from their fifty-three acres to buy a 1942 Packard Clipper. This brief euphoria came to a sudden and sober end, however, when Japan attacked Pearl Harbor on December 7 and plunged America into World War II.[183]

\*   \*   \*

In the weeks that followed, MAWC leaders urged the federal government to create the conditions that would allow citizens who labored in cotton fields to do their part for the war. This followed a pledge made collectively by the CIO, the Communist Party, and the American Federation of Labor to the Roosevelt administration that they would not take action that would endanger the nation's war effort. They vowed to expand production, prohibit strike action, and submit to federal wage and hour guidelines in exchange for federal policies that benefited labor later.[184] In addition to achieving higher chopping wages, activists in the Bootheel were intent on pressuring the FSA into finalizing its planned Sugar Tree cooperative settlement in Mississippi County. Modelled on La Forge, Sugar Tree was to house seventy black families on 2,900 acres near the predominately white town of East Prairie.[185]

During a trip to Washington and in numerous letters to federal agencies in mid-December, Whitfield assured New Deal officials about the loyalty of Bootheel agricultural workers, who were outraged by the predations of "ALMOND EYED MURDERERS." He claimed that if the FSA could help farm workers get on the Sugar Tree land and acquire tools and livestock, then the farmers could raise food to support the war. Farmers were desperate to join the effort, he said, and "to form an army behind the army, an army of food producers, instead of food consumers and relief clients." But they could not do so without FSA help. Should that help not come, Whitfield warned, their mood might turn dangerous. He reminded federal officials of Takis's work in the Bootheel in 1934, when "some ten or more thousands of negroes" were "convinced that the JAP is the negro's best friend." He urged the government to "beat these foreign agents to the punches" with economic incentives. "Give these great mass of people some kind of employment so they can have something to make them proud of," because, Whitfield explained, a "hungry

drifting people does not look to safeguard his flag as one who has [an] oc-
cupation and plenty of the necessities of life." If farmers were not allowed
to work like citizens, he suggested, how could they perform the duties of
citizenship? "Give us more to fight for."[186]

Mirroring the conservative backlash sweeping the country, Bootheel authorities launched their own version of national defense aimed at the enemies—unionists and blacks—they perceived in their midst.[187] They targeted
Sugar Tree. Local elites, led again by Representative Zimmerman, again ob-
jected to a collective farm for blacks in a white section. They denounced it as
a "radical scheme" that would "result in much unpleasantness, trouble and
possibly even worse circumstances," an allusion to mayhem that arsonists
helped clarify by burning several buildings at the proposed site.[188] At the
same time, in Pemiscot County, planter-backed vigilantes launched assaults
against STFU members. In one incident, Scottie Spears was severely beaten
and shot at as he fled. Despite pressure from the Department of Justice and
the American Civil Liberties Union, local police refused to investigate the
attacks.[189] Against this backdrop, on January 25, white vigilantes lynched
and burned Cleo Wright, an African-American wage worker, in Sikeston.[190]
His murder shocked the nation and violated the national ethos of calls for
patriotic service to defend democracy. It led, among other things, to the
formal launch by the African-American press of the Double-V campaign
for victory over fascism abroad and over racial discrimination in the United
States.[191] In the Bootheel it had the immediate effect of turning the tide of
opinion against Sugar Tree. A Charleston editor predicted that "there will
be trouble, and serious trouble [in East Prairie], unless that project is shifted
to another location."[192] Soon after that, the FSA announced that Sugar Tree
would be postponed for fear of inciting further racial violence.[193] "To allow
race prejudice to defeat this very worthy project," Whitfield lamented, "would
be a shameful blot on the escutcheon of democracy."[194]

The demise of Sugar Tree outraged MAWC activists. They began talking
about a strike in the upcoming chopping season. The communists in the
UCAPAWA, however, were among the strongest supporters of the wartime
promise they had given Roosevelt not to strike. Sensing the rising tension,
Whitfield urged local leaders Peter Wilderness and E. L. Hughes (who was
now president of the MAWC), to "do all that they felt necessary for the
benefit of our people."[195] He would not be there to help, however, because
UCAPAWA had again sent him to organize in Memphis.[196] As an alternative
course, UCAPAWA leader Donald Henderson advised the MAWC to petition their congressmen to approve full funding for the FSA, which by that

point was being attacked in the U.S. Congress. With little hope of swaying Representative Zimmerman's vote, Hughes's Morley Local 384 sent their petition to him. Without these funds, they argued, FSA clients could not participate in the government's Food for Victory program, which promoted domestic food production to supplement the war effort. "The farmers are the front line in this battle," members of Local 384 reminded him.[197] These efforts were unsuccessful; in July 1942, after heated debates over the president's budget in the late spring and early summer, Congress slashed 43 percent from the funding amount requested for the FSA.[198] Their New Deal threatened, Wilderness and the members of Lilbourn Local 313 asked the UCAPAWA in March what they should do next, since planters seemed to be colluding to keep chopping wages below $1.20 for a ten-hour day. Committed to the no-strike pledge, Henderson replied that they should negotiate a minimum wage and issue "pamphlets and leaflets for determining" the scale.[199]

Frustrated by such timid tactics, the MAWC prepared for all-out confrontation with area planters and with the communist leaders of the UCAPAWA if necessary. Sometime in March, Local 313 leaders Peter Wilderness, Booker T. Clark, and Rev. W. L. Echols began making preparations for a wildcat strike. They had help from C. L. R. James, then a little-known scholar from Trinidad who had been sent to report on Bootheel unionists in the aftermath of the Wright lynching for *Labor Action,* the newspaper of the Trotskyite Socialist Workers Party. Throughout April, local activists, along with James, mobilized union members and sympathizers to join the strike that would take place at the height of May chopping season. Word spread quickly. The STFU's Mitchell told organizer J. E. Clayton that "some Negro who is a Trotskyite communist has been in there [around Sikeston] and is trying to get something started."[200] James suggested that union leaders issue a pamphlet stating their reasons and goals for the strike. This was, after all, what Henderson had told them to do. Rather than write it himself, as the leaders initially requested, James suggested that he simply present their demands and justifications. Five or six of the leaders "said what they thought," he later recalled, "and I put it together."[201] The Socialist Workers Party likely provided money for printing. The one-cent pamphlet, *Down With Starvation Wages in South-East Missouri,* appeared on International Workers' Day, May 1.[202]

The strike leaders argued that they were resisting dependence and degradation in order to perform their duties as patriotic citizens. The government and planters "tell us to sacrifice for the war" instead of organizing, the pamphlet stated, but "we have nothing to sacrifice with." They demanded 30 cents per hour for chopping cotton, not $1.25 a day. They knew that cotton planters, who were "prosperous," could pay that rate. "Only we who produce the cotton are starving," they said. Wage workers were hungry, living in hovels, and wearing rags. This system robbed landless people of their humanity, the pamphlet said: "We are not men and women, we are just animals." They understood that New Deal agricultural legislation had made this system possible. "They are fooling themselves if they think that they are fooling us," the leaders concluded. "We can't go on like this." Local 313 pointed out that everything landless people in the Bootheel had, mainly Delmo, was a result of their demonstrations in 1939 and 1940. Now, they declared, "to get a decent wage we must struggle again." The members of the MAWC local emphasized that they were American citizens and that their labor had "built this country." They emphasized their loyalty to the U.S. government: "We don't want any Hitler, or Mussolini or any Japanese ruling us." Yet at the same time, they could not tolerate oppression at the hands of wealthy planters. "A man who has to live on 12 cents an hour . . . is a citizen in name [only]," they declared. "In reality he is a slave." The pamphlet combined older producerist ideas about the centrality of labor with an emerging belief in the inviolability of citizenship as the basis for economic justice. This conception of the relationship between work and rights was more akin to the burgeoning civil rights unionism in regional cities than with earlier modes of agrarian thought.[203] Whereas before, Bootheel farmers had emphasized that they needed land to produce enough to support their families and perform the duties of full citizens, now they were arguing that they needed decent wages because they were loyal citizens with all the rights that status entailed. "We may have to die for democracy in Java or in Iceland," the leaders concluded, so they might as well risk death "for 30¢ an hour here first."[204]

On May 10, Wilderness, Clark, and Echols held a rally in Lilbourn. More than 350 wage workers, most of them black, attended. They elected a strike committee that consisted of unionists from Charleston, Lilbourn, Matthews, Wardell, Morley, Essex, and Cropperville. Many of these supporters lived at Delmo. They considered the strike necessary to defend their ability to continue living on the projects. As many as 8,000 laborers laid down their hoes and went on strike following the meeting.[205]

One month after the strike began, the members of Local 313 wrote to the regional FSA director to explain their motivation. "We are grateful to the FSA for the homes," they said, but the low wages the landlords were paying threatened their ability to pay their rent: "Unless we can get a wage of 30¢ per hour or above, we will be unable to continue on the project." They hinted that landlords were well aware of this economic equation. "The landlords are against our program," they said, a likely reference to Delmo.[206]

The strike caused problems for the CIO because of the no-strike pledge it had made at the outset of the war. Henderson denounced it as illegal and assured readers of the planter-friendly *Enterprise-Courier* that the UCAPAWA had no role in it. He accused the strike leaders of being "Trotskyites" bent on wrecking the UCAPAWA and the CIO. He warned that unless the strike stopped, all who were involved would be expelled from the CIO and that he would help have them jailed.[207] Many unionists outside the Bootheel, however, lent crucial support to the strikers. The St. Louis CIO Industrial Union Council claimed that its solidarity with the strikers was "in accordance with the highest traditions and best interests of the CIO" and promised to support them. The council accused Henderson of being more concerned with his Communist Party affiliations than with the workers in his union. Communists like Henderson, they argued, would gladly sacrifice American workers in order to fulfil the foreign policies of the Soviet Union, which had ordered support for the war effort following the Nazi invasion in 1941. "We know that today since Russia's alliance with the USA you seek to grind the workers in the dust and chain the workers organizations hand and foot to the most reactionary elements in the employing class," the council wrote to Henderson.[208]

The strike depended, however, on how fast weeds could grow. Whitfield chose to defy Henderson. "Now is the time to battle for 30 cents per hour," he argued on June 11, because heavy summer rains would encourage the weeds and weaken the planters. "Every rain is in our favor," Whitfield said, and "all workers should take advantage of this rainy season to demand a living wage."[209] Local MAWC leaders, meanwhile, appealed directly to Roosevelt for support. They said they needed the 30-cent wage scale in order to make a positive contribution to the war effort. "The average plantation owner in the South is not concerned with defeating Hitler and the Japs," the MAWC told FDR, "but instead is concerned with defeating the efforts of farm labor to obtain a wage that will enable them to feed their starving wives and children."[210] The transition away from landed agrarianism was now so complete that local unionists were using producerist rhetoric about independent manhood to justify higher wages. This would have been unthinkable to earlier generations who considered waged work akin to enslavement, let alone a platform for achieving agrarian goals.

In early July, with weeds choking the cotton, the strikers won their demands. Theirs was the first victory of rank-and-file unionists since the war had begun.[211] Outflanked, Henderson changed direction by calling a conference in Cape Girardeau where the UCAPAWA set a wage scale for southern field workers and established the Southeast Missouri Organizing Committee to see that the wage scale was won. The committee demanded $3 per 100 pounds picked. UCAPAWA now justified this demand by declaring that "the present starvation wages are not only unjust, but a direct threat to winning the war, since they prevent efficient work on the Food for Victory program."[212] The convention also called for Roosevelt to establish by executive order an agricultural board to oversee relations between farm workers and employers, as the National War Labor Board did for industrial workers.[213] For his part, Whitfield proposed that the FSA should "organize an army of harvesters" to meet regional labor shortages so that "no perishable foodstuffs go to waste during the great crisis."[214]

The chopping strike loomed over the conference. Henderson was determined to reassert control over the MAWC and punish the strike leaders. The only officers on the May strike committee to receive appointments to the UCAPAWA's new Organizing Committee were Fred Coleman and E. L. Hughes. Henderson refused to appoint anyone from Local 313 until all of its members signed oaths reaffirming their loyalty to the UCAPAWA. Furthermore, he placed the entire local on three months' probation, during which time it would be under the control of the new Organizing Committee. "Because Lilbourn 313 had been led recently to set themselves in opposition to UCAPAWA," Henderson explained, "it was necessary to take these steps to get them straightened out."[215] Wilderness, Clark, and Echols refused to submit to Henderson's punishment. All three left the union. They never returned. Thirty years later, Clark was still bitterly suspicious of Henderson, recalling how "it seemed to me that Don Henderson was mostly out for what he could get for Don Henderson."[216]

STFU members in the Bootheel joined the agitation for higher wages. By the summer of 1942, the STFU presence in Missouri had stabilized to about ten active locals anchored by three groups on Delmo projects. The strongest of the Delmo locals was at the white North Wardell project and was led by Bill Johnson. STFU activists argued that they could no longer comply with the terms of the no-strike pledge and that to continue do so would not only prevent them from supporting the war but would run counter to the values it was being fought to preserve.[217] "We ask your help in our effort to win for all our people, white and negro," the union said, "the right to live as decent human beings." Now appealing to citizenship rights more than ever, the STFU explained that "while our boys from the cotton fields are fighting on the seven seas and in far off lands to defeat tyranny and to establish the rights of free people throughout the world, their folks at home are being offered the right to starve at" low wages. "We are eager to do our part in this great war effort," the appeal concluded, "but we cannot do much so long as we are regarded as subjects for exploitation by those who own and rule the land." They also demanded $3 per hundred pounds picked.[218]

The strike failed. Bootheel planters actually reduced picking wages to $1.50 per hundred and threatened to ensure that anyone who failed to work would be sent into the military. The STFU was too weak to resist. Henderson never supported the strike. All his demands remained rhetoric only. Without greater support and the leaders of Local 313, the MAWC folded. When Wilderness, Clark, and Echols left the union, they took most rank-and-file members with them. They left no record to explain the collapse other than the bitter disappointment they registered after the spring strike. It seems safe to say, however, that Henderson's actions convinced rural unionists that neither the UCAPAWA nor the CIO represented their interests.[219] What use was an organization that rejected its most talented, courageous leaders at a moment of great need and potential victory? No MAWC locals outside of Cropperville registered any activity after the summer of 1942. Bogged down in Memphis, Whitfield could do little about it; he focused his spare efforts on securing a lasting solution for Cropperville Local 349. In less than a year, during which time the union had won a massive victory, MAWC membership fell from as many as 8,000 to less than 100. The STFU maintained about 200 members, most of whom lived on Delmo projects.[220]

In some ways, the efforts of landless farmers in the Bootheel to make a New Deal for themselves had succeeded. The roadside demonstration of 1939 and the symbolic protest of 1940, together with intense lobbying on the part of the MAWC and the STFU, had brought unprecedented federal attention to the poorest citizens—so much so that P. G. Beck, the FSA's regional director, stated that "southeast Missouri offers an interesting laboratory for stabilization of the farm population and the farm labor supply."[221] New Deal experimentation addressed many issues at the heart of the rural working-class movement, including housing, access to subsistence plots, and improved diets. None of this, however, stopped evictions, demotion, and the shift to a wage labor system. Instead, the FSA programs attempted to ease that transition by supporting landless families as they rebuilt their lives in a new rural economy. The aim was, in Beck's words, to make them into a stable "farm labor supply." Measured against the aspirations and hopes that tens of thousands of migrants had brought with them to the Bootheel, the victory rural activists had won was pyrrhic. Union activists had abandoned the goal of independent homesteads to achieve partial measures that, despite helping thousands of desperate people, promised nothing certain as landless farmers transitioned toward an unknown and likely difficult future. In the end, the rural working-class movement had won a New Deal for landless farmers by accepting a system of wage labor. The struggle to win "land for the landless" was over. In the transaction, traditional agrarian producerist ideals gave way to a more universalist emphasis on citizenship as the basis for rights, both economic and civil. While this concept threatened to undermine ingrained rural notions of manhood and womanhood, household composition, and community cooperation, it was transportable and easier to deploy, whether one picked cotton or worked in a steel mill.

# Epilogue

In 1943 Orville Zimmerman sat on a select committee in the House of Representatives to investigate the activities of the FSA. The agency, he said, was driven by a communistic intent to "go out and lease all of the land in the United States and have these associations created so that you will have these men in these houses and the Farm Security will be one gigantic supervising agency over all the land in the United States." One had to look no further than the Delmo Labor Homes Project, which, he claimed, was infested with union agitators. To ensure the domination of "certain social leaders," Zimmerman continued, the FSA made the projects a "mecca for these organizers that come in and cause confusion in the community."[1]

The attack succeeded. The investigation led to Public Law 76, which outlawed the use of federal funds to improve the wages, hours, or living conditions of agricultural workers. As intended, the measure decimated the FSA's programs, although Delmo and a few other migrant labor projects survived under the authority of the War Food Administration so workers could supply food for the war effort. The War Food Administration, however, was dominated by administrators from the Department of Agriculture's Cooperative Extension Service, which had little interest in the FSA's programs to help landless farmers. Meanwhile, under pressure from Zimmerman, the Dunklin County Medical Society pulled out of the Southeast Missouri Health Service. Doctors claimed that the service's federal subsidies constituted unfair competition.[2]

By early 1945, with the war in Europe drawing to a close, Delmo's enemies began their final offensive. In January, the War Food Administration declared that it no longer needed the housing communities for its wartime program and shifted them back to the FSA, which was now under the control of the very politicians seeking to destroy it. Frank Hancock, the new FSA director, claimed that Delmo was unprofitable and that enough housing existed for farm workers elsewhere. In March, the FSA announced it would liquidate the projects altogether by private auction and subcontract the Southeast Missouri Health Service to Blue Cross, a private medical insurer.[3]

Activists in the Delmo communities launched a vigorous campaign to stop the liquidation process. Bill Johnson, an STFU leader in Wardell, reported that residents were "storming me for petitions to rebel against" the FSA's decision.[4] Within days Johnson had organized a committee of representatives from each project to petition against the planned closure.[5] The first petition of the Tenants Committee, which was signed by members of all 606 client families, protested "the sale of our rental homes and lands at public auction." They thanked the FSA and the War Food Administration for helping them secure and enjoy "liberty, good housing, and the benefits of community life." If, however, the homes were sold, they warned, all of this would be lost and "we will be homeless or living in old shacks, and we will once again face the future without hope." Having fought so hard for their New Deal, they wanted the federal government to uphold its end of the bargain. "In the name of liberty, patriotism and justice," they asked that their "homes remain under the supervision of the Federal Government."[6] Tommie Hamilton, a veteran of the roadside demonstration, signed, as did Peter Wilderness's two brothers, Calvin and Earl.[7] Many vowed to leave the Bootheel and farming for good if their homes were sold. "We won't go back to the plantations," one black resident declared, "no matter what. Where will I go, you ask? Well someplace," he concluded, "up North, East or West, but I won't stay here." Another resident invoked memories of the roadside demonstrations that had precipitated the creation of Delmo in the first place, saying that if they were forced out "it's going to be out yonder on the road—another highway demonstration."[8]

The STFU joined the fight. STFU leader H. L. Mitchell sent David Burgess, a white preacher, to coordinate the union effort with Johnson. Through his connections in the Congregational Church, Burgess tapped a network of liberal and labor organizations for help: the Missouri Council of Churches, the League of Women Voters, the St. Louis CIO Industrial Union Council, the Urban League of St. Louis, the NAACP of St. Louis, the Episcopal Diocese of Missouri, the American Civil Liberties Union, the American Federation of Labor Central Trades and Labor Union, and the Liberal Voters League.[9] Backed by this array of allies, Johnson and the Tenant Committee filed a final appeal. By "fighting for the working man," they said, the FSA has "given us hope in ourselves and in the future." Privatizing Delmo, the new petitioners claimed, would subject client families to the whims of planters, who wanted them "back on the farms so that they can have greater control over" them. In short, they would lose their independence. Holding fast to service and citizenship as guarantors against dependence, they pointed out that "at least 300 of the fathers or sons in the armed forces" came from Delmo; they were fighting for the same liberty that local planters would deny them.[10]

Armed with their petition, representatives of the Tenants Committee, Mitchell and Burgess went to Washington in early April. The group made their case to sympathetic congressmen at a meeting covered by the St. Louis and national press. The group met the FSA's director of projects sales, who said that although he would not oppose any offer by the clients to buy the homes, he could not extend the sale deadline. Before leaving, the group lodged its petition with the White House. President Roosevelt never heard their case; he died a few days later in Georgia. Once they realized that Delmo was sure to be sold, Burgess and Johnson began canvassing clients to find out who wanted to buy their homes. Nearly everyone was interested.[11] But there was a problem.

While preaching in Mississippi County, Whitfield happened to visit the black project at South Wyatt during the week before the STFU delegation was due to brief clients on these developments. Whitfield held an emergency meeting the night before their arrival and "blasted the hell out of [Mitchell] and his STFU." Although he no longer worked for the CIO, Whitfield claimed that the STFU was only trying to keep the CIO out of Delmo.[12] When the STFU organizers spoke the following night, they received a lukewarm response. In frantic efforts throughout the summer, Whitfield and his wife Zella worked hard to pry the other Delmo communities away from the STFU by advocating a rival scheme to buy the homes. The South Wyatt clients were the first to contribute money to Whitfield.[13]

The STFU-led effort, meanwhile, gained ground. In early July, the FSA announced that it would delay the sale of Delmo for another sixty days in order to allow the residents time to put together an offer. Given breathing space, Burgess, William Scarlett, bishop of the Episcopal Diocese of Missouri, and Edwin Meissner, president of the St. Louis Car Company, created the Delmo Housing Corporation (DHC) in early August to pool the clients' money, raise additional funds, and lead negotiations with the FSA.[14] They were gaining support. The *Washington Post,* for example, attacked the liquidation scheme on its editorial page. Gardner Jackson, head of the new Farmers' Union, and Alfred Schindler, Under Secretary of Commerce, appealed directly to President Harry Truman to support the DHC plan. Under growing media scrutiny, Truman ordered the FSA to postpone the sale again until October. He wanted the "Delmo residents to be able to retain their homes," but only "if they could buy them from the government at fair market prices."[15]

Despite clear progress by the DHC, the South Wyatt clients stuck with Whitfield, who refused to join the STFU's bid.[16] He claimed to have raised over $25,000 toward the purchase of the project, although no record exists of any negotiations on his part with the FSA. Yet as late as September 25, he still hoped to organize the purchase, though the situation, he admitted, was "hanging Fire."[17] Too mistrustful to compromise with the STFU and too entrepreneurial to back off, Whitfield continued to complicate the effort to preserve the claims of all Delmo residents.

While the DHC had already entered negotiations to buy the other nine projects, the South Wyatt community drifted toward disaster. With little fanfare, the FSA sold South Wyatt Homes in early October 1945 to a local alfalfa mill. Whitfield never entered a bid. The owners of the mill immediately raised the rent to $20 a month, far more than any farm worker could pay. Thirty black families unceremoniously left the homes they had lived in since 1941 and vanished from the historical record. They were victims of Whitfield's unresolved struggle with the demons of political sectarianism.[18]

The financial support and political contacts of Delmo's liberal allies and heartfelt appeals from the residents themselves saved the other projects. In mid-November, the FSA accepted the DHC's bid of $285,000 for the remaining eight communities. The purchase included houses, lots, household furnishings, community buildings, and roads within community borders but not the adjoining land. Contributions from sympathetic donors covered most of the $73,000 down payment, including $12,500 donated by department store magnate Marshall Field, $4,500 by the STFU's National Sharecroppers Fund, and $1,000 by the NAACP. The DHC then sold the homes to the inhabitants for $800 each to be paid for with a $100 down payment and affordable monthly payments of $7.50 for eight years.[19] For once, the remaining residents contemplated a future with some security, dignity, and autonomy; they would offer a lasting reminder of the movement for justice in the fields.

It had been a long struggle. As he witnessed the birth of the agricultural revolution that would remake life and work in southeast Missouri, *Scott County Kicker* editor Phil Hafner had warned in 1907 that unless farmers resisted the power of corporations and capitalist speculators, they would be "doomed to wage slavery." Worse still, he asked, "What better chance have your children?"[20] The same fear motivated Whitfield and those who went to the roadsides in 1939. Farmers "must join together in one strong labor movement," Whitfield argued, "to free themselves and their wives and children from wage slavery." This was the only way to "get some of the things that God prepared for us" in the promised lands of the Bootheel, he said.[21]

The tens of thousands of rural men and women who rallied to these calls shared a faith in the moral certainties of an agrarian cosmology rooted in the political and cultural world of the late nineteenth century. That belief system rested on the idea that farmers who, in Whitfield's words, earned "a living by the sweat of their brow, as god said do," also earned the product of their labor, their autonomy on the land, and their independence as citizens.[22] These were "the things that God prepared for us." "We feel that we are entitled to this," the roadside demonstrators had declared, "since we want to work and since we are Americans and since we helped to make America what it is today."[23] *Justice* editor John Scott had used the same logic almost thirty years earlier to denounce tenancy and wage work when he argued that "God Almighty and labor produces all the wealth of the world and labor is entitled to all it produces."[24]

As this book has shown, the efforts of landless farmers to restore their agrarian faith drew upon an abiding sense of moral justice inspired by democratic religious fellowship and fired by rebellious revival. This was more than just a poor people's religion. Agrarian producerism revolved around duty to God, to work, to kin, and to society. Anything that impeded a farmer's efforts to meet those duties was wrong, immoral. "Discontented farmers," one historian has written about agrarian rebels in the 1890s, "understood contemporary issues through the restorationist and millennialist language that was a deep part of their religious worlds."[25] That same frame of reference shaped the views of rural people well into the twentieth century, even as the causes of their discontent multiplied. The great grassroots revivals in Pentecostal-Holiness and schismatic Baptist churches gave farmers who felt discarded economically and socially the intellectual tools—the prophetic power—to seek to restore the balance in the agrarian cosmology. Although often escapist, as others have documented, this rebellious theological tradition could also, according to one historian of southern religion, "offer hope in this world, hope for a miracle, hope that could bypass the repressive machinery of society."[26] One did not need a preacher or a church building to hear God speak. Indeed, the call to salvation and mission could be heard as loud, if not louder, while cradling a child struck with malaria, while walking down a dark dirt road following a revival meeting, or while enjoying the cool dusk after a hard day's work in the fields.

Were they alive, however, the first generation of migrants to the Bootheel no doubt would have looked with sadness on the ultimate failure of rebellious, righteous farmers to stop the triumph of an agricultural economy based on wage labor. While the children of Hafner's generation carried forward the fight against large-scale mechanized farming and its displacement of families, their grandchildren would not. True, agrarian activists won a New Deal, but not without relinquishing their claims to the land and accepting wage labor. By the 1940s, rural people were leaving the Bootheel almost as fast as they had entered it decades earlier. Between 1940 and 1945 alone, the rural population of the region dropped by 27 percent. People unwilling or unable to find agricultural labor left for better opportunities elsewhere. More than 75 percent of the rural people who remained, meanwhile, relied solely on farm wage work.[27]

Yet that outcome was not the most crushing defeat. Despite the failure to reverse the structural changes in the cotton economy, the frequent turns to racial division, and the implied or actual appeals to violence, it was the corrosive effects of political sectarianism that brought landless people low. Scriptural references and religious rhetoric pervaded the written records of rural rebellion in the Bootheel up to the roadside demonstration of 1939. Those allusions dwindled in the record that followed. As dreams of landed agrarianism went down to final defeat, so too did the cosmology that defined rural lives, labors, and citizenship. In place of this ideal, rural people embraced more than ever before a universal—what some might call a more modern—faith in their rights as American citizens.[28] What was lost in the process, however, was considerable.

Historians of twentieth-century America have been quick to dismiss the agrarian rebellions that swept southern fields as late as the 1940s. Most scholars interested in the history of progressive and reactionary politics, labor unions, the fight for civil rights, and modern African American history have focused their inquiries either on people in cities or people moving to cities.[29] This focus on urban and suburban settings has fostered a view of rural America, and especially the South, as a place of torpor, of hopelessness, and of people with no future or ambitions outside the city.[30]

By neglecting the struggles of these activists, historians have overlooked an alternative American protest tradition that combined beliefs in the democratic potential of evangelical religion, the primacy of family and community groups, the centrality of work to citizenship, and the role of the state in safeguarding the social and economic health of the people. At its best, this vision called for a reciprocal relationship between hardworking small producers and the commonwealth. As sectarianism, displacement, and domestic anticommunism finally destroyed the agrarian movement in the 1940s, threads of these protests survived as tens of thousands of rural people moved into southern and northern cities. Many of them joined labor unions in places such as Memphis, Winston-Salem, and Detroit. Former agrarians contributed to nascent civil rights unionism a spirit of radical religiosity, experience in community organizing, and belief in the responsibilities and power of the state.

Despite defeat, the people who made the agrarian movement in the Bootheel left behind remnants of their struggles. Roy Cooper, who migrated with his father to Pemiscot County in 1923, bought 103 acres of farmland in 1940 through the FSA's Tenant Ownership Program, which was introduced in southeast Missouri as a result of the roadside demonstrations. He was one of the first African American farmers to get such a loan. In the following years, Cooper, who had always been a sharecropper, planted about thirty acres of cotton and devoted the rest of his land to food and forage crops, mainly corn, oats, soybeans, and hay. His family also raised hogs and chickens. When he died, Cooper passed his farm to his children. Sixty years later they still own the farm, to which they have added even more land. Every August the Cooper family gathers together to celebrate their well-being, their future success, and the meaning of those original 103 acres. At some point during the festivities, someone evokes the words of advice that have come down through the generations.[31] "Land is the most valuable thing," Roy Cooper Jr. recalled his father saying.[32] Echoing the same demands for independence, self-sufficiency, and self-possession that roused Whitfield and Hafner, he remembered "this thing my grandfather always said," which was to "own something if it's just one board over your head" because that "shows some progress." After attending college, Roy Cooper Jr. became a loan officer for the Rural Housing Administration in the Bootheel, where he ran a program similar to the one that enabled his father to buy his farm.[33] His brother Alex went on to serve as the director of the DHC.

The security and independence enjoyed by the residents of the Delmo homes was the greatest lasting achievement of the Bootheel's agrarian radicals. The buildings themselves offer a physical reminder of a proud and bitter struggle. In the years after the families bought their homes, most worked to modernize and improve them. "The home owners are farm workers, mechanics, teachers and preachers," a report later found. Agriculture remained an important part of their lives, however, as more than half still performed farm work of some kind. Many continued their "seasonal work, picking peaches in

Illinois, tomatoes in Indiana and fruits in Michigan."[34] In 1947, these families earned an average of $1,353, a dramatic increase over the $257 that an average family of rural wage workers had earned in 1935. And they endured. In 1994, 80 percent of the original families still owned their homes.[35]

The Delmo communities kept alive the vision of the agrarian movement that had created them; they remind us of a lost progressive alternative. The rural New Deal that was won on the roadsides worked (albeit for a smaller number than activists hoped): Delmo is a rare example of successful public housing, the loan programs have enabled good farmers to maintain small operations in an era of agribusiness, and various projects have bound whites and blacks together in cooperation despite larger racial tensions. Roy Cooper's land was situated in the midst of white farms. He chose the location. "Dad would want to prove that people could live together," Roy Cooper Jr. explained. Cooper's children were sorry, however, that the rural New Deal was not extended further. Roy Cooper said of the notions of righteousness, justice, and collective wealth that had motivated these programs, "Now we call it socialism." This political label caused unnecessary suffering, he believed, because it suffocated projects such as Delmo that were right and moral. "We're talking about America helping people," he exclaimed. "We're talking about back to the Bible type of thing. Jesus helped people and that's what we need to do." Cooper concluded: "We need to help people to get above, because it's going to continue to go down."[36]

# Notes

## Abbreviations

| | |
|---|---|
| Barnes Papers | Charles M. Barnes Papers, WHMC-C |
| Bootheel Project Records | Bootheel Project Records, 1993–1997, WHMC-C |
| Carey Papers | Scott Carey Papers, 1917–1961, WHMC-C |
| Caverno Papers | Xenophon Caverno Papers, 1917–1941, WHMC-C |
| Cook Papers | Fannie Frank Cook Papers, 1874–1949, MHM |
| DCL | Dunklin County Library |
| ER Papers | Eleanor Roosevelt Papers, FDR Library |
| FDR Library | Franklin D. Roosevelt Presidential Library and Museum |
| Gideon-Anderson Papers | Gideon-Anderson Lumber & Mercantile Company Papers, 1901–1985, WHMC-R |
| Hadley Papers | Herbert Spencer Hadley Papers, WHMC-C |
| Hyde Papers | Arthur Mastick Hyde Papers, 1913–1954, WHMC-C |
| IPHCA | International Pentecostal-Holiness Church Archives and Research Center |
| KL | Special Collections and Archives, Kent Library, Southeast Missouri State University |
| LOC | Library of Congress |
| MHM | Missouri History Museum Library and Research Center, St. Louis, Missouri |
| NAACP Records | National Association for the Advancement of Colored People Records, LOC |
| NARA | National Archives and Records Administration |

| Park Papers | Guy Brasfield Park Papers, 1933–1937, WHMC-C |
| PMOH | Politics in Missouri Oral History Project Records, WHMC-C |
| Records of the FHA | Records of the Farmers Home Administration and Predecessor Agencies, RG 96, NARA |
| Snow Papers | Thad Snow Papers, WHMC-S |
| Stark Papers | Lloyd Crow Stark Papers, 1931–1941, WHMC-C |
| STFU Papers | Southern Tenant Farmers' Union Papers, 1934–1973, Microfilming Corporation of America |
| WHMC-C | Western Historical Manuscript Collection–Columbia |
| WHMC-R | Western Historical Manuscript Collection–Rolla |
| WHMC-S | Western Historical Manuscript Collection–St. Louis |
| Williams Papers | Claude Williams Papers, Walter P. Reuther Library |

## Introduction

1. Owen Whitfield, "What Was Done," Spring 1939, Folder 3, Box 6, Fannie Frank Cook Papers, MHM (hereafter Cook Papers).

2. Case No. 16 (Mose Daniels), Case No. 72 (Ike Tripp), Case No. 74 (Henry Tripp), Folder "Tenant Farming, 1939–1944," Box 1, Official File 1650, FDR Library; U.S. Census, Manuscript Schedules, 1930 ( "Ikey Tripp," Elk, Stoddard County, Missouri; and "Mose Daniel," Oak Bluff, Clay County, Arkansas).

3. "We the Undersigned," ca. February 1939, Folder 1939, Lloyd Crow Stark Papers, C0004, WHMC-C.

4. For more on the places they came from, see Blevins, *Hill Folks*, 30–48; Hahn, *A Nation under Our Feet*, 412–64; and Waldrep, *Night Riders*, 5–35.

5. Walker, *Southern Farmers and Their Stories*, 78–79, quote on 216.

6. Thomas M. Inge, "Introduction," in Inge, *Agrarianism*, xiv. See also Reid, *Reaping a Greater Harvest*, xxi–xxii.

7. C. F. Bruton, *The Modern Promised Land* (1919), 5–7, Folder 1, *The Modern Promised Land*, R701, WHMC-R.

8. N. G. Silvermaster quoted in Cantor, *A Prologue to the Protest Movement*, 5.

9. For more on the development of this frontier, see Woodruff, *American Congo*, 8–37; Willis, *Forgotten Time*; Whayne, *A New Plantation South*; and Cobb, *The Most Southern Place on Earth*, 69–183.

10. Cohen, *The Reconstruction of American Liberalism*, 29.

11. Stromquist, "The Crisis of 1894 and the Legacies of Producerism," in Schneirov, Stromquist, and Salvatore, *The Pullman Strike and the Crisis of the 1890s*, 181.

12. For the roots of agrarian producerism, see Hild, *Greenbackers, Knights of Labor, and Populists*, 8–24, 217–18; Hahn, *A Nation under Our Feet*, 135–46, 414–25; Kazin, *The Populist Persuasion*, 3–35; Hahn, *The Roots of Southern Populism*, 1–11, 252; Creech, *Righteous Indignation*, 86–89; and Stromquist, *Reinventing "The People,"* 5, 13–16.

13. See Kantrowitz, *Ben Tillman and the Reconstruction of White Supremacy*, 18,

106–10; Edwards, *Gendered Strife and Confusion*, 18; and Stanley, *From Bondage to Contract*, 172–73.

14. Owen Whitfield, "What Was Done," Spring 1939, Folder 3, Box 6, Cook Papers; George H. Crumb, Bloomfield, to Louis Houck, March 6, 1900, Folder 18, Box 1523, Series I, Louis Houck Papers, KL.

15. Creech, *Righteous Indignation*, 30.

16. "The Omaha Platform, 1892," reprinted in Tindall, *A Populist Reader*, 90. See also Wayne Flynt, "One in the Spirit, Many in the Flesh: Southern Evangelicals," in Harrell, *Varieties of Southern Evangelicalism*, 27–30; Creech, *Righteous Indignation*, 35–38; and Flynt, *Poor but Proud*, 232–36.

17. Harvey, *Freedom's Coming*, 5–46; Harvey, *Redeeming the South*, 197–255; Hahn, *A Nation under Our Feet*, 230–34, 451–63; Creech, *Righteous Indignation*, 76–78; Giggie, *After Redemption*, 59–200; Fred Arthur Bailey, "That Which God Hath Put Asunder: White Baptists, Black Aliens, and the Southern Social Order, 1890–1920," in Feldman, *Politics and Religion in the White South*, 11–33.

18. Kazin, *The Populist Persuasion*, 3–4 (quotes), 33; Creech, *Righteous Indignation*, xiv–xx.

19. Creech, *Righteous Indignation*, xxvii–iii (quote), 17–19, 180; Woodward, *Origins of the New South*, 172–73; Stephens, *The Fire Spreads*, 9, 67–68; Harvey, *Redeeming the South*, 86–88, 206–26.

20. Glass, *Strangers in Zion*, 16–17 (quote); Stephens, *The Fire Spreads*, 56–64.

21. Stephens, *The Fire Spreads*, 66, 137; Creech, *Righteous Indignation*, 30–31.

22. Stephens, *The Fire Spreads*, 137–38, 167–72; Weber, *In the Shadow of the Second Coming*, 9–40, 63–91; Glass, *Strangers in Zion*, 1–32.

23. Cox, *Fire from Heaven*, 114, 120–21.

24. Hatch, *The Democratization of American Christianity*, 5, 216–17.

25. Hobsbawm, *Primitive Rebels*, 6, 57–64; Billings, "Religion as Opposition," 2, 27; Payne, *I've Got the Light of Freedom*, 274. For an ethnographic example of this oppositional impulse, see Scott, "They Don't Have to Live by the Old Traditions," 238–39. Kelley mentioned this dynamic in *Hammer and Hoe*, 107–8.

26. Adas, *Prophets of Rebellion*, xx.

27. Chappell, *A Stone of Hope*, 3–4 (first two quotes); Adas, *Prophets of Rebellion*, xxvii (final quote).

28. All of these studies are inspired in part by Lizabeth Cohen's pioneering *Making a New Deal*. For recent works that extended this argument to include the industrial South, see Korstad, *Civil Rights Unionism*, 7; and Irons, *Testing the New Deal*, 3–7.

29. Cohen, *The Reconstruction of American Liberalism*, 5.

30. Hild, *Greenbackers, Knights of Labor, and Populists*, 217. Other examples include Creech, *Righteous Indignation*, 177–83; Goodwyn, *Democratic Promise*, 516–31; and Hahn, *The Roots of Southern Populism*, 287–88.

31. Sanders, *Roots of Reform*, 1.

32. The most potent examples of this discovery include Steinbeck, *The Grapes of*

*Wrath*; Lange and Taylor, *American Exodus*; and Agee and Evans, *Let Us Now Praise Famous Men*.

33. Sullivan, *Days of Hope,* 3.

34. Grubbs, *Cry from the Cotton*; Gilmore, *Defying Dixie*; Kelley, *Hammer and Hoe*; Rolinson, *Grassroots Garveyism*.

35. Harvard Sitkoff, "The Impact of the New Deal on Black Southerners," in Cobb and Namorato, *New Deal and the South,* 120.

36. For a similar conclusion, see Rolinson, *Grassroots Garveyism,* 14.

37. Green, *Grass-Roots Socialism,* 397; Woodruff, *American Congo,* 4–7; Gilmore, *Defying Dixie,* 4–7, 15–154; Kelley, *Hammer and Hoe,* 228–31; Rolinson, *Grassroots Garveyism,* 21–23, 192–96. See also Fannin, *Labor's Promised Land*; Bissett, *Agrarian Socialism*; Dunbar, *Against the Grain*; and Foley, *White Scourge*.

38. The most prominent examples include Payne, *I've Got the Light of Freedom,* 274; Chappell, *A Stone of Hope,* 87–104; Kazin, *The Populist Persuasion*; Creech, *Righteous Indignation*; Harvey, *Freedom's Coming*; Cox, *Fire from Heaven*; Craig, *Religion and Radical Politics*; and (to some extent) De Jong, *A Different Day*.

39. Dunbar, *Against the Grain*; Craig, *Religion and Radical Politics,* 130–63; Harvey, *Freedom's Coming,* 77–84, 97–103; Cobb, *Radical Education in the Rural South,* 161–89.

40. Sernett, *Bound for the Promised Land,* 4, 57–179; Korstad, *Civil Rights Unionism,* 3, 30–31; Kimberley L. Phillips, "Making a New Church Home: African-American Migrants, Religion, and Working-Class Activism," in Arnesen, Greene, and Laurie, *Labor Histories,* 230–56; Phillips, *AlabamaNorth,* 164–80. Important exceptions that gesture toward the importance of rural roots are Honey, *Southern Labor and Black Civil Rights,* 71; Kelley, *Hammer and Hoe,* 107–8; and Best, *Passionately Human, No Less Divine*.

41. McLoughlin, *Revivals, Awakenings, and Reform,* 2 (first quote), xiii (second quote). For studies of this process, see Fields, *Revival and Rebellion in Colonial Central Africa,* 3–23; Adas, *Prophets of Rebellion*; and Cebula, *Plateau Indians and the Quest for Spiritual Power*.

42. Hobsbawm, *Primitive Rebels,* 1–12; Hatch, *The Democratization of American Christianity,* 210–19.

43. Korstad, on the other hand, interpreted the working-class political movements of the 1940s and 1950s as the product of the "social learning" involved in the rural-to-urban and southern-to-northern migration. Korstad, *Civil Rights Unionism,* 2–3. See also Honey, *Southern Labor and Black Civil Rights,* 68; Phillips, *AlabamaNorth*; and Gregory, *Southern Diaspora*.

## 1. A Modern Promised Land

1. Dickens, "The Banks of the Mississippi" and "The Settlement of Eden," in Slater, *Dickens on America,* 140 (first and final two quotes), 198–199 (middle two quotes).

2. Ogilvie, "Development of Southeast Missouri," 1–31; Kochtitzky, *Story of a Busy*

*Life,* 69–70; Studabaker, *What They "Showed Me,"* 7; Sweet, Tillman, and Krusekopf, *Soil Survey of Dunklin County,* 8–12; Otto, *Final Frontiers,* xi–xii, 115; Woodruff, *American Congo,* 8–10.

3. Studabaker, *What They "Showed Me,"* 7; Sweet, Tillman, and Krusekopf, *Soil Survey of Dunklin County,* 8–12; DeYoung and Wildermuth, *Soil Survey of Mississippi County,* 551–552.

4. U.S. Bureau of the Census, *Eleventh Census of the United States: 1890,* vol. 5, *Reports on the Statistics of Agriculture in the United States,* 158–61; U.S. Bureau of the Census, *Eleventh Census of the United States: 1890,* vol. 9, *Report on the Statistics of Churches in the United States,* 70–71; Douglass, *History of Southeast Missouri,* 387–89, 524; Krusekopf, "Delta Soils," 4–7.

5. Houck quoted in Stepenoff, "Last Tree," 62 (quotes one and two); and Rhodes, "Father of Southeast Missouri," 77 (quote three).

6. Otto, *Final Frontiers,* 1–12; Ogilvie, "Development of Southeast Missouri," 78, 88–110; McDowell, "Development by Drainage," 184–205; Nolen, *Missouri's Swamp,* 18; Woodward, *Origins of the New South,* 120–23, 186–87; Flamming, *Creating the Modern South,* 9–35; Wright, *Old South, New South,* 124–97.

7. Houck quoted in Rhodes, "Father of Southeast Missouri," 77.

8. Ogilvie, "Development of Southeast Missouri," 43–56; Kochtitzky, *Story of a Busy Life,* 150–52; Otto, *Final Frontiers,* 21; Woodward, *Origins of the New South,* 120–23.

9. Otto, *Final Frontiers,* 26–27; "History," ca. 1923, Levee District No. 3 Papers, R326, WHMC-R.

10. Fries, *Empire in Pine,* 239–242; Ogilvie, "Development of Southeast Missouri," 100–101; Jones, *The Tribe of Black Ulysses,* 17–20; Otto, *Final Frontiers,* 30–31.

11. Ophelia Wade, "Deering," in Wade, *Deering,* 13–16; McDowell, "Development by Drainage," 217–218; Ogilvie, "Development of Southeast Missouri," 52–55, 99–102; Kochtitzky, *Story of a Busy Life,* 107–16; "Scope and Content Notes," Himmelberger-Harrison Papers, KL; "Scope and Content Notes," Gideon-Anderson Lumber & Mercantile Company Papers, 1901–1985, R449, WHMC-R (hereafter Gideon-Anderson Papers); Stepenoff, "Last Tree," 61–78.

12. Ogilvie, "Development of Southeast Missouri," 110–24.

13. McDowell, "Development by Drainage," 254; Woodruff, *American Congo,* 11–17; Willis, *Forgotten Time,* 54–56; Otto, *Final Frontiers,* 31; Brandfon, *Cotton Kingdoms,* 67; J. F. Duggar quoted in Woodward, *Origins of the New South,* 118.

14. *St. Louis Mirror,* September 12, 1912, quoted in Stepenoff, "Last Tree," 73.

15. Woodward, *Origins of the New South,* 272–274; Sklar, *Corporate Reconstruction,* 49–50; Painter, *Standing at Armageddon,* 110–128; Dawley, *Struggles for Justice.*

16. Waldrep, *Night Riders,* 23–24.

17. "New Departure" Democrats advocated the industrial and commercial development of Kentucky in the years after the Civil War in opposition to Bourbon Democrats, who sought to defend local autonomy. Waldrep, *Night Riders,* 114–15.

18. Shapiro, *New South Rebellion,* 237–238 (quotes); Waldrep, *Night Riders,* 22–23, 29–30; Marshall, *Violence in the Black Patch,* 107–110.

19. Blevins, *Hill Folks*, 31–48, 75–77, 93–94; Steinson, "Rural Life in Indiana," 214–215, 238; Adams, "How Can a Poor Man Live?" 94, 103–104.

20. Ogilvie, "Development of Southeast Missouri," 529.

21. Snow, *From Missouri*, 134–135.

22. John Case, "A Tribute to the Builders," ca. 1935, Folder 46, FC 2.2, Clippings Collection, 1871–2001, KL; Wade, "Deering," Willie Baxter, "My Life in Deering and Pondertown," "1910 Census, Braggadocio Township," all in Wade, *Deering*, 11–39, 48–50, 243–255; Stepenoff, "Last Tree," 68; U.S. Bureau of the Census, *Twelfth Census of the United States: 1900*, vol. 9, *Manufactures Part III: Special Reports on Selected Industries*, 822; Jones, *The Tribe of Black Ulysses*, 15–42.

23. U.S. Bureau of the Census, *Twelfth Census of the United States: 1900*, vol. 9, *Manufactures Part III: Special Reports on Selected Industries*, 818; "Logging Camp around 1910," Item 5.02, Folder 5, Himmelberger-Harrison Papers, KL; "Rates of Wages—Time Workers," Folder 3, Gideon-Anderson Papers; Pat Richardson, "The Farm Managers, Number Two—William Richardson," in Wade, *Deering*, 149; Case, "A Tribute to the Builders," Folder 46, Box FC 2.2, Clippings Collection, 1871–2001, KL; McDowell, "Development by Drainage," 254; Stepenoff, "Last Tree," 66; Flynt, *Poor but Proud*, 147–150.

24. Kochtitzky, *Story of a Busy Life*, 131–132.

25. Nolen, *Missouri's Swamp*, 14–15.

26. Mercer Wilson, "Great Bargain on Cutover Land," n.d., Folder 10, Gideon-Anderson Papers.

27. McDowell, "Development by Drainage," 210–225; Kochtitzky, *Story of a Busy Life*, 133–135.

28. Otto, *Final Frontiers*, 37; Little River Drainage District, *Little River Drainage District of Southeast Missouri*, 1–13; McDowell, "Development by Drainage," 252, 256; Ogilvie, "Development of Southeast Missouri," 120–128.

29. Howe, *What Hath God Wrought*, 285.

30. A. E. Chamberlain, International Harvester, testimony reprinted in U.S. Congress, *Mississippi River Floods: Hearings before the United States House Committee on Flood Control, 64th Congress, First Session, on Mar. 16, 1916*, 194–195.

31. "Syrilda Dement's Memories," in *Cardwell Then and Now*, 17–18, DCL; Willie Baxter, "My Life in Deering and Pondertown," Mary Williams, "Deering: My Hometown," and Mary Stillman-Wright, "My Recollections of Deering," in Wade, *Deering*, 45, 54, 103; Snow, *From Missouri*, 133–134; Krusekopf, "Delta Soils," 24; Sweet, Tillman, and Krusekopf, *Soil Survey of Pemiscot County*, 12–13.

32. W. F. James, Caruthersville, interview, March 14, 1994, A.C. 8, Side A, Bootheel Project Records, 1993–1997, C3928, WHMC-C (hereafter Bootheel Project Records); Ogilvie, "Development of Southeast Missouri," 208–12.

33. U.S. Bureau of the Census, *Historical Statistics of the United States*, 517; Wright, *Old South, New South*, 118; U.S. Bureau of the Census, *Twelfth Census of the United States: 1900*, vol. 6, pt. 2, *Agriculture, Crops and Irrigation*, 171–73, 248–49; U.S. Bureau of the Census, *Thirteenth Census of the United States: 1910*, vol. 6, *Agriculture: Reports by States, Alabama–Montana*, 928–38.

34. U.S. Bureau of the Census, *Historical Statistics of the United States,* 517.

35. U.S. Bureau of the Census, *Census of Religious Bodies: 1916,* pt. 1, *Summary and General Tables,* 280–83.

36. U.S. Census, Manuscript Schedules, 1910 (Dwelling 36, Como, New Madrid County, Missouri); 1900 ("William Gander" and "Alvah Gander," Campbell, Warrick County, Indiana; "Oliver Proffer," Welch, Cape Girardeau County, Missouri; and "Tully Raburn," Bardwell, Carlisle County, Kentucky); and 1880 ("Alvah Gander," Campbell, Warrick County, Indiana).

37. Mercer Wilson, "Great Bargain on Cutover Land," n.d., Folder 10, Gideon-Anderson Papers; Painter, *Standing at Armageddon,* 141–175.

38. Kochtitzky, *Story of a Busy Life,* foreword.

39. Nolen, *Missouri's Swamp,* 14–15.

40. C. F. Bruton, *The Modern Promised Land* (1919), Folder 1, *The Modern Promised Land,* R701, WHMC-R.

41. George H. Crumb, Bloomfield, to Louis Houck, March 6, 1900, Folder 18, Box 1523, Series I, Houck Papers, KL.

42. U.S. Bureau of the Census, *Fourteenth Census of the United States: 1920,* vol. 6, pt. 1, *Agriculture: The Northern States,* 578–88; U.S. Bureau of the Census, *Thirteenth Census of the United States: 1910,* vol. 2, *Population: Reports by States, Alabama-Montana,* 1070–86; Ogilvie, "Development of Southeast Missouri," 529.

43. Ogilvie, "Development of Southeast Missouri," 356–57.

44. "The Scott County Kicker Is the People's Paper," *Scott County Kicker,* June 2, 1906; Ogilvie, "Populism and Socialism," 159–183.

45. Salvatore, *Eugene V. Debs,* 183–219.

46. "Observations by the Kicker," *Scott County Kicker,* November 3, 1906; Ogilvie, "Development of Southeast Missouri," 356–357.

47. Green, *Grass-Roots Socialism,* xxi (quote); see also Postel, *Populist Vision,* vii-viii, 4–9.

48. "Farmer and Socialism," *Scott County Kicker,* May 16, 1908.

## 2. Jerusalem

1. "Socialism Is Being Discussed Everywhere," *Scott County Kicker,* February 2, 1907.

2. Russell quoted in Painter, *Standing at Armageddon,* 214–15.

3. Little River Drainage District, *Little River Drainage District of Southeast Missouri,* 6; Bratton, "Geography of the St. Francis," 6–7; "World's Biggest Drainage District Is in S. E. Missouri" (1925) and "Little River Project Reclaims 500,000 Acres" (ca. 1917), both in Folder 46, Box FC 2.2, Clippings Collection, 1871–2001, KL.

4. "Farmers, Are You Blind?" *Scott County Kicker,* October 19, 1907.

5. "From Butler County," *Scott County Kicker,* February 22, 1908.

6. Rodgers, *The Work Ethic in Industrial America,* 30–63; Hackney, *Populism to Progressivism in Alabama,* 81–82; Kantrowitz, *Ben Tillman and the Reconstruction of White Supremacy,* 106–22; Fink, *Workingmen's Democracy,* 3–4.

7. Hahn, *The Roots of Southern Populism*, 3.

8. "Observations by the Kicker," *Scott County Kicker*, July 11, 1908.

9. Debs quoted in Salvatore, *Eugene V. Debs*, 224.

10. Green, *Grass-Roots Socialism*, xi.

11. Stephens, *The Fire Spreads*, 186–229.

12. Stromquist, *Reinventing "The People,"* 7.

13. Kantrowitz, *Ben Tillman and the Reconstruction of White Supremacy*, 2–18; Dawley, *Struggles for Justice*, 136–38, 161–62; Painter, *Standing at Armageddon*, 220–25; Simon, *A Fabric of Defeat*, 11–35; Hackney, *Populism to Progressivism in Alabama*, 318–30; Woodward, *Origins of the New South*, 350–95.

14. For those who see no continuation of producerist political challenges in the Progressive era, see Kantrowitz, *Ben Tillman and the Reconstruction of White Supremacy*, 7; Hackney, *Populism to Progressivism in Alabama*, 111–12; Hahn, *The Roots of Southern Populism*, 287–88; and Hild, *Greenbackers, Knights of Labor, and Populists*, 217–18. For explorations of these rural uprisings, see Green, *Grass-Roots Socialism*; and Waldrep, *Night Riders*.

15. "In a Nut Shell," *Scott County Kicker*, December 1, 1906.

16. "Private Ownership of the Earth Is a Crime Against Mankind," *Scott County Kicker*, August 22, 1908.

17. "In a Nut Shell," *Scott County Kicker*, December 1, 1906.

18. "Something to Think About," *Scott County Kicker*, July 9, 1910.

19. Smith, *Civic Ideals*, 412–13.

20. "Something to Think About," *Scott County Kicker*, July 9, 1910.

21. Ibid.

22. "A Farmer Writes," *Scott County Kicker*, October 26, 1907.

23. "The Time Is Now," *Scott County Kicker*, December 3, 1910.

24. "The Scott County Kicker Is the People's Paper," *Scott County Kicker*, June 2, 1906.

25. "From Sikeston," *Scott County Kicker*, April 2, 1910.

26. "Observations by the Kicker," *Scott County Kicker*, August 10, 1910.

27. "The Night Riders," *Scott County Kicker*, November 21, 1908.

28. "Observations by the Kicker," *Scott County Kicker*, August 10, 1910.

29. Rodgers, *The Work Ethic in Industrial America*, 30–33; Roediger, *The Wages of Whiteness*, 44–47.

30. "With the Beanville Natives," *Scott County Kicker*, January 9, 1909.

31. "Farmer and Socialism," *Scott County Kicker*, May 16, 1908.

32. "A Debate," *Scott County Kicker*, February 8, 1908.

33. "Here and Yonder," *Scott County Kicker*, May 30, 1908.

34. "The Blodgett Picnic," *Scott County Kicker*, September 4, 1909.

35. *Official Manual of the State of Missouri, 1905–06*, 442–43; *Official Manual of the State of Missouri, 1909–10*, 673–720; "Intelligent Voter," *Scott County Kicker*, March 7, 1908; "Socialist Convention," *Scott County Kicker*, March 21, 1908.

36. "Get Busy Socialists," *Scott County Kicker,* October 22, 1910.

37. "In Adjoining Counties," *Scott County Kicker,* August 8, 1908.

38. "It Just Will Grow," *Scott County Kicker,* September 10, 1910.

39. "Socialists Meet and Adopt Platform," *Scott County Kicker,* August 13, 1910.

40. *Official Manual of the State of Missouri, 1905–06,* 442–43; *Official Manual of the State of Missouri, 1909–10,* 673–720; *Official Manual of the State of Missouri, 1911–1912,* 736–81; "It Just Will Grow," *Scott County Kicker,* September 10, 1910; U.S. Bureau of the Census, *Historical Statistics of the United States,* 510–11; U.S. Bureau of the Census, *Fourteenth Census of the United States: 1920,* vol. 6, pt. 1, *Agriculture: Reports for the States,* 578–88.

41. *Pemiscot Argus,* October 5, 1911, quoted in Wyllie, "Race and Class Conflict," 185–86.

42. Wyllie, "Race and Class Conflict," 185.

43. Snow, *From Missouri,* 154.

44. "Around Benton," *Scott County Kicker,* August 28, 1908.

45. "Circuit Court Doings," *Scott County Kicker,* October 24, 1907, November 2, 1908.

46. Wyllie, "Race and Class Conflict," 185.

47. "Kennett News," *Justice,* October 9, 1914.

48. Gorn, "Social Significance of Fighting," 37. See also Flynt, *Poor but Proud,* 217, 243–44 and Ownby, *Subduing Satan.*

49. Ogilvie, "Development of Southeast Missouri," 29–30, 235–37, 529; U.S. Bureau of the Census, *Thirteenth Census of the United States: 1910,* vol. 2: *Population: Reports by States, Alabama–Montana,* 1100–21; U.S. Bureau of the Census, *Fourteenth Census of the United States: 1920,* vol. 6, pt. 1, *Agriculture: Reports for the States,* 578–88.

50. H. R. Post, Parma, to Governor Herbert Hadley, November 9, 1911, Folder 292, Herbert Spencer Hadley Papers, C0006, WHMC-C (hereafter Hadley Papers).

51. Seth Barnes, Marston, to Governor Hadley, March 12, 1911, Folder 322, Hadley Papers.

52. "Negro Stabs Two," *Daily Republican,* October 3, 1911.

53. "Two Negroes Shot by Mob; Thrown in River," *Daily Republican,* October 11, 1911.

54. Hadley Papers: Seth Barnes, Marston, to Governor Hadley, October 12, 1911, Folder 282; J. S. Gossom to Governor Hadley, October 17, 1911, Folder 283; H. R. Post, Parma, to Governor Hadley, November 9, 1911, Folder 292; H. R. Post to Governor Hadley, December 5, 1911, Folder 299; Governor Hadley to J. S. Gossom, October 14, 1911. See also Wyllie, "Race and Class Conflict," 185–86.

55. Hobsbawm, *Primitive Rebels,* 2–3.

56. Seth Barnes to Governor Hadley, October 21, 1911, Folder 285, Hadley Papers.

57. H. R. Post to Governor Hadley, November 9, 1911, Folder 292, and Rumbold to Governor Hadley, December 6, 1911, Folder 299, Hadley Papers

58. Gossom to Governor Hadley, October 17, 1911, Folder 283, Hadley Papers.

59. Echols, "Early History of the First Assembly of God," 3–4, DCL.

60. Higgins, *Pioneering in Pentecost,* 14.

61. Echols, "Early History of the First Assembly of God," 4.

62. Stephens, *The Fire Spreads,* 149–50, 214–15.

63. Barrett, *The Holy Spirit and the Gospel Tradition,* 160.

64. R. Stronstad and J. B. Shelton quoted in Dunn, "Baptism in the Spirit," 7 (first quote) and 8 (second quote).

65. Various historical discussions of Pentecostalism include Stephens, *The Fire Spreads*; Wacker, *Heaven Below*; Blumhofer, *Restoring the Faith*; and Anderson, *Vision of the Disinherited.*

66. "Kennett, Mo.," *Christian Evangel,* December 19, 1914.

67. Echols, "Early History of the First Assembly of God," 4. See also Roll, "From Revolution to Reaction," 5–29.

68. "Moorehouse, Mo.," *Word and Witness,* December 20, 1912.

69. Fields, "Charismatic Religion," 323–25.

70. Stephens, *The Fire Spreads,* 205–06.

71. Thompson, *The Making of the English Working Class,* 382; Green, *Grass-Roots Socialism,* 173.

72. Fields, "Charismatic Religion," 322–25.

73. See, for example, Stephens, *The Fire Spreads,* 206–15. Flynt recognized this denominational blindness in "One in the Spirit," in Harrell, *Varieties of Southern Evangelicalism,* 36.

74. Higgins, *Pioneering in Pentecost,* 16.

75. *Official Manual of the State of Missouri, 1913–14,* 755–56; Ogilvie, "Development of Southeast Missouri," 364.

76. *Justice,* January 16, 1914, 1. *Justice* frequently printed articles without titles; these are cited here with page numbers.

77. "Renters Union," *Justice,* May 8, 1914.

78. "From Mac," *Justice,* October 30, 1914.

79. *Justice,* April 24, 1914, 1.

80. *Justice,* January 23, 1914, 1.

81. *Justice,* May 29, 1914, 1.

82. *Justice,* June 5, 1914, 4.

83. "Malden Matters," *Justice,* June 12, 1914.

84. "Work That Counts," *Justice,* March 6, 1914.

85. Green, *Grass-Roots Socialism,* 162–63; Bissett, *Agrarian Socialism,* 85–87; Goulder, *Luke,* 462.

86. *Justice,* May 22, 1914, 4.

87. Drury, *Luke,* 78.

88. "Comrade Jesus," *Justice,* June 26, 1914.

89. "Kennett News," *Justice,* June 5, 1914.

90. *Justice,* June 12, 1914, 1.

91. "Kennett News," *Justice,* January 9, 1914.

92. "Plum Island," *Justice,* May 15, 1914.

93. Burns, "Soul of Socialism," 113; Green, *Grass-Roots Socialism,* 163–65.

94. "The Socialist Party Platform of 1912," available at www.sagehistory.net/progressive/SocialistPlat1912.htm (accessed July 10, 2009).

95. "Dunklin County Socialist Platform," *Justice,* October 30, 1914.

96. *Justice,* August 14, 1914, 1.

97. "Kennett News," *Justice,* January 9, 1914.

98. "Great Socialist Meeting a Splendid Success," *Justice,* January 30, 1914.

99. "Debs Meeting a Big Success," *Justice,* November 6, 1914.

100. *Justice,* May 29, 1914, 4.

101. *Justice,* May 22, 1914, 4.

102. *Justice,* May 29, 1914, 4.

103. *Justice,* June 12, 1914, 4.

104. "Kennett News," *Justice,* January 16, 1914.

105. U.S. Bureau of the Census, *Thirteenth Census of the United States: 1910,* vol. 6: *Agriculture: Reports by States, Alabama–Montana,* 917–27; U.S. Bureau of the Census, *Fourteenth Census of the United States: 1920,* vol. 6, pt. 1, *Agriculture: Reports for the States,* 578–88; Sweet, Mann, and Krusekopf, *Survey of Pemiscot County, Missouri,* 15; U.S. Bureau of the Census, *Historical Statistics of the United States,* 517; Green, *Grass-Roots Socialism,* 287.

106. *Justice,* January 9, 1914, 4.

107. *Justice,* March 6, 1914, 4.

108. *Justice,* June 12, 1914, 4.

109. Debs quoted in Salvatore, *Eugene V. Debs,* 230.

110. "Renters Union in Pemiscot County," *Justice,* November 13, 1914.

111. *Justice,* May 29, 1914, 4.

112. "Renters Union," *Justice,* November 13, 1914.

113. *Justice,* January 9, 1914, 4.

114. *Justice,* April 3, 1914, 4.

115. *Justice,* January 9, 1914, 4; Horton, *Race and the Making of American Liberalism,* 113–19.

116. *Justice,* August 7, 1914, 4.

117. "The Mudsills," *Justice,* March 19, 1914.

118. "Gideon Injustice," *Justice,* May 22, 1914.

119. U.S. Census, Manuscript Schedules, 1910 ("William Cunningham," Lewis, New Madrid County, Missouri); Roediger, *The Wages of Whiteness,* 47.

120. Foley, *The White Scourge,* 92–117; Salvatore, *Eugene V. Debs,* 226–27; Green, *Grass-Roots Socialism,* 236–37.

121. *Justice,* January 23, 1914, 4.

122. *Justice,* January 9, 1914, 1.

123. O'Hare, "Nigger Equality," in Foner and Miller, *Kate Richards O'Hare,* 46.

124. Davis quoted in Hild, *Greenbackers, Knights of Labor, and Populists,* 162.

125. *Justice,* May 29, 1914, 4.

126. *Justice,* June 5, 1914, 4.

127. *Justice,* June 19, 1914, 4.

128. *Justice,* August 21, 1914, 4.

129. *Justice,* January 9, 1914, 1.

130. *Justice,* May 29, 1914, 4.

131. *Justice,* September 11, 1914, 4.

132. "Their Reason Applied," *Justice,* April 10, 1914.

133. *Justice,* July 31, 1914, 1.

134. "Election Returns," *Justice,* November 6, 1914.

135. *Justice,* June 19, 1914, 4.

136. "Election Returns," *Justice,* November 6, 1914; *Justice,* November 13, 1914, 1.

137. Green, *Grass-Roots Socialism,* 295–99; Hild, *Greenbackers, Knights of Labor, and Populists,* 213.

138. "Burns Doings," *Justice,* September 4, 1914.

139. *Justice,* November 13, 1914, 4.

140. Ogilvie, "Development of Southeast Missouri," 217–18.

141. "The Negro Situation," *Critic,* March 19, 1915.

142. "Night Riders at Tallapoosa," *Dunklin Democrat,* October 29, 1915; "New Madrid Night Riders," *Dunklin Democrat,* November 5, 1915; "Battle with the Night Riders," *Dunklin Democrat,* December 24, 1915; "Night Rider Outrage," *Standard,* November 12, 1915.

143. "Night Riders Held," *Sikeston Standard,* December 10, 1915; "Night Rider Outrages," *Sikeston Standard,* December 17, 1915.

144. Roll, "Gideon's Band," 483–85; N. C. Anderson, Gideon, to Whom It May Concern, May 12, 1917, Folder 2, Scott Carey Papers, 1917–1961, C2336, WHMC-C (hereafter Carey Papers).

145. "Land Barons Back Prosecution of 67 for Night Riding," *Post-Dispatch,* January 24, 1916.

146. Ibid.

147. "Guard Doubled to Prevent Effort to Free Night Riders," *Post-Dispatch,* January 22, 1916; "Night Riders Held," *Standard,* December 10, 1915; Ogilvie, "Development of Southeast Missouri," 219.

148. "33 Night Riders Given Preliminary," *Scott County Democrat,* December 16, 1915; "Last of the Night Riders in the Toils," *Weekly Record,* December 25, 1915.

149. *State of Missouri v. Ed Miller, et al.,* no. 450, January Term 1916 (New Madrid County Circuit Court), witness subpoena.

150. "Night Riders Held," *Standard,* December 10, 1915; "Guard Doubled to Prevent Effort to Free Night Riders," *Post-Dispatch,* January 22, 1916.

151. Waldrep, *Night Riders,* 72.

152. "Guard Doubled to Prevent Effort to Free Night Riders," *Post-Dispatch,* January 22, 1916.

153. "Land Barons Back Prosecution of 67 for Night Riding," *Post-Dispatch,* January 24, 1916.

154. "Editorial," *Standard,* December 24, 1915.

155. N. C. Anderson to Whom It May Concern, May 12, 1917, Folder 2, Carey Papers.

156. "Editorial," *Citizen,* December 17, 1915.

157. "Night Riders Held," *Standard,* December 10, 1915. *State of Missouri v. Ed Miller, et al.,* no. 450, January Term 1916 (New Madrid County Circuit Court) provides further descriptions of the accused.

158. "2 Are Convicted, 3 Plead Guilty to Night Riding," *Post-Dispatch,* January 21, 1916; *State of Missouri v. Ed Miller, et al.,* no. 450, January Term 1916 (New Madrid County Circuit Court); *Criminal Record,* Docket E, June 1915–October 1920 (New Madrid County Circuit Court), 119–69.

159. Green, *Grass-Roots Socialism,* 303 (second quote), 308 (first quote).

160. Cunningham testimony quoted in "Guard Doubled to Prevent Effort to Free Night Riders," *Post-Dispatch,* January 22, 1916.

161. State of *Missouri v. Ed Miller, et al.,* nos. 448–450, January Term 1916 (New Madrid County Circuit Court); "Editorial," *Standard,* January 28, 1916.

162. "35 Plead Guilty in Night Rider Cases; Paroled," *Post-Dispatch,* January 25, 1916.

163. *Official Manual of the State of Missouri, 1915–16,* 484–86; *Official Manual of the State of Missouri, 1917–18,* 431–56; *Official Manual of the State of Missouri, 1919–20,* 411–12; Ogilvie, "Development of Southeast Missouri," 372–74; Weinstein, *The Decline of Socialism in America,* 119–76; Salvatore, *Eugene V. Debs,* 262–302.

164. Kantrowitz, *Ben Tillman and the Reconstruction of White Supremacy,* 7.

## 3. Saviors of Agriculture

1. "Thousands of Negroes Driven from a Missouri Town in America; An Indication of What Will Happen to Negroes without Organization," *The Negro World,* March 10, 1923.

2. U.S. Census, Manuscript Schedules, 1920 ("Alex Cooper," Hector, Mississippi County, Arkansas). The total number of rural blacks living in Dunklin, Mississippi, New Madrid, Pemiscot, Scott, and Stoddard counties rose from approximately 5,500 in 1920 to 20,696 in 1924, or from about 5 percent of the rural population in 1920 to over 20 percent in 1924. U.S. Bureau of the Census, *Fourteenth Census of the United States: 1920,* vol. 3, *Population,* 551–61; U.S. Bureau of the Census, *U.S. Census of Agriculture: 1925,* pt. 1, *The Northern States,* 904–33, 949–63.

3. Helms, "Just Lookin' for a Home," 281–314; Higgs, "Boll Weevil," 349; Daniel,

*Standing at the Crossroads,* 77–78; Jones, *The Dispossessed,* 123; Sydney Nathans, "Fortress without Walls," in Hall and Stack, *Holding onto the Land and the Lord,* 60; U.S. Census, Manuscript Schedules, 1900 ("Alex Cooper," Louisville, Winston County, Mississippi).

4. Grim, "African American Landlords," 405–16; Rogers, *Life and Death in the Delta,* 75–78; Reid, "African-American Farm Families," 336–40; Schweninger, *Black Property Owners in the South,* 162–64, 208; Debra A. Reid, "African Americans, Community Building," in Stock and Johnston, *The Countryside in the Age of the Modern State,* 39; Reid, *Reaping a Greater Harvest,* xxi–xxii; Hahn, *A Nation under Our Feet,* 135–67.

5. Roy Cooper Jr. and Alex Cooper, Hayti, interview with Will Sarvis, August 4, 1998, 26, PMOH, C3929.

6. R. Douglas Hurt, "Introduction," in Hurt, *African American Life in the Rural South,* 1. Others that take this approach include McMillen, *Dark Journey,* 122; Litwack, *Trouble in Mind,* 135; Cobb, *The Most Southern Place on Earth,* 115–16; and Woodruff, *American Congo,* 22–23. For recent exceptions to this portrayal, see Rolinson, *Grassroots Garveyism*; Reid, *Reaping a Greater Harvest*; and Walker, *Southern Farmers and Their Stories.*

7. Figures based on lists in Hill, *The Marcus Garvey and Universal Negro Improvement Association Papers,* 7:986–96; Rolinson, *Grassroots Garveyism,* 197–99; and Membership Record Card File, 1925–1927, Box 22B, UNIA Central Division Records, Schomburg Center, New York Public Library.

8. Rolinson, *Grassroots Garveyism,* 8, 47.

9. Garvey, January 1924, quoted in Wintz, *African American Political Thought,* 234.

10. "U.N.I.A., Nearing the Greatest World Conference of Race, Calls upon Negroes Everywhere to Rise Up and Be Men," *The Negro World,* April 27, 1929.

11. Mitchell, *Righteous Propagation,* 144–45, 218–39; Stein, *The World of Marcus Garvey,* 226–47. Helen Bradford charts a similar process among rural South Africans whereby "Garveyism was domesticated" to correspond to existing millenarian beliefs. See Bradford, *A Taste of Freedom,* 214–18.

12. Giggie, *After Redemption,* 95.

13. "Preach the Gospel of Conservation of Race Resources," *The Negro World,* August 13, 1927.

14. Fulop, "Millennialism and Black Americans," 78; Rolinson, *Grassroots Garveyism,* 1–8.

15. "Scott County Acreage Goes to 15,000," *Southeast Missourian,* January 23, 1923, "Cotton Facts," *Southeast Missourian,* September 12, 1923; Hudson, "Rise of Cotton Production in Southeast Missouri," 66; Jenkins, "History of Cotton Production in Southeast Missouri," 23, 36–37; U.S. Bureau of the Census, *Historical Statistics of the United States,* 511, 517; Tindall, *The Emergence of the New South,* 111–12.

16. Jenkins, "History of Cotton Production in Southeast Missouri," 36–37.

17. C. M. Barnes to the Editor, *Southeast Missourian*, May 24, 1923.

18. A. S. Hulit, Charleston, to Governor Arthur Hyde, December 16, 1922, Folder 106, Arthur Mastick Hyde Papers, 1913–1954, C0007, WHMC-C (hereafter Hyde Papers); "20,000 Acres of Cotton; Outlook for this County," *Enterprise-Courier*, December 14, 1922.

19. Hudson, "Rise of Cotton Production in Southeast Missouri," 57, 68–69; Helms, "Just Lookin' for a Home," 257, 269, 320–21.

20. Hulit to Governor Hyde, December 16, 1922, Folder 106, Hyde Papers.

21. "City Hosts Cotton Growing Conference," *Southeast Missourian*, February 9, 1923.

22. Alex Cooper, Portageville, interview by unidentified researcher, March 11, 1994, A.C. 3, Side A, Folder 50, Bootheel Project Records; Maxwell Williams, Gideon, interview by unknown researcher, March 16, 1994, Folder 50, Bootheel Project Records; *Southeast Missourian*, January 3, 1923, quoted in Hudson, "Rise of Cotton Production in Southeast Missouri," 61.

23. "What Class Shall Run Southeast Missouri?" *Standard*, January 19, 1923.

24. U.S. Census, Manuscript Schedules, 1930 ("George Washington," LeSieur, New Madrid County, Missouri); 1920 ("George Washington," Holly, Desha County, Arkansas).

25. "Southern Negroes Flocking Up North," *Democrat-Argus*, December 8, 1922; "White Man and Negro Must Hit the Road," *Standard*, January 26, 1923 (quote).

26. Roy Cooper Jr. and Alex Cooper, interview with Will Sarvis, 1, PMOH.

27. Helms, "Just Lookin' for a Home," 320–21.

28. "Editorial," *Standard*, January 19, 1923.

29. Hahn, *A Nation under Our Feet*, 457–61; Clark, *Defining Moments*, 67; Sitton and Conrad, *Freedom Colonies*, 4–5, 121; Schweninger, *Black Property Owners in the South*, 182–84.

30. Washington quoted in Harlan, *Booker T. Washington*, 218.

31. Ayers, *The Promise of the New South*, 326.

32. U.S. Census, Manuscript Schedules, 1930 ("George Washington," LeSieur, New Madrid County, Missouri); Rolinson, *Grassroots Garveyism*, 41.

33. "What Class Shall Run Southeast Missouri?" *Standard*, January 19, 1923.

34. "People Flocking to Cotton District," *Southeast Missourian*, January 5, 1923.

35. "Cotton Is King Again," *Enterprise-Courier*, December 14, 1922.

36. "Postal Card Brings 31 Families to Mississippi County," *Southeast Missourian*, January 19, 1923.

37. "Cotton Production in Missouri," Bulletin 299, 4–6; U.S. Bureau of the Census, *Fourteenth Census of the United States: 1920*, vol. 3, *Population*, 551–61; U.S. Bureau of the Census, *Fifteenth Census of the United States: 1930: Population*, vol. 3, pt. 1, *Alabama–Missouri*, 1347–54, 1370–86; U.S. Bureau of the Census, *U.S. Census of Agriculture: 1925*, pt. 1, *The Northern States*, 904–33, 949–63.

38. U.S. Bureau of the Census, *Fourteenth Census of the United States: 1920*, vol. 6, pt. 1, *Agriculture: The Northern States*, 578–88; U.S. Bureau of the Census, *U.S. Census of Agriculture: 1925*, pt. 1, *The Northern States*, 904–33.

39. Sitton and Conrad, *Freedom Colonies*, 143; Rogers, *Life and Death in the Delta*, 74 (quote), 78, 117; Lynn-Sherow, *Red Earth*, 42.

40. Washington quoted in Wintz, *African American Political Thought*, 76.

41. U.S. Bureau of the Census, *Fourteenth Census of the United States: 1920*, vol. 6, pt. 1, *Agriculture: The Northern States*, 578–88; U.S. Bureau of the Census, *U.S. Census of Agriculture: 1925*, pt. 1, *The Northern States*, 904–33; Kirby, *Rural Worlds Lost*, 143–44; Wright, *Old South, New South*, 99–102; Fite, *Cotton Fields No More*, 4–6; Alex Cooper, interview by author, November 30, 2003; "Lease contract, Marston Real Estate Company," 1924, Folder 196, Charles M. Barnes Papers, C2802, WHMC-C (hereafter Barnes Papers).

42. Roy Cooper Jr. and Alex Cooper, interview with Will Sarvis, 1, PMOH.

43. Kirby, *Rural Worlds Lost*, 143–44; Fite, *Cotton Fields No More*, 4–6.

44. Roy Cooper Jr., interview with unidentified researcher, March 17, 1994, A. C. 11, Side A, Bootheel Project Records; U.S. Census, Manuscript Schedules, 1930 ("Alex Cooper," Concord, Pemiscot County, Missouri; and "Gideon Caffee," La Font, New Madrid County, Missouri).

45. Grim, "African American Landlords," 405, 407; Sitton and Conrad, *Freedom Colonies*, 61–64.

46. Jones, *Labor of Love, Labor of Sorrow*, 96–109; Rogers, *Life and Death in the Delta*, 51–2.

47. Roy Cooper Jr. and Alex Cooper, interview with Will Sarvis, 1, PMOH.

48. Louise Newman, "Moving beyond the Accommodation/Resistance Divide: Race and Gender in the Discourse of Booker T. Washington," in Brundage, *Booker T. Washington and Black Progress*, 183–84 (second quote), 186–87 (first quote).

49. Henry H. Hooker to James Weldon Johnson, December 28, 1923, Folder "River, Mo.," Container 109, Series G, Records of the National Association for the Advancement of Colored People, Library of Congress (hereafter NAACP Records); U.S. Bureau of the Census, *Census of Religious Bodies: 1926*, vol. 1:63–39; 2:133, 997.

50. Clark, *Defining Moments*, 64–5 (quotes); Mitchell, *Righteous Propagation*, 52–4; Lincoln and Mamiya, *The Black Church in the African American Experience*, 68.

51. Roy Cooper Jr. and Alex Cooper, interview with Will Sarvis, 2, PMOH.

52. James Jackson, Caruthersville, to Governor Hyde, Jefferson City, November 5, 1922, Folder 366, Hyde Papers.

53. "Thinning out of Negroes in North End of County," *Democrat-Argus*, February 6, 1923; "Homes of Negroes Are Riddled; Cotton Workers Driven Away," *Southeast Missourian*, February 6, 1923.

54. "Whites Who Sought Higher Pay Warn Negroes," *Standard*, March 9, 1923; "Klan Said to Have Stopped Negro Exodus from Southeast Missouri by Warning Disturbers to Leave," *Star*, March 4, 1923; "Negro Killed on Stone Plantation" and

"Editorial," *Vindicator,* April 27, 1923; "Three Men Held in Connection with Slaying of Negro Worker," *Southeast Missourian,* April 30, 1923.

55. Carl F. Bloker, Caruthersville, to Governor Hyde, March 1, 1923, Folder 107, Hyde Papers; "Negro Farmers Being Intimidated," *Standard,* January 12, 1923.

56. "Klan Said to Have Stopped Negro Exodus from Southeast Missouri by Warning Disturbers to Leave," *Star,* March 4, 1923.

57. "Whites Who Sought Higher Pay Warn Negroes," *Standard,* March 9, 1923.

58. "Negro Farmers Being Intimidated," *Standard,* January 12, 1923.

59. Governor Hyde to James Jackson, Caruthersville, November 10, 1922, Folder 366, Hyde Papers.

60. "Klan Said to Have Stopped Negro Exodus from Southeast Missouri by Warning Disturbers to Leave," *Star,* March 4, 1923.

61. "Ku Klux Klan Issues Warning," ca. 1923, Folder 20, Box FC 3.1, Clippings Collection, 1871–2001, KL.

62. Major A. C. Thrower to Adjutant General of Missouri, April 24, 1923, Folder 107, Hyde Papers; "Race Riot at Parma," *Carter County News,* ca. 1923, Folder 20, Box FC 3.1, Clippings Collection, 1871–2001, KL.

63. "Negroes Swarm to this District from the South," *Southeast Missourian,* October 19, 1923; Jenkins, "History of Cotton Production in Southeast Missouri," 36–37; Ogilvie, "Development of Southeast Missouri," 183–84.

64. "Locations of UNIA Divisions and Chapters," in Hill, *The Marcus Garvey and Universal Negro Improvement Association Papers,* 7:986–96; Rolinson, *Grassroots Garveyism,* 197–99; Membership Record Card File, 1925–1927, Box 22B, UNIA Central Division Records, Schomburg.

65. "Thinks *The Negro World* Should Be in Every Home," *The Negro World,* September 13, 1924.

66. U.S. Census, Manuscript Schedules, 1920 ("D. D. Daniels," Canadian, Mississippi County, Arkansas); D. D. Daniels, "Convention Report," August 8, 1924, in Hill, *The Marcus Garvey and Universal Negro Improvement Association Papers,* 5:685; *The Negro World,* June 16, 30, 1923.

67. U.S. Census, Manuscript Schedules, 1920 ("Stonewall Jackson," Badgett, Pulaski County, Arkansas).

68. U.S. Census, Manuscript Schedules, 1930 ("Will Jones," Ohio, Mississippi County, Missouri); "Wyatt, Missouri, Div.," *The Negro World,* August 29, 1931.

69. U.S. Census, Manuscript Schedules, 1920 ("James Milton," Mississippi, Mississippi County, Missouri; "S. H. Marris," Tywhappity, Mississippi County, Missouri).

70. "Charleston, Mo.," *The Negro World,* August 7, 1926, "Wyatt, Mo.," *The Negro World,* September 3, 1927; Hahn, *A Nation under Our Feet,* 471–72; Stein, *The World of Marcus Garvey,* 223; Rolinson, *Grassroots Garveyism,* 109.

71. See Rolinson, *Grassroots Garveyism,* 103.

72. Membership Record Card File, 1925–1927, Box 22B, UNIA Central Division Records, Schomburg.

73. "African Redemption Fund Appeal," in Hill, *The Marcus Garvey and Universal Negro Improvement Association Papers*, 3:745.

74. "Marcus Garvey's Defense Fund," *The Negro World*, June 16 and June 30, 1923.

75. "Marcus Garvey's Defense Fund," *The Negro World*, June 16 and September 8, 1923.

76. "Preach the Gospel of Conservation of Race Resources," *The Negro World*, August 13, 1927.

77. Harold, *The Rise and Fall of the Garvey Movement in the Urban South*, 68–69. For further analysis of urban Garveyites, see Phillips, *AlabamaNorth*, 186–88.

78. Rolinson, *Grassroots Garveyism*, 3 (quote); Clark, *Defining Moments*, 67–167.

79. Gaines, *Uplifting the Race*, 2.

80. Stein, *The World of Marcus Garvey*, 223.

81. Owen and Zella Whitfield family, oral history, November 14, 1982, A.C. "Tom," Side A, Box 107, Oral History 500, Wagner Labor Archives, Tamiment Library.

82. "Wyatt, Mo.," *The Negro World*, December 8, 1928.

83. Burkett, *Garveyism as a Religious Movement*, 49 (quote), 59.

84. "Grapple with Problems in a Practical Way," *The Negro World*, July 25, 1925.

85. "Working Hard Now with Eye on Future," *The Negro World*, September 5, 1925.

86. "Renters Union in Pemiscot County," *Justice*, November 13, 1914.

87. Barbara Bair, "True Women, Real Men: Gender, Ideology, and Social Roles in the Garvey Movement," in Helly and Reverby, *Gendered Domains*, 156.

88. "Thousands of Negroes Driven from a Missouri Town in America; An Indication of What Will Happen to Negroes without Organization," *The Negro World*, March 10, 1923.

89. Ogilvie, "Development of Southeast Missouri," 260–61.

90. Clark, *Defining Moments*, 77; Rolinson, *Grassroots Garveyism*, 135–36.

91. Bair, "True Women, Real Men," in Helly and Reverby, *Gendered Domains*, 155 (quote); O'Donovan, *Becoming Free in the Cotton South*, 191–93.

92. Stein, *The World of Marcus Garvey*, 236; Taylor, *Veiled Garvey*, 44.

93. "Wyatt, Mo., Div.," *The Negro World*, October 4, 1930.

94. "Charleston, Mo.," *The Negro World*, August 7, 1926.

95. Mitchell, *Righteous Propagation*, 225–37.

96. See, for example, "Marcus Garvey Defense Fund," *The Negro World*, June 16, 30, September 8, 1923; "Convention and General Fund," *The Negro World*, July 12, August 2, September 6, 1924, and December 11, 1926.

97. See "Rehabilitation and Expansion Fund," *The Negro World*, May 15, 1926, June 26, 1926; Rolinson, *Grassroots Garveyism*, 152–53.

98. "Defense Fund Subscribers Whose Liberality We Gratefully Acknowledge," *The Negro World*, September 22, 1923.

99. Giggie, *After Redemption*, 60 (quote); Phillips, *AlabamaNorth*, 180–81.

100. Clark, *Defining Moments*, 227.

101. Hahn, *A Nation under Our Feet,* 464 (quote); Harvey, *Redeeming the South,* 243–55; Giggie, *After Redemption,* 76–93.

102. Burkett, *Garveyism as a Religious Movement,* 5–33.

103. Clark, *Defining Moments,* 207.

104. "Charleston, Mo.," *The Negro World,* August 7, 1926.

105. "Wyatt, Mo.," *The Negro World,* December 8, 1928.

106. Burkett, *Garveyism as a Religious Movement,* 5–9, 23–29; Rolinson, *Grassroots Garveyism,* 45–47, 92–94; Garvey, August 14, 1921, in Hill, *The Marcus Garvey and Universal Negro Improvement Association Papers,* 3:665.

107. "Wyatt, Mo.," *The Negro World,* October 27, 1928.

108. Marcus Garvey speech, Liberty Hall, Harlem, August 14, 1921, in Hill, *The Marcus Garvey and Universal Negro Improvement Association Papers,* 3:665.

109. Burkett, *Garveyism as a Religious Movement,* 29. The "Universal Ethiopian Anthem," also known as "Ethiopia, Land of My Fathers," was adopted as the official anthem of the UNIA in 1920. Penned by UNIA members Arnold Ford and Benjamin Burrell, the "Universal Ethiopian Anthem" captured the militant, quasi-martial atmosphere of Harlem in the early 1920s. See "The Universal Ethiopian Anthem and How It Came to Be Written," *The Negro World,* August 25, 1923; and Wilmore, *African American Religious Studies,* 81n49.

110. Barnes, *Journey of Hope,* 133–34 (quote); Campbell, *Songs of Zion,* 296–300; Montgomery, *Under Their Own Vine and Fig Tree,* 225–29.

111. Fulop, "Millennialism and Black Americans," 78–91; Giggie, *After Redemption,* 73 (quote).

112. Hahn, *A Nation under Our Feet,* 469.

113. "Cape Girardeau, Mo.," *The Negro World,* November 15, 1924.

114. "Hermondale, Missouri," *The Negro World,* April 18, 1925.

115. Ezek. 34:12–13.

116. Emmanuel Street, Charleston, to the Editor, *The Negro World,* July 26, 1924.

117. "Charleston, Missouri," *The Negro World,* December 15, 1923.

118. D. D. Daniel and R. H. Starks, New Madrid, to the Attorney General, November 1, 1925, Folder 9, Box 1160A, Record 42, Pardon Case Files, RG 204, NARA, College Park.

119. "Charleston, Missouri," *The Negro World,* December 15, 1923.

120. "New Madrid, Ill.," *The Negro World,* October 27, 1923. Note that the article is incorrectly titled; it should read "New Madrid, Mo."

121. "Proceedings of Fourth International Convention," *The Negro World,* August 16, 1924.

122. "Charleston, Mo.," *The Negro World,* July 19, 1924.

123. For more on the politics of Garveyites in the urban South, see Harold, *The Rise and Fall of the Garvey Movement in the Urban South,* 9, 91–92.

124. "Application for Charter, Caruthersville, Mo. Branch, December 31, 1920," Container 107, Series G, NAACP Records.

125. Container 107, Series G, NAACP Records: Jewell Murphy, Commerce, to NAACP, December 2, 1926, Folder "Commerce, Mo."; Claude A. Davis, East Prairie, to J. E. Spingarn, October 25, 1924, Folder "East Prairie, Mo." Container 109, Series G, NAACP Records: J. G. Hopkins, Oran, to NAACP, September 20, 1926, Folder "Oran, Mo."

126. "Convention Report," August 4, 1924, in Hill, *The Marcus Garvey and Universal Negro Improvement Association Papers,* 5:652.

127. "Report of Activities in UNIA Divisions and Garvey Clubs," March 1936, in Hill, *The Marcus Garvey and Universal Negro Improvement Association Papers,* 7:673.

128. Ogilvie, "Development of Southeast Missouri," 257–58; "Negro Farmers Being Intimidated," *Standard,* January 12, 1923 (quote).

129. Stein, *The World of Marcus Garvey,* 154–55.

130. Ibid., 186–204; Rolinson, *Grassroots Garveyism,* 156.

131. Harry McHolland, Charleston, to President Calvin Coolidge, March 1, 1925, Folder 1, Box 1161, Record 42, Pardon Case Files, RG 204, NARA, College Park.

132. McHolland to John Sargent, Washington, D.C., May 3, 1925, Folder 4, Box 1161, Record 42, Pardon Case Files, RG 204, NARA, College Park.

133. D. D. Daniel and R. H. Starks, New Madrid, to the Attorney General, November 1, 1925, Folder 9, Box 1160A, Record 42, Pardon Case Files, RG 204, NARA, College Park.

134. See numerous examples in Folder 6, Box 1160B, Record 42, Pardon Case Files, RG 204, NARA, College Park.

135. "New Madrid Suffers Worst Flood in Its History," *Weekly Record,* April 29, 1927; "Red Cross Supervising Relief among Refugees," *Dunklin Democrat,* April 26, 1927; American National Red Cross, *The Mississippi Valley Flood Disaster of 1927,* 126.

136. "Summary Statistics of Losses in the State of Missouri," August 2, 1928, Folder "Mississippi River Valley Flood, Statistics by States," Box 735, DR 220–02, Group 2, Red Cross Records: 1917–1934, ARC 304957, NARA, College Park; U.S. Bureau of the Census, *U.S. Census of Agriculture: 1925,* pt. 1, *The Northern States,* 904–16.

137. "Flood Water Recedes," *Weekly Record,* May 6, 1927.

138. "Tells of Flood in Dorena District," *Enterprise-Courier,* May 12, 1927.

139. "Statistics of Losses in the State of Missouri," August 2, 1928, Folder "Mississippi River Valley Flood, Statistics by States," Box 735, and "Preliminary Health Report of Southeastern Missouri Flood Area," April 19, 1927, Folder "Mississippi River Valley Flood, Missouri," Box 738, both in DR 220–02, Group 2, Red Cross Records: 1917–1934; American National Red Cross, *The Mississippi Valley Flood Disaster of 1927,* 120–21; Spencer, "Contested Terrain," 170–81; Daniel, *Deep'n As It Come,* 91–108.

140. Robert E. Bondy, "Report of Conference on Mississippi Valley Flood Situation," July 19–20, 1928, Folder "Mississippi Valley Flood, Reports and Statistics," Box

734, and "Meeting of the Missouri chapters of the Red Cross," June 5, 1927, Folder "Mississippi River Valley Flood, Missouri," Box 738, both in DR 220–02, Group 2, Red Cross Records: 1917–1934; Jenkins, "History of Cotton Production in Southeast Missouri," 39.

141. Hawes, "Drainage and Its Financial Obligations," Folder 46, Box FC 2.2, Clippings Collection, 1871–2001, KL; U.S. Bureau of the Census, *U.S. Census of Agriculture: 1925*, pt. 1, *The Northern States*, 904–33, 949–78; U.S. Bureau of the Census, *Fifteenth Census of the United States: 1930: Agriculture*, vol. 3, pt. 1, *Type of Farm, The Northern States*, 747–54, 796–803; U.S. Bureau of the Census, *Fifteenth Census of the United States: 1930: Population*, vol. 3, pt. 1, *Alabama–Missouri*, 1356–57.

142. Membership Record Card File, 1925–1927, 22B, UNIA Central Division Records, Schomburg.

143. "Wyatt, Missouri," *The Negro World*, September 3, 1927.

144. "Wyatt, Mo.," *The Negro World*, December 8, 1928. After visiting the United Kingdom and France, Garvey journeyed to Canada, from where rumors emerged that he would attempt to enter the United States. He did not. See Grant, *Negro with a Hat*, 425–26.

145. Jacob Harris, Charleston, to NAACP, October 1927, "Application for Charter of Mississippi County, Mo Branch," February 18, 1928, Folder "Charleston, Mo., 1928–1940," Container 107, Series G, NAACP Records.

146. A. L. Halloway to NAACP, March 24, 1929, Folder "Charleston, Mo., 1928–1940," Container 107, Series G, NAACP Records.

147. "Introduction," in Hill, *The Marcus Garvey and Universal Negro Improvement Association Papers*, 7: xxxvii–xliv.

148. Report of UNIA Secretary General Henrietta Vinton Davis, May 3, 1930, in Hill, *The Marcus Garvey and Universal Negro Improvement Association Papers*, 7: 403–04.

149. "Poplar Bluff, Mo.," *The Negro World*, May 10, 1930.

150. "Wyatt, Mo., Div.," *The Negro World*, October 4, 1930.

151. See "Wyatt, Missouri, Div.," *The Negro World*, August 29, 1931; and Joseph Gray's report mentioned in "Report of Activities in UNIA Divisions and Garvey Clubs," March 1936, in Hill, *The Marcus Garvey and Universal Negro Improvement Association Papers*, 7:673.

## 4. No More Mourning

1. Versions of Whitfield's story are in Cantor, *A Prologue to the Protest Movement*, 31; Whitfield, interview by Howard Emerson, March 1963, quoted in Emerson, "Sharecropper's Strike," 38; and Belfrage, "Cotton-Patch Moses," 97 (quotes).

2. *Southeast Missourian*, June 25, 1934, quoted in Jenkins, "History of Cotton Production in Southeast Missouri," 63–64.

3. Wright, *Old South, New South*, 226–35; Pete Daniel, "The New Deal, Southern Agriculture, and Economic Change," in Cobb and Namaroto, *The New Deal and the South*, 41–42, 50.

4. Belfrage, "Cotton-Patch Moses," 97.

5. Cox, *Fire from Heaven*, 71; Kirby, *Rural Worlds Lost*, 184; Harvey, *Redeeming the South*, 255; Oltman, *Sacred Mission, Worldly Ambition*, 161, 182; Phillips, *Alabama-North*, 173–78.

6. Stephens, *The Fire Spreads*, 161–65, 195–98; Phillips, *AlabamaNorth*, 173–74; Cox, *Fire from Heaven*, 114.

7. Pinn, *Why, Lord?* 157.

8. Kelley, *Race Rebels*, 42 (quote); Cox, *Fire from Heaven*, 114.

9. Belfrage, "Cotton-Patch Moses," 97.

10. See Woodruff, *As Rare as Rain*; and Hamilton, "Hoover and the 1930 Drought," 850–75.

11. "Reports from County Agents," Folder "Reports of Crop Losses and Farmers Needs," Box 767, DR 401, Group 2, Red Cross Records: 1917–1934, ARC 304957, NARA, College Park; "Local Showers Bring Little Relief; Senath Farmers Ask for Feed Aid," *Dunklin Democrat*, August 12, 1930.

12. U.S. Bureau of the Census, *Fifteenth Census of the United States: 1930, Population*, vol. 6, *Families*, 745–51; U.S. Bureau of the Census, *U.S. Census of Agriculture: 1935*, vol. 1, *Farms, Farm Acreage, and Value*, 262–71; William Baxter to DeWitt Smith, "Weekly Drouth Relief Report," September 13, 1930, Folder "Weekly Reports, 9/13/30," Box 769, DR 401, Group 2, Red Cross Records: 1917–1934, ARC 304957, NARA, College Park.

13. *Democrat-Argus*, October 3, 1930, quoted in Bright, "Farm Wage Workers," 31–32.

14. Baxter to Smith, "Weekly Drouth Relief Report," September 13, 1930, Folder "Weekly Reports, 9/13/30"; Baxter to Smith, "Drouth Relief Report for Missouri and Illinois," September 27, 1930, Folder "Weekly Reports, 9/27/30"; both in Box 769, DR 401, Group 2, Red Cross Records: 1917–1934, ARC 304957, NARA, College Park.

15. Xenophon Caverno, Canalou, to Scott W. Julian, New Madrid, October 19, 1930, Folder 77, Xenophon Caverno Papers, 1917–1941, C0059, WHMC-C (hereafter Caverno Papers).

16. Baxter to Governor Henry Caulfield, Jefferson City, December 29, 1930, Folder "Missouri Reports and Statistics," Baxter to Stratton Shartel, December 29, 1930, Folder "Missouri, by Counties," Box 773, DR 401, Group 2, Red Cross Records: 1917–1934, ARC 304957, NARA, College Park.

17. "Missouri," Folder "Statistics as of June 30, 1931," Box 768, DR 401, Group 2, Red Cross Records: 1917–1934, ARC 304957, NARA, College Park. Percent population calculated from U.S. Bureau of the Census, *Fifteenth Census of the United States: 1930: Population*, vol. 3, pt. 1, *Alabama–Missouri*, 1347–54.

18. Baxter to Frieser, June 23, 1931, Folder "Missouri, by Counties," Box 773, DR 401, Group 2, Red Cross Records: 1917–1934, ARC 304957, NARA, College Park.

19. Ogilvie, "Development of Southeast Missouri," 195; Jenkins, "Cotton Production in Southeast Missouri," 39; Snow, *From Missouri*, 164–65; Daniel, *Breaking the Land*, 92.

20. Caverno to Baxter, June 28, 1932, Folder 77, Caverno Papers; Ogilvie, "Development of Southeast Missouri," 197; Snow, *From Missouri*, 169.

21. *Daily Dunklin Democrat*, March 31, 1993, quoted in Wade, *Deering Plantation*, 108; Hart, "Study of Levels of Living," 44; Bright, "Farm Wage Workers," 64.

22. Testimony of Andrew Puckett, South Lilbourn, in U. S. Congress, *Hearings before the Select Committee Investigating National Defense Migration, House of Representatives, 77th Congress, First Session, Part 23, St. Louis, November 26, 1941*, 9172–74.

23. Caverno to Julian, October 19, 1930, Folder 77, Caverno Papers.

24. United States Army Corps of Engineers, *Final Report of the Mississippi River Flood Control Board to the President of the United States*, 6; L. T. Berthe, *Analysis of the Plans of the United States Army Corps of Engineers, Presented to the Committee on Flood Control, January 17, 1928*, 2–25; *Scott County Democrat*, January 31, 1929, quoted in Shrum, *Super Floods Raging in Wide Spread Area*, 1–2.

25. Snow, *From Missouri*, 172–73.

26. "Rich Land, Poor People," Report File on the Southeast Missouri Study, 1937, Tables 1–7, Entry 52, Records of the Farmers Home Administration, RG 96, NARA, Great Lakes Region (hereafter Records of the FHA).

27. Stokes, "Housing Conditions in Southeast Missouri," 104.

28. "The Farmers' Column," *Chicago Defender*, February 13, 1932 (quote); "Mississippi Farmers Save by Co-Operative Marketing," *Chicago Defender*, July 19, 1930; McMillen, *Dark Journey*, 135.

29. "The Farmers' Column," *Chicago Defender*, July 9 (first quote); "The Farmers' Column," *Chicago Defender*, February 27, 1932 (second quote).

30. "Mississippi Farmers Save by Co-Operative Marketing," *Chicago Defender*, July 19, 1930. See also "Arkansas Farmers Fail to Form Co-Operatives," *Chicago Defender*, July 26 and "Federation of Farmers Granted Corporate Charter," *Chicago Defender*, December 6, 1930.

31. "Boler Advises Colored People Remain on Farm," *Enterprise-Courier*, February 10, 1931.

32. "Red Cross to Aid All Stricken Farmers," *Chicago Defender*, January 17, 1931 and "Tell of Methods to Get Farm Loans," *Chicago Defender*, January 24, 1931.

33. *Official Manual of the State of Missouri for Years 1933–34*, 269–361.

34. Container 107, Series G, NAACP Records: Rev. Shepherd to Walter White, December 18, 1933, Folder "Caruthersville, Mo., 1920–1924." Container 111, Series G, NAACP Records: Rev. McNewerell to NAACP, June 1, 1933, Folder "Sikeston, Mo.";

C. H. Smith to NAACP, March 2, 1933, Folder "Vanduser, Mo., 1931–1934"; John Polk to NAACP, August 22, 1933, Folder "Wardell, Mo., 1933."

35. McNewerell to NAACP, June 1, 1933, Folder "Sikeston, Mo.," Container 111, Series G, NAACP Records.

36. See Fairclough, *Better Day Coming*, 147; and Goluboff, *The Lost Promise of Civil Rights*, 174–82. African-American allegiance to the Republican Party still remained strong, however, as the party of emancipation.

37. Smith to NAACP, April 12, 1933, Folder "Vanduser, Mo., 1931–1934," Container 111, NAACP Records.

38. Calvin B. Hoover, "Human Problems in Acreage Reduction in the South," Folder "AAA, 1934," Box 1, Gardner Jackson Papers, FDR Library.

39. Daniel, *Breaking the Land*, 92, 100–01.

40. Ogilvie, "Development of Southeast Missouri," 271; Wright, *Old South, New South*, 228–32; Fite, *Cotton Fields No More*, 128; Conrad, *The Forgotten Farmers*, 55–58.

41. Ogilvie, "Development of Southeast Missouri," 271; "Cotton Fields Labor Suffers with New Deal," *Daily Tribune*, May 23, 1934.

42. Caverno to Friant, Department of Agriculture, February 11, 1934, Folder 60, Caverno Papers.

43. Snow to Victor Anderson, AAA, October 20, 1934, Folder 1, Thad Snow Papers, SL 88, WHMC-S (hereafter Snow Papers).

44. Bright, "Farm Wage Workers," 58.

45. Ibid., 65, 108 (quote); Wright, *Old South, New South*, 231–32.

46. U.S. Bureau of the Census, *U.S. Census of Agriculture: 1935*, vol. 2, *Farms and Farm Acreage by Size*, 284–93; "Rich Land, Poor People," 10, Report File on the Southeast Missouri Study, Entry 52, Records of the FHA, Great Lakes; Woods, *Development Arrested*, 13; Tolnay, *The Bottom Rung*, 19.

47. Stokes, "Housing Conditions in Southeast Missouri," 58, 73, 97–101.

48. "Rich Land, Poor People," 9, 19, 24–26, Report File on the Southeast Missouri Study, Entry 52, Records of the FHA, Great Lakes; *Southeast Missouri*, 6; McWilliams, *Ill Fares the Land*, 286. For a description of similar living conditions in other parts of the South, see Fite, *Cotton Fields No More*, 37–38.

49. Kirby, *Rural Worlds Lost*, 184.

50. Bright, "Farm Wage Workers," 200–05; "The Church," Project Notes, 1 (quote), 11–12, Report File on the Southeast Missouri Study, Entry 52, Records of the FHA, Great Lakes.

51. U.S. Bureau of the Census, *Census of Religious Bodies, 1936*, 1:778–81; Schall, "Negro in New Madrid County," 123–24. For more on the social demographics in the AME, see Larry Little, "One Church Indivisible," in Best, *Black Religious Leadership*, 133–37; and Lincoln and Mamiya, *The Black Church in the African American Experience*, 68.

52. U.S. Bureau of the Census, *Census of Religious Bodies, 1936*, 1:778–81.

53. Giggie, *After Redemption*, 180 (quote); Wills, *Democratic Religion*, 137.

54. U.S. Bureau of the Census, *Census of Religious Bodies, 1936*, 1:778–81.

55. Bright, "Farm Wage Workers," 201–02; Harvey, *Freedom's Coming*, 114–20, 142; Oltman, *Sacred Mission, Worldly Ambition*, 50–55.

56. "Association Notes," *Charleston Spokesman*, August 31, 1934.

57. "Minutes of the Second Annual Session of Missouri," July 22, 1925, 3–7, in 1925 Alabama Conference Book, IPCHA; Church Deeds, Folder 6915, Reel 262, U.S. Works Progress Administration, Historical Records Survey, C3551, WHMC-C. For an extended view of the process of institutionalization in Pentecostal churches and its effect on theology, see Douglas Jacobsen, "Knowing the Doctrines of Pentecostals: The Scholastic Theology of the Assemblies of God, 1930–1955," in Blumhofer, Spittler, and Wacker, *Pentecostal Currents*, 90–91, 100–1.

58. Church listings, Folder 6915, Reel 262; Folder 6941, Reel 263; Folder 13980, Reel 459; Folder 16197, Reel 528, U.S. Works Progress Administration, Historical Records Survey; Harvey, *Freedom's Coming*, 142–48; Sanders, *Saints in Exile*, 3–21. Although Pentecostal-Holiness believers differed in the details of their interpretation of sanctification, they generally understood it to encompass the experience of "the Holy Spirit descending upon them, purifying them of sin, blessing them with supernatural powers, and assuring them of eternal reward." See Giggie, *After Redemption*, 166.

59. "The Church," 12, Report File on the Southeast Missouri Study, Entry 52, Records of the FHA, Great Lakes.

60. Ibid., 3–4, 11–14; Bright, "Farm Wage Workers," 201–04.

61. "Victory Temple Church of God in Christ History," available at http://www .netministries.org/see/churches/ch10628?frame=N (accessed September 2008).

62. "Rich Land, Poor People," 45, Report File on the Southeast Missouri Study, Entry 52, Records of the FHA, Great Lakes.

63. Ibid., 44; Bright, "Farm Wage Workers," 203–04 (quote).

64. "New Sikeston Church for Working People," *Democrat-Argus*, September 19, 1930.

65. Harvey, *Freedom's Coming*, 114, 127.

66. Althouse, "The Ideology of Power in Early American Pentecostalism," 99 (first quote); Menzies, *The Development of Early Christian Pneumatology with Special Reference to Luke-Acts*, 48 (second quote).

67. Althouse, "The Ideology of Power in Early American Pentecostalism," 105.

68. Harvey, *Freedom's Coming*, 126; "The Church," 3–4, Report File on the Southeast Missouri Study, Entry 52, Records of the FHA, Great Lakes.

69. For descriptions of this outlook among the Bootheel faithful, see "Rich Land, Poor People," 45, Report File on the Southeast Missouri Study, Entry 52, Records of the FHA, Great Lakes; and Bright, "Farm Wage Workers," 205. For general descriptions of this strain of Pentecostal-Holiness eschatology, see Harvey, *Freedom's Coming*, 136–46; and Stephens, *The Fire Spreads*, 214.

70. Pope, *Millhands and Preachers*, 165–6.

71. Althouse, "The Ideology of Power in Early American Pentecostalism," 115.

72. Dewar, *The Holy Spirit and Modern Thought*, 47; Dempster, "Christian Social Concern," 55–58.

73. Harvey, *Freedom's Coming*, 147.

74. Ibid., 148–52.

75. "The Church," 1; "Rich Land, Poor People," 11, Report File on the Southeast Missouri Study, Entry 52, Records of the FHA, Great Lakes.

76. See especially Stephens, *The Fire Spreads*, 214–15.

77. "Co-Operation," *Charleston Spokesman*, August 18, 1934.

78. C. D. Wilson, Crosno, to J. Edgar Hoover, April 26, 1934, Microfilm Series 1440, Reel 6, File 10218–446/1, Records of the Military Intelligence Division, RG 165, NARA, College Park.

79. Evanzz, *The Messenger*, 108–10; Gallicchio, *The African American Encounter with Japan & China*, 95–101; Allen, "Black Messianic Nationalism," 24; Allen, "Waiting for Tojo," 18–22.

80. Takis quoted in Evanzz, *The Messenger*, 108.

81. Takis quoted in Gallicchio, *The African American Encounter with Japan & China*, 95.

82. Allen, "Waiting for Tojo," 18–19.

83. Allen, "Black Messianic Nationalism," 24; Allen, "Waiting for Tojo," 22.

84. "Sikeston among Towns Organized by Negro 'Benevolent' Order," Folder 20, Box FC 3.1, Clippings Collection, 1871–2001, KL; "OAPMOTW," *Charleston Spokesman*, August 18, 1934.

85. "Local Negro Organizer in Court Battle," *Enterprise-Courier*, August 23, 1934.

86. "Sikeston among Towns Organized by Negro 'Benevolent' Order"; Allen, "Waiting for Tojo," 21–22.

87. "'Fifth Column' Propaganda among Negroes in St. Louis Area Traced to Japanese," *Post-Dispatch*, March 5, 1942.

88. "Sikeston among Towns Organized by Negro 'Benevolent' Order"; C. D. Wilson to J. Edgar Hoover, April 26, 1934, Microfilm Series 1440, Reel 6, File 10218–446/1, Records of the Military Intelligence Division, RG 165, NARA, College Park.

89. Whitfield quoted in *Post-Dispatch*, March 6, 1942.

90. "Statement obtained from Policarpio Manansala," Pittsburgh Immigration Office, Pennsylvania, April 17, 1934, Microfilm Collection 1440, Reel 4, File 10218–446/1, Records of the Military Intelligence Division, RG 165, NARA, College Park.

91. Allen, "Black Messianic Nationalism," 27–28; *Post-Dispatch*, March 5, 1942; "Sikeston among Towns Organized by Negro 'Benevolent' Order."

92. Evanzz, *The Messenger*, 103.

93. "Further Details of Jap Agitator's 5th Column Work," *Post-Dispatch*, March 6, 1942.

94. Ibid.

95. "Sikeston among Towns Organized by Negro 'Benevolent' Order"; "Negroes Beaten by Mob at Steele," September 12, 1934, Folder 1420, Guy Brasfield Park Papers, 1933–1937, C0008, WHMC-C (hereafter Park Papers).

96. "OAPMOTW," *Charleston Spokesman*, August 18, 1934; "Application for Char-

ter of Mississippi County," February 18, 1928, Folder "Charleston, Mo., 1928–1940," Container 107, Series G, NAACP Records.

97. "Negro Agitators Held," *Democrat-Argus,* September 11, 1934.

98. "Agitators Arrested," *Enterprise,* September 13, 1934.

99. "Organizers Are Attacked in Mo.," *Argus,* September 14, 1934; "Negro Agitators Held," *Democrat-Argus,* September 11, 1934.

100. "Organizers Are Attacked in Mo.," *Argus,* September 14, 1934.

101. "Negro Organizers Beaten in Court Face 2-Year Term," *Post-Dispatch,* September 14, 1934.

102. "Negro Agitators Held," *Democrat-Argus,* September 11, 1934.

103. "Negro Organizers Beaten in Court Face 2-Year Term," *Post-Dispatch,* September 14, 1934.

104. "Disband Unit of the 'Pacific Movement' Here," *Democrat-Argus,* September 18, 1934.

105. "Sikeston among Towns Organized by Negro 'Benevolent' Order."

106. "Agitators Arrested," *Enterprise,* September 13, 1934.

107. "Charleston gets 1934 National N. F. C. F. Convention," *Charleston Spokesman,* August 25, 1934; "Noted Leaders Speak at National Confab of Farmers," *Chicago Defender,* November 17, 1934.

108. "Noted Leaders Speak at National Confab of Farmers," *Chicago Defender,* November 17 and "New Deal will get Real Hearing at Farmers' Meet," *Chicago Defender,* October 20, 1934 (quote).

109. Bellamy, "Henry A. Hunt and Black Agricultural Leadership in the New South," 474–75; "Noted Leaders Speak at National Confab of Farmers," *Chicago Defender,* November 17, 1934.

110. "Expect Big Delegation at Farmers' Annual Convention," *Chicago Defender,* September 15, 1934.

111. "Noted Leaders Speak at National Confab of Farmers," *Chicago Defender,* November 17, 1934 (all quotes).

112. "Missouri Farmers Gain 37 Tracts," *Chicago Defender,* November 17, 1934.

113. U.S. Bureau of the Census, *Fifteenth Census of the United States: 1930: Agriculture,* vol. 3, pt. 1, *Type of Farm, The Northern States,* 796–803; U.S. Bureau of the Census, *U.S. Census of Agriculture: 1935,* vol. 1, *Farms, Farm Acreage, and Value,* 277–863; "Extent of AAA Crop Curb for S.E. Missouri," *Southeast Missourian,* December 31, 1934.

114. Snow, *From Missouri,* 182.

115. "Rich Land, Poor People," 79, Report File on the Southeast Missouri Study, Entry 52, Records of the FHA, Great Lakes.

116. Caverno, 1934, quoted in Ogilvie, "Development of Southeast Missouri," 203; Caverno to Friant, December 5, 1934, Folder 61, Caverno Papers.

117. "Rich Land, Poor People," 7, Report File on the Southeast Missouri Study, Entry 52, Records of the FHA, Great Lakes.

118. Historians who emphasize the role of the STFU's leadership include Ross, "Rise and Fall," 34, 96; Fannin, *Labor's Promised Land*, 111–21; Dunbar, *Against the Grain*, 84–96; and Grubbs, *Cry from the Cotton*, 27–29. Scholars who focus on the union's rank and file include Naison, "Black Agrarian Radicalism," 53–58; Biegert, "Legacy of Resistance," 74–75; and Woodruff, *American Congo*, 165–70.

119. Fannin, *Labor's Promised Land*, xxiii; "Instructions to Organizers, Number 1," March 2, 1935, Reel 1, Southern Tenant Farmers' Union Papers, 1934–1973, Microfilming Corporation of America (hereafter STFU Papers).

120. Woodruff, *American Congo*, 170; Fannin, *Labor's Promised Land*, 94–112.

121. Grubbs, *Cry from the Cotton*, 47, 84–6, 94–5.

122. Handcox, Charleston, to Mitchell, June 1, 1936, Reel 2, STFU Papers.

123. Fannin, *Labor's Promised Land*, 162–64.

124. Handcox, Charleston, to Mitchell, June 1, 1936, Reel 2, STFU Papers.

125. Handcox, Charleston, to Mitchell, June 8, 1936 (A), "Application for Community Council," Snow's Local, June 20, 1936, Reel 2, STFU Papers.

126. Handcox to Mitchell, July 23, 1936, Reel 2, STFU Papers.

127. Handcox, Charleston, to Mitchell, June 8, 1936 (B), and J. W. Davis, Wyatt, to J. R. Butler, July 27, 1936, both on Reel 2, STFU Papers. These locals included Wyatt #92, Bird Mill #160, Fish Lake #142, Texas Bend #53, Snow's Local, and Henson Local.

128. Fannin, *Labor's Promised Land*, 299; Dunbar, *Against the Grain*, 90–96.

129. *The Disinherited Speak* quoted in Alex Lichtenstein, "Introduction," in Kester, *Revolt among the Sharecroppers*, 39.

130. Goulder, *Luke*, 462.

131. Handcox, East Prairie, to Mitchell, c.a. 1936, in *The Disinherited Speak*, Reel 4, STFU Papers.

132. Handcox, interview with Joe Glazer and Michael Honey, May 15, 1985.

133. "Last of the Legendary Labor Poets," *San Francisco Chronicle*, February 5, 1988 (quote); "Songwriter for Labor Activism of the 1930s Gets Long-Due Praise," *Los Angeles Times*, April 14, 1985.

134. "O Freedom," in Sandilands, *Negro Spirituals*, 69. Handcox recorded all of the songs in the American Folklore Center collection in March 1937 at Snow's plantation. Handcox, "No More Mourning," March 1937, AFS 3238, Sides A1/2, Missouri Field Recordings, LOC. See also "No More Mournin'" in Lomax, Guthrie, and Seeger, *Hard Hitting Songs*, 262–63; and Schroeder and Lance, "Sharecropper Troubador," 123, 127–28, Folder 4, Bootheel Project Records.

135. Handcox, "In My Heart," March 1937, AFS 3237, Side B2, Missouri Field Recordings, LOC; Sandilands, *Negro Spirituals*, 53.

136. Handcox, "Join the Union Tonight," March 1937, AFS 3237, Side B1, Missouri Field Recordings, LOC.

137. Handcox, "Going to Roll the Union On," March 1937, AFS 3237, Side A2, Missouri Field Recordings.

138. "Resolution on Land," "Official Report of the Second Annual Convention," January 1936, Reel 2, STFU Papers.

139. Handcox, "The Planter and the Sharecropper," March 1937, AFS 3239, Side A, Missouri Field Recordings, LOC.

140. Charter, Snow's Local, included in Handcox, Charleston, to H. L. Mitchell, June 8, 1936 (A), Reel 2, STFU Papers; Case No. 91 (Will Jones), Folder "Tenant Farming, 1939–1944," Box 1, Official File 1650, FDR Library.

141. Handcox, Henson, to Mitchell, October 12, 1936, Reel 3, STFU Papers.

142. Fannin, *Labor's Promised Land,* 221–53; Grubbs, *Cry from the Cotton,* 66–69; Handcox, interview with Michael Honey, May 19, 1990.

143. Handcox to Mitchell, July 23, 1936; Handcox to Mitchell, August 7, 1936, Reel 2, STFU Papers.

144. J. W. Davis, Charleston, to Mitchell, October 5, 1936, Reel 3, STFU Papers.

145. Handcox to Mitchell, June 14, 1936, Reel 2, STFU Papers.

146. Handcox to Mitchell, September 28, 1936, Reel 3, STFU Papers.

147. Handcox, interview with Glazer and Honey, May 15, 1985.

148. Handcox, Charleston, to Mitchell, September 28, 1936, Reel 3, STFU Papers.

149. Claude Williams quoted in Belfrage, *Let My People Go,* 311.

150. Claude Williams quoted in ibid., 313.

151. "Union Meetings," n.d. 1936, Reel 3, STFU Papers.

152. "Union Organized in Missouri," *Sharecropper's Voice,* September 1936, Reel 58, STFU Papers.

153. "Application for Membership," December 1936; and "Application for Charter of the New Madrid-Stoddard Counties Branch," April 12, 1937; both in Folder "Stoddard-New Madrid Counties, Mo., 1936–1937," Container 111, Series G, NAACP Records.

154. Rev. Johnson, Rev. Wherry, and Dolly Wherry, Essex, to Harry S. Truman, January 28, 1937, Folder "Stoddard-New Madrid Counties, Mo., 1936–1937," Container 111, Series G, NAACP Records.

155. "Organized Race Farmers Close Meeting," *Chicago Defender,* November 14, 1936.

## 5. Bear Our Burdens Together

1. C. H. Williams, Charleston, to Gardner Jackson, January 16, 1937, Folder "Farm Organizations," Box 24, Gardner Jackson Papers, FDR Library; "STFU Annual Convention Proceedings, 1937," Reel 5, STFU Papers.

2. President Franklin D. Roosevelt, Second Inaugural Address, January 20, 1937; Baldwin, *Poverty and Politics,* 167.

3. Handcox, Charleston, to Mitchell, February 8, 1937, Reel 4, STFU Papers; "Flood Expected at New Madrid Soon," *Weekly Record,* January 29, 1937; "Levee Blasted," *Enterprise-Courier,* January 28, 1937; "Nation's Most Disastrous Flood Raging," *East*

*Prairie Eagle,* January 29, 1937; Snow, *From Missouri,* 205–10, 214–15; "Narrative Report—Emergency Period, 1937, Region H," Box 1271, DR 735, Group 2, Red Cross Records: 1935–1946, ARC 304957, NARA, College Park; Shrum, *Super Floods Raging in Wide Spread Area,* 1–3.

4. The literature on the deleterious effect of the AAA on landless farmers is deep. For the most important works, see Kirby, *Rural Worlds Lost,* 60–65; Wright, *Old South, New South,* 226–32; Daniel, *Breaking the Land,* 92–101; Fite, *Cotton Fields No More,* 131–43; Grubbs, *Cry from the Cotton,* 22–25; and Conrad, *The Forgotten Farmers,* 53–77.

5. Goluboff, *The Lost Promise of Civil Rights,* 28–29; Gordon, *Pitied but Not Entitled,* 3–6.

6. On the diversity and flexibility of the STFU, see Fannin, *Labor's Promised Land.*

7. Mitchell, *Mean Things Happening in This Land,* 83.

8. Green, *Grass-Roots Socialism,* 424–28; Grubbs, *Cry from the Cotton,* 157–59; Kirby, *Rural Worlds Lost,* 267.

9. Pinn, *Why, Lord?* 15.

10. Zieger, *The CIO,* 42–65.

11. "Nation's Most Disastrous Flood Raging," *East Prairie Eagle,* January 29, 1937; "Levee Blasted," *Enterprise-Courier,* January 28, 1937; "Total Number Flood Refugees Reaches 8400," *Enterprise-Courier,* February 11, 1937; "Statistical Summary of Relief Operations, February 19, 1937," Box 1252, DR 735, Group 2, Red Cross Records: 1935–1946, ARC 304957, NARA, College Park.

12. "Final Statistical Statement, Region H, Missouri," Box 1253, "Narrative Report—Emergency Period, 1937, Region H," Box 1271, DR 735, Group 2, Red Cross Records: 1935–1946, ARC 304957, NARA, College Park; U.S. Census, 1935, Agriculture, Volume 2, Missouri, County Table 4.

13. Thomas Carson, Charleston, to Mitchell, January 30, 1937, Reel 4, STFU Papers.

14. H. Laws, Charleston, to Mitchell, February 15, 1937, Reel 4, STFU Papers.

15. "Membership Report from the Third Annual Convention, STFU," January 1937, Reel 4, STFU Papers.

16. "Flood Bulletin," ca. January 1937; "To Officers and Locals of the Southern Tenant Farmers' Union," January 1937, both on Reel 5, STFU Papers.

17. W. H. Nelson, Charleston, to Mitchell, February 1, 1937, Reel 4, STFU Papers.

18. Mule Ridge Local to Mitchell, February 4, 1937, Reel 4, STFU Papers.

19. Handcox, Charleston, to Mitchell, February 8, 1937, Reel 4, STFU Papers.

20. Mule Ridge Local to Mitchell, February 4, 1937, Reel 4, STFU Papers.

21. Handcox, Charleston, to Mitchell, February 8, 1937, Reel 4, STFU Papers.

22. Mule Ridge Local to Mitchell, February 4, 1937, Reel 4, STFU Papers.

23. Parker, *Portrait of Missouri,* 55–56; "Disaster Nursing Service Report," 12–13,

Box 1271, DR 735, Group 2, Red Cross Records: 1935–1946, ARC 304957, NARA, College Park; "River Reaches Crest at Cairo," *East Prairie Eagle,* February 5, 1937.

24. Butler speech, "Proceedings of the STFU Fifth Annual Convention," February 25, 1938, Reel 7, STFU Papers; Handcox, Charleston, to Mitchell, February 8, 1937, Scottie Spears, Charleston, to Mitchell, February 16, 1937, Reel 4, STFU Papers.

25. Butler to Handcox, Charleston, February 14, 1937, Reel 4, STFU Papers.

26. "Minutes of the Refugees of STFU CC," February 15, 1937, Reel 4, STFU Papers.

27. Ibid.

28. Ibid.

29. "Super Flood Drives Thousands of Union Members from Homes," *Sharecropper's Voice,* February 1937, Reel 58, STFU Papers.

30. Fannin, *Labor's Promised Land,* 112. See, for example, "STFU Report to the Governor's Commission on Tenancy," September 1936, Reel 3, STFU Papers.

31. Fannin, *Labor's Promised Land,* 164–80.

32. "Crop Loans in Spillway to Be Made," *Enterprise-Courier,* March 11, 1937; "Three Agencies Making Loans in Flood Area," *Enterprise-Courier,* March 18, 1937; "Flood Loans May Total $300,000," *Enterprise-Courier,* March 25, 1937 (quote); Mr. Dillon to Mr. Griesemer, April 3, 1937, Box 1253, DR 735, Group 2, Red Cross Records: 1935–1946, ARC 304957, NARA, College Park.

33. "Huge Task Caring for Victims of Flood Ends," *Enterprise-Courier,* April 1, 1937; Rosa Schladweiler to Lona Trott, Sikeston, March 26, 1937, Box 1270, DR 735, Group 2, Red Cross Records: 1935–1946, ARC 304957, NARA, College Park.

34. Handcox, Charleston, to Butler, February 19, 1937, Reel 4, STFU Papers.

35. Rev. D. C. Johnson, Rev. D. W. Wherry, and Dolly Wherry, Essex, to Truman, January 28, 1937, Folder "Stoddard-New Madrid Counties, Mo., 1936–1937," Container 111, Series G, NAACP Records.

36. A. M. Mitchell to William Pickens, February 18, 1937, Folder "Stoddard-New Madrid Counties, Mo., 1936–1937," Container 111, Series G, NAACP Records.

37. Rev. A. M. Mitchell, Marston, to Walter White, February 5, 1937 (first quote) and February 11, 1937, Folder "Mississippi Flood Control, Jan. 1–Feb. 27, 1937," Container 383, Series C, NAACP Records; Mitchell to White, March 20, 1937 (second quote), Folder "Stoddard-New Madrid Counties, Mo., 1936–1937," Container 111, Series G, NAACP Records.

38. See Goluboff, *The Lost Promise of Civil Rights,* 174–82.

39. Handcox, Charleston, to Butler, April 8, 1937, Reel 4, STFU Papers.

40. Whitfield, East Prairie, to Butler, June 15, 1937, Reel 4, STFU Papers.

41. Joe Kelly, Charleston, to Walter White, June 21, 1937, Folder "Mississippi Flood Control, March 2–October 28, 1937," Container 383, Series C, NAACP Records.

42. Whitfield, East Prairie, to Butler, June 15, 1937, Reel 4, STFU Papers; Butler to Whitfield, East Prairie, July 1, 1937, Reel 5, STFU Papers; Zieger, *The CIO,* 66–89; Kelley, *Hammer and Hoe,* 173–74.

43. *Enterprise-Courier,* April 15, 22, and May 27, 1937.

44. W. M. Harvey, Wyatt, to Butler, July 20, 1937, Reel 5, STFU Papers.

45. W. M. Harvey, Wyatt, to Mitchell, July 17, 1937, Reel 5, STFU Papers.

46. Baldwin, *Poverty and Progress,* 122–90.

47. Handcox, Charleston, to Butler, February 19, 1937, Reel 4, STFU Papers.

48. Braxton Taylor, Charleston, to Butler, May 23, 1937, Reel 4, STFU Papers.

49. W. M. Harvey, Wyatt, to Mitchell, July 17, 1937, Reel 5, STFU Papers.

50. Lee Munday, Deventer, to Mitchell, July 19, 1937, Reel 5, STFU Papers.

51. T. R. Hollingsworth, Caruthersville, to Butler, July 10, 1937, Reel 5, STFU Papers.

52. W. F. Steele, Cooter, to Mitchell, September 2, 1937, Reel 5, STFU Papers.

53. McConnell, Caruthersville, to Butler, August 20, 1937; Carl Hollis, Caruthersville, to Mitchell, August 28, 1937; McConnell, Caruthersville, to Mitchell, August 29, 1937; all on Reel 5, STFU Papers. For more on Mexican cotton pickers in the Bootheel, see Kirby, *Rural Worlds Lost,* 66.

54. Local Secretary's Reports, Holland Local #296, July, August, and September 1937, Reel 6, STFU Papers.

55. Monthly Report of Organizer McConnell, August 18, 1937, Reel 6, STFU Papers.

56. Butler to E. S. Marshall, Holland, September 8, 1937; Butler to E. S. Marshall, Holland, September 15, 1937; Ive L. Renfrow, Cooter, to Butler, September 15, 1937; Butler to Governor Lloyd Stark, Jefferson City, September 20, 1937; and Norman Thomas to *Post Dispatch,* September 18, 1937; all on Reel 5, STFU Papers.

57. McConnell, Caruthersville, to Butler, November 15, 1937, Reel 5, STFU Papers.

58. W. M. Harvey, Wyatt, to Butler, August 20, 1937, Reel 5, STFU Papers.

59. Whitfield to Mitchell, October 1, 1937, Reel 5, STFU Papers. The number of paid members varied from month to month, as did the number of reporting locals. These totals reflect the sum of the average of the highest number of paying members reported by each of the twenty-six locals in late 1937. See the following sources on STFU Papers, Reel 5: "Proceedings of the STFU Fourth Annual Convention," 1937; "Organization Fees, July 1937." On STFU Papers, Reel 6, see the various questionnaires, secretaries' reports, and organizers' reports for membership data from the Bootheel locals. See also "Locals of the Southern Tenant Farmers Union" (ca. 1937), Reel 6, STFU Papers.

60. McConnell to Butler, January 6, 1938, Reel 7, STFU Papers.

61. Whitfield to Mitchell, April 19, 1938, Reel 8, STFU Papers.

62. "What Is Cotton Laborer's Condition in This Section?" *Standard,* January 14, 1938.

63. Mertz, *New Deal Policy and Southern Rural Poverty,* 43–44.

64. Ogilvie, "Development of Southeast Missouri," 285–87; Caverno to H. R. Tolley, AAA, January 21, 1938, Folder 24, Caverno Papers; Wright, *Old South, New South,*

232; Snow, *From Missouri*, 294; Cantor, *A Prologue to the Protest Movement*, 21, 42; U.S. Federal Bureau of Investigation, *Investigation Concerning the Sharecropper Situation Existing in Southeast Missouri*, 6.

65. E. J. Holcomb, "Farm Organization," in Holcomb, Murray, Folsom, and Turner, *Report to the Tolan Committee on the Cooperative Study of Farm Labor and Tenancy in Southeast Missouri*, 1–14.

66. Bright, "Farm Wage Workers," 50, 61; Hoffman and Bankson, "Crisis in Missouri's Boot Heel," 4–5; Testimony of Thad Snow and Andrew Puckett, reprinted in United States Congress, *Hearings before the Select Committee Investigating National Defense Migration*, 9145–9148, 9168, 9173; U.S. Federal Bureau of Investigation, *Investigation Concerning the Sharecropper Situation Existing in Southeast Missouri*, 13–14; Daniel, *Breaking the Land*, 170–75.

67. "What Is Cotton Laborer's Condition in this Section?" *Standard*, January 14, 1938.

68. Holcomb, Folsom, Murray, "Analysis of Sub-Tenant and Wage Labor Records," in Holcomb, Murray, Folsom, Turner, *Report to the Tolan Committee on the Cooperative Study of Farm Labor and Tenancy in Southeast Missouri*, 3–7, 32–38; "What Is Cotton Laborer's Condition in this Section?" *Standard*, January 14, 1938.

69. Tolnay, *The Bottom Rung*, 18.

70. C. H. Williams, Charleston, to Gardner Jackson, January 16, 1937, Folder "Farm Organizations," Box 24, Gardner Jackson Papers, FDR Library.

71. Testimony of Snow, in United States Congress, *Hearings before the Select Committee Investigating National Defense Migration*, 9145.

72. "Negro Sharecropper Who Made Trip to Washington Gives His Opinion on Problem Confronting Semo District," *Enterprise-Courier*, December 23, 1937.

73. Ibid.

74. Ibid.

75. On the patriarchal implications of family wage rhetoric, see Simon, *A Fabric of Defeat*, 23–24, 63; Cohen, *Making a New Deal*, 247–49; and Gordon, *Pitied but Not Entitled*, 290–91.

76. Mitchell, *Mean Things Happening in This Land*, 124; Fannin, *Labor's Promised Land*, 104, 120–21.

77. Sid Mitchell, Charleston, to Mitchell, January 23, 1938, Reel 7, STFU Papers.

78. "Preliminary Reports, Labor Displacement on Cotton Plantations," 15 January 1938, Reel 7, STFU Papers.

79. Clifton Dickerson, Wyatt, to Mitchell, January 18, 1938, Reel 7, STFU Papers.

80. James W. Lomax, Charleston, to Mitchell, January 9, 1938, Reel 7, STFU Papers.

81. Mitchell to Whitfield, East Prairie, January 13, 1938, Reel 7, STFU Papers.

82. "Nearly 500 Ex-Tenants Apply for Relief Jobs," *Enterprise-Courier*, April 28, 1938.

83. U.S. Federal Bureau of Investigation, *Investigation Concerning the Sharecropper Situation Existing in Southeast Missouri*, 22–23.

84. Zieger, *For Jobs and Freedom*, 115. For discussions of racism in the CIO as well as examples of interracial cooperation, see Nelson, *Divided We Stand*, xxi–xxvii; Honey, *Southern Labor and Black Civil Rights*, 93–144; and Feurer, *Radical Unionism in the Midwest*, 137–76.

85. See, for example, Woodruff, *American Congo*, 184–89.

86. "Negro Sharecropper Who Made Trip to Washington Gives His Opinion on Problem Confronting Semo District," *Enterprise-Courier*, December 23, 1937 (quotes); "More Than 1000 Negroes Attend Lincoln Program," *Enterprise-Courier*, February 17, 1938.

87. U.S. Federal Bureau of Investigation, *Investigation Concerning the Sharecropper Situation Existing in Southeast Missouri*, 23.

88. Cantor, *A Prologue to the Protest Movement*, 32.

89. Whitfield to Mitchell, December 27, 1937, Reel 4, STFU Papers; Whitfield to Mitchell, January 10, 1938, Reel 7, STFU Papers.

90. McConnell to Mitchell, September 6, 1937, Reel 5, STFU Papers; McConnell to Butler, January 6, 1938 (quote), Reel 7, STFU Papers.

91. McConnell to Butler, January 6, 1938, Reel 7, STFU Papers.

92. "Negroes Announce Food Program," *Standard*, January 21, 1938.

93. For a full account of the tortuous infighting between Henderson and the STFU leadership, see Green, *Grass-Roots Socialism*, 428–29; Grubbs, *Cry from the Cotton*, 166–87; Kelley, *Hammer and Hoe*, 169.

94. "Proceedings of the STFU Annual Convention," February 25, 1938, Reel 7, STFU Papers.

95. Burnette, "'Upon This Rock,'" available at http://www.bible.org/page.php?page_id=2702 (accessed January 14, 2009).

96. "Minutes of the Executive Council Meeting," May 21–22, 1938, Reel 8, STFU Papers.

97. Cantor, *A Prologue to the Protest Movement*, 43; Whitfield to Mitchell, January 22, 1938, Reel 7, STFU Papers.

98. Whitfield to Mitchell, March 28, 1938, Reel 7, STFU Papers.

99. Brenda J. Taylor, "The Farm Security Administration and Rural Families in the South," in Green, *New Deal and Beyond*, 30–35; Grey, *New Deal Medicine*, 62–97; Holley, *Uncle Sam's Farmers*, ix, 134–35; Baldwin, *Poverty and Progress*, viii–ix, 194–201.

100. "La Forge Farms," Box 411, Entry 4A, Records of the FHA, College Park; "5000 Ask to Be Made Tenants on U.S. Farm," *Enterprise-Courier*, June 16, 1938.

101. "La Forge Farms," Box 411, Entry 4A, Records of the FHA, College Park; "Second Anniversary, La Forge Farms Resettlement Project, 20 December 1939," Folder 772, O. R. Johnson Papers, 1910–1959, C3483, WHMC-C; Chase, "From the Lower Depths," 109–11; "New Homes for LaForge Farmers," *East Prairie Eagle*, March 25,

1938; "Modern Houses, Barns Rise Overnight on LaForge Tract," *Standard*, March 22, 1938.

102. "La Forge Farms," and "Farm Security Administration, Southeast Missouri Project," both in Box 411, Entry 4A, Records of the FHA, College Park; Chase, "From the Lower Depths," 111; *Standard*, October 18, 1938; U.S. Federal Bureau of Investigation, *Investigation Concerning the Sharecropper Situation Existing in Southeast Missouri*, 37.

103. "Whitfield's Family Moves from La Forge," *Enterprise-Courier*, March 2, 1939; Whitfield to Mitchell, June 6, 1938, Reel 8, STFU Papers. Whitfield did not live in New Madrid County, nor did he live on the land that became La Forge. The FBI reported that he was recommended because he had successfully repaid a loan from the Resettlement Administration in 1937, likely a loan issued after the flood crisis; see U.S. Federal Bureau of Investigation, *Investigation Concerning the Sharecropper Situation Existing in Southeast Missouri*, 36. Other reports claimed that Thad Snow secured Whitfield's place on the project; see Belfrage, "Cotton-Patch Moses," 99; Stepenoff, *Thad Snow*, 81–82.

104. "Farm Security Administration, Southeast Missouri Project," Box 411, Entry 4A, Records of the FHA, College Park.

105. Taylor, "FSA and Rural Families in the South," in Green, *New Deal and Beyond*, 302–32.

106. Whitfield to Mitchell, April 19, 1938, Reel 8, STFU Papers.

107. "Moore to Work in Missouri," *STFU News*, April 1938, Reel 58, STFU Papers; Mitchell to Whitfield, April 5, 1938, Reel 8, STFU Papers.

108. Whitfield to Mitchell, June 30, 1938, Reel 8, STFU Papers.

109. Reel 8, STFU Papers: W. B. Moore, New Madrid, to Mitchell, April 12, 1938; Whitfield to Mitchell, May 6, 1938; Ruth Sharp, Dorena, to Mitchell, July 27, 1938.

110. Whitfield to Butler, August 4, 1938, Reel 8, STFU Papers. Also Whitfield to Claude Williams, August 9, 1938, Folder 10, Box 2, Claude Williams Papers, Walter P. Reuther Library (hereafter Williams Papers).

111. Peter Wilderness and Willie Scott, Portageville, to Mitchell, June 3, 1938, Reel 8, STFU Papers; "Monthly Report of Membership and Fees, Cyprus Grove #353, Essex, Mo.," Reel 10, STFU Papers.

112. Snow, *From Missouri*, 232.

113. Membership data compiled from "Monthly Report of Membership and Fees," 1938, Reels 8, 9, 10, STFU Papers.

114. "Minutes of National Executive Council Meeting," September 16–17, 1938, Reel 9, STFU Papers.

115. Reel 9, STFU Papers: Albert Presson, Charleston, to Butler, September 5, 1938; Whitfield to Butler, September 6, 1938; Whitfield to Mitchell, November 8, 1938; "Resolutions of the Fifth Annual Convention," January 1 1939.

116. McConnell to Mitchell, ca. September 1, 1938, Reel 9, STFU Papers; Butler to

McConnell, September 6, 1938, Reel 9, STFU Papers; Whitfield to Claude Williams, August 9, 1938, Folder 10, Box 2, Williams Papers.

117. Lewis Adams, East Prairie, to Butler, August 24, 1938, Reel 8, STFU Papers.

118. "How the Farm Program Works in Washington but Fails to on the Farm," *Enterprise-Courier,* May 19, 1938.

119. "Requests for WPA Cotton Pickers Light; No Sikeston Projects Are Shut Down but Demand Elsewhere Is Heavy," *Standard,* September 27, 1938; "Farmers Demand WPA Workers for Cotton Picking," *Enterprise-Courier,* September 22, 1938.

120. "Requests for WPA Cotton Pickers Light; No Sikeston Projects Are Shut Down but Demand Elsewhere Is Heavy," *Standard,* September 27, 1938; "Farmers Demand WPA Workers for Cotton Picking," *Enterprise-Courier,* September 22, 1938; "Cotton Strike Apparently Near the End," *Enterprise-Courier,* September 29, 1938; "The Sharecroppers' Demonstration," ca. 1939, Folder 48, "Sharecroppers," Box FC 2.3, Clippings Collection, 1871–2001, KL.

121. "Unfair to Labor?" *Enterprise-Courier,* September 29, 1938; "CIO Cotton Pickers Strike at Charleston," *Standard,* September 27, 1938.

122. "The Bald Headed Sharecropper Expresses His Views on the Recent Cotton Strike," *Enterprise-Courier,* October 20, 1938.

123. Whitfield, "Minutes of the National Executive Council meeting of the STFU," September 16–17, 1938, quoted in Cantor, *A Prologue to the Protest Movement,* 35.

124. Whitfield to John T. Clark, St. Louis Urban League, August 3, 1938, Folder 15, Box 7, Cook Papers.

125. Whitfield, interview by Howard Emerson, March 1963, quoted in Emerson, "Sharecropper's Strike," 41; U.S. Federal Bureau of Investigation, *Investigation Concerning the Sharecropper Situation Existing in Southeast Missouri,* 22–24.

126. Stepenoff, *Thad Snow,* 89.

127. They could also have gleaned the concept of the roadside demonstration from the numerous CIO sit-down strikes in the late 1930s or from a very small roadside demonstration that occurred during a cotton-picking strike of STFU members in Arkansas in 1936. See Cantor, *A Prologue to the Protest Movement,* 57–58.

128. Whitfield to Mitchell, December 1, 1938, Reel 9, STFU Papers. Mitchell saw the letter after the event.

129. Josephine Johnson, St. Louis, to Mitchell, December 21, 1938, Reel 9, STFU Papers.

130. Cantor, *A Prologue to the Protest Movement,* 54–55.

131. "Program, Dedication of Southeast Missouri Project, 20–21 December 1938," Box 412, Entry 4A, Records of the FHA, College Park.

132. Cantor, *A Prologue to the Protest Movement,* 50–52.

133. Butler to Whitfield, December 24, 1938, Reel 9, STFU Papers.

134. Whitfield to Mitchell, December 30, 1938, Reel 9, STFU Papers.

135. Grubbs, *Cry from the Cotton,* 181; Cantor, *A Prologue to the Protest Movement,* 54–55.

136. Belfrage, "Cotton-Patch Moses," 100; Stepenoff, *Thad Snow*, 90; U.S. Federal Bureau of Investigation, *Investigation Concerning the Sharecropper Situation Existing in Southeast Missouri*, 25.

137. Drury, *Luke*, 114; Goulder, *Luke*, 462.

138. If we accept that Whitfield's audience understood the Biblical context of the verses he quoted, which was highly likely for such fervent Christians, and that the Biblical context evoked concepts that a simple literal interpretation of single verses did not, we can extrapolate a richer understanding of his sermon. Likening the protestors to the Son of Man was to recall Christ's promise from the same chapter of Luke that in such misery lay the power to "preach the kingdom of God" (Luke 9:60). It is also likely that listeners would have had in mind the opening verses of the chapter, which describe how Jesus gave his disciples "power and authority over all devils, and to cure diseases" and "sent them to preach the kingdom of God." "And he said unto them, Take nothing for your journey, neither staves, nor scrip, neither bread, neither money; neither have two coats apiece." "And whosoever will not receive you, when ye go out of that city, shake off the very dust from your feet for a testimony against them" (Luke 9:1–5). By hewing so closely to the Lukan discourse, which foretells of the outpouring of the Holy Spirit to come in the book of Acts, Whitfield fed the upcoming protest from its roots in the Pentecostal-Holiness revivals of the early 1930s.

139. "Sharecroppers, Ordered Evicted, to Camp on Road," *Post-Dispatch*, January 8, 1939; Whitfield, interview by Emerson, quoted in Emerson, "Sharecroppers' Strike," 41–43; Belfrage, "Cotton-Patch Moses," 94–95; Cantor, *A Prologue to the Protest Movement*, 60–61.

## 6. On Jordan's Stormy Banks

1. Officials from the National Youth Administration recorded the recent life histories of individual demonstrators during the roadside protest. These files offer unique information about where the protestors came from and what they hoped to achieve. Case No. 7 (Alonzo J. Julian), Case No. 19 (Allen Sellars), Case No. 22 (Robinson Shirley), all in Folder "Tenant Farming, 1939–1944," Box 1, Official File 1650, FDR Library.

2. "Sharecroppers Evicted, Camp along Highways," *Post-Dispatch*, January 10, 1939 (quote); "Sharecroppers in Mass Move; Appeal to Federal Officials," *Standard*, January 13, 1939; "Army of Sharecroppers Trek from Homes; Protest Missouri Landlords' Wage Plans," *New York Times*, January 11, 1939; John C. Wilson, "Report of the 1939 Roadside Demonstration," January 19, 1939, F. 841, Box 1217, Group 3, Red Cross Records: 1935–1946, ARC 304957, NARA, College Park; Case No. 1 (Willie Scott), Case No. 14 (Peter Wilderness), both in Folder "Tenant Farming, 1939–1944," Box 1, Official File 1650, FDR Library.

3. Snow, *From Missouri*, 242.

4. "Sharecroppers Evicted, Camp along Highways," *Post-Dispatch,* January 10, 1939.

5. Herbert Little to Aubrey Williams, January 16, 1939, Folder "Tenant Farming, 1939–1944," Box 1, Official File 1650, FDR Library; Colonel B. M. Casteel to Governor Stark, January 20, 1939, Folder 1959, Lloyd Crow Stark Papers, 1931–1941, C0004, WHMC-C (hereafter Stark Papers); Snow, *From Missouri,* 240–41.

6. Natanson, *The Black Image in the New Deal,* 4.

7. Ibid., 113–19.

8. McWilliams, *Ill Fares the Land,* 290.

9. Eleanor Roosevelt, "My Day," syndicated newspaper column, January 31, 1939, available at http://www.gwu.edu/~erpapers/myday/ (accessed September 7, 2009).

10. Herbert Little to Aubrey Williams, January 16, 1939; Herbert Little to Aubrey Williams, January 16, 1939; Aubrey Williams to FDR, January 19, 1939; FDR to Henry Wallace, January 19, 1939 (quote); all in Folder "Tenant Farming, 1939–1944," Box 1, Official File 1650, FDR Library .

11. Henry Wallace to Eleanor Roosevelt, June 7, 1939, Folder "Henry Wallace, 1939," Box 335, Eleanor Roosevelt Papers, FDR Library (hereafter ER Papers).

12. Eleanor Roosevelt to Wallace, June 15, 1939, Folder "Henry Wallace, 1939," Box 335, ER Papers.

13. Will Alexander to Eleanor Roosevelt, November 29, 1939, Folder "WW Alexander, September–December 1939," Box 328, ER Papers.

14. "Sharecroppers, Ordered Evicted, to Camp on Road," *Post-Dispatch,* January 8, 1939.

15. Booker T. Clark, interview by Mitchell, quoted in Mitchell, "The 1939 Highway Sitdown in Southeast Missouri," Rural Revolt in Missouri, SL 427, WHMC-S; U.S. Federal Bureau of Investigation, *Investigation Concerning the Sharecropper Situation Existing in Southeast Missouri,* 25–26.

16. "Sharecropper Horde Hit by Snowstorm," *New York Times,* January 13, 1939; Snow, *From Missouri,* 248; Cantor, *A Prologue to the Protest Movement,* 79–80; Whitfield to Mitchell, January 10, 1939, Reel 10, STFU Papers (quote).

17. "Sharecroppers Evicted, Camp along Highways," *Post-Dispatch,* January 10, 1939.

18. Cases No. 1–16, 32–102, Folder "Tenant Farming, 1939–1944," Box 1, Official File 1650, FDR Library. (Cases 17–31 are missing.) See also L. B. Boler, Charleston, to Governor Stark, January 18, 1939, Folder 1938, Stark Papers.

19. Cases No. 1–16, 32–102, Folder "Tenant Farming, 1939–1944," Box 1, Official File 1650, FDR Library .

20. Case No. 76 (Melvin Smith), Case No. 14 (Peter Wilderness), Case No. 101 (Walter Johnson), Case No. 72 (Ike Tripp), Case No. 41 (Daniel McClenton), Case No. 7 (Alonzo Julian), all in Folder "Tenant Farming, 1939–1944," Box 1, Official File 1650, FDR Library.

21. Aubrey Williams to FDR, January 19, 1939, Folder "Tenant Farming, 1939–1944," Box 1, Official File 1650, FDR Library.

22. Craig Winfrey to Governor Stark, January 11, 1939, Folder 1958, Stark Papers.

23. Case No. 51 (Dave Coffey), Folder "Tenant Farming, 1939–1944," Box 1, Official File 1650, FDR Library.

24. "Stories Told by Sharecroppers Camped on Cold Highways," *Daily American Republic,* ca. January 1939, Folder 48, Box FC 2.3, Clippings Collection, 1871–2001, KL.

25. Alonzo J. Julien, New Madrid, in "Letters Written on Backs of Survey Blanks," ca. January 1939, Reel 10, STFU Papers.

26. Colonel Casteel to Governor Stark, January 20, 1939, Folder 1959, Stark Papers.

27. Elijah Moore, Canalou, in "Letters Written on Backs of Survey Blanks," ca. January 1939, Reel 10, STFU Papers.

28. Irene Nickerson, Portageville, in "Letters Written on Backs of Survey Blanks," ca. January 1939, Reel 10, STFU Papers.

29. U.S. Federal Bureau of Investigation, *Investigation Concerning the Sharecropper Situation Existing in Southeast Missouri,* 45.

30. Case No. 52 (Floyd Topps), Folder "Tenant Farming, 1939–1944," Box 1, Official File 1650, FDR Library.

31. Case No. 99 (Charlie Rogers), Folder "Tenant Farming, 1939–1944," Box 1, Official File 1650, FDR Library.

32. Cases No. 1–16, 32–102, Folder "Tenant Farming, 1939–1944," Box 1, Official File 1650, FDR Library.

33. Harry E. Dudley, Missouri National Guard, to Governor Stark, January 20, 1939, Folder 1959, Stark Papers.

34. Case No. 86 (Henry MacAdory), Folder "Tenant Farming, 1939–1944," Box 1, Official File 1650, FDR Library.

35. Clark, interview by Mitchell, quoted in Mitchell, "The 1939 Highway Sitdown in Southeast Missouri," Rural Revolt in Missouri, SL 427, WHMC-S.

36. See Cases No. 1–16, 32–102, particularly Case No. 47 (John Nesbitt), Case No. 55 (Spencer Nesbitt), Case No. 72 (Ike Tripp), Case No. 74 (Henry Tripp), and Case No. 77 (Tommie Clark), Folder "Tenant Farming, 1939–1944," Box 1, Official File 1650, FDR Library.

37. Case No. 64 (H. P. Miller), Case No. 77 (Tommie Clark), Case No. 3 (Walter Johnson), Folder "Tenant Farming, 1939–1944," Box 1, Official File 1650, FDR Library.

38. Case No. 14 (Peter Wilderness), Case No. 60 (Gold Richardson), Case No. 77 (Tommie Clark), Case No. 80 (B. L. Randolph), Folder "Tenant Farming, 1939–1944," Box 1, Official File 1650, FDR Library; "Application for Charter of the New Madrid–Stoddard Counties Branch," April 12, 1937, Folder "Stoddard–New Madrid Counties, Mo., 1936–1937," Container 111, Series G, NAACP Records.

39. See Cases No. 1–16, 32–102, especially Case No.1 (Willie Scott), Folder "Tenant Farming, 1939–1944," Box 1, Official File 1650, FDR Library.

40. Case No. 7 (Alonzo J. Julian), Folder "Tenant Farming, 1939–1944," Box 1, Official File 1650, FDR Library.

41. *Post-Dispatch,* January 11, 1939; Cantor, *A Prologue to the Protest Movement,* 80; "On Jordan's Stormy Banks I Stand," http://www.hymnsite.com/lyrics/umh724 .sht (accessed September 7, 2009).

42. Snow, *From Missouri,* 243–44, 252–56; Alex Cooper, Hayti, interview with author, November 30, 2003.

43. Harry E. Dudley to Governor Stark, January 20, 1939, Folder 1959, Stark Papers.

44. Ibid. (quote); "Resolution of the Mississippi County Citizen's Committee," January 12, 1939, Folder 1957; E. R. Rafferty, Wyatt, to Governor Stark, January 11, 1939, Folder 1935, all in Stark Papers.

45. Colonel Franklin to Colonel Bull, January 13, 1939, Folder "Tenant Farming, 1939–1944," Box 1, Official File 1650, FDR Library.

46. William M. Baxter to James Frieser, January 10, 1939, Folder 841, Box 1217, Group 3, Red Cross Records: 1935–1946, ARC 304957, NARA, College Park (quote); "Evicted Campers on Roads Await Food from State," *Post-Dispatch,* January 11, 1939.

47. Cantor, *A Prologue to the Protest Movement,* 73.

48. Colonel Franklin to Colonel Bull, January 13, 1939, Folder "Tenant Farming, 1939–1944," Box 1, Official File 1650, FDR Library.

49. "Evicted Farmers Short of Food in Road Camps," *Post-Dispatch,* January 12, 1939; "Police Put Head of Tenant Union Out of Missouri," *Post-Dispatch,* January 15, 1939; Press Releases, January 14, 16, 1939, Reel 10, STFU Papers. For more on the Federal Surplus Commodities Corporation, see Blau with Abramowitz, *The Dynamics of Social Welfare Policy,* 438.

50. Harry Parker to Governor Stark, January 19, 1939, Folder 1938, Stark Papers (all quotes).

51. "Move to End Trek by Sharecroppers," *New York Times,* January 14, 1939.

52. Harry E. Dudley to Governor Stark, January 20, 1939, Folder 1959, Stark Papers; Wilson, "Report of the 1939 Roadside Demonstration," F. 841, Box 1217, Group 3, Red Cross Records: 1935–1946.

53. MacAdory quoted by Clark, interview by Mitchell, quoted in Mitchell, "1939 Highway Sitdown," Rural Revolt in Missouri, SL 427, WHMC-S; Kim Ruehl, "'I Shall Not Be Moved': History of an American Folk Song," available at http://folkmusic .about.com/od/folksongs/qt/ShallNotBeMoved.htm (accessed September 7, 2009).

54. MacAdory quoted by Clark, interview by Mitchell, quoted in Mitchell, "1939 Highway Sitdown," Rural Revolt in Missouri, SL 427, WHMC-S.

55. "Police Put Head of Tenant Union out of Missouri," *Post-Dispatch,* January 15, 1939.

56. Herbert Little to Aubrey Williams, January 16, 1939, Folder "Tenant Farming,

1939–1944," Box 1, Official File 1650, FDR Library; Clark, interview by Mitchell, in Mitchell, "1939 Highway Sitdown," Rural Revolt in Missouri, SL 427, WHMC-S.

57. Herbert Little to Aubrey Williams, January 16, 1939, Folder "Tenant Farming, 1939–1944," Box 1, Official File 1650, FDR Library.

58. Herbert Little, transcript of telephone conversation with Aubrey Williams, January 15, 1939, Folder "Tenant Farming, 1939–1944," Box 1, Official File 1650, FDR Library.

59. Herbert Little to Aubrey Williams, January 16, 1939, FDR to Henry Wallace, January 19, 1939, Folder "Tenant Farming, 1939–1944," Box 1, Official File 1650, FDR Library .

60. "Police Move 500 Share-Croppers into Swamp Area," Post-Dispatch, January 16, 1939.

61. Ibid.

62. Herbert Little to Aubrey Williams, dictated over the telephone, January 16, 1939, Folder "Tenant Farming, 1939–1944," Box 1, Official File 1650, FDR Library; U.S. Federal Bureau of Investigation, Investigation Concerning the Sharecropper Situation Existing in Southeast Missouri, 1; "Demonstrating Farm Laborers Are Moved from Highway to Co. Farm," Weekly Record, January 20, 1939.

63. Clark, interview by Mitchell, in Mitchell, "1939 Highway Sitdown," Rural Revolt in Missouri, SL 427, WHMC-S.

64. FDR to Henry Wallace, January 19, 1939, Folder "Tenant Farming, 1939–1944," Box 1, Official File 1650, FDR Library.

65. "Sheriff Disarms Sharecroppers Near New Madrid," Post-Dispatch, January 17, 1939.

66. FDR to Wallace, January 19, 1939, Folder "Tenant Farming, 1939–1944," Box 1, Official File 1650, FDR Library.

67. "Police Move 500 Share-Croppers into Swamp Area," Post-Dispatch, January 16, 1939; Will Alexander to Henry Kannee, The White House, ca. January 14, 1939; Alexander to Mitchell, January 11, 1939, Reel 10, STFU Papers; Cantor, A Prologue to the Protest Movement, 89–90.

68. "Sharecroppers Moved with U.S. Tents on the Way," Post-Dispatch, January 20, 1939.

69. "Sharecropper Campers Forced to Move Again," Post-Dispatch, January 19, 1939; Snow, From Missouri, 281; Cantor, A Prologue to the Protest Movement, 89–90.

70. Cases Nos. 90–102, Folder "Tenant Farming, 1939–1944," Box 1, Official File 1650, FDR Library.

71. U.S. Federal Bureau of Investigation, Investigation Concerning the Sharecropper Situation Existing in Southeast Missouri, 1; "Report of Contact Men in Missouri," January 21, 1939, Reel 10, STFU Papers; "Sharecroppers' Health Menaced in Drafty Houses," Post-Dispatch, January 25, 1939; Whitfield, St. Louis, to Thurgood Marshall, NAACP, January 24, 1939, Folder "Southern Tenant Farmers Union, Jan. 23–Dec. 20, 1939," Container 406, Series C, NAACP Records.

72. Fannie Cook to Eleanor Roosevelt, November 10, 1939, Folder "Folder C. Harrington, 1939," Box 329, ER Papers; Cantor, *A Prologue to the Protest Movement,* 90.

73. Whitfield to Thurgood Marshall, January 24, 1939, Folder "Southern Tenant Farmers Union, Jan. 23–Dec. 20, 1939," Container 406, Series C, NAACP Records.

74. "Flood of Checks Ordered Stopped Pending Probe by Federal Agents," *Enterprise-Courier,* February 9, 1939.

75. Willie Scott, New Madrid, to Butler, January 25, 1939, Reel 10, STFU Papers.

76. Daniel McClenton, Kewanee, to Butler, January 24, 1939, Reel 10, STFU Papers.

77. Alonzo Julian, New Madrid, to Butler, January 31, 1939; and Alonzo J. Julien, New Madrid, in "Letters Written on Backs of Survey Blanks," ca. January 1939, both Reel 10, STFU Papers.

78. Unknown, Charleston, to Butler, January 26, 1939, Reel 10, STFU Papers.

79. Ike Tripp, Lilbourn, to Butler, February 2, 1939, Reel 10, STFU Papers.

80. R. A. McAdory, Matthews, to Mitchell, January 31, 1939, Reel 10, STFU Papers.

81. Mitchell to FDR, January 18, 1939, Folder "Tenant Farming, 1939–1944," Box 1, Official File 1650, FDR Library; Mitchell to St. Clair Drake, ca. January 1939, Mitchell to Howard Kester, ca. January 1939, both Reel 9, Mitchell to FDR, January 22, 1939, Mitchell to All STFU locals, January 17, 1939, Mitchell to Union Officers in Missouri, January 15, 1939, Mitchell to All STFU locals, January 17, 1939, Press Release, January 23, 1939, "Report of Relief Distribution in Southeast Missouri, January 10–February 18," 1939, Mitchell to Houston Turner, Wyatt, February 14, 1939, all Reel 10, STFU Papers.

82. Al Murphy to T. J. North, Charleston, January 18, 1939, Reel 10, STFU Papers; Donald Henderson to Governor Stark, January 11, 1939, Folder 1935, Stark Papers; "Sharecroppers Evicted from State Highways under Order of Missouri Health Commissioner," *Enterprise-Courier,* January 19, 1939; Cantor, *A Prologue to the Protest Movement,* 78, 81; Greene, "Lincoln University's Involvement with the Sharecropper Demonstration in Southeast Missouri," 31–32.

83. "God's Chosen People," *Enterprise-Courier,* February 2, 1939.

84. Cantor, *A Prologue to the Protest Movement,* 100–1; "New Sharecropper Grants Are Held Up," *Post-Dispatch,* February 9, 1939.

85. Conservative Democrats joined with Republicans to pass the Hatch Act in July 1939, which aimed to stop the use of relief money for "pernicious political activities." For more on the congressional politics of agricultural relief and the FSA, see Patterson, *Congressional Conservatism and the New Deal,* 316; and Baldwin, *Poverty and Politics,* 198–201.

86. "Biggest Snow in 20 Years," *Enterprise-Courier,* February 9, 1939.

87. Savannah Warr, Charleston, to Mitchell, February 11, 1939, Reel 10, STFU Papers.

88. Harlan McField, Charleston, to Butler, February 6, 1939, Reel 10, STFU Papers.

89. Houston Turner, Charleston, to Butler and Mitchell, February 17, 1939, Reel 10, STFU Papers.

90. "Six Here to Seek Aid for Sharecroppers," *Post-Dispatch,* February 12, 1939.

91. Peter Wilderness, Marston, to J. R. Butler, February 10, 1939, Reel 10, STFU Papers.

92. Whitfield, New York, to All Locals in Missouri, February 5, 1939 (all quotes), Whitfield to All STFU Officers and Members in Missouri, February 11, 1939, both in Reel 10, STFU Papers.

93. Essex Local #383 to Mitchell, February 17, 1939, Reel 10, STFU Papers.

94. Peter Wilderness, Marston, to Butler, February 10, 1939, Reel 10, STFU Papers.

95. Cantor, *A Prologue to the Protest Movement,* 102–4, 108.

96. Ibid., 105.

97. Mitchell to Houston Turner, Wyatt, February 14, 1939, Reel 10, STFU Papers.

98. Cantor, *A Prologue to the Protest Movement,* 116.

99. Whitfield to F. R. Betton, Cotton Plant, Arkansas, February 27, 1939, Reel 10, STFU Papers.

100. Whitfield to Missouri locals of the STFU, February 24, 1939, Reel 10, STFU Papers.

101. "Butler, Mitchell Removed from UCAPAWA and CIO," *UCAPAWA News,* July 1939; "Farm Union Members Are Detained Here," *Enterprise-Courier,* March 16, 1939; Membership Referendum Local 385, Membership Referendum Local 502, Membership Referendum Local 380, Membership Referendum Local 515, F. L. Thompson, Parma, to J. R. Butler, March 17, 1939, all Reel 11, STFU Papers; Cantor, *A Prologue to the Protest Movement,* 118–22.

102. Priscilla, Anchorage, KY, to STFU Headquarters, July 5, 1939, Reel 12, STFU Papers.

103. J. F. Moore, Matthews, to Mitchell, March 16, 1939, Reel 11, STFU Papers.

104. Willie Scott, New Madrid, to Butler, March 7, 1939, Reel 11, STFU Papers.

105. Peter Wilderness, Marston, to Butler, February 10, 1939, Reel 10, STFU Papers; "Application for Charter of the New Madrid–Stoddard Counties Branch," April 12, 1937, Folder "Stoddard–New Madrid Counties, Mo., 1936–1937," Container 111, Series G, NAACP Records; "We the Undersigned," ca. March 1939, Folder 1939, Stark Papers.

106. This interpretation draws on Payne, *I've Got the Light of Freedom,* 274.

107. William Fischer and Whitfield to Donald Henderson, March 20, 1939, Folder 19, Box 16, Williams Papers.

108. Cook to Eleanor Roosevelt, December 8, 1939, Box 411, Missouri, Entry 4A, Records of the FHA, College Park.

109. Priscilla, Anchorage, KY, to STFU Headquarters, July 5, 1939, Reel 12, STFU Papers.

110. Whitfield, "What Was Done," Spring 1939, Folder 3, Box 6, Cook Papers.

111. "We the Undersigned."

112. U.S. Federal Bureau of Investigation, *Investigation Concerning the Sharecropper Situation Existing in Southeast Missouri*, 58 (first quote); "We the Undersigned" (second quote).

113. "We the Undersigned," ca. February 1939, Folder 1939, Stark Papers.

114. Whitfield, "What Was Done."

115. Whitfield, "What It Stands For," Spring 1939, Folder 3, Box 6, Cook Papers.

116. Fannie Cook to Edna Gellhorn, April 17, 1939, Folder 2, Box 5, Cook Papers.

117. "Sweet Home Squatters Face Ejectment," *Enterprise-Courier*, April 27, 1939.

118. "New Camp Is Planned for Sharecroppers," *Enterprise-Courier*, June 15, 1939 (quote); Cadle, "'Cropperville' from Refuge to Community," 39–40; Cantor, *A Prologue to the Protest Movement*, 93.

119. Whitfield to the MAWC, June 10, 1939, quoted in Greene, "Lincoln University's Involvement with the Sharecropper Demonstration in Southeast Missouri," 42–43.

120. O. R. Dyck to H. C. Albin, December 1, 1939, Folder "Pa–Pe, 1939," Box 333, ER Papers; Cadle, "'Cropperville' from Refuge to Community," 40–41, 62; "'Croppers Now on 90-A Farm in Butler Co.," *Enterprise-Courier*, June 22, 1939.

121. H. Laws, Charleston, to Mitchell, February 15, 1937, Reel 4, STFU Papers; Priscilla, Anchorage, KY, to STFU Headquarters, July 5, 1939, Reel 12, STFU Papers; "Resolution of Cropperville Residents," June 29, 1939, Folder 1939, Stark Papers.

122. "Resolution of Cropperville Residents."

123. Petition to FDR, W. W. Alexander, and P. G. Beck, July 9, 1939, Folder 3, Box 5, Cook Papers (quotes); Belfrage, "Cotton-Patch Moses," 102; "'Croppers Now on 90-A Farm in Butler Co.," *Enterprise-Courier*, June 22, 1939.

124. Priscilla, Anchorage, KY, to STFU Headquarters, July 5, 1939, Reel 12, STFU Papers.

125. "Missouri Council Buys Land for Union Camp," *UCAPAWA News*, December 1939.

126. J. W. Littlefield, Hayti, to the Editor, *UCAPAWA News*, August 1939.

127. "Until Hell Freezes Over," *UCAPAWA News*, December 1939.

128. *UCAPAWA News*, February 1940, quoted in Kelley, *Hammer and Hoe*, 174.

129. "Complete List of Locals in Missouri," ca. July 1939, Reel 9, STFU Papers.

130. J. F. Hynds to Butler, August 16, 1939, Reel 12, STFU Papers.

131. Isaac Wells to Butler, October 9, 1939; Bradford to Butler, November 25, 1939; both in Reel 13, STFU Papers.

132. Butler to Mitchell, August 16, September 23, 1939, Reel 12, STFU Papers.

133. W. M. Buck to Butler, September 10, 1939, Reel 12, STFU Papers; Priscilla,

Anchorage, KY, to STFU Headquarters, July 5, 1939, Reel 12, STFU Papers; Butler to Isaac Wells, November 17, 1939, Reel 13, STFU Papers.

134. Fannie Cook to Eleanor Roosevelt, November 10, 1939, Folder "F. C. Harrington, 1939," Box 329, ER Papers; O. R. Dyck to H. C. Albin, December 1, 1939, Folder "Pa–Pe, 1939," Box 333, ER Papers.

135. "Missouri Roadside Demonstrators Struggle for Life in Their Own Camp," *UCAPAWA News,* September 1939.

136. Unknown, Portageville, to Butler, January 1, 1940, Reel 14, STFU Papers; James McLeash, Hayti, to Mitchell, January 1940, Reel 14, STFU Papers; George Rogers, Matthews, to Governor Stark, January 5, 1940, Folder 1942, Stark Papers; Sherman Fish, Holcomb, to Governor Stark, February 12, 1940, Folder 1942, Stark Papers.

137. Whitfield to Eleanor Roosevelt, January 2, 1940, Folder "We–Wh, 1940," Box 348, ER Papers.

138. Will Alexander to Eleanor Roosevelt, November 29, 1939, Folder "WW Alexander, September–December 1939," Box 328, ER Papers; "Press Release," STFU, December 20, 1939, Reel 13, STFU Papers.

139. STFU Memorandum to FSA, November 30, 1939, Reel 13, STFU Papers.

140. Governor Stark, "Press Release," December 29, 1939, Folder 1941, Stark Papers.

141. "Stark calls FSA Head to Discuss Sharecroppers," *Enterprise-Courier,* January 4, 1940; Cantor, *A Prologue to the Protest Movement,* 134–36.

142. "Roadside Signs Cite Plight of Sharecroppers," *Post-Dispatch,* January 8, 1940; "Sharecropper Handbill," Folder 32, Snow Papers; "Drafts: Roadside Demonstration," Folder 32, Snow Papers.

143. Sharecroppers' Conference, "Press Release," January 7, 1940, Folder 1942, Stark Papers; "Gov. Stark Asks Landowners to Delay Evictions," *Post-Dispatch,* January 6, 1940; "Sharecroppers Stay on Day of Eviction," *Post-Dispatch,* January 10, 1940.

144. "National Council to Aid Agricultural Workers," Folder 4, Box 5, Cook Papers; Eleanor Roosevelt to Jackson, February 27, 1940, Folder "National Sharecropper Week 1940," Box 73, Gardner Jackson Papers, FDR Library; Cantor, *A Prologue to the Protest Movement,* 138, 143.

145. *Southeast Missouri,* 5–8; "Stark Requests Second Delay in Farm Eviction," *Post-Dispatch,* February 2, 1940; Carl Wideking to Jewell Mayes, February 13, 1940, Reel 14, STFU Papers.

146. "Rural Survey Basis for FSA Study" and "FSA Leases Second Rehabilitation Tract," *Standard,* February 9, 1940; "Tract of 2650 Acres Leased by the FSA," *Enterprise-Courier,* February 15, 1940; "New FSA Plan for Semo Farmers Gets Under Way," *Enterprise-Courier,* March 7, 1940.

147. P. G. Beck, memorandum, May 9, 1940, Folder 1954, Stark Papers; Ogilvie, "Development of Southeast Missouri," 300.

148. Beck, memorandum, May 9, 1940, Folder 1954, Stark Papers (quote); "Release on Eight Groups," June 17, 1940, Folder 1954, Stark Papers; Ellison, "Camp Lost

Colony," 18–19; Brown, "Farm Labor in Southeast Missouri," 11–13; Cocalis, "They Came from Missouri," 15–19.

149. "Amounts Received from Local Secretaries," February 1940, Reel 14, STFU Papers.

150. "2500 at Missouri Meeting," *UCAPAWA News,* May–June, 1940; Walter Johnson to Committee for the Rehabilitation of the Sharecroppers, November 30, 1940, Folder 5, Box 5, Cook Papers.

151. Cadle, "'Cropperville' from Refuge to Community," 69–71. For more on Whitfield's work in Memphis, see Roll and Gellman, "Whitfield and the Gospel of the Working Class," 308–48.

152. "We Won't Pick His Cotton," *UCAPAWA News,* September–October 1940.

153. "Release on Eight Groups," June 17, 1940, Folder 1954, Stark Papers.

154. P. G. Beck to C. B. Baldwin, February 11, 1941, Box 414, Missouri, Entry 4A, Records of the FHA, College Park; McWilliams, *Ill Fares the Land,* 293–94.

155. *Post-Dispatch,* March 15, 1941, quoted in Emerson, "Sharecroppers' Strike," 75.

156. Grey, *New Deal Medicine,* 113–28.

157. Ogilvie, "Development of Southeast Missouri," 325–29.

158. *Southeast Missouri: A Laboratory for the Cotton South.*

159. Testimony of Orville Zimmerman, in U.S. Congress, *Hearings before the Select Committee of the House Committee on Agriculture, to Investigate the Activities of the Farm Security Administration,* 691–93.

160. P. E. Bussert to Zimmerman, February 15, 1941 (quote); W.H. Foster to Zimmerman, February 15, 1941; Oscar Fuller to Zimmerman, February 17, 1941; O.A. Knight to Zimmerman, February 17, 1941; J. I. Murlison to Zimmerman, February 17, 1941, all in Box 414, Missouri, Entry 4A, Records of the FHA, College Park.

161. U.S. Bureau of the Census, *U.S. Census of Agriculture: 1935,* vol. 1, *Farms, Farm Acreage, and Value,* 262–71; U.S. Bureau of the Census, *Sixteenth Census of the United States: 1940, Agriculture,* vol. 1, pt. 2, *Statistics for Counties,* 254–63.

162. "A Petition to the FSA," February 1941, Folder 4, Box 6, Cook Papers.

163. "A Petition to the FSA," March 1941, Box 414, Missouri, Entry 4A, Records of the FHA, College Park.

164. "First Family Moves in Group Labor Home," *Standard,* March 7, 1941.

165. Robert Wicker, Charleston, to STFU, ca. October 1936, Reel 3, STFU Papers.

166. Martin Lechner to Thad Snow, Charleston, January 27, 1941, Folder 7, Snow Papers.

167. U.S. Bureau of the Census, *Sixteenth Census of the United States: 1940, Agriculture,* vol. 1, pt. 2: *Statistics for Counties,* 254–63; U.S. Bureau of the Census, *U.S. Census of Agriculture: 1935,* vol. 1, *Farms, Farm Acreage, and Value,* 262–71.

168. Bright, "Farm Wage Workers," 48–50; E. J. Holcomb, "Farm Organization," in Holcomb, Murray, Folsom, and Turner, *Report to the Tolan Committee,* 3–13.

169. *Southeast Missouri,* 1.

170. Ibid., 2; McWilliams, *Ill Fares the Land,* 283; Testimony of P. G. Beck, in U.S. Congress, *Hearings before the Select Committee Investigating National Defense Migration,* 9243–45.

171. Testimony of P. G. Beck, in U.S. Congress, *Hearings before the Select Committee Investigating National Defense Migration,* 9244–45.

172. Graham to STFU, July 8, 1941, Reel 18, STFU Papers.

173. Press Release, May 12, 1941, Reel 18, STFU Papers.

174. Mitchell to Clayton, April 27, 1941, Reel 18, STFU Papers.

175. "Missouri Locals Form District Council" and "Missouri Farm Wages Go Up," *Tenant Farmer,* July 5, 1941, Reel 58, STFU Papers.

176. Press Release, May 12, 1941, Reel 18, STFU Papers.

177. Mitchell to Clayton, June 11, 1941, Reel 18, STFU Papers; Mitchell to Betton, June 6, 1941, Reel 18, STFU Papers; Graham to Butler, June 17, 1941, Reel 18, STFU Papers; "STFU Paid Membership," Summer 1941, Reel 19, STFU Papers.

178. "Special Missouri Call to Third Annual Convention," June 1941, Reel 11, STFU Papers.

179. Lichtenstein, *Labor's War at Home,* 60–66; Zieger, *The CIO, 1935–1955,* 121–22, 130–41; Isserman, *Which Side Were You On?* 135.

180. Whitfield, Kirkwood, to J. E. Clayton, July 15, 1941, Reel 18, STFU Papers; Whitfield, "Foreward to the Big Four Program," mid-1941, Reel 20, STFU Papers.

181. Mitchell to Thad Snow, April 20, 1941; Mitchell to F. R. Betton, May 6, 1941; Mitchell to F. R. Betton, May 14, 1941, all on Reel 18, STFU Papers.

182. Whitfield, "Foreward to the Big Four Program," mid-1941, Reel 20, STFU Papers.

183. Testimony of Thad Snow, in U.S. Congress, *Hearings before the Select Committee Investigating National Defense Migration,* 9166; "Food for the Hungry," *UCAPAWA News,* September 22, 1941; "Union Doubles Cotton Picking Pay," *UCAPAWA News,* October 27, 1941; Frame, "Cost of Producing Cotton," 3; "Sharecroppers Living High Now That They Are Prosperous," October 17, 1941, Folder 48, Box FC 2.3, Clippings Collection, 1871–2001, KL; "Editorial," *Standard,* October 17, 1941.

184. Zieger, *The CIO, 1935–1955,* 142–44; Isserman, *Which Side Were You On?* 136–39; Honey, *Southern Labor and Black Civil Rights,* 189–90; Lichtenstein, *Labor's War at Home,* 66, 145.

185. John Stewart to Fannie Cook, January 21, 1942, Folder 11, Box 7, Cook Papers; Fannie Cook to E. L. Hughes, February 2, 1942, Folder 8, Box 5, Cook Papers; Cadle, "'Cropperville' from Refuge to Community," 81.

186. Whitfield, Kirkwood, to Julia Katz, December 16, 1941, Reel 7, Frames 679–681, Series 3, *Papers of the National Negro Congress* (Bethesda, MD: University Publications of America, 1988; 94 reels); "Sharecropper Leader Wins Government Help," *UCAPAWA News,* December 22, 1941; "Further Details of Jap Agitator's 5th Column Work," *Post-Dispatch,* March 6, 1942 (last quote).

187. Lichtenstein, *Labor's War at Home,* 95–96.

188. "Club Protests FSA Project; East Prairie Lions Object to Negro Farms," *Southeast Missourian*, January 22, 1942 (quotes); C. B. Baldwin to Eleanor Roosevelt, March 4, 1942, Folder "C.B. Baldwin, 1942," Box 365, ER Papers; Cadle, "'Cropperville' from Refuge to Community," 82.

189. Mitchell to W. M. Tanner, January 12, 1942; "Mass Meeting," Caruthersville, January 16, 1942; Roy E. Raley to Governor Forrest Donnell, Jefferson City, January 1942; "Statement of W. M. Tanner," January 1942; Frank McAllister to Mitchell, January 24, 1942; Press Release, ca. February 1942 (all on Reel 20, STFU Papers). Also "Missouri Planters Break Up Union Meeting," *Tenant Farmer*, January 15, 1942, Reel 58, STFU Papers; "FBI May Act in Missouri," *Tenant Farmer*, February 15, 1942, Reel 58, STFU Papers; "Tenant Union Meeting Calm; Speakers Get Hearing in Pemiscot Gathering," *Southeast Missourian*, January 24, 1942; "Trouble Comes Up at Organization of Tenant Labor," *Democrat-Argus*, January 20, 1942; "Union Promotion Meeting Attended Mostly by Planters," *Democrat-Argus*, January 27, 1942; "Donnell Orders Protection for Farm Union Meeting; Also Asks Pemiscot County Officials to Investigate Charge That Gathering Was Broken Up," *Post-Dispatch*, January 19, 1942.

190. "Sikeston Mob Lynches Negro; Town Incensed by Attack on Woman" and "Second Lynching within 17 Years," *Southeast Missourian*, January 26, 1942.

191. For more on the Double-V campaign, see Fairclough, *Better Day Coming*, 185–86.

192. "Mob Action," *Enterprise-Courier*, January 29, 1942 (quote); Mr. and Mrs. L. Benoist, "Informal Report on Attitudes in Southeast Missouri Relative to the Lynching of Cleo Wright, Negro, January 25, 1942," pgs. 5–6, Part 7, Series A, Reel 27, *Microfilm Edition of the Papers of the NAACP*; Capeci, *The Lynching of Cleo Wright*, 1–3, 21–22; Gallicchio, *The African American Encounter with Japan & China*, 116.

193. "East Prairie Airs Protest; FSA Officials Told Objections to Project," *Southeast Missourian*, January 29, 1942.

194. John Stewart to Fannie Cook, January 27, 1942, Folder 11, Box 7, Cook Papers; Whitfield to the FSA, February 27, 1942 (quote), Folder 11, Box 7, Cook Papers; John Stewart to Edward Miller, February 7, 1942, Folder 11, Box 7, Cook Papers; C. B. Baldwin to Eleanor Roosevelt, March 4, 1942, Folder "C.B. Baldwin, 1942," Box 365, ER Papers; Cadle, "'Cropperville' from Refuge to Community," 83.

195. St. Louis Industrial Union Council to Henderson, June 1942, Reel 21, STFU Papers.

196. Honey, *Southern Labor and Black Civil Rights*, 125–34.

197. "FSA Battle in Senate" and "Demand Land to Raise Hogs," both in *UCAPAWA News*, March 27, 1942.

198. Grey, *New Deal Medicine*, 132–34; Sullivan, *Days of Hope*, 129; Holley, *Uncle Sam's Farmers*, 243–45; Baldwin, *Poverty and Politics*, 262.

199. St. Louis Industrial Union Council to Henderson, June 1942, Reel 21, STFU Papers.

200. Worcester, *C. L. R. James,* 70; Mitchell to Clayton, April 18, 1942, Reel 20, STFU Papers.

201. "Down with Starvation Wages," in James, *The Future in the Present,* 89.

202. Worcester, *C. L. R. James,* 70–71.

203. See Korstad and Lichtenstein, "Opportunities Found and Lost"; and Goluboff, *The Lost Promise of Civil Rights,* 51–80.

204. "Down with Starvation Wages," 89–94.

205. "Negro Laborers Ask $3.00 Per Day to Chop," *Charleston Democrat,* May 21, 1942; Arthur McDowell to Frank McAllister, June 2, 1942, Reel 21, STFU Papers; St. Louis Industrial Union Council to Henderson, June 1942, Reel 21, STFU Papers.

206. "Owe Back Rent; Must Get 30c," *UCAPAWA News,* May 28, 1942 (quote). This is a reprinted version of a letter to P. G. Beck.

207. Arthur McDowell to Frank McAllister, June 2, 1942, Reel 21, STFU Papers.

208. Reel 21, STFU Papers: "Resolution of St. Louis CIO Industrial Union Council," May 27, 1942; Arthur McDowell to Frank McAllister, June 2, 1942; St. Louis Industrial Union Council to Henderson, June 1942 (quote).

209. Whitfield to Secretaries, Delmo Homes Projects, June 11, 1942, Reel 21, STFU Papers.

210. "Planters Defy Govt."; "Croppers Call on FDR," both in *UCAPAWA News,* June 15, 1942.

211. Worcester, *C. L. R. James,* 72.

212. "'Croppers Set $3 per 100 Cotton Picking Scale," *UCAPAWA News,* August 1, 1942.

213. Fannie Cook to Eleanor Roosevelt, July 23, 1942, Folder "Co, 1942," Box 511, ER Papers; FDR to Eleanor Roosevelt, July 30, 1942, Folder "Co, 1942," Box 511, ER Papers; Eleanor Roosevelt to Wallace, August 3, 1942, Folder "Henry Wallace 1942," Box 775, ER Papers.

214. "Army of Harvesters from South; Only 'Shortage' Is Decent Wages," *UCAPAWA News,* May 28, 1942 (quote); "'Croppers Mobilize to Further Wage Campaign," *UCAPAWA News,* July 15, 1942.

215. "'Croppers Set $3 per 100 Cotton Picking Scale," *UCAPAWA News,* August 1, 1942.

216. Clark, interview by Mitchell, quoted in Mitchell, *Mean Things Happening in This Land,* 181.

217. "Missouri Locals," June 1942, Reel 21, STFU Papers; Bill Johnson to Mitchell, October 10, 1942, Reel 22, STFU Papers; "Delegate from Missouri" and "Proceedings, Mid-South Cotton Picking Conference," September 7, 1942, both in Folder "H. L. Mitchell, 1938–1940," Box 49, Gardner Jackson Papers, FDR Library .

218. Mitchell to Whom It May Concern, September 29, 1942 (quotes), Reel 21, STFU Papers; Bill Johnson to Mitchell, October 12, 1942, Reel 22, STFU Papers.

219. For an excellent discussion of the negative impact of communist ideology on African-American labor organizing, see Arnesen, "No 'Graver Danger.'"

220. Woodruff, "Pick or Fight," 80–81; Whitfield to Fannie Cook, November 4, 1942, Folder 4, Box 6, Cook Papers; Whitfield to Claude Williams, November 3, 1942, and December 3, 1942, Folder 24, Box 15, Williams Papers. On Reel 24, STFU Papers: "Sharecroppers Plea Gov't for Chance to Grow Food," *UCAPAWA News*, February 1943; "Standing of Locals Southern Tenant Farmers Union," August 1, 1943; Mitchell to Rosemary Freil, August 20, 1943; Mitchell to B. C. Deweese, September 14, 1943. Also "Organization Report" 1943 Annual Convention; "Missouri Locals—Active List," late 1943; "Missouri Dead Locals," late 1943, all on Reel 25, STFU Papers.

221. Testimony of P. G. Beck, in U.S. Congress, *Hearings before the Select Committee Investigating National Defense Migration*, 9185.

## Epilogue

1. Testimony of Orville Zimmerman, in U.S. Congress, *Hearings before the Select Committee of the House Committee on Agriculture, to Investigate the Activities of the Farm Security Administration*, 527 (final quote), 691 (second quote), 701–02, 708 (first quote).

2. Hancock to Zimmerman, April 10, 1945, Folder 1, David Burgess Papers, Part 4, Reel 17, *The Green Rising, 1910–1977: A Supplement to the Southern Tenant Farmers' Union Papers* (hereafter *The Green Rising*); Hahamovitch, *The Fruits of Their Labor*, 173–74; Sullivan, *Days of Hope*, 129; Ogilvie, "Development of Southeast Missouri," 315, 32–33; Grey, *New Deal Medicine*, 128.

3. Hancock to Zimmerman, April 10, 1945, Folder 1, David Burgess Papers, Reel 17, *The Green Rising*; Towle, "Delmo Saga," 2, Folder 5, Bootheel Project Records, 1993–1997, WHMC-C (hereafter Bootheel Project Records); Ogilvie, "Development of Southeast Missouri," 333–36.

4. Bill Johnson, Wardell, to Mitchell, March 2, 1945, Reel 29, STFU Papers.

5. "First Meeting of the Tenant Committee," March 20, 1945, Reel 29, STFU Papers; Mitchell to David Burgess, 1945, Reel 31, STFU Papers.

6. Mitchell to Evelyn Smith, March 13, 1945, Reel 29, STFU Papers; Tenants Committee to Marvin Jones, March 20, 1945, Reel 29, STFU Papers; Towle, "Delmo Saga," 2 (quotes).

7. Petition, Lilbourn Homes, March 1945, Reel 29, STFU Papers.

8. Towle, "Delmo Saga," 2, 20–21.

9. Ibid., 2; Burgess, interview by Jacquelyn Hall and Bill Finger, September 25, 1974, Folder 87, David Burgess Papers, Reel 17, *The Green Rising*; Burgess to Thomas A. Tripp et al., March 1945, Reel 29, STFU Papers.

10. W. A. Johnson, Wardell, to Stephen Hughes, April 21, 1945, Folder 1, David Burgess Papers, Reel 17, *The Green Rising*.

11. "Report of the Washington Delegation," April 1945, Reel 29, STFU Papers; North Lilbourn Tenant Council to the Congress of the United States, April 4, 1945, Reel 29, STFU Papers; Mrs. Robert Wicker to Whom it May Concern, March 23,

1945, Reel 29, STFU Papers; Burgess to Tripp et al., April 30, 1945, Reel 29, STFU Papers.

12. Whitfield to Fannie Cook, April 7, 1945, Folder 7, Box 6, Cook Papers.

13. Mitchell to Delmo Labor Homes Committee, April 16, 1945, Reel 29, STFU Papers; Whitfield to Claude Williams, Detroit, July 11, 1945, Folder 25, Box 15, Williams Papers.

14. Mitchell to Delmo Labor Homes Committee, July 16, 1945 and Burgess to Mitchell, August 5, 1945, both on Reel 30, STFU Papers; Burgess to Charles Johnson, August 16, 1945, Folder 1 and Burgess, interview by Jacquelyn Hall and Bill Finger, September 25, 1974, Folder 87, both David Burgess Papers, Reel 17, *The Green Rising*.

15. Harry Truman to Frank E. Hook, October 2, 1945, Folder 1, David Burgess Papers, Reel 17, *The Green Rising*; Burgess to Tripp et al., August 31, 1945, Reel 30, STFU Papers; Towle, "Delmo Saga," 22.

16. Burgess to Tripp et al., August 31, 1945, Reel 30, STFU Papers.

17. Whitfield to Claude Williams, Detroit, August 13, 1945 and September 25, 1945, both in Folder 25, Box 15, Williams Papers.

18. Wilson and Burgess to Prospective Buyers, October 16, 1945, Reel 31, STFU Papers.

19. Charles C. Wilson, St. Louis, to Friends, November 16, 1945, Reel 31, STFU Papers; "Delmo Housing Committee Contributions," Folder 88, David Burgess Papers, Reel 17, *The Green Rising*; Emerson, "The Sharecroppers' Strike, 1939," 83–84.

20. "Farmers, Are You Blind?" *Scott County Kicker,* October 19, 1907.

21. Whitfield, "What Was Done," Spring 1939, Folder 3, Box 6, Cook Papers.

22. Whitfield, "Forward to the Big Four Program," ca. mid-1941, Reel 20, STFU Papers.

23. "We the Undersigned," ca. March 1939, Folder 1939, Stark Papers.

24. *Justice,* April 24, 1914, 1.

25. Harvey, *Freedom's Coming,* 50.

26. David Edwin Harrell Jr., "The South: Seedbed of Sectarianism," in Harrell, *Varieties of Southern Evangelicalism,* 56.

27. U.S. Bureau of the Census, *U.S. Census of Agriculture: 1945,* vol. 1, pt. 100, *Statistics for Counties,* 18–61; U.S. Bureau of the Census, *Sixteenth Census of the United States: 1940, Agriculture,* vol. 1, pt. 2, *Statistics for Counties,* 254–63, 326–34.

28. Roy Cooper Jr. and Alex Cooper, Hayti, Missouri, interview with Will Sarvis, August 4, 1998, 17, PMOH, C3929.

29. Notable exceptions include Woodruff, *American Congo*; Fannin, *Labor's Promised Land*; De Jong, *A Different Day*; Bissett, *Agrarian Socialism in America*; Foley, *The White Scourge,* 28–39; Whayne, *A New Plantation South*; Dunbar, *Against the Grain*; Green, *Grass-Roots Socialism*; and Grubbs, *Cry from the Cotton.*

30. See, for example, Ted Ownby, "'A Crude and Raw Past': Work, Folklife, and Anti-Agrarianism in Twentieth-Century African American Autobiography," 27–53, and Peter Coclanis and Bryant Simon, "Exit, Voice, and Loyalty: African American

Strategies for Day-to-Day Existence/Resistance in the Early-Twentieth-Century Rural South," 189–209, both in Hurt, *African American Life in the Rural South.*

31. Roy Cooper, Hayti, Missouri, interview by unidentified researcher, August 13, 1994, Audio Cassette 15–16, Sides A–B; Roy Cooper Jr., interview by unidentified researcher, 1994, A.C. 101, Side A; Roy Cooper, Portageville, Missouri, interview by unidentified researcher, March 11, 1994, A.C. 3, Sides A–B; Roy Cooper Jr., interview by unidentified researcher, March 17, 1994, A.C. 11, Side B. All in Bootheel Project Records.

32. Roy Cooper Jr., interview by unidentified researcher, March 17, 1994, A.C. 11, Side A.

33. Roy Cooper Jr. and Roy Cooper, Hayti, Missouri, interview by Will Sarvis, August 4, 1998, 6, 26, PMOH.

34. "Happy New Year for Delmo Colonists," *Post-Dispatch,* January 6, 1948.

35. Towle, "Delmo Saga," 27; Roy Cooper, Portageville, Missouri, interview by unknown researcher, March 11, 1994, A.C. 3, Side A.

36. Roy Cooper Jr. and Roy Cooper, Hayti, Missouri, interview with Will Sarvis, August 4, 1998, 2 (first quote), 23 (final quote), PMOH.

# Bibliography

## Manuscript Collections

**LOCAL HISTORY ROOM, DUNKLIN COUNTY LIBRARY, KENNETT, MISSOURI (DCL)**

*Cardwell Then and Now, 1894–1994.* Cardwell, 1994.
Echols, E. T. "Early History of the First Assembly of God Church." Senath, Mo., 1989 (unpublished typescript)

**FRANKLIN D. ROOSEVELT PRESIDENTIAL LIBRARY AND MUSEUM, HYDE PARK, NEW YORK (FDR LIBRARY)**

Eleanor Roosevelt Papers
Gardner Jackson Papers
Official Files

**INTERNATIONAL PENTECOSTAL-HOLINESS CHURCH ARCHIVES AND RESEARCH CENTER, OKLAHOMA CITY, OKLAHOMA (IPHCA)**

Conference Minute Books, 1925

**LIBRARY OF CONGRESS, WASHINGTON, D.C. (LOC)**

Missouri Field Recordings, American Folklife Center
National Association for the Advancement of Colored People Records, 1842–1999 (NAACP Records)

**MISSOURI HISTORY MUSEUM LIBRARY AND RESEARCH CENTER, ST. LOUIS, MISSOURI (MHM)**

Fannie Frank Cook Papers, 1874–1949

**NATIONAL ARCHIVES AND RECORDS ADMINISTRATION (NARA), ARCHIVES II, COLLEGE PARK, MARYLAND**

RG 96, Records of the Farmers Home Administration and Predecessor Agencies, 1918–1980
RG 165, Records of the Military Intelligence Division
RG 204, Pardon Case Files, 1853–1946
ARC 304957, Records of the American National Red Cross

**NATIONAL ARCHIVES AND RECORDS ADMINISTRATION, GREAT LAKES REGION, CHICAGO, ILLINOIS**

RG 96, Records of the Farmers Home Administration and Predecessor Agencies

**NEW MADRID COUNTY COURT HOUSE, NEW MADRID, MISSOURI (NMCH)**

County Court Dockets, 1915–1920

**WALTER P. REUTHER LIBRARY, WAYNE STATE UNIVERSITY, DETROIT, MICHIGAN**

Claude C. Williams Papers, 1929–1979

**SCHOMBURG CENTER FOR RESEARCH IN BLACK CULTURE, NEW YORK PUBLIC LIBRARY, NEW YORK, NEW YORK**

Universal Negro Improvement Association, Central Division Records, Membership Record Card File, 1925–1927

**SPECIAL COLLECTIONS AND ARCHIVES, KENT LIBRARY, SOUTHEAST MISSOURI STATE UNIVERSITY, CAPE GIRARDEAU, MISSOURI (KL)**

Julien Friant Papers
Himmelberger-Harrison Lumber Company Papers
Louis Houck Papers, 1886–1943
Clippings Collection, 1871–2001

**WAGNER LABOR ARCHIVES, TAMIMENT LIBRARY, NEW YORK UNIVERSITY**

Oral History Collection 500

**WESTERN HISTORICAL MANUSCRIPTS COLLECTION–COLUMBIA (WHMC-C)**

Bootheel Project Records, 1993–1997 (C3928)
Charles Merlin Barnes Papers, 1892–1965 (C2802)
Scott Carey Papers, 1917–1961 (C2336)
Xenophon Caverno Papers, 1917–1941 (C0059)
Papers of Herbert Spencer Hadley, 1830–1943 (C0006)
Papers of Arthur Mastick Hyde, 1921–1954 (C0007)
O. R. Johnson Papers, 1910–1959 (C3483)

Guy Brasfield Park Papers, 1933–1937 (C0008)
Lloyd Crow Stark Papers, 1931–1941 (C0004)
Politics in Missouri Oral History Project Records, 1966–(C3929).
U.S. Works Progress Administration, Historical Record Survey, 1935–1942 (C3551)

**WESTERN HISTORICAL MANUSCRIPTS COLLECTION–ROLLA (WHMC-R)**

Levee District No. 3 Papers (R326)
Papers of the St. Francis Levee District, 1893–1980 (R076)
Papers of the Mississippi Levee District No. 1 (R326)
Gideon-Anderson Lumber & Mercantile Company Papers, 1901–1985 (R449)
*The Modern Promised Land* (R701)

**WESTERN HISTORICAL MANUSCRIPTS COLLECTION–ST. LOUIS (WHMC-S)**

Rural Revolt in Missouri (SL47)
Thad Snow Papers, 1921–1954 (SL88)

## Microfilmed Collections

*The Green Rising: Supplement to the Papers of the Southern Tenant Farmers' Union.*
    17 reels. Glen Rock, N.J.: Microfilming Corporation of America, 1978. (*The Green
    Rising*)
Meier, August, John H. Bracey, and Robert L. Zingrando, eds. *Microfilm Edition of
    the Papers of the NAACP. Part 7, The Anti-Lynching Campaign, 1912–1955.* Series
    A: *Anti-Lynching Investigative Files.* 30 reels. Frederick, Md.: University Publica-
    tions of America
Schipper, Martin Paul, Eric Gallagher, and David H. Werning, eds. *Papers of the National
    Negro Congress.* 94 reels. Frederick, Md.: University Publications of America.
*Southern Tenant Farmers' Union Papers, 1934–1973.* 65 reels. Microfilming Corpora-
    tion of America. (STFU Papers)

## Interviews

Cooper, Alex. Telephone interview with the author, November 30, 2003.
Handcox, John. Interview with Michael Honey, May 19, 1990. Unpublished transcript
    in possession of Michael Honey.
Handcox, John. Interview with Joe Glazer and Michael Honey, May 15, 1985. Unpub-
    lished audio recording in possession of Michael Honey.

## Newspapers

**ARKANSAS**

*Word and Witness* (Malvern)

**MISSOURI**

*Argus* (St. Louis)
*Citizen* (Campbell)
*Critic* (Hayti)
*Daily Dunklin Democrat* (Kennett)
*Daily Republican* (Cape Girardeau)
*Democrat* (Charleston)
*Democrat-Argus* (Caruthersville)
*Dunklin Democrat* (Kennett)
*Eagle* (East Prairie)
*Enterprise* (Steele)
*Enterprise-Courier* (Charleston)
*Justice* (Kennett and Gibson)
*Pemiscot-Argus* (Caruthersville)
*Post-Dispatch* (St. Louis)
*Scott County Banner* (Morley)
*Scott County Democrat* (Benton)
*Scott County Kicker* (Benton)
*Southeast Missourian* (Cape Girardeau)
*Spokesman* (Charleston)
*Standard* (Sikeston)
*Star* (St. Louis)
*Twice-a-Week Democrat* (Caruthersville)
*Victor* (Parma)
*Weekly Record* (New Madrid)

**OHIO**

*Christian Evangel* (Findlay)

**TENNESSEE**

*Farm Worker* (Memphis)
*Sharecropper's Voice* (Memphis)
*STFU News* (Memphis)

**NATIONAL AND MAJOR CITY DAILIES**

*Chicago Defender*
*Daily Tribune* (Chicago)
*Los Angeles Times*
*The Negro World* (New York)
*New York Times*
*San Francisco Chronicle*
*UCAPAWA News* (Philadelphia)

## Other Primary Sources

Agee, James, and Walker Evans. *Let Us Now Praise Famous Men: Three Tenant Families*. Boston, 1969, first ed., 1941.

American National Red Cross. *The Final Report of the Colored Advisory Commission, Mississippi Valley Flood Disaster, 1927.* Washington, 1929.

———. *The Mississippi Valley Flood Disaster of 1927: Official Report of the Relief Operations*. Washington, 1929.

Belfrage, Cedric. "Cotton-Patch Moses." *Harper's Magazine* 197 (November 1948): 94–103.

———. *Let My People Go*. London, 1940.

Berthe, L. T. *Analysis of the Plans of the United States Army Corps of Engineers, presented to the Committee on Flood Control, January 17, 1928*. Washington, 1928.

Bratton, Samuel T. "The Geography of the St. Francis Basin." *The University of Missouri Studies* 1 (July 1926): 1–54.

Bright, Margaret L. "Farm Wage Workers in Four Southeast Missouri Cotton-Producing Counties." MA thesis, University of Missouri–Columbia, 1944.

Brown, Phillip. "Farm Labor in Southeast Missouri." *The Agricultural Situation* 24 (April 1940): 11–13.

Chase, Stuart. "From the Lower Depths." *Reader's Digest* 38 (May 1941): 109–11.

Cocalis, Virginia. "They Came from Missouri." *Land Policy Review* 4 (February 1941): 15–19.

*Cotton Production in Missouri*. Agricultural Experiment Station Bulletin 299. Columbia, Mo., 1931.

DeYoung, William, and Robert Wildermuth. *Soil Survey of Mississippi County, Missouri*. Washington, D.C., 1924.

Douglass, Robert S. *History of Southeast Missouri: A Narrative Account of Its Historical Progress, Its People and Its Principal Interests*. New York, 1912.

Ellison, Ralph. "Camp Lost Colony." *New Masses* 34 (February 6, 1940): 18–19.

Frame, B. H. "Cost of Producing Cotton in Southeast Missouri, 1941." Agricultural Extension Service Bulletin 467. Columbia, Mo., 1943.

Hart, Grace E. "Study of Levels of Living in Three Southeast Missouri Counties." MA Thesis, University of Missouri–Columbia, 1937.

Higgins, Walter. *Pioneering in Pentecost: My Experiences of 46 Years in the Ministry*. Bostonia, Calif.: Walter Higgins, 1958.

Hill, Robert A., ed. *The Marcus Garvey and Universal Negro Improvement Association Papers*. 10 vols. Berkeley, 1983–2006.

Hoffman, Charles S., and Virgil L. Bankson. "Crisis in Missouri's Boot Heel." *Land Policy Review* 3 (January–February 1940): 1–14.

Holcomb, E. J., G. M. Murray, J. C. Folsom, and H. A. Turner. *Report to the Tolan Committee on the Cooperative Study of Farm Labor and Tenancy in Southeast Missouri*. Washington, 1941.

Hudson, Charles E. "A Geographic Study Examining the Major Elements Involved in the Rise of Cotton Production in Southeast Missouri, 1922–1925." MA thesis, Western Michigan University, 1967.

James, C. L. R. *The Future in the Present: Selected Writings.* Westport, 1977.

Johnson, Charles S., Edwin R. Embree, and W. W. Alexander. *The Collapse of Cotton Tenancy: Summary of Field Studies and Statistical Surveys, 1933–35.* Chapel Hill, 1935.

Kester, Howard. *Revolt among the Sharecroppers.* Knoxville, rcv. ed. 1999.

Kochtitzky, Otto. *The Story of a Busy Life.* Cape Girardeau, 1957.

Krusekopf, H. H. "Delta Soils of Southeast Missouri." Agricultural Experiment Station Bulletin 854. Columbia, Mo., 1962.

Lange, Dorothea, and Paul Taylor. *American Exodus: A Record of Human Erosion.* New York, 1939.

Little River Drainage District. *Little River Drainage District of Southeast Missouri, 1907–Present.* Cape Girardeau, Mo., 1989.

Lomax, Alan, Woody Guthrie, and Pete Seeger. *Hard Hitting Songs for Hard-Hit People.* New York, 1967.

McWilliams, Carey. *Ill Fares the Land.* Boston, 1942.

Mitchell, H. L. *Mean Things Happening in This Land: The Life and Times of H. L. Mitchell, Co-Founder of the Southern Tenant Farmers Union.* Montclair, 1979.

Nolen, John N. *Missouri's Swamp and Overflowed Lands and Their Reclamation.* Jefferson City, Mo., 1913.

*Official Manual of the State of Missouri, 1905–06.* Jefferson City, 1905.

*Official Manual of the State of Missouri, 1909–10.* Jefferson City, 1909.

*Official Manual of the State of Missouri, 1911–12.* Jefferson City, 1911.

*Official Manual of the State of Missouri, 1913–14.* Jefferson City, 1913.

*Official Manual of the State of Missouri, 1915–16.* Jefferson City, 1915.

*Official Manual of the State of Missouri, 1917–18.* Jefferson City, 1917.

*Official Manual of the State of Missouri, 1919–20.* Jefferson City, 1919.

*Official Manual of the State of Missouri for Years 1933 and 1934.* Jefferson City, 1933.

*Official Manual of the State of Missouri for Years 1939 and 1940.* Jefferson City, 1939.

Richards, Henry I. *Cotton under the Agricultural Adjustment Act: Developments up to July 1934.* Washington, D.C., 1934.

Ridpath, Ben M. "The Case of the Missouri Sharecroppers." *The Christian Century* 56 (February 1939): 146–48.

Roosevelt, Eleanor. "My Day." Syndicated Newspaper Column. Available at http://www.gwu.edu/~erpapers/myday/ (accessed September 7, 2009).

Sandilands, Alexander, ed. *A Hundred and Twenty Negro Spirituals.* Lesotho, 1981.

Schall, Jesse. "The Negro in New Madrid County." MA Thesis, University of Missouri–Columbia, 1930.

Shrum, Edison. *Super Floods Raging in Wide Spread Area: The Scott County Democrat's Account of the 1937 Mississippi-New Madrid County Jadwin Floodway Disaster.* Benton, 1994.

Slater, Michael, ed. *Dickens on America and the Americans*. Austin, 1978.

Snow, Thad. *From Missouri*. Boston, 1954.

*Southeast Missouri: A Laboratory for the Cotton South*. Farm Security Administration, Washington, 1940.

Steinbeck, John. *The Grapes of Wrath*. New York, 1939.

Stokes, Joseph H. "Some Factors Relating to Housing Conditions in Southeast Missouri." M.A. thesis, University of Missouri–Columbia, 1937.

Studabaker, Hugh D. *What They "Showed Me" in Southeast Missouri*. Valparaiso, 1913.

Sweet, A. T., C. J. Mann, and H. Krusekopf. *Soil Survey of Pemiscot County, Missouri*. United States Department of Agriculture, Bureau of Soils. Washington, 1912.

Sweet, A. T., B. W. Tillman, and H. H. Krusekopf. *Soil Survey of Dunklin County, Missouri*. United States Department of Agriculture, Bureau of Soils. Washington, D.C., 1916.

Tindall, George Brown, ed. *A Populist Reader: Selections from the Works of American Populist Leaders*. New York, 1966.

U.S. Army Corps of Engineers. *Final Report of the Mississippi River Flood Control Board to the President of the United States*. Washington, 1928.

U.S. Bureau of the Census. *Census of Religious Bodies: 1916*. Part 1, *Summary and General Tables*. Washington, 1919.

U.S. Bureau of the Census. *Census of Religious Bodies, 1926*. 2 vols. Washington, 1930.

U.S. Bureau of the Census. *Census of Religious Bodies, 1936*. Volume 1. Washington, 1940.

U.S. Bureau of the Census. *Eleventh Census of the United States: 1890*. Volume 5, *Reports on the Statistics of Agriculture in the United States*. Washington, 1895.

U.S. Bureau of the Census. *Eleventh Census of the United States: 1890*. Volume 9, *Report on the Statistics of Churches in the United States*. Washington, 1894.

U.S. Bureau of the Census. *Fifteenth Census of the United States: 1930: Agriculture*. Volume 3, Part 1, *Type of Farm, The Northern States*. Washington, 1932.

U.S. Bureau of the Census. *Fifteenth Census of the United States: 1930: Population*. Volume 3, Part 1, *Alabama–Missouri*. Washington, 1932.

U.S. Bureau of the Census. *Fifteenth Census of the United States: 1930, Population*. Volume 6, *Families*. Washington, 1933.

U.S. Bureau of the Census. *Fourteenth Census of the United States: 1920*. Volume 3, *Population*. Washington, 1922.

U.S. Bureau of the Census. *Fourteenth Census of the United States: 1920*. Volume 6, Part 1, *Agriculture: The Northern States*. Washington, 1922.

U.S. Bureau of the Census. *Historical Statistics of the United States, Colonial Times to 1970*. Washington, 1975.

U.S. Bureau of the Census. Manuscript Census Schedules (1900, 1910, 1920, 1930).

U.S. Bureau of the Census. *Sixteenth Census of the United States: 1940, Agriculture*. Volume 1, Part 2, *Statistics for Counties*. Washington, 1942.

U.S. Bureau of the Census. *Thirteenth Census of the United States: 1910.* Volume 2: *Population: Reports by States, Alabama–Montana.* Washington, 1913.

U.S. Bureau of the Census. *Thirteenth Census of the United States: 1910.* Volume 6, *Agriculture: Reports by States, Alabama–Montana.* Washington, 1913.

U.S. Bureau of the Census. *Twelfth Census of the United States: 1900.* Volume 6, Part 2, *Agriculture, Crops and Irrigation.* Washington, 1902.

U.S. Bureau of the Census. *Twelfth Census of the United States: 1900.* Volume 9, *Manufactures Part III: Special Reports on Selected Industries.* Washington, 1903.

U.S. Bureau of the Census. *U.S. Census of Agriculture: 1925.* Part 1, *The Northern States.* Washington, 1927.

U.S. Bureau of the Census. *U.S. Census of Agriculture: 1935.* Vol. 1, *Farms, Farm Acreage, and Value.* Washington, 1937.

U.S. Bureau of the Census, *U.S. Census of Agriculture: 1935.* Vol. 2, *Farms and Farm Acreage by Size* (Washington: Government Printing Office, 1937)

U.S. Bureau of the Census. *U.S. Census of Agriculture: 1945.* Volume 1. Part 100: *Statistics for Counties.* Washington, 1946.

U.S. Congress. *Mississippi River Floods: Hearings before the United States House Committee on Flood Control, 64th Congress, First Session, on Mar. 16, 1916.* Washington, 1916.

U.S. Congress. *Hearings before the Select Committee of the House Committee on Agriculture, to Investigate the Activities of the Farm Security Administration, House of Representatives, 78th Congress, First Session, Pursuant to H. Res. 119, a Resolution Creating a Select Committee to Investigate the Activities of the Farm Security Administration.* Washington, 1943.

U. S. Congress. *Hearings before the Select Committee Investigating National Defense Migration, House of Representatives, 77th Congress, First Session, Part 23, St. Louis, November 26, 1941.* Washington, 1942.

U.S. Federal Bureau of Investigation. *Investigation Concerning the Sharecropper Situation Existing in Southeast Missouri.* Washington, D.C., 1939.

Wade, Ophelia R., ed. *Deering Plantation: Sixty Thousand Acres in the Bootheel of Missouri.* Caruthersville, 1999.

Wintz, Cary D., ed. *African American Political Thought, 1890–1930: Washington, Du Bois, Garvey and Randolph.* Armonk, N.Y., 1996.

## Books, Articles, and Dissertations

Adams, Jane. "'How Can a Poor Man Live?' Resistance to Capitalist Development in Southern Illinois, 1870–1890." *Rural History* 3 (1992): 87–110.

Adas, Michael. *Prophets of Rebellion: Millenarian Protest Movements against the European Colonial Order.* Chapel Hill: University of North Carolina Press, 1979.

Aiken, Charles S. *The Cotton Plantation South since the Civil War.* Baltimore, 1998.

Allen, Ernest, Jr. "Waiting for Tojo: The Pro-Japan Vigil of Black Missourians, 1932–1943." *Gateway Heritage* 15 (Fall 1994): 38–55.

———. "When Japan Was 'Champion of the Darker Races': Satokata Takahashi and the Flowering of Black Messianic Nationalism." *The Black Scholar* 24 (Winter 1994): 23–46.

Alter, Robert and Frank Kermode, eds. *The Literary Guide to the Bible.* Cambridge, 1987.

Althouse, Peter. "The Ideology of Power in Early American Pentecostalism." *Journal of Pentecostal Theology* 13 (2004): 97–115.

Anderson, David M., and Douglas H. Johnson, eds. *Revealing Prophets: Prophecy in Eastern African History.* London, 1995.

Anderson, Robert Mapes. *Vision of the Disinherited: The Making of American Pentecostalism.* New York, 1979.

Arnesen, Eric, Julie Greene, and Bruce Laurie, eds. *Labor Histories: Class, Politics, and the Working-Class Experience.* Urbana, 1998.

Arnesen, Eric. "No 'Graver Danger': Black Anticommunism, the Communist Party, and the Race Question." *Labor* 3 (2006): 13–52.

Ayers, Edward L. *The Promise of the New South: Life after Reconstruction.* New York, 1992.

Baldwin, Sidney. *Poverty and Politics: The Rise and Decline of the Farm Security Administration.* Chapel Hill, 1968.

Barnes, Kenneth C. *Journey of Hope: The Back-to-Africa Movement in Arkansas in the Late 1800s.* Chapel Hill, 2004.

Barrett, C. K. *The Holy Spirit and the Gospel Tradition.* London, 1966.

Bellamy, Donnie D. "Henry A. Hunt and Black Agricultural Leadership in the New South." *Journal of Negro History* 60 (October 1975): 464–79.

Best, Felton O., ed. *Black Religious Leadership from the Slave Community to the Million Man March.* Lewiston, 1998.

Best, Wallace D. *Passionately Human, No Less Divine: Religion and Culture in Black Chicago, 1915–1952.* Princeton, 2007.

Biegert, M. Langley. "Legacy of Resistance: Uncovering the History of Collective Action by Black Agricultural Workers in Central East Arkansas from the 1860s to the 1930s." *Journal of Social History* 32 (Fall 1998): 73–99.

Biles, Roger. *The South and the New Deal.* Lexington, 1994.

Billings, Dwight B. "Religion as Opposition: A Gramscian Analysis." *American Journal of Sociology* 96 (July 1990): 1–31.

Bissett, Jim. *Agrarian Socialism in America: Marx, Jefferson, and Jesus in the Oklahoma Countryside, 1904–1920.* Norman, 1999.

Blau, Joel with Mimi Abramowitz. *The Dynamics of Social Welfare Policy.* New York, 2004.

Blevins, Brooks. *Hill Folks: A History of Arkansas Ozarkers and Their Image.* Chapel Hill, 2002.

Blumhofer, Edith L. *Restoring the Faith: The Assemblies of God, Pentecostalism, and American Culture.* Urbana, 1993.

Blumhofer, Edith L., Russell P. Spittler, and Grant A. Wacker, eds. *Pentecostal Currents in American Protestantism*. Urbana, 1999.

Bradford, Helen. *A Taste of Freedom: The ICU in Rural South Africa, 1924–1930*. New Haven, 1987.

Brandfon, Robert L. *Cotton Kingdoms of the New South: A History of the Yazoo Mississippi Delta from Reconstruction to the Twentieth Century*. Cambridge, 1967.

Brundage, W. Fitzhugh, ed. *Booker T. Washington and Black Progress: Up from Slavery 100 Years Later*. Gainesville, 2003.

Burkett, Randall K. *Garveyism as a Religious Movement: The Institutionalization of a Black Civil Religion*. Metuchen, 1978.

Burnette, Brittany C. "'Upon This Rock': An Exegetical and Patristic Examination of Matthew 16:18." Available at http://www.bible.org/page.php?page_id=2702 (accessed July 1, 2009).

Burns, Dave. "The Soul of Socialism: Christianity, Civilization, and Citizenship in the Thought of Eugene Debs." *Labor* 5 (Summer 2008): 113.

Cadle, Jean Douglas. "'Cropperville' from Refuge to Community: A Study of Missouri Sharecroppers Who Found an Alternative to the Sharecropper System." MA thesis, University of Missouri–St. Louis, 1993.

Campbell, James T. *Songs of Zion: The African Methodist Episcopal Church in the United States and South Africa*. Chapel Hill, 1998.

Cantor, Louis. *A Prologue to the Protest Movement: The Missouri Sharecropper Roadside Demonstration of 1939*. Durham, 1969.

Capeci, Dominic J., Jr. *The Lynching of Cleo Wright*. Lexington, 1998.

Cebula, Larry. *Plateau Indians and the Quest for Spiritual Power, 1700–1850*. Lincoln, 2003.

Chamberlain, Charles D. *Victory at Home: Manpower and Race in the American South during World War II*. Athens, 2003.

Chappell, David L. *A Stone of Hope: Prophetic Religion and the Death of Jim Crow*. Chapel Hill, 2004.

Clark, Kathleen Ann. *Defining Moments: African American Commemoration & Political Culture in the South, 1863–1913*. Chapel Hill, 2005.

Cobb, James C. *The Most Southern Place on Earth: The Mississippi Delta and the Roots of Regional Identity*. New York, 1992.

———, and Michael V. Namorato, eds. *The New Deal and the South*. Jackson, 1984.

Cobb, William H. *Radical Education in the Rural South: Commonwealth College, 1922–1940*. Detroit, 2000.

Cohen, Lizabeth. *Making a New Deal: Industrial Workers in Chicago, 1919–1939*. Cambridge, 1990.

Cohen, Nancy. *The Reconstruction of American Liberalism, 1865–1914*. Chapel Hill, 2002.

Cohen, William. *At Freedom's Edge: Black Mobility and the Southern White Quest for Racial Control, 1861–1915.* Baton Rouge, 1991.

Conrad, David E. *The Forgotten Farmers: The Story of Sharecroppers in the New Deal.* Urbana, 1965.

Cox, Harvey. *Fire from Heaven: The Rise of Pentecostal Spirituality and the Reshaping of Religion in the Twenty-First Century.* Cambridge, 2001.

Craig, Robert H. *Religion and Radical Politics: An Alternative Christian Tradition in the United States.* Philadelphia, 1992.

Creech, Joe. *Righteous Indignation: Religion and the Populist Revolution.* Urbana, 2006.

Cronon, E. David. *Black Moses: The Story of Marcus Garvey and the Universal Negro Improvement Association.* Madison, rev. ed. 1969.

Daniel, Pete. *Breaking the Land: The Transformation of Cotton, Tobacco, and Rice Cultures since 1880.* Urbana, 1985.

———. *Deep'n as It Come: The 1927 Mississippi River Flood.* New York, 1977.

———. *Standing at the Crossroads: Southern Life since 1900.* New York, 1986.

Dawley, Alan. *Struggles for Justice: Social Responsibility and the Liberal State.* Cambridge, 1991.

De Jong, Greta. *A Different Day: African American Struggles for Justice in Rural Louisiana, 1900–1970.* Chapel Hill, 2002.

———. "'With the Aid of God and the F.S.A': The Louisiana Farmers' Union and the African American Freedom Struggle in the New Deal Era." *Social History* 34 (2000): 105–39.

Dempster, Murray W. "Christian Social Concern in Pentecostal Perspective: Reformulating Pentecostal Eschatology." *Journal of Pentecostal Theology* 1 (1993): 51–64.

Dewar, L. *The Holy Spirit and Modern Thought: An Inquiry into the Historical, Theological, and Psychological Aspects of the Christian Doctrine of the Holy Spirit.* New York, 1959.

Drury, John. *Luke.* London, 1973.

Dunbar, Anthony P. *Against the Grain: Southern Radicals and Prophets, 1929–1959.* Charlottesville, 1981.

Dunn, James D. G. "Baptism in the Spirit: A Response to Pentecostal Scholarship on Luke-Acts." *Journal of Pentecostal Theology* 1 (1993): 3–27.

Edwards, Laura F. *Gendered Strife and Confusion: The Political Culture of Reconstruction.* Urbana, 1997.

Emerson, Howard. "The Sharecroppers' Strike, 1939." Senior Honors Thesis, Southeast Missouri State University, 1963.

Evanzz, Karl. *The Messenger: The Rise and Fall of Elijah Muhammad.* New York, 1999.

Fairclough, Adam. *Better Day Coming: Blacks and Equality, 1890–2000.* New York, 2001.

Fannin, Mark. *Labor's Promised Land: Radical Visions of Gender, Race, and Religion in the South.* Knoxville, 2003.

Fauset, Arthur H. *Black Gods of the Metropolis: Negro Religious Cults in the Urban North.* Philadelphia, second ed., 1971.

Feldman, Glenn, ed. *Politics and Religion in the White South.* Lexington, 2005.

Feurer, Rosemary. *Radical Unionism in the Midwest, 1900–1950.* Urbana, 2006.

Fields, Karen E. "Charismatic Religion as Popular Protest: The Ordinary and the Extraordinary in Social Movements." *Theory and Society* 11 (May 1982): 322–25.

———. *Revival and Rebellion in Colonial Central Africa.* Princeton, 1985.

Fink, Leon. *Workingmen's Democracy: The Knights of Labor and American Politics.* Urbana, 1983.

Fite, Gilbert C. *Cotton Fields No More: Southern Agriculture, 1865–1980.* Lexington, 1984.

Flamming, Douglas. *Creating the Modern South: Millhands and Managers in Dalton, Georgia, 1884–1984.* Chapel Hill, 1992.

Flynt, Wayne. *Dixie's Forgotten People: The South's Poor Whites.* Bloomington, 1979.

———. *Poor but Proud: Alabama's Poor Whites.* Tuscaloosa, 1989.

Foley, Neil. *The White Scourge: Mexicans, Blacks, and Poor Whites in Texas Cotton Culture.* Berkeley, 1997.

Foner, Philip. *American Socialism and Black Americans: From the Age of Jackson to World War II.* Westport, 1977.

Foner, Philip, and Sally Miller, eds. *Kate Richards O'Hare: Selected Writings and Speeches.* Baton Rouge, 1982.

Fraser, Walter J., R. Frank Saunders Jr., and Jon L. Wakelyn, eds. *The Web of Southern Social Relations: Women, Family, and Education.* Athens, 1985.

Fries, Robert F. *Empire in Pine: The Story of Lumbering in Wisconsin, 1830–1900.* Madison, 1951.

Fulop, Timothy E. "'The Future Golden Day of the Race': Millennialism and Black Americans in the Nadir, 1877–1901." *Harvard Theological Review* 84 (1991): 75–99.

Gaines, Kevin K. *Uplifting the Race: Black Leadership, Politics, and Culture in the Twentieth Century.* Chapel Hill, 1996.

Gallicchio, Mark. *The African American Encounter with Japan & China: Black Internationalism in Asia, 1895–1945.* Chapel Hill, 2000.

Giggie, John M. *After Redemption: Jim Crow and the Transformation of African American Religion in the Delta, 1875–1915.* New York, 2008.

Gilmore, Glenda. *Defying Dixie: The Radical Roots of Civil Rights.* New York, 2008.

Glass, William R. *Strangers in Zion: Fundamentalists in the South, 1900–1950.* Macon, 2001.

Goff, James R. *Fields White unto Harvest: Charles F. Parham and the Missionary Origins of Pentecostalism.* Fayetteville, 1988.

Goluboff, Risa L. *The Lost Promise of Civil Rights.* Cambridge, 2007.

Goodwyn, Lawrence. *Democratic Promise: The Populist Moment in America.* New York, 1976.

Gordon, Linda. *Pitied but Not Entitled: Single Mothers and the History of Welfare, 1890–1935.* New York, 1994.

Gorn, Elliott J. "'Gouge and Bite, Pull Hair and Scratch': The Social Significance of Fighting in the Southern Backcountry." *American Historical Review* 90 (1985): 18–43.

Goulder, Michael D. *Luke: A New Paradigm.* Vol. II. Sheffield, 1989.

Grant, Colin. *Negro with a Hat: The Rise and Fall of Marcus Garvey.* London, 2009.

Green, Elna C., ed. *The New Deal and Beyond: Social Welfare in the South since 1930.* Athens, 2003.

Green, James R. *Grass-Roots Socialism: Radical Movements in the Southwest, 1895–1943.* Baton Rouge, 1978.

Greene, Lorenzo J. "Lincoln University's Involvement with the Sharecropper Demonstration in Southeast Missouri, 1939–1940." *Missouri Historical Review* 82 (October 1987): 24–50.

Gregory, James N. *Southern Diaspora: How the Great Migrations of Black and White Southerners Transformed America.* Chapel Hill, 2005.

Grey, Michael R. *New Deal Medicine: The Rural Health Programs of the Farm Security Administration.* Baltimore, 1999.

Grim, Valerie. "African American Landlords in the Rural South, 1870–1950." *Agricultural History* 72 (Spring 1998): 399–416.

Grubbs, Donald H. *Cry from the Cotton: The Southern Tenant Farmers' Union and the New Deal.* Chapel Hill, 1971.

Hackney, Sheldon. *Populism to Progressivism in Alabama.* Princeton, 1969.

Hagood, Margaret J. *Mothers of the South: Portraiture of the White Tenant Farm Woman.* Chapel Hill, 1939.

Hahamovitch, Cindy. *The Fruits of Their Labor: Atlantic Coast Farmworkers and the Making of Migrant Poverty, 1870–1945.* Chapel Hill, 1997.

Hahn, Steven. *A Nation under Our Feet: Black Political Struggles in the Rural South from Slavery to the Great Migration.* Cambridge, 2003.

———. *The Roots of Southern Populism: Yeoman Farmers and the Transformation of the Georgia Upcountry.* New York, 1983.

Hall, Robert L., and Carol B. Stack, eds. *Holding onto the Land and the Lord: Kinship, Ritual, Land Tenure, and Social Policy in the Rural South.* Athens, 1982.

Hamilton, David E. "Herbert Hoover and the 1930 Drought." *Journal of American History* 68 (March 1982): 850–75.

Haney, Wava G., and Jane B. Knowles, eds. *Women and Farming: Changing Roles, Changing Structures.* Boulder, 1988.

Harlan, Louis R. *Booker T. Washington: The Wizard of Tuskegee, 1901–1915.* New York, 1983.

Harold, Claudrena N. *The Rise and Fall of the Garvey Movement in the Urban South, 1918–1942*. London, 2007.

Harrell, David Edwin, Jr., ed. *Varieties of Southern Evangelicalism*. Macon, 1981.

Harvey, Paul. *Freedom's Coming: Religious Culture and the Shaping of the South from the Civil War through the Civil Rights Era*. Chapel Hill, 2005.

———. *Redeeming the South: Religious Cultures and Racial Identities among Southern Baptists, 1865–1925*. Chapel Hill, 1997.

Hatch, Nathan O. *The Democratization of American Christianity*. New Haven, 1989.

Helly, Dorothy O., and Susan M. Reverby, eds. *Gendered Domains: Rethinking Public and Private in Women's History*. Ithaca, 1992.

Helms, Douglas. "Just Lookin' for a Home: The Cotton Boll Weevil and the South." Ph.D. diss., Florida State University, 1977.

Higgs, Robert. "The Boll Weevil, the Cotton Economy, and Black Migration, 1910–1930." *Agricultural History* 50 (April 1976): 335–50.

Hild, Matthew. *Greenbackers, Knights of Labor, and Populists: Farmer-Labor Insurgency in the Late-Nineteenth-Century South*. Athens, 2007.

Hobsbawm, E. J. *Primitive Rebels: Studies in Archaic Forms of Social Movement in the 19th and 20th Centuries*. New York, 1965.

Holley, Donald. *The Second Great Emancipation: The Mechanical Cotton Picker, Black Migration, and How They Shaped the Modern South*. Fayetteville, 2000.

———. *Uncle Sam's Farmers: The New Deal Communities in the Lower Mississippi Valley*. Urbana, 1975.

Honey, Michael K. *Southern Labor and Black Civil Rights: Organizing Memphis Workers*. Urbana, 1993.

Horton, Carol A. *Race and the Making of American Liberalism*. New York, 2005.

Howe, Daniel Walker. *What Hath God Wrought: The Transformation of America, 1815–1848*. New York, 2008.

Hurt, R. Douglas, ed. *African American Life in the Rural South, 1900–1950*. Columbia, 2003.

Inge, M. Thomas, ed. *Agrarianism in American Literature*. New York, 1969.

Irons, Janet. *Testing the New Deal: The General Textile Strike of 1934 in the American South*. Urbana, 2000.

Isserman, Maurice. *Which Side Were You On? The American Communist Party during the Second World War*. Urbana, 1993.

James, Winston. *Holding Aloft the Banner of Ethiopia: Caribbean Radicalism in Early Twentieth-Century America*. London, 1998.

Jenkins, Paul. "The History of Cotton Production in Southeast Missouri." MA Thesis, University of Missouri–Columbia, 1935.

Jones, Jacqueline. *The Dispossessed: America's Underclasses from the Civil War to the Present*. New York, 1992.

———. *Labor of Love, Labor of Sorrow: Black Women, Work, and the Family from Slavery to the Present*. New York, 1995.

Jones, William P. *The Tribe of Black Ulysses: African American Lumber Workers in the Jim Crow South.* Urbana, 2005.

Kantrowitz, Stephen. *Ben Tillman and the Reconstruction of White Supremacy.* Chapel Hill, 2000.

Kazin, Michael. *The Populist Persuasion: An American History.* New York, 1995.

Kearney, Reginald. *African American Views of the Japanese: Solidarity or Sedition?* Albany, N.Y., 1998.

Kelley, Robin D. G. *Hammer and Hoe: Alabama Communists during the Great Depression.* Chapel Hill, 1990.

———. *Race Rebels: Culture, Politics, and the Black Working Class.* New York, 1994.

Kirby, Jack T. *Rural Worlds Lost: The American South, 1920–1960.* Baton Rouge, 1987.

Korstad, Robert R. *Civil Rights Unionism: Tobacco Workers and the Struggle for Democracy in the Mid-Twentieth-Century South.* Chapel Hill, 2003.

———, and Nelson Lichtenstein. "Opportunities Found and Lost: Labor, Radicals, and the Early Civil Rights Movement." *Journal of American History* 75 (December 1988): 786–811.

Lerner, Gerda. "Reconceptualizing Differences among Women." *Journal of Women's History* 1 (Winter 1990): 237–48.

Letwin, Daniel. *The Challenge of Interracial Unionism: Alabama Coal Miners, 1878–1921.* Chapel Hill, 1998.

Lewis, Ronald L. *Transforming the Appalachian Countryside: Railroads, Deforestation, and Social Change in West Virginia, 1880–1920.* Chapel Hill, 1998.

Lichtenstein, Alex. "Was the Emancipated Slave a Proletarian?" *Reviews in American History* 26 (1998): 133–37.

Lichtenstein, Nelson. *Labor's War at Home: The CIO in World War II.* Cambridge, 1982.

Lincoln, C. Eric, and Lawrence H. Mamiya. *The Black Church in the African American Experience.* Durham, 1990.

Link, William A. *The Paradox of Southern Progressivism, 1880–1930.* Chapel Hill, 1992.

Litwack, Leon F. *Trouble in Mind: Black Southerners in the Age of Jim Crow.* New York, 1998.

Lynn-Sherow, Bonnie. *Red Earth: Race and Agriculture in Oklahoma Territory.* Lawrence, Kans., 2004.

MacLean, Nancy. *Behind the Mask of Chivalry: The Making of the Second Ku Klux Klan.* New York, 1994.

MacRobert, Iain. *The Black Roots and White Racism of Early Pentecostalism in the USA.* New York, 1988.

Mann, Susan A. *Agrarian Capitalism in Theory and Practice.* Chapel Hill, 1990.

———. "Slavery, Sharecropping, and Sexual Inequality." *Signs* 14 (Summer 1989): 795–98.

Marshall, Suzanne. *Violence in the Black Patch of Kentucky and Tennessee.* Columbia, 1994.

Martin, Tony. *Race First: The Ideological and Organizational Struggles of Marcus Garvey and the Universal Negro Improvement Association.* Westport, Conn., 1976.

McDowell, Gary L. "Local Agencies and Land Development by Drainage: The Case of 'Swampeast' Missouri." PhD diss., Columbia University, 1965.

McLoughlin, William G. *Revivals, Awakenings, and Reform: An Essay on Religion and Social Change in America, 1607–1977.* Chicago, 1978.

McMath, Robert C., Jr. *American Populism: A Social History, 1877–1898.* New York, 1993.

McMillen, Neil. *Dark Journey: Black Mississippians in the Age of Jim Crow.* Urbana, 1989.

Menzies, R. P. *The Development of Early Christian Pneumatology with Special Reference to Luke-Acts.* Sheffield, 1991.

Mertz, Paul E. *New Deal Policy and Southern Rural Poverty.* Baton Rouge, 1978.

Miller, Worth Robert. *Oklahoma Populism: A History of the People's Party in the Oklahoma Territory.* Norman, 1987.

Mitchell, Michelle. *Righteous Propagation: African Americans and the Politics of Racial Destiny after Reconstruction.* Chapel Hill, 2004.

Montgomery, William E. *Under Their Own Vine and Fig Tree: The African-American Church in the Rural South, 1865–1900.* Baton Rouge, 1993.

Mooney, Patrick H., and Theo J. Majka. *Farmers' and Farm Workers' Movements: Social Protest in American Agriculture.* New York, 1995.

Naison, Mark. "Black Agrarian Radicalism in the Great Depression: The Threads of a Lost Tradition." *Journal of Ethnic Studies* 1 (Fall 1973): 47–65.

———. "Claude and Joyce Williams: Pilgrims of Justice." *Southern Exposure* 1 (Winter 1974): 38–50.

Natanson, Nicholas. *The Black Image in the New Deal: The Politics of FSA Photography.* Knoxville, 1992.

Nelson, Bruce. *Divided We Stand: American Workers and the Struggle for Black Equality.* Princeton, 2001.

O'Donovan, Susan Eva. *Becoming Free in the Cotton South.* Cambridge: Harvard University Press, 2007.

Ogilvie, Leon P. "The Development of the Southeast Missouri Lowlands." PhD diss., University of Missouri–Columbia, 1967.

———. "Populism and Socialism in the Southeast Missouri Lowlands." *Missouri Historical Review* 65 (January 1971): 159–83.

Oltman, Adele. *Sacred Mission, Worldly Ambition: Black Christian Nationalism in the Age of Jim Crow.* Athens, 2008.

Otto, John Solomon. *The Final Frontiers, 1880–1930: Settling the Southern Bottomlands.* Westport, 1999.

Ownby, Ted. *Subduing Satan: Religion, Recreation, and Manhood in the Rural South, 1865–1920*. Chapel Hill, 1990.

Painter, Nell Irvin. *Standing at Armageddon: The United States, 1877–1919*. New York, 1987.

Parker, Paul E. *A Portrait of Missouri, 1935–1943: Photographs from the Farm Security Administration*. Columbia, 2002.

Patterson, James T. *Congressional Conservatives and the New Deal: The Growth of the Conservative Coalition in Congress, 1933–1939*. Lexington, 1967.

Payne, Charles M. *I've Got the Light of Freedom: The Organizing Tradition and the Mississippi Freedom Struggle*. Berkeley, 1995.

Payne, Elizabeth Ann. "The Lady Was a Sharecropper: Myrtle Lawrence and the Southern Tenant Farmers' Union." *Southern Cultures* 4 (Summer 1998): 5–27.

Phillips, Kimberley L. *AlabamaNorth: African-American Migrants, Community, and Working-Class Activism in Cleveland, 1915–45*. Urbana, 1999.

Pinn, Anthony B. *Why, Lord? Suffering and Evil in Black Theology*. New York, 1995.

Pitts, Walter F. *Old Ship of Zion: The Afro-Baptist Ritual in the African Diaspora*. New York, 1993.

Pope, Liston. *Millhands and Preachers: A Study of Gastonia*. New Haven, 1942.

Postel, Charles. *The Populist Vision*. New York, 2007.

Reich, Steven. "Soldiers of Democracy: Black Texans and the Fight for Citizenship, 1917–1921." *Journal of American History* 82 (March 1996): 1478–1504.

Reid, Debra A. "Furniture Exempt from Seizure: African-American Farm Families and Their Property in Texas, 1880s-1930s." *Agricultural History* 80 (Summer 2006): 336–57.

———. *Reaping a Greater Harvest: African Americans, the Extension Service, and Rural Reform in Jim Crow Texas*. College Station, 2007.

Rhodes, Joel P. "The Father of Southeast Missouri: Louis Houck and the Coming of the Railroad." *Missouri Historical Review* 100 (January 2006): 72–86.

Rodgers, Daniel T. *The Work Ethic in Industrial America, 1850–1920*. Chicago, 1978.

Roediger, David R. *The Wages of Whiteness: Race and the Making of the American Working Class*. London, rev. ed., 1999.

Rogers, Kim Lacy. *Life and Death in the Delta: African American Narratives of Violence, Resilience, and Social Change*. New York, 2006.

Rolinson, Mary G. *Grassroots Garveyism: The Universal Negro Improvement Association in the Rural South, 1920–1927*. Chapel Hill, 2007.

Roll, Jarod H. "From Revolution to Reaction: Early Pentecostalism, Radicalism and Race in Southeast Missouri, 1910–1930." *Radical History Review* 90 (August 2004): 5–29.

———. "Gideon's Band: From Socialism to Vigilantism in Southeast Missouri, 1907–1916." *Labor History* 43 (November 2002): 483–503.

———, and Erik S. Gellman. "Owen Whitfield and the Gospel of the Working Class in New Deal America, 1936–1946." *Journal of Southern History* 72 (May 2006): 303–48.

Ross, James D., Jr. "'I ain't got no home in this world': The Rise and Fall of the Southern Tenant Farmers' Union in Arkansas." Ph.D. diss., Auburn University, 2004.

Saloutos, Theodore. *The American Farmer and the New Deal.* Ames, 1982.

Salvatore, Nick. *Eugene V. Debs: Citizen and Socialist.* Urbana, 1982.

Sanders, Cheryl J. *Saints in Exile: The Holiness-Pentecostal Experience in African American Religion and Culture.* New York, 1996.

Sanders, Elizabeth. *Roots of Reform: Farmers, Workers, and the American State, 1877–1917.* Chicago, 1999.

Schneirov, Richard, Shelton Stromquist, and Nick Salvatore, eds. *The Pullman Strike and the Crisis of the 1890s: Essays on Labor and Politics.* Urbana, 1999.

Schweninger, Loren. *Black Property Owners in the South, 1790–1915.* Urbana, 1990.

Scott, Shaunna L. "'They Don't Have to Live by the Old Traditions': Saintly Men, Sinner Women, and an Appalachian Pentecostal Revival." *American Ethnologist* 21 (1994): 227–44.

Seavoy, Ronald E. *The American Peasantry: Southern Agricultural Labor and Its Legacy, 1850–1995.* Westport, 1998.

Sernett, Milton C. *Bound for the Promised Land: African American Religion and the Great Migration.* Durham, 1997.

Shapiro, Karin A. *A New South Rebellion: The Battle against Convict Labor in the East Tennessee Coalfields, 1871–1896.* Chapel Hill, 1998.

Sharpless, Rebecca. *Fertile Ground, Narrow Choices: Women on Texas Cotton Farms, 1900–1940.* Chapel Hill, 1999.

Shore, Elliott. *Talkin' Socialism: J. A. Wayland and the Radical Press.* Lawrence, 1988.

Simon, Bryant. *A Fabric of Defeat: The Politics of South Carolina Millhands, 1910–1948.* Chapel Hill, 1998.

Sitton, Thad and James H. Conrad. *Freedom Colonies: Independent Black Texans in the Time of Jim Crow.* Austin, 2005.

Sklar, Martin J. *Corporate Reconstruction of American Capitalism, 1890–1916.* Cambridge, 1988.

Smith, Rogers M. *Civic Ideals: Conflicting Visions of Citizenship in U.S. History.* New Haven, 1997.

Spencer, Robyn. "Contested Terrain: The Mississippi Flood of 1927 and the Struggle to Control Black Labor." *The Journal of Negro History* 79 (Spring 1994): 170–81.

Stanley, Amy Dru. *From Bondage to Contract: Wage Labor, Marriage, and the Market in the Age of Slave Emancipation.* Cambridge, 1998.

Stave, Bruce, ed. *Socialism and the Cities.* Port Washington, 1975.

Stein, Judith. *The World of Marcus Garvey: Race and Class in Modern Society.* Baton Rouge, 1986.

Steinson, Barbara J. "Rural Life in Indiana, 1800–1950." *Indiana Magazine of History* 90 (September 1994): 203–50.

Stepenoff, Bonnie. "'The Last Tree Cut Down': The End of the Bootheel Frontier, 1880–1940." *Missouri Historical Review* 90 (October 1995): 61–78.

———. *Thad Snow: A Life of Social Reform in the Missouri Bootheel.* Columbia: University of Missouri Press, 2003.

Stephens, Randall J. *The Fire Spreads: Holiness and Pentecostalism in the American South.* Cambridge, 2008.

Stock, Catherine M., and Robert D. Johnston, eds. *The Countryside in the Age of the Modern State: Political Histories of Rural America.* Ithaca, 2001.

Street, Paul. "The 'Best Union Members': Class, Race, Culture, and Black Worker Militancy in Chicago's Stockyards during the 1930s." *Journal of American Ethnic History* 20 (Fall 2000): 18–49.

Stromquist, Shelton. *Reinventing "The People": The Progressive Movement, the Class Problem, and the Origins of Modern Liberalism.* Urbana, 2006.

Sullivan, Patricia. *Days of Hope: Race and Democracy in the New Deal Era.* Chapel Hill, 1996.

Summers, Martin. *Manliness and Its Discontents: The Black Middle Class and the Transformation of Masculinity, 1900–1930.* Chapel Hill, 2004.

Taylor, Ula Yvette. *The Veiled Garvey: The Life & Times of Amy Jacques Garvey.* Chapel Hill, 2002.

Thelen, David R. *Paths of Resistance: Tradition and Dignity in Industrializing Missouri.* New York, 1986.

Thompson, E. P. *The Making of the English Working Class.* New York, 1966.

Tindall, George Brown. *The Emergence of the New South, 1913–1945.* Baton Rouge, 1967.

Tolnay, Stewart E. *The Bottom Rung: African American Family Life on Southern Farms.* Urbana, 1999.

Trotter, Joe W., Jr. *Coal, Class, and Color: Blacks in Southwest Virginia, 1929–1945.* Urbana, 1990.

Vincent, Theodore G. *Black Power and the Garvey Movement.* Berkeley, 1971.

Wacker, Grant. *Heaven Below: Early Pentecostals and American Culture.* Cambridge, 2001.

Waldrep, Christopher. *Night Riders: Defending Community in the Black Patch, 1890–1915.* Durham: Duke University Press, 1993.

Walker, Melissa. *Southern Farmers and Their Stories: Memory and Meaning in Oral History.* Lexington, 2006.

Weber, Timothy P., Jr. *In the Shadow of the Second Coming: American Premillennialism, 1875–1925.* New York, 1979.

Weinstein, James. *The Decline of Socialism in America, 1912–1925.* New York, 1967.

Weisiger, Marsha L. *Land of Plenty: Oklahomans in the Cotton Fields of Arizona, 1933–1942.* Norman, 1995.

Whayne, Jeannie M. *A New Plantation South: Land, Labor, and Federal Favor in Twentieth-Century Arkansas.* Charlottesville, 1996.

Willis, John C. *Forgotten Time: The Yazoo-Mississippi Delta after the Civil War*. Charlottesville, 2000.

Wills, Gregory A. *Democratic Religion: Freedom, Authority, and Church Discipline in the Baptist South, 1785–1900*. New York, 1997.

Wilmore, Gayraud S., ed. *African American Religious Studies: An Interdisciplinary Anthology*. Durham: Duke University Press, 1989.

Woodruff, Nan. *American Congo: The African American Freedom Struggle in the Delta*. Cambridge, 2003.

———. *As Rare as Rain: Federal Relief in the Great Southern Drought of 1930–31*. Urbana, 1985.

———. "Pick or Fight: The Emergency Farm Labor Program in the Arkansas and Mississippi Deltas during World War II." *Agricultural History* 64 (Spring 1990): 74–85.

Woods, Clyde. *Development Arrested: The Blues and Plantation Power in the Mississippi Delta*. London, 1998.

Woodward, C. Vann. *Origins of the New South, 1877–1913*. Baton Rouge, 1951.

———. *Tom Watson: Agrarian Rebel*. New York, 1963, first ed., 1938.

Worcester, Kent. *C. L. R. James: A Political Biography*. Albany, 1996.

Wright, Gavin. *Old South, New South: Revolutions in the Southern Economy since the Civil War*. New York, 1986.

Wyllie, Irvin J. "Race and Class Conflict on Missouri's Cotton Frontier." *Journal of Southern History* 20 (May 1954): 183–96.

Zieger, Robert H. *The CIO, 1935–1955*. Chapel Hill, 1995.

———. *For Jobs and Freedom: Race and Labor in America since 1865*. Lexington, 2007.

# Index

**JAROD ROLL** teaches American history at the University of Sussex, England, where he is founder and director of the Marcus Cunliffe Center for the Study of the American South. He is coauthoring, with Erik Gellman, a biography of Claude Williams and Owen Whitfield that explores their use of a "revolutionary Gospel" to organize black and white workers during the 1930s and 1940s.

Worker City, Company Town: Iron and Cotton-Worker Protest in Troy and Cohoes, New York, 1855–84   *Daniel J. Walkowitz*

Life, Work, and Rebellion in the Coal Fields: The Southern West Virginia Miners, 1880–1922   *David Alan Corbin*

Women and American Socialism, 1870–1920   *Mari Jo Buhle*

Lives of Their Own: Blacks, Italians, and Poles in Pittsburgh, 1900–1960   *John Bodnar, Roger Simon, and Michael P. Weber*

Working-Class America: Essays on Labor, Community, and American Society   *Edited by Michael H. Frisch and Daniel J. Walkowitz*

Eugene V. Debs: Citizen and Socialist   *Nick Salvatore*

American Labor and Immigration History, 1877–1920s: Recent European Research   *Edited by Dirk Hoerder*

Workingmen's Democracy: The Knights of Labor and American Politics   *Leon Fink*

The Electrical Workers: A History of Labor at General Electric and Westinghouse, 1923–60   *Ronald W. Schatz*

The Mechanics of Baltimore: Workers and Politics in the Age of Revolution, 1763–1812   *Charles G. Steffen*

The Practice of Solidarity: American Hat Finishers in the Nineteenth Century   *David Bensman*

The Labor History Reader   *Edited by Daniel J. Leab*

Solidarity and Fragmentation: Working People and Class Consciousness in Detroit, 1875–1900   *Richard Oestreicher*

Counter Cultures: Saleswomen, Managers, and Customers in American Department Stores, 1890–1940   *Susan Porter Benson*

The New England Working Class and the New Labor History   *Edited by Herbert G. Gutman and Donald H. Bell*

Labor Leaders in America   *Edited by Melvyn Dubofsky and Warren Van Tine*

Barons of Labor: The San Francisco Building Trades and Union Power in the Progressive Era   *Michael Kazin*

Gender at Work: The Dynamics of Job Segregation by Sex during World War II   *Ruth Milkman*

Once a Cigar Maker: Men, Women, and Work Culture in American Cigar Factories, 1900–1919   *Patricia A. Cooper*

A Generation of Boomers: The Pattern of Railroad Labor Conflict in Nineteenth-Century America   *Shelton Stromquist*

Work and Community in the Jungle: Chicago's Packinghouse Workers, 1894–1922   *James R. Barrett*

Workers, Managers, and Welfare Capitalism: The Shoeworkers and Tanners of Endicott Johnson, 1890–1950   *Gerald Zahavi*

Men, Women, and Work: Class, Gender, and Protest in the New England Shoe Industry, 1780–1910   *Mary Blewett*

The University of Illinois Press
is a founding member of the
Association of American University Presses.

———————————————————————————

Composed in 10.5/13 Adobe Minion Pro
with Meta display
by Celia Shapland
at the University of Illinois Press
Manufactured by Sheridan Books, Inc.

University of Illinois Press
1325 South Oak Street
Champaign, IL 61820-6903
www.press.uillinois.edu